Time Out

Stockholm

timeout.com/stockholm

Published by Time Out Guides Ltd, a wholly owned subsidiary of Time Out Group Ltd.
Time Out and the Time Out logo are trademarks of Time Out Group Ltd.

© **Time Out Group Ltd 2008**
Previous editions 2003, 2005.

10 9 8 7 6 5 4 3 2 1

This edition first published in Great Britain in 2008 by Ebury Publishing
A Random House Group Company
20 Vauxhall Bridge Road, London SW1V 2SA

Random House Australia Pty Limited 20 Alfred Street, Milsons Point, Sydney, New South Wales 2061, Australia
Random House New Zealand Limited 18 Poland Road, Glenfield, Auckland 10, New Zealand
Random House South Africa (Pty) Limited Isle of Houghton, Corner Boundary
Road & Carse O'Gowrie, Houghton 2198, South Africa

Random House UK Limited Reg. No. 954009

For further distribution details, see www.timeout.com

ISBN 10: 1-84670-001-9
ISBN 13: 9781846700019

A CIP catalogue record for this book is available from the British Library

Printed and bound by Firmengruppe APPL, aprinta druck, Wemding, Germany

The Random House Group Limited supports the Forest Stewardship Council (FSC), the leading international forest
certification organisation. All our titles that are printed on Greenpeace approved FSC certified paper carry the FSC logo.
Our paper procurement policy can be found at www.rbooks.co.uk/environment.

Time Out Guides Limited
Universal House
251 Tottenham Court Road
London W1T 7AB
Tel + 44 (0)20 7813 3000
Fax + 44 (0)20 7813 6001
Email guides@timeout.com
www.timeout.com

Editorial

Editor Dominic Earle
Deputy Editor Francis Gooding
Listings Editor Victoria Hesselius
Proofreader Marion Moisy
Indexer Sam Le Quesne

Managing Director Peter Fiennes
Financial Director Gareth Garner
Editorial Director Ruth Jarvis
Deputy Series Editor Dominic Earle
Editorial Manager Holly Pick
Assistant Management Accountant Ija Krasnikova

Design

Art Director Scott Moore
Art Editor Pinelope Kourmouzoglou
Senior Designer Henry Elphick
Graphic Designer Gemma Doyle
Junior Graphic Designer Kei Ishimaru
Digital Imaging Simon Foster
Ad Make-up Jodi Sher

Picture Desk

Picture Editor Jael Marschner
Deputy Picture Editor Katie Morris
Picture Researcher Helen McFarland
Picture Desk Assistant Troy Bailey

Advertising

Sales Director Mark Phillips
International Advertising Manager Kasimir Berger
International Sales Consultant Ross Canadé
International Sales Executive Charlie Sokol
Advertising Sales (Stockholm) Arenholm
Advertising Assistant Kate Staddon

Marketing

Group Marketing Director John Luck
Marketing Manager Yvonne Poon
Sales and Marketing Director North America Lisa Levinson

Production

Group Production Director Mark Lamond
Production Manager Brendan McKeown
Production Coordinator Caroline Bradford
Production Controller Susan Whittaker

Time Out Group

Chairman Tony Elliott
Financial Director Richard Waterlow
Group General Manager/Director Nichola Coulthard
Time Out Magazine Ltd MD Richard Waterlow
Time Out Communications Ltd MD David Pepper
Time Out International MD Cathy Runciman
Group Art Director John Oakey
Group IT Director Simon Chappell

Contributors

Introduction Dominic Earle. **History** James Savage. **Stockholm Today** James Savage. **Made in Sweden** James Savage.
Where to Stay Stephen Whitlock. **Sightseeing** Chad Henderson, Elizabeth Dacey. **Restaurants** Stephen Whitlock. **Bars**
Jonas Leijonhufvud. **Cafés** Kathleen Archery. **Shops & Services** Stephen Whitlock, Victoria Hesselius. **Festivals & Events**
Elizabeth Dacey. **Children** Lisa del Papa. **Clubs** Kristoffer Poppius. **Film** Elizabeth Dacey (*Lasse come home* Simon Cropper).
Gay & Lesbian Stephen Whitlock. **Music** Kristoffer Poppius. **Sport & Fitness** Paul Eade. **Theatre & Dance** Kristoffer Poppius.
Directory Victoria Hesselius. **My Stockholm features** Stephen Whitlock.

Maps john@jsgraphics.co.uk
Map on p256 courtesy of SL (www.sl.se)

Photography by Tove K Breitstein except page 12 Time & Life Pictures/Getty Images; page 15 ullstein bild/akg-images;
page 16 Nationalmuseum, Stockholm, Sweden/Bridgeman Art Library; page 19 Mary Evans Picture Library; page 22 Anders
Wiklund/ Scanpix/Reuters/Corbis; page 179 Mattia Olsson; page 164 published by Rabén & Sjögren; page 170 Matthew Lea;
page 190 AFP/Getty Images; page 199 Mats Bäcker.

The following image was provided by the featured establishment/artist: page 171.

The Editor would like to thank First Hotel Reisen, Nordic Light Hotel, Stockholm Tourist Office and all contributors to previous
editions of *Time Out Stockholm*, whose work forms the basis of parts of this book.

Contents

Introduction

If you thought the Brits were obsessed with the weather, then come to Stockholm, where there are whole festivals devoted to the passing of the seasons, from Walpurgis Night in April to Lucia Day in December. And long may it continue – in these days of wildly unpredictable climate change, there is something very refreshing about a country that still clings to its clearly defined seasons.

Stockholm's shortest day (22 December) sees the sun rise at 8.44am and disappear again at 2.49pm, a miserly six hours and five minutes of light therapy, while the longest day (21 June) stretches for 20 hours and 37 minutes, with sunrise at 3.31am and sunset at 9.08pm. What this means for locals and, indirectly, for visitors, is that this is a city whose modus operandi is ruled by the heavens. Visit in March and you might catch a ski race around the Royal Palace (the equivalent of a schuss down the Mall), but come back in midsummer and it's all crayfish parties on the beach, park theatre and midnight marathons.

Whatever time of year you visit, though, you will notice that Stockholm offers that rarest of urban commodities – space to think. Sweden covers an area the size of California, but its population is smaller than that of London, and the capital itself is made up of one-third water and one-third green space, which means just one-third urbanity. And if you still can't get enough fresh air in your lungs, then you can hop on a ferry to the archipelago, a playground of more than 24,000 islands starting just a few miles east of the city.

All that thinking space might just help to explain the roll call of homegrown success stories: from Strindberg and Bergman to H&M and Ericsson, this is a place positively bursting with creative genius. But that creativity is first and foremost born of functional simplicity – a mantra at the very root of Sweden's soul. Ikea owner Ingvar Kamprad may be worth $33 billion, and ten per cent of Europeans currently alive may have been conceived in one of his beds, but he still drives an old Volvo and takes the metro to work. The local word for it is *lagom*, or 'just enough', and it sums up principles of fairness, equality and modesty.

Unfortunately, *lagom* is not a word that applies to Stockholm's price tags, and however crafty you are with your holiday kronor, there's no getting away from the fact that the city makes a pretty expensive weekend getaway. From tucking into a large beer and a plate of meatballs to finding a hotel room, nothing comes cheap in the Venice of the North. But in return you get a triumph of substance and style, with over 100 galleries and 70 museums, northern Europe's largest and best-preserved medieval city, plus more than enough Nordic chic to fill your baggage allowance on the way home.

ABOUT TIME OUT CITY GUIDES

This is the third edition of *Time Out Stockholm*, one of an expanding series of Time Out guides produced by the people behind the successful listings magazines in London, New York and Chicago. Our guides are all written by resident experts who have striven to provide you with all the most up-to-date information you'll need to explore the city or read up on its background, whether you're a local or a first-time visitor.

THE LIE OF THE LAND

The centre of Stockholm is small and easy to get around on foot, but we've also given details of the nearest Tunnelbana (metro) station and bus routes for venues listed. To make the city even easier to navigate, we've divided Stockholm into areas and assigned each one its own chapter in our Sightseeing section (for an introduction to central Stockholm, see p50). Wherever possible, a map reference is provided for venues listed; the maps can be found at the back of the book.

ESSENTIAL INFORMATION

For all the practical information you might need for visiting the area – including visa and customs information, details of local transport, a listing of emergency numbers, information on local weather and a selection of useful websites and books relating to the city – turn to the Directory at the back of this guide. It begins on page 216.

THE LOWDOWN ON THE LISTINGS

We have tried to make this book as easy to use as possible. Addresses, phone numbers, bus information, opening times and admission prices are all included in the listings. However,

businesses can change their arrangements at any time. Before you go out of your way, we'd strongly advise you to phone ahead to check opening times and other particulars. While every effort and care has been made to ensure the accuracy of the information contained in this guide, the publishers cannot accept responsibility for any errors it may contain.

PRICES AND PAYMENT

We have noted where venues such as shops, hotels, restaurants, museums and theatres accept the following credit cards: American Express (AmEx), Diners Club (DC), MasterCard (MC) and Visa (V).

The prices we've listed in this guide should be treated as guidelines, not gospel. If prices vary wildly from those we've quoted, ask whether there's a good reason. If not, go elsewhere. Then please let us know. We aim to give the best and most up-to-date advice, so we want to know if you've been badly treated or overcharged.

Advertisers

We would like to stress that no establishment has been included in this guide because it has advertised in any of our publications and no payment of any kind has influenced any review. The opinions given in this book are those of Time Out writers and entirely independent.

TELEPHONE NUMBERS

The area code for Stockholm is 08, but you don't need to use it when phoning from within the city. Throughout the guide we've listed phone numbers as dialled from within Stockholm. If you're calling Stockholm from abroad, you must dial 46 (the code for Sweden) then 8 then the number. For more on telephones and codes, see page 225.

MAPS

The map section at the back of this book includes an overview map of the city, plus detailed street maps and a transport map showing all the Tunnelbana (metro) routes. The maps start on page 238, and now pinpoint the specific locations of hotels (**①**), restaurants (**①**), bars (**①**) and cafés (**①**). There is also a Trips Out of Town map on page 202, which covers day trips and the archipelago.

LET US KNOW WHAT YOU THINK

We hope you enjoy *Time Out Stockholm*, and we'd like to know what you think of it. We welcome tips for places that you consider we should include in future editions and take note of your criticism of our choices. You can email us at guides@timeout.com.

There is an online version of this book, along with guides to over 100 international cities, at **www.timeout.com**.

Time Out
Travel Guides

Worldwide

All our guides are
written by a team of
local experts with a
unique and stylish
insider perspective.
We offer essential tips,
trusted advice and
honest reviews for
everything you need
to know in the city.

Over 50 destinations
available at all good
bookshops and at
timeout.com/shop

Time Out
Guides

BERNS SALONGER

In Context

History

The blond ambition tour – from Viking mythology
to cradle-to-grave ideology.

Compared with many European capitals,
Stockholm is a relative newcomer. While
human activity in the region around Lake
Mälaren dates back thousands of years, the city
itself wasn't founded until the 13th century,
and it took until the 15th century for Stockholm
to be widely recognised as Sweden's political
and economic centre.

The earliest evidence of human habitation
in Sweden is of nomadic reindeer hunters
from continental Europe, who appear to have
followed the receding glaciers north into
Scandinavia at the end of the last Ice Age in
approximately 11000 BC. By about 7500 BC
Mesolithic hunter-gatherers had migrated to

the coastal areas of central and northern
Sweden. Between 4000 and 2800 BC, villages
dotted the southern half of the country and
people eked out a living as farmers. Sweden's
inhabitants began establishing trading links
with the wider world during the Bronze Age
(1500 to 500 BC). They had access to abundant
supplies of fur and amber, which they traded
for raw metals, weapons and decorative objects.

Between AD 550 and 1000 two main rival
groups emerged in Sweden – the Svear, who
were based in the Lake Mälaren region, and
the Götar, who controlled a swathe of territory
to the west and south. The geographical
terms Svealand and Götaland are still in use

today, and *Sverige*, Sweden's modern name in Swedish, comes from *Svea rike* – the Svea kingdom.

The Viking culture emerged in various parts of Scandinavia in the early ninth century. The word 'Viking' is thought to come from the *viks* (Old Norse for 'inlets') in which they harboured their long ships. Extremely capable mariners, by the mid ninth century they had reached both the Black and Caspian Seas, where they launched attacks on Byzantium and north-east Iran. While often violent, the Vikings of Sweden were somewhat more business-minded than those of Denmark and Norway, and they successfully developed lucrative trading contacts with Byzantium.

Taken as a group, the Vikings effectively dominated the political and economic life of Europe until the mid 11th century. Remnants of their civilisation have been uncovered at a number of sites not far from Stockholm's city limits, most notably at Birka, a town founded in about AD 700 that was Sweden's leading trading centre in the early tenth century. Gamla Uppsala is even older than Birka, with some of its royal graves dating back to the sixth century. Stockholm's Historiska Museet has an excellent exhibition introducing visitors to a wealth of information and artefacts that cast light on Viking culture.

The Swedes were among the last Europeans to abandon paganism. In spite of the efforts of a number of crusading monks and priests, and the baptism of King Olof Skötkonung in 1008 (and all his successors after him), many Swedes stubbornly remained true to the old Norse gods until the end of the 11th century. By the middle of the 12th century, the church had finally gained a foothold and Sweden's first archbishopric was established in Uppsala. The first Swedish archbishop, appointed in 1164, was an English monk called Stephen. King Erik Jedvardsson (1156-60), who had led a crusade to christianise the Finns, was chosen to become Sweden's patron saint. He is commemorated in place names such as St Eriksplan and St Eriksgatan; his remains are entombed at Uppsala Cathedral.

BIRTH OF A CITY

The foundation of Stockholm is intimately connected to the power struggles between the monarchy and the nobility that characterised Swedish history after the collapse of Viking culture. Both the physical city and its name can be traced to Sweden's 13th-century ruler, Birger Jarl.

Birger Jarl came to power in 1229, after the then king, Erik Erikssen, had been deposed. He is remembered for two main accomplishments:

the long and turbulent process he initiated to centralise political power in Sweden, and the founding of the city of Stockholm. In 1247-51 he made significant progress towards achieving his first goal by using German money and soldiers to successfully defeat a rebellion led by noblemen in the area around Lake Mälaren. Shortly after this victory he offered good trading terms to German merchants, especially those from Lübeck, which led to Sweden's long-lasting ties to the Hanseatic League.

The 13th-century Swedish kingdom consisted of the area around Lake Mälaren, the Stockholm and Åland archipelagos, and the Gulf of Finland all the way to Viborg (now part of Russia). Low sea levels meant that the passage from the Baltic Sea into Lake Mälaren was restricted to a narrow channel now known as Norrström, just north of Gamla Stan. This passage became a vital trade route and a key defensive position, and in 1252 Birger Jarl constructed a mighty fortress on the site: the Tre Kronor (on the site of the present-day Kungliga Slottet). It would grow to become the city of Stockholm.

'In the mid 14th century, a third of the population was killed by the bubonic plague.'

In that same year, Birger Jarl wrote two letters in which the name 'Stockholm' is mentioned for the first time. The origin of the name is unclear, but it may be derived from from the fact that logs (*stockar*) were used to build up the small island (*holme*) upon which the fortress was built.

The settlement at Tre Kronor soon became one of Sweden's most important economic centres. Ships from Lübeck and other Hanseatic towns traded enthusiastically with the expatriate Germans who were setting up copper and iron-ore mines in Sweden, while products from the interior of the country (fur, grain and iron) were traded with merchants from across northern Europe.

Birger Jarl's son Magnus took power in 1275. A renewed repression of the country's unruly nobles concentrated power in his hands, and the various edicts and rulings with which he limited the power of the nobility are credited with forestalling the development of feudalism in Sweden. After his death in 1290, power shifted briefly back to the nobility before Magnus's son Birger then assumed the throne in 1302, but his rule was blighted by a prolonged power struggle with his brothers, who demanded that he divide the kingdom between them. In 1317 he had them arrested, thrown in prison and starved to death. The horrified nobility promptly deposed him, forcing him to flee the country, and began to search for a successor.

They settled on Magnus, the child of a Swedish duke and, at the age of three, already king of Norway. Upon reaching adulthood Magnus assumed the throne and set about making some important changes to the Swedish social order. He abolished *träldom*, a form of slavery, in 1335, and established Sweden's first national legal code in 1350. His dual kingdom was huge – after the signing of the treaty of Novgorod in 1323 Finland had officially become part of the Swedish realm – but the vast majority of his subjects lived in abject poverty. During the mid 14th century the kingdom was hit by the bubonic plague, and approximately a third of the population was killed.

By the mid 1300s King Magnus was in serious trouble. Long-running disputes about the then Danish provinces of Skåne and Blekinge resulted in devastating Danish attacks on Swedish targets. In the early 1360s the nobility lost all patience with Magnus and enlisted the help of Duke Albrecht of Mecklenburg (1364-88) to unseat him. Albrecht and his forces quickly conquered Stockholm and assumed nominal control over the kingdom, while the nobles carved up the country for themselves.

NORDIC ALLIANCE

Upon the death in 1386 of Bo Jonsson Grip – chief of Sweden's ruling nobles – the union turned to Margaret, daughter of Danish King Valdemar and wife of Magnus's son King Håkon of Norway. Since the deaths of her father and husband she had already been made regent in both Denmark and Norway for her son Olof. Though Olof died in 1387, she retained her hold on power in the three kingdoms. In 1389 she was proclaimed ruler of Sweden and in return she confirmed all the privileges of the Swedish nobility. When they asked her to choose a king she nominated 14-year-old Erik VII of Pomerania. As he was already king of Norway and Denmark, Scandinavia now had just one ruler. However, Margaret was the real power behind the throne and remained so until her death in 1412.

In 1397 she formalised a Nordic alliance called the Kalmar Union, whose purpose was to limit both the commercial and political influence of the Hanseatic League. By the start of the 15th century the union encompassed Norway, Sweden, Finland, Iceland and the immensity of Greenland, making it the largest kingdom in Europe. The union was threatened many times over the next 125 years by Swedish rebellion against Danish forces.

Christopher of Bavaria ruled the union from 1439 to 1448, after being elected by the nobility. Upon his death, the noble families of Norway, Sweden and Denmark could not agree on a single candidate to fill the kingships. Sweden's nationalists, led by the Sture family, seized this opportunity to attempt to free Sweden from the union. This led to vicious fighting with Sweden's unionist faction, which was led by the Oxenstierna family. Finally, in 1470, the nationalists had the upper hand and Sten Sture the Elder (1471-97, 1501-3) was appointed the 'Guardian of the Realm'. A year later the Battle of Brunkeberg broke out in what is now the centre of Stockholm, resulting in the decimation of the unionist forces. The statue of St George and the Dragon in Storkyrkan was donated by Sture to commemorate the victory.

STOCKHOLM BLOODBATH

Aside from his crucial military victories, Sten Sture the Elder is remembered for the many technological, cultural and educational steps forward that Sweden made under his leadership. He established Sweden's first university in Uppsala in 1477, and in 1483 Sweden's first printing press was set up. Decorative arts became more sophisticated, as shown by the many fine German- and Dutch-style paintings that adorn Swedish churches of this period. Stockholm continued to grow throughout the 15th century, and by the early 16th century the city had between 6,000 and 7,000 inhabitants, most of them living in present-day Gamla Stan.

Though these numbers made Stockholm Sweden's largest town, by continental standards it was tiny. In 1500 Bremen and Hamburg both had about 20,000 inhabitants, while Lübeck had 25,000 and Paris more than 100,000. The *Parhelion Painting* in Storkyrkan gives an idea of how the city looked around this time; it depicts an unusual light phenomenon seen in 1535.

From the start, the population of Stockholm was a mix of people from different parts of Sweden and other areas of Europe. The largest 'foreign' contingent – between 10 and 20 per cent of the population – was made up of Finns, largely a result of Finland's status, since the mid 12th century, as a Swedish province. The Germans comprised a smaller, but much more powerful, proportion; since the city had been founded with Hanseatic support, wealthy German merchants had been living in Stockholm from its beginnings. By the 1580s, at least 12 per cent of the city's population was of German extraction, and Germans

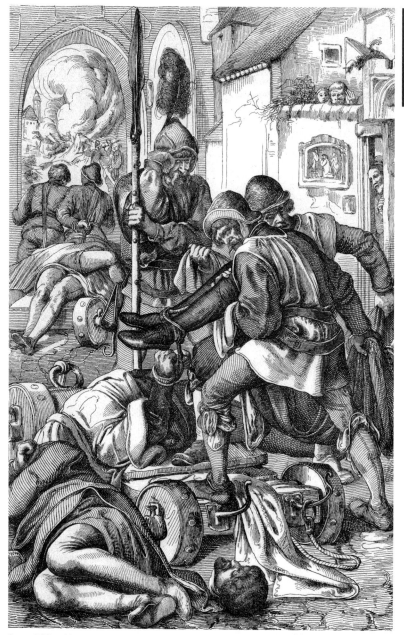

Around 90 noblemen were slaughtered during the **Stockholm Bloodbath**. *See p17.*

A monarch with flair

If asked to name their favourite monarch, most Swedes would plump for Gustav III. Extravagant, cultured and with a flair for the dramatic, Gustav left behind a cultural legacy unparalleled by any other Swedish monarch. He was controversial – not least for stripping power from the parliament (the Riksdag of the Estates) and installing himself as an absolute ruler, something that later led to his murder by his aristocratic enemies. Suitably enough, he met his end after being shot at a midnight masked ball at the Royal Swedish Opera, an institution he himself had founded.

The opera was not his only legacy: he is widely viewed as the founder of Swedish theatre, and wrote a number of his own plays. He established numerous other cultural institutions too, including the Royal Swedish Academy of Music and the Swedish Academy, the guardian of the Swedish language.

Gustav's founding of the Swedish Academy provides an indication of his taste for the whimsical: while plans were already in place for the foundation, he declared that his institution would have 18 members rather than his original proposal of 20. This, he said, was because the Swedish word for 18, 'aderton', had a nicer ring to it.

Many of Gustav III's contributions to Swedish culture have stood the test of time. While the opera house in which he was shot has since been replaced, the magnificent theatre he built at Grippsholm Castle is preserved in more or less its original state, and his collection of classical sculpture forms the basis of the Gustav III Museum of Antiquities in the Royal Palace, which opened in 1794. The collection is still open to the public today, making it one of Europe's oldest museums.

dominated Stockholm's city council until 1471, when a decision was made at a national level that Germans would be banned from participating in city politics. Dutch, Scottish, French, English, Italian, Danish, Russian and Polish merchants and traders also became increasingly significant in Stockholm during the 15th century.

By the late 15th century, most Swedes thought the Kalmar Union was a thing of the past, but the alliance was still popular in Denmark and Sweden's rulers had to deal with numerous Danish attacks. When Christian II assumed the Danish throne in 1513, the unionist movement rejoiced, thinking it had now finally found a leader who would be able to crush the Swedish nationalists.

Sure enough, Christian attacked Sweden and killed the then ruler, Sten Sture the Younger (1512-20). After Sture's death, Christian gathered leading members of the Swedish nobility together at Tre Kronor castle under the guise of granting them amnesty for their opposition to the union. After three days of feasting and celebrating, he locked the doors to the castle and arrested his guests.

Around 90 men were sentenced to death and taken to Stortorget, outside the castle, where they were killed one by one. The event came to be known as the Stockholm Bloodbath (*photo p15*), and it earned Christian II the name Christian the Tyrant. After the killings, Sture's followers were ruthlessly persecuted. This proved counter-productive, as it provoked widespread opposition to Danish rule and finally resulted in the complete breakdown of the union in 1521-23. Sweden then became a totally independent country under the leadership of Gustav Eriksson, who was crowned King Gustav Vasa (1523-60).

AGE OF EMPIRE

During Gustav Vasa's long reign Sweden was changed in two fundamental ways: it was unified under a strong hereditary monarch, and it became a Protestant country. Gustav Vasa was never a particularly religious man, and his Reformation had more to do with politics and economics than it did with theology. Lacking the wealth he required to fulfil his ambitions, he confiscated Church property, re-assigned it to the Crown, and began a propaganda campaign that stressed the negative role the Church's leadership had played in the past – in particular, Archbishop Gustav Trolle's support for Christian the Tyrant. These measures resulted in the eventual adoption of the Lutheran faith as the state religion.

The Reformation led to the state-sanctioned destruction of scores of Swedish monasteries, convents and churches, their riches going directly to an increasingly wealthy and powerful king. Gustav Vasa even had plans to tear down Storkyrkan because he felt it was situated too close to the royal residence at Tre Kronor castle, thereby complicating its defence. But public opinion was strongly opposed to the outright destruction of Stockholm's spiritual heart, so the king relented and decided only to make minor alterations. (Gustav Vasa's son Johan was more interested in both architecture and religion than his father, and in the 1580s he had a number of Stockholm's demolished churches rebuilt.)

His larder full and his domestic goals largely accomplished, Gustav Vasa launched a campaign to weaken Russia, Poland and Denmark and thereby make Sweden the dominant Baltic power, beginning with a modestly successful war against Russia in 1555-57. After his death in 1560, his sons, King Erik XIV, King Johan III and King Karl IX, took up the mission. Gustav Vasa is seen as the monarch who was most responsible for turning Sweden into a nation. He created a modern army, navy and civil service, and the intellectual figures he brought to his court connected Sweden with the Renaissance revolution in the arts and sciences.

'By the end of the 17th century Sweden was the most powerful nation in northern Europe.'

In 1570-95 Sweden fought another war against Russia, with some success. But Denmark was harder to beat – in spite of the break-up of the Kalmar Union, it had remained the most powerful country in the region, as Sweden learned to its cost in the expensive wars of 1563-70 and 1611-13. It was not until the Thirty Years War, which began in Germany in 1618, that the tide finally turned decisively in Sweden's favour in its rivalry with the Danes. After suffering a devastating defeat at the hands of the Swedes in the battle of Lutter-am-Barenburg in 1626, Denmark was forced to pull out of the war. In 1630 Sweden officially entered the war on the side of the Protestants. The resulting peace treaty of 1648 gave Sweden new provinces in northern Germany, and by 1658 a severely weakened Denmark had been forced to surrender parts of Norway plus all Danish provinces east of Öresund. As a result, by the end of the 17th century Sweden had become the most powerful nation in northern Europe.

Gustav II Adolf and his chancellor, Axel Oxenstierna, were eager to develop Stockholm and make it the political and administrative centre of the growing Swedish empire. They strengthened Stockholm's position as a centre of foreign trade, founded Sweden's Supreme Court in the city and reorganised the national assembly into four estates; nobility, clergy, burghers and farmers. This too was based in Stockholm. The medieval wall was torn down so that the city could expand to the north and south and the old wooden buildings that dominated Södermalm and Norrmalm were replaced by new, straight streets lined with stone buildings.

After Gustav II Adolf's death his young daughter, Christina, became queen, with Oxenstierna as regent until 1644. In 1654 Christina converted to Catholicism, renounced the throne and moved to Rome, where she lived out her life building up one of the finest art and book collections in Europe. She left the throne to Karl X Gustav (1654-60), who is remembered best for his invasion and defeat of Denmark in 1657, thereby creating the largest Swedish empire ever. He was succeeded by his son, Karl XI (1660-97), who in 1682 pronounced himself to be Sweden's first absolute monarch, answerable only to God.

Stockholm's population grew rapidly during Sweden's age of empire; by the 1670s the city had between 50,000 and 55,000 citizens. Literacy rates were rising, grammar schools were being established, and creativity flourished under the likes of George Stiernhielm (1598-1672), the father of modern Swedish poetry. Architecturally this was the age of the Tessins, who completed the fabulous Drottningholms Slott in 1686. It was truly a golden age for Swedish history, in military, cultural, economic and social terms.

RISE OF THE ARISTOCRACY

It was during the reign of Karl XII (1697-1718) – who assumed the throne at the tender age of 15 – that Sweden lost her empire. Between 1700 and 1721 Sweden fought the Great Northern War against a number of opponents, notably the defensive alliance of Saxony-Poland, Russia and Denmark. The young king fought valiantly against the odds to hold on to all of Sweden's far-flung possessions, but suffered a terrible loss to Russia's Peter the Great at the Battle of Poltava in 1709. His bravery in battle is still revered in Sweden's far-right circles to this day. He was finally killed in Norway by a sniper's bullet in 1718. Since he had no heir, the period after Karl's death was marked by a weakening of the monarchy and the rise of the aristocracy.

In 1719 the role of the monarch was reduced to that of nominal head of state, and with the government dominated by cabals of squabbling noblemen, the economy was left to stagnate, and political and social reforms were slow in coming.

By the end of the Great Northern War in 1721, Sweden had lost parts of Pomerania in Germany, as well as its strongholds in modern-day Estonia, Latvia, north-west Russia and Finland. Disastrous attempts were made to reconquer some of these territories by fighting wars with Russia in 1741-43 and 1788-90. Participation in the Seven Years War (1756-63) resulted in the loss of Swedish territory to Prussia. Sweden was no longer the great power it had been.

This was also a trying time for the citizens of Stockholm – on top of coping with their country's political and military difficulties, their city was ravaged by fire and disease. In 1697 it was devastated by a fire that completely destroyed Tre Kronor, the royal palace and pride of Stockholm. In 1710 plague swept through, killing about a third of the population.

Later in the century Stockholm suffered three more devastating fires, which resulted in a municipal ban on wood as a building material for new houses. Over the course of the 18th century the population stayed static at about 70,000 inhabitants. Unsanitary conditions, overcrowding, cold and disease all contributed to the fact that Stockholm's death rate was among the highest of all European cities.

But there was a brighter side. In the decades leading up to 1754, Stockholm buzzed with the building of the new Kungliga Slottet to replace Tre Kronor. The construction work was a huge stimulus for the city's artisans, and for Stockholm's economy overall. There was an influx of skilled workers from overseas, many of whom stayed on in the city, and new industries began to grow up in Stockholm. The city's foreign trade was also developing rapidly – not only with Europe but also with the Far East and the Americas.

Many of Stockholm's burghers used their increasing wealth to build larger and larger houses, especially along Skeppsbron in Gamla Stan. New residential neighbourhoods sprang up on Södermalm and Norrmalm, and many of the old houses on Gamla Stan were renovated.

SCIENTIFIC PROGRESS

The 18th century was also an age of scientific and intellectual advance in Stockholm, and throughout Sweden. Key figures included the famous botanist Carl von Linné (aka Linnaeus; 1707-78); Anders Celsius (1701-44), inventor of the centigrade temperature scale; and mystical

August Strindberg. *See p20.*

philosopher Emanuel Swedenborg (1688-1772). Sweden's best-loved poet, Carl Michael Bellman (1740-95), did much to encourage Swedish nationalism. Religious life became less strictly constrained; Jews were allowed to settle in Sweden in 1744, and in 1781 Catholics were permitted to establish a church in Stockholm for the first time since the Reformation.

The monarchy regained some of its old power under Gustav III (1771-92; *see p16* **A monarch with flair**). Seeing that the Riksdag (Parliament) was divided, the king seized the opportunity to force through a new constitution that would make the nobility share power with the Crown. Gustav III was initially popular with his subjects because he built hospitals, allowed freedom of worship and lessened economic controls. He was also a man of culture who imported French opera, theatre and literature to Sweden, and in 1782 he founded Stockholm's first opera house. During his reign, several newspapers were established, and political and cultural debate flourished. The nobility were not so happy with his increasingly tyrannical behaviour, however, especially after the start of the French Revolution. In 1792 Gustav III was shot by an assassin at a masked ball at the Kungliga Operan; he died two weeks later.

In 1805 Gustav III's successor, Gustav IV Adolf (1792-1809), was drawn into the Napoleonic Wars on the British side. This resulted in a number of gains and losses; most significantly, Sweden lost Finland to Russia and gained Norway from Denmark. All this upheaval resulted in political changes, notably the constitution of 1809, which established a system whereby a liberal monarchy would be responsible to an elected Riksdag.

The union with Norway was established in 1814, and was formalised in the 1815 Act of Union. The settlement took account of the Norwegian desire for self-government, declaring Norway a separate nation from Sweden. However, King Karl XIII (1748-1818) was now sovereign over Norway. The tension between the Swedish desire to strengthen the union, and the Norwegian wish for further autonomy, was set to increase over the century that followed.

Following the death of Karl XIII in 1818, one of Napoleon's generals, Jean-Baptiste Bernadotte, was invited to assume the Swedish throne. He accepted the offer and took the name Karl XIV Johan (1818-44). In spite of the fact that he spoke no Swedish and had never even visited Scandinavia prior to accepting the kingship, Sweden prospered under his rule.

His successor, Oscar I (1844-59), gave women inheritance rights equal to those of their brothers in 1845, passed an Education Act (1842) and a Poor Care law (1855), and reformed the restrictive craftsmen's guilds. The reign of his son, Karl XV (1859-72), is remembered for the reformation of the Riksdag in 1866 – the old four estates were replaced with a dual-chamber representative parliament. This act marked the beginning of the end for the monarch's role in politics, essentially reducing the role to that of a figurehead.

INDUSTRIAL REVOLUTION

Industrialisation arrived late to Sweden, and the mechanisation of what little industry did exist (mining, forestry and the like) was half-hearted – hardly what you would call a revolution. Meanwhile, the rural population had grown steadily through the first half of the 19th century. There was neither enough land, nor jobs in the cities, to support everyone. A severe famine during 1867-68 tipped the scales, and over one million Swedes emigrated to North America between 1860 and 1910 – a traumatic event for a country whose population in 1860 was only four million.

> **'In 1876, Ericsson opened his telephone company, and soon the city had more phones per capita than any other city in Europe.'**

In the 1860s, Sweden's first railway lines finally opened reliable communications between Stockholm and the country's southern regions; by 1871 the railway to the north was complete. The railways were a boon for nascent industry. High-quality, efficiently made steel and safety matches (a Swedish invention) were to become the two most notable Swedish manufactured products. By the late 19th century a number of large industries had been established in Stockholm; for example, a shoe factory on Södermalm, a huge Bolinders factory on Kungsholmen producing steam engines, cast-iron stoves, and other household items. In 1876, Lars Magnus Ericsson opened his Ericsson telephone company in Stockholm, and soon the city had more phones per capita than any other city in Europe.

By 1900 almost one in four Swedes lived in a city, and industrialisation was finally in full swing. Stockholm's factories attracted workers from all over the country, causing the capital's population to grow from 100,000 in 1856 to 300,000 in 1900. Conditions in many factories

were appalling, and unions emerged to fight for the rights of workers. The unions formed a confederation in 1898 but found it difficult to make progress under harsh laws on picketing.

Living conditions in the city were nearly as bad as working conditions. In response to Stockholm's growing housing crisis, the city planners – led by Claes Albert Lindhagen – put forward a proposal in 1866 to build wide boulevards and esplanades similar to those in Paris, which would create some green space within the city as well as allowing traffic to move freely. The plan resulted in the construction of some of the city's key arteries, such as Birger Jarlsgatan, Ringvägen, Karlavägen and, perhaps most impressive of all, Strandvägen. In just one decade, the 1880s, Stockholm's population increased by 46 per cent – more buildings were constructed in the 1880s than during the previous 70 years. Neighbourhoods such as Östermalm, Vasastaden, Kungsholmen, Hornstull and Skanstull were created at this time.

The late 19th century also saw the arrival of Stockholm's first continental-style hotels, cafés, restaurants, shopping galleries and department stores, to serve the city's upper classes and the beginnings of a tourist industry.

The arts and academies also prospered. Swedish dramatist August Strindberg (*photo p19*) achieved critical success across Europe, and folk historian Artur Hazelius founded the Nordiska Museet and open-air museum Skansen to preserve Sweden's rich cultural heritage. The Academy of Stockholm (now the University of Stockholm) was founded in 1878, and in 1896 Alfred Nobel donated his fortune to fund the Nobel Prizes.

SOCIAL DEMOCRACY TO THE FORE

In 1905 the union between Sweden and Norway finally dissolved. Norway took full control of its own affairs, and the Swedish state assumed its current shape.

At the outbreak of World War I Sweden declared itself neutral, in spite of its German sympathies. The British demanded that Sweden enforce a blockade against Germany. When Sweden refused to co-operate, the British blacklisted Swedish goods and interfered with Swedish commercial shipping, going so far as to seize ships' cargoes. The economy suffered dramatically and inflation shot through the roof. The British tactics led to rationing, as well as severe food shortages. Demonstrations broke out in 1917-18, partly inspired by the Russian Revolution. The demonstrators focused on food shortages and demands for democratic reforms, particularly the extension of voting rights to women.

The privations of the war helped social democracy make its breakthrough. By the end of the war, the Social Democrat party had been active for some time – its first member had been elected to the Riksdag in 1902 – though it remained marginal. After the Russian Revolution, they presented a less extreme alternative to communism in Sweden, and gained popularity. In 1920 Hjalmar Branting became Sweden's first Social Democrat prime minister, and reforms quickly followed: women were awarded the vote; the state-controlled alcohol-selling system was established; and the working day was limited to eight hours.

The Social Democrats' dominance of political affairs began in earnest in the 1930s. From 1932, the party enjoyed an unbroken 40 years in power. This made it possible to take the first steps towards building the notion of a People's Home (*Folkhemmet*), in which higher taxes would finance a decent standard of living for all. The first components of the welfare system were unemployment benefits, paid holidays, family allowances and increased old-age pensions.

At the outbreak of World War II there was little sympathy in Sweden for the Germans – unlike in 1914. Sweden declared neutrality but was in a difficult position. Germany was allied with Finland against the Soviet Union, and the relationship between Sweden and Finland was traditionally close – with Russia the age-old enemy. But when the Soviets invaded Finland in 1939, Sweden was only drawn in to a certain degree, providing weapons, volunteers and refuge to the Finns, but refusing to send regular troops. Sweden's position became even more uncomfortable in 1940, when Germany invaded Denmark and Norway, thus isolating Sweden and compelling it to supply the Nazis with iron ore and to allow them to transport their troops across Swedish territory and in Swedish waters. In 1942 the Swedish navy fought an undeclared war against Soviet submarines.

On the other hand, western allied airmen were rescued in Sweden and often sent back to Britain, and Danish and Norwegian armed resistance groups were organised on Swedish soil in 1942-43. Jewish lives were also saved, notably by Swedish businessman Raoul Wallenberg, who managed to prevent about 100,000 Hungarian Jews from being deported by the SS. After the Soviet conquest of Budapest in January 1945, Wallenberg was arrested as a suspected spy and disappeared. For years, rumours flew about whether or not he had died in a Moscow prison in 1947; Soviet documents unearthed in 1989 indicated this was what had most likely happened.

The main goal for the Swedish government during the war was not strict neutrality but rather to avoid Sweden being dragged into the conflict – this was accomplished at high diplomatic and moral cost.

At the start of the Cold War, in 1948-49, Sweden tried to form a defensive alliance with Denmark and Norway, but the plans failed

Age of destruction

'A tourist asked whether it was the Germans or the Russians who had destroyed Stockholm. He received the answer that we did this all by ourselves.'

This legendary quotation entered Swedish popular consciousness in the 1970s, in reference to the demolition of huge swathes of the capital during the preceding two decades. The demolition was focused on the Klara district in the city centre, with city councillors claiming unsentimentally that the buildings erected in the preceding four centuries were slum-like, and unfit for Stockholmers to live in. The inhabitants would move out to the shiny new suburbs, and the city centre would be left as an area for shopping and communal services. The buildings torn down would also make way for wider roads and ease the construction of the city's new underground rail network.

Plans for the demolition were laid out in the 1930s; by the time the authorities got round to carrying through the programme in the 1960s and 1970s, those parts of the city that had not originally been run down had become shabby as they served out their prolonged death sentence.

The price of the planners' municipal idealism was high: among over 500 buildings torn down were several from the 17th century and two churches. The demolition men would have gone further – plans had been laid out to demolish large parts of Gamla Stan, the city's medieval heart. But before the wrecking balls started swinging, a mixture of popular revolt and economic recession turned the tide in favour of preservation. The destruction was stopped, but not before one of Europe's biggest peacetime demolitions of historic buildings had been carried out.

partly because the other two countries wanted close links with the western allies. When the Danes and Norwegians became members of NATO in 1949, Sweden remained outside, ostensibly to prevent Finland becoming isolated in the face of the Soviet Union. In recent years it has emerged that Sweden was, in fact, in secret co-operation with NATO from as far back as the early 1950s.

A CHANGING SKYLINE

After the end of World War II, a large-scale transformation of Stockholm's city centre began, despite the fact that Stockholm was one of the few European capitals to survive the war unscathed. Once the rebuilding process on the continent was in full swing, with American-style skyscrapers rising from the ashes of all the bombed-out cities, Sweden felt left out. The city government began to tear down many of its decaying old buildings and construct anew.

As more and more people moved to Stockholm in the post-war period (the capital's population more than doubled in the 20th century), the city once again developed a severe housing crisis. Stockholm's Tunnelbana system was inaugurated in 1950 and new suburbs were built along it, to the south and north-west.

Under the leadership of Tage Erlander (1946-69), the Social Democrats introduced models for industrial bargaining and full employment that were successful in boosting the economy. At the same time, the country created a national health service and a disability benefits system, improved the quality of its schools and instituted free university education. Sweden established itself as a leading industrial country and was proud of its 'Third Way', a blending of corporate capitalism with a cradle-to-grave social safety net for all.

In 1953 Swedish diplomat Dag Hammarskjöld was appointed secretary-general of the United Nations. A controversial figure who tried to use his position to broker peace in the conflicts of the period, he became a thorn in the side of the superpowers. He died in 1961 in a mysterious plane crash over northern Rhodesia while on a mission to try to solve the Congo crisis. News of his death caused profound sadness across Sweden, as he personified the Swedes' perception of themselves as the world's conscience.

Sweden's booming post-war economy produced a great demand for labour that the national workforce could not meet. From about 1950, Sweden began to import skilled labour, primarily from the Nordic countries but also from Italy, Greece and Yugoslavia. This immigration continued unrestricted until the mid 1960s, reaching its peak in 1969-70, when more than 75,000 immigrants were entering Sweden each year. Thereafter numbers fell significantly, although Sweden continued to welcome political refugees from around the globe. By the mid 1990s, 11 per cent of Sweden's population – over a million people – were foreign-born.

The murder of foreign minister Anna Lindh in 2003 shocked the nation.

In the 1970s international economic pressures began to put the squeeze on Sweden's social goals, and it was under Prime Minister Olof Palme's leadership (1982-86) that the Third Way began to falter. Palme spent a lot of time and energy on building up Sweden's international image, while Sweden's high-tax economy was sliding into stagnation. When an unknown assailant murdered Palme on a Stockholm street in 1986 it created a national trauma.

The end of the Cold War in the late 1980s led to a serious re-evaluation of Sweden's position in international politics. The early 1990s saw the Social Democrats replaced by a centre-right coalition. This coincided with an economic crisis; long-term economic stagnation and budgetary problems led to a massive devaluation of the krona. A programme of austerity measures was then implemented, but it wasn't enough. Sweden suffered its worst recession since the 1930s and unemployment soared to a record 14 per cent. In 1994 the Social Democrats were returned to power.

'On 26 December 2004, 543 Swedes were killed in the Asian tsunami.'

With its economy and national confidence severely shaken, Sweden voted (by a very narrow margin) to join the European Union, its membership taking effect on 1 January 1995.

Since then, the economy has improved considerably, with both unemployment and inflation falling greatly, particularly during the IT boom of the 1990s. The bursting of the IT bubble seemed to threaten this renewed prosperity, but the industry picked itself up and by 2007 was booming once more.

Sweden's relationship with the EU remained controversial, with many on the left fearing that closer co-operation with other European countries threatened to undermine the tenets of the welfare state. These arguments were given a good airing in the referendum in 2003 on the euro. Despite support for membership from almost all the major parties, voters chose to stay outside the single currency zone. After the vote, the prime minister, Göran Persson, declared that Sweden would not hold another referendum on the issue for at least ten years.

The referendum came just two days after the murder of Anna Lindh, the popular foreign minister, in a Stockholm department store. A young Swede of Serbian origin, Mijailo Mijailovic, was convicted of her killing. A clear motive was never established, but Mijailovic was later ruled to have been suffering from a mental illness at the time of the attack.

The killing came as a huge shock to Swedes, and to the Social Democrat Party. It was to be the first of a number of blows to Prime Minister Göran Persson that would culminate in his defeat in the 2006 general election.

TSUNAMI TRAGEDY

A tragedy of much greater proportions befell Sweden on 26 December 2004, when 543 Swedes were killed in the Asian tsunami. The number of Swedes killed was greater even than in the 1994 Estonia ferry disaster, in which 501 Swedes died. With most ministers and civil servants at home for Christmas, it took a whole day for the government to realise that thousands of Swedes were holidaying in the area. The episode dented the government's reputation, and the next two years were dominated by inquiries into the handling of Sweden's response to the disaster.

The opposition found themselves in a good position to capitalise on the Social Democrats' discomfort. The four centre-right parties – the Moderate Party, the Liberal People's Party, the Centre Party and the Christian Democrats – agreed to campaign on a joint manifesto. Calling themselves the Alliance for Sweden, they went on to win the election in September 2006, promising modest tax cuts and cuts to some benefits. The aim, they said, was to reduce Sweden's hidden unemployment, which by some measures was between 15 and 20 per cent.

Moderate leader Fredrik Reinfeldt was the first non-Social Democrat prime minister for 12 years. He was also a rarity from the longer-term perspective – the Social Democrats had ruled Sweden for 67 of the previous 76 years. He was the youngest prime minister for 80 years, and his cabinet included the first Swedish minister of African descent and the first gay minister.

While his tax cuts and benefit cuts were small, he also put into action plans to privatise state industries such as Vin&Sprit, maker of Absolut Vodka, and sell the state's stakes in companies like telephone operator Telia Sonera.

There was to be no honeymoon period for Reinfeldt, however. Within days of appointing his cabinet, two ministers had been forced to resign – his trade minister for not paying all the social fees for her nanny, his culture minister for not paying her television licence fee.

Emboldened by these early victories, the Social Democrats continued to attack the new government, particularly focusing on its plans to cut benefits to the unemployed. In this, they were able to draw on support from their powerful allies in the unions. But whatever blows the left landed on the government, with the centre-right expected to remain in power until at least 2010, the shape of Sweden's welfare state is set to be changed permanently.

Stockholm Today

It's all change at the top, but the script remains the same: high taxes, healthy welfare, happy people.

For a country of just nine million people, Sweden makes a big impression on the world. A recent study concluded that if Sweden was a commercial brand, it would be worth $464 billion, significantly more than its Scandinavian neighbours and more than many much larger nations.

Indeed, few other countries of the same size have produced pop bands to match the success of Abba while at the same time boasting international firms of the stature of Ikea, Saab, Electrolux and Ericsson, and becoming a magnet for foreign politicians in search of an ideology.

These politicians were, until recently, usually of a left-wing bent. They looked to Sweden to confirm their view that a country could be a socialist paradise and have a thriving economy at the same time. They were to be sorely disappointed in September 2006 when Sweden, for the first time in 12 years, kicked the Social Democrats out of government and replaced them with a centre-right coalition under the leadership of Prime Minister Fredrik Reinfeldt.

Not that Swedes have changed overnight from being highly taxed lovers of the welfare state to free-wheeling dog-eat-dog capitalists. In fact, the new government came to power by promising to leave the fundamental structure of the Social Democratic state intact. Tax cuts have been focused on normal wage-earners rather than the super-rich and jobs have been promised for the large numbers of people who were living on various forms of welfare payment.

While the policies may not be radical, the new government nonetheless presented a big change, given that the Social Democrats had ruled Sweden for 65 of the past 74 years. Indeed, familiarity with former Prime Minister Göran Persson had bred a certain amount of contempt, and for many voters Reinfeldt provided a fresh face who promised to introduce any changes gradually and painlessly.

CHANGING FACES

The changing nature of the country's inhabitants is also confounding the stereotypes. The image of Swedes as blonde, pigtailed Ingas and strapping bearded Viking Svens is rapidly getting out of date as the pace of immigration accelerates. Refugees from troubled corners of the world such as Bosnia, Somalia and, more recently, Iraq have followed earlier immigrants from southern Europe, Turkey and South America. More people migrated to Sweden in 2006 than during any other year since records began, 131 years ago. These included 9,700 Iraqis; indeed, in 2006, more Iraqis are believed to have moved to Södertälje, a city in Stockholm's commuter belt, than to the whole of the United States.

'Swedes refer to the rest of Europe as "the continent" as though it were some distant entity.'

This immigration is having an effect on the language. The large immigrant-dominated suburbs have a dialect of their own, with words from languages such as Turkish and Arabic mixing with Swedish. Last year's dictionary from the Swedish Academy included *guzz* (Turkish for 'girl') and *keff* (Arabic for 'bad'). Sweden's culinary dictionary is also getting updated, with Lebanese eateries popularising meze buffets, a concept that goes down well with Swedes brought up on *smörgåsbord*.

The impact of immigration on politics has also been visible. While most Swedes remain pragmatically liberal on the issue, there are pockets of dissent, and anti-immigrant parties increased their share of the vote in the 2006 elections. The Sweden Democrats, whose policies include paying for the repatriation of immigrants, gained 2.8 per cent of the vote, putting them within shouting distance of the four per cent needed to enter parliament.

Globalisation has affected Sweden in other ways too. The cherished Swedish model, in which unions and employers bash out wage agreements for their workers without interference from the government, has taken something of a beating as union membership declines, particularly among the young. In this way, as in others, Sweden has moved slowly towards the European norm.

Unions have attempted to go on the offensive and blockade firms to force them to sign up to collective agreements. This has led to tensions, with the media and public opinion often siding against the unions, such as when a young salad-bar owner in Gothenburg was forced to sell up after a strident campaign by union activists.

Such blockades have not been confined to Swedish companies – companies from other European countries have also faced blockades

for not first signing deals with unions, leading to questions over whether the Swedish model is at odds with membership of the EU.

NATIONHOOD AND IDENTITY

Indeed, Sweden shares with its Scandinavian neighbours an ambivalence to the whole EU project. While Swedes are in many ways good Europeans – many speak multiple languages, travel widely and are well informed about international affairs – they have a strong sceptical streak. Like many Brits, they refer to the rest of Europe as simply 'Europe' or 'the continent', as though it were a distant entity of which they were not really part.

This sense of being set apart was one reason why in a 2003 referendum Sweden rejected membership of the European single currency, the euro. Polls in late 2006 showed that another three years on the outside had strengthened opposition to Sweden joining, with only 35 per cent in favour.

There is one thing, however, that Swedes love about Europe – the Eurovision Song Contest. The Swedish heats for the event, known as *Melodifestivalen* (the 'Melody Festival') are the most-watched entertainment show of all time in Sweden, and remain one of the country's most popular programmes.

But even in Eurovision, there are signs that Sweden is running out of sympathy with its European partners. While some other European nations take the pan-European final with a pinch of salt, for the Swedes it is no laughing matter. An unimpressive performance by the Swedish entry is followed by agonised analysis in both tabloids and the quality press. In 2007, when Sweden came 18th, leader writers harrumphed that if Swedish songs couldn't win, then maybe the country should consider whether it wants to participate at all.

In the political arena, Euroscepticism is based on a perception that the EU threatens Sweden's particular brand of welfare state. Particularly, many harbour suspicions that EU bureaucrats are itching to bring Swedish taxes further into line with European norms, to abolish the alcohol and gambling monopolies that protect Swedes from themselves, and to cajole the historically neutral country into joining military alliances such as NATO.

The sceptics brandish a succession of rulings from the European courts, which have slowly chipped away at Swedish exceptionalism, such as when in June 2007 they overturned a ban on Swedes importing cheap booze bought online. For many who support the Systembolaget alcohol monopoly shops, this was a sign that Europe was intent on undermining the Swedish way of doing things.

Who's holding the baby?

in one of the fleet of designer prams parked between the tables. There is also a better chance in Stockholm than in many other capital cities that those lattes will be being sipped by a man.

Swedish couples are given 450 days of state-funded leave to look after every child. Most of this can be split between the parents as they see fit, but the mother and father must each take 60 days' leave. If they don't, the other parent cannot take their 60 days. The aim of this is explicit – fathers are expected to do their bit. This 'daddy quota' aims to encourage fathers to take more time off. Yet Swedish men have resisted using more of their allotted days.

They're now under pressure to use more – not from their partners, but from the politicians. A bold parenting agenda – and a heated debate – are currently underway. Certain policy-shapers are proposing that fathers and mothers must split the parental time 50-50 or else lose the time (and the benefit pay). They believe that only such a drastic measure will help ensure complete gender equality at home and at work.

The generous allowances for parental leave are one explanation given for the rise in births in the capital – more than 25,000 children were born in the city in 2006, compared to 19,000 in 1999. In addition, children aged one and above are given free daycare – something that for many parents allows them to keep one foot in the workplace while bringing up their youngsters. For parents in Stockholm, support is never far away.

What makes women happy, lowers the divorce rate and increases male life expectancy? No, it's not the latest miracle drug. It's dads who spend more time at home raising the kids, according to several recent Swedish studies. And dads in Stockholm are leading the way. Walk past a city coffee shop on a weekday during working hours, and the chances are the establishment will have been colonised by hordes of parents, sipping on lattes while their children gurgle contentedly

At the root of this suspicion of European meddling is a deep-rooted confidence that Sweden could teach the world a thing or two about quality of life. Despite paying what are still the highest taxes in the world, Swedes have the right to feel a bit smug. The World Bank's Human Development Index, which ranks countries according to their quality of life, puts it in second place after Australia.

Sweden comes out well in a wide variety of international surveys. Generous parental leave has helped it to be named the best country in the world to be a mother; it also has the lowest levels of high blood pressure, the second-highest rate of female representation in parliament and one of the lowest rates of teenage pregnancy in the western world.

Little wonder, then, that Swedes are a nation of unashamed flag-wavers. Drive through a Stockholm suburb on a summer evening and you will see flags fluttering from many a garden flagpole. Birthday cakes are often decorated with small Swedish flags attached to cocktail sticks, and buses fly the blue and yellow ensign to mark occasions ranging from Midsummer to King Carl XVI Gustaf's birthday.

The king and his family might be low-key by European standards, but they remain one of the main focuses of Swedish patriotism. Despite having the last vestiges of formal power removed in 1974, the royals retain a central role in national life. The highlight of the royal year is the Nobel Prize banquet held at Stockholm City Hall. The whole event is broadcast live on national television, and although presenters always explain dutifully the prizewinners' world-changing discoveries, the hushed tones are usually reserved to comment on Princess Madeleine's dress or Queen Silvia's tiara.

The royal children provide the staple diet of Sweden's army of celebrity magazines, with endless speculation about when and to whom they will get married. After years of unfulfilled predictions that Victoria was about to announce her engagement to boyfriend Daniel Westling, whom she met in 2002, the tabloids decided in 2007 that the wedding was off.

'Disdain for Stockholmers has inspired northerners to describe the capital as the mire of queens.'

The middle-class Westling was simply not viewed by royal flunkeys as suitable prince material, the tabloids claimed, and promptly produced a list of alternative grooms. These included a bevvy of Swedish television presenters and international celebrities such as Justin Timberlake. The royals themselves rise above the tittle-tattle, managing to maintain a dignified silence about their private lives, despite the ferocious interest of the press.

CITY AND COUNTRY
Any city that dominates the political, commercial and media life of a country as comprehensively as Stockholm does, tends to have an uneasy relationship with the provinces. This is particularly true in Sweden, which has a population of just nine million spread over the third-largest land area in western Europe.

With 1.9 million inhabitants, the Stockholm region is home to just under a quarter of the Swedish population, and has around twice as many inhabitants as Gothenburg. The Stockholm-centric nature of the media, politics and business grates with many outside the capital, particularly inhabitants of the sparsely populated north. Disdain for the hair-gelled, suited, fake-tanned Stockholmers has even inspired northerners to coin the term *fjollträsk*, roughly translated as 'mire of queens', to describe the capital.

If Stockholmers are viewed in the provinces as effete and snooty, city-dwellers' views of the country are more affectionate. Many own second homes in the countryside, something that even today is possible for people with relatively modest means. The dream of waking up on a summer's day in a simple, red wooden cottage by a lake is one that has endured for generations of urban Swedes.

Stockholmers' reputation in the rest of Scandinavia is little better, and recent efforts by the city to brand itself as the 'Capital of Scandinavia' have scarcely made it more popular in Oslo and Copenhagen. But the city authorities point out that Stockholm is the largest city in the largest country in Scandinavia, and the most important financial centre in the region.

The town–country divide was in evidence in the results of the 2006 general election. While Stockholm and much of the more densely populated south voted for the centre-right administration of Fredrik Reinfeldt, the north would have much preferred to stick to Sweden's traditional Social Democratic path.

The environment was a hot issue in Swedish politics long before the current wave of concern about global warming. The country's wealth of lakes and trees, the people's love of outdoor pursuits and the dramatic contrast between Swedish seasons mean that Swedes pay close attention to nature. In a referendum held alongside the 2006 election, Stockholmers approved a congestion charging scheme. This will mean that drivers will pay tolls to use the city's roads during peak hours, unless they are one of the increasing number of people driving hybrid cars or cars that use alternative fuels such as ethanol or biogas. Around 15 per cent of all cars sold in Sweden in 2006 were 'green' cars.

MONEY MATTERS
For such a small country, Sweden is home to a large number of international brands. Car-makers Volvo and Saab may have been sold off to US car giants, but furniture retailer Ikea, clothes chains H&M and Gant and telecoms giant Ericsson all remain in Swedish hands.

The many Swedish companies owned by the state could soon find themselves under foreign ownership, however, as the current government pushes through its privatisation programme. Among the companies on the for-sale list are telecoms company Telia Sonera and Vin&Sprit, makers of Absolut Vodka, the third-largest brand of alcoholic spirits in the world.

Music is another area in which Sweden has a global presence. Abba may have kick-started Swedish international success, but since then the music industry has taken on a life of its own and Sweden is now the world's third-largest music exporter, thanks to acts such as the Cardigans and the Hives.

Sweden might punch above its weight, but it would be uncharacteristic of Swedes to boast openly of their country's achievements. Yet under the naturally modest outer shell, this is a country that feels comfortable with its place in the world.

Svenskt Tenn.

Made in Sweden

Never forget the three Fs: form, function and flat-packing.

In the world of furniture, glassware, industrial and increasingly fashion design, Swedes have carved out a profitable niche, creating products that are functional and effortlessly stylish. The result is big business around the world, with Swedish design flying off the shelves from Tallinn to Tokyo.

The roots of Swedish design are everywhere to be seen. Ikea, the biggest exporter of the Swedish functionalist concept, still furnishes the majority of Sweden's homes. Alternatively, walk around the boutiques of Östermalm or the fashionable SoFo district of Södermalm, and you'll find achingly simple furniture at achingly high prices.

But while sleek and functional is still the order of the day in most Stockholm studios, a new generation of designers is less bound to the philosophy that underpins the minimalist tradition. Today, designers of glassware, furniture, wallpaper and industrial products are looking abroad to the rest of Europe, the Middle East, Africa and Asia for inspiration.

Combining the well-known Swedish look with more colourful, daring and flamboyant styles, the new generation is leading the country's design tradition in an exciting new direction (*see p30* **Minimalist no more?**).

DEVELOPMENT

Though modern Swedish design dates back roughly 100 years, its aesthetic roots can be traced further back. The highly influential Gustavian style, which came about during the reign of King Gustav III in the 18th century, marked a move away from elaborate baroque to a more classical, restrained elegance characterised by white wood and simple curves. Then, in the late 1800s, the Swedish elite was first exposed to German art nouveau, a new style that dramatically changed the way well-to-do Swedes thought about their homes.

It marked a further shift towards organic forms and sinewy curves, inspired by nature, and led to even less fancy and more ergonomic furniture and household accessories.

The paintings of late 19th-century artist **Carl Larsson** (1853-1919) played a significant role in the development of Swedish interior design. In 1899 he created a widely reproduced series of watercolours called *Ett Hem* ('A Home'), featuring the simple furniture and pale-coloured textiles created by his wife Karin, who was inspired by local design traditions, the English Arts and Crafts movement and art nouveau trends on the continent. In Larsson's paintings, it is easy to recognise the rural wooden floors and rectangular woven rag rugs that are still common in nearly every Swedish home. The striped patterns on the simple white-painted chairs are also strikingly similar to those sold today by Swedish interior decorating monolith Ikea which, with more than 200 branches worldwide, seems to be rapidly taking over the refurbishment of the world's homes.

In an essay entitled 'Beauty for All' ('Skönhet för Alla'; 1899) inspired by the Larssons' aesthetics, Swedish social critic Ellen Key defined the democratic ideals embodied in the Larssons' rustic home: 'Not until nothing ugly can be bought, when the beautiful is as cheap as the ugly, only then can beauty for all become a reality.' These democratic principles, as well as those expressed by Gregor Paulsson in 1919 in his book *More Beautiful Things for Everyday Use*, still inform Swedish society and influence new design.

'Fresh air and natural light became the defining characteristics of Swedish home design.'

Many of the classics of Swedish design came out during the creatively fertile 1930s, as modernism blossomed throughout northern Europe. The movement made its breakthrough in Sweden at the Stockholm Exhibition in 1930, organised by influential Swedish architect **Gunnar Asplund** (1885-1940), and the Swedish offshoot came to be known as functionalism. Some speculate that Sweden was especially receptive to the gospel of functionalism – and later to minimalist severity – because of sober Swedish Lutheranism, as well as a national penchant for social engineering.

The fresh air, natural light and access to greenery extolled by Asplund's functionalism quickly became the defining characteristics of Swedish home design and urban planning. During the next two decades, as news of the practical and beautiful designs coming out of the Nordic region spread to other parts of

Europe, as well as North America, the reputation of Scandinavian style became firmly established.

DESIGN ICONS

The demigods of Swedish furniture design – Carl Malmsten and Bruno Mathsson – both flourished during the dynamic pre-war period. **Carl Malmsten** (1888-1972) sought forms that some described as 'rural rococo', and aspired to a craft-oriented and functional approach to furniture design. The company he founded 60 years ago – **Carl Malmsten Inredning** (*see p155*) – is still in the same family. His counterpart, **Bruno Mathsson** (1907-88), is famous for his groundbreaking work with bentwood. Mathsson's light and simple modernistic designs can be seen in Stockholm at **Studio B3**'s permanent showroom (Barnhusgatan 3, Norrmalm, 08 21 42 31, www.scandinaviandesign.com/b3).

A third giant of the pre-war design era was modernist architect and designer **Josef Frank** (1885-1967), an Austrian exile in Sweden, who created elegant furniture and vibrant floral textiles. Frank was so ahead of his time that his brilliant patterns look like they could have been created yesterday, and are still very popular. Frank's colourful fabrics can be seen at **Svenskt Tenn** (*see p156*), the design emporium on Strandvägen in Östermalm.

The term 'Scandinavian design' was coined in the 1950s when the exhibition 'Design in Scandinavia' toured northern America, and Nordic design, with its clean lines, high-level functionality and accessibility, became the most internationally influential design movement of the time. The latter half of the 20th century inevitably brought some variance from the founding facets of Swedish design, with designers responding to the times and experimenting. For instance, in the 1960s an 'anti-functional' movement took root as Swedish designers looked to their Italian counterparts for inspiration. Free from the rules of functionalism, they began to produce chairs, lamps and sofas in all sizes, shapes and colours, and in a variety of new and unusual materials, notably plastic.

During the economic boom of the 1980s, eclecticism and postmodernism took over as designers such as **Jonas Bohlin** (born 1953) and **Mats Theselius** (born 1956) began creating 'work of art' furniture in limited editions for sale to collectors. Bohlin's breakthrough came in 1980 with 'Concrete', a chair made out of – you guessed it – concrete.

A kind of neo-functionalist minimalism had taken over by the 1990s. Suddenly every bar and restaurant in the city, it seemed, was painted white, with unobtrusive furniture and almost no decoration on the walls or tables. This Scandinavian ultra-simplicity quickly spread to the rest of the world, in no small part owing to the praise it earned from international style magazines such as *Wallpaper**.

FRESH FACES

These days, a fresh generation of creators, inspired by everything from Japanese cartoons to baroque furniture, are bringing a playful and often witty twist to the local design scene.

Designers Anna Holmquist and Chandra Ahlsell of industrial design firm **FolkForm** (www.folkform.se) are good examples of this. Their masonite tabletop embedded with a real butterfly won them the prestigious main prize at Future Design Days, a cutting-edge international design festival.

Held in Stockholm every November, **Future Design Days** (www.futuredesigndays.com) is a key event in the calendar. The festival takes the stance that all design should have a purpose, and is therefore all-encompassing. Previous guests at the festival have included **Christian von Koenigsegg** (www. koenigsegg.com), founder of the Swedish company bearing his name that makes the fastest street-legal cars in the world (sleekly designed, with oodles of sex appeal); **Ulrika Hydman-Vallien**, the inspiring glassware designer who makes colourful vases that radiate personality; and **Jonas Blanking**, who created the innovative hard-shelled, high-tech Boblbee urban backpack (www.boblbee.com) that has been marketed around the world.

Another Stockholm designer making waves at the moment is **Damian Williamson**. Williamson's 'Silent Supper' exhibition at the Stockholm Furniture Fair in 2007 drew on Leonardo da Vinci's *The Last Supper* for inspiration, replacing the disciples with objects. The purpose, he said, was to explore how objects communicate with humans.

PRODUCT PLACEMENT

Many of these young designers' cool creations – ranging from ceramics and jewellery to wine carriers and axes – can be found in Stockholm's seven **DesignTorget** stores (see p150), the largest of which is located in Kulturhuset at Sergels Torg. Other upscale design outlets include the **NK** department store (see p137), **R.O.O.M** (see p155) and **Asplund** (see p155).

If money's no issue, head for high-profile **Svenskt Tenn** (see p156). The company was founded in 1924 by art teacher Estrid Ericson and pewter artist Nils Fougstedt. The name means 'Swedish Pewter', and it still produces exquisite objects made of the alloy. Today, however, it is perhaps best known for Josef Frank's textile designs, with rich nature-inspired patterns. The 300th anniversary of the birth of Swedish botanist Carolus Linnaeus

Minimalist no more?

The *International Herald Tribune* recently declared that Swedish design was 'minimalist no more'. Few would go that far, and Swedish designers such as Thomas Bernstrand, Anna von Schewen and Jonas Bohlin remain keen disciples of the clean lines and functionalism that have characterised the country's fashion, furniture and industrial design.

However, a new generation of creative talent is breaking out of the mould established over the past few decades, creating in the process a new opulent, witty Swedish style.

Jewellery designers **David & Martin** (www.davidandmartin.com) are among those leading this trend. Favoured by Karl Lagerfeld and winners of numerous prizes on home turf, the pair's creations are extravagant and original. The bracelets, brooches and necklaces in their Chicken Feet Collection are decorated, as the name would suggest, with golden chicken feet. The Bone Collection has a similarly surreal edge to it.

In the world of wallpaper, **Hanna Werner**'s 2006 collection 'By Hanna', produced by Borås Tapeter (www.borastapeter.se), is challenging Swedes to jettison their monochromal interior design tastes and become a bit more daring. Rich floral patterns of reds, blacks, golds and greens give a warm, luxurious feeling.

In clothing too, Stockholm designers are beginning to exhibit a more decadent streak. The likes of **Martin Bergström** (www.martinbergstrom.com) and knitwear designer **Sandra Backlund** (www.sandra backlund.com) shy away from the chic but practical lines of high-street darlings Filippa K and Johan Lindeberg, instead allowing their imaginations to run riot with bright colours and floral inspiration.

The result of all this is a design scene in Stockholm that, while loyal in many ways to its minimalist heritage, is daring to think outside the monochrome box.

Design Torget gives young designers the chance to sell their work on a commission basis.

was marked by Svenskt Tenn launching a new edition of a classic chest of drawers, decorated with reproductions of the botanical wall charts Linnaeus used as wallpaper in his Stockholm bedroom.

'To get a taste of the alternative design culture, take a safari around SoFo.'

To get a taste of the alternative side of Stockholm's design culture, take a safari around **SoFo**, on the hip south side of town. SoFo comprises the area south of Folkungagatan and east of Götgatan on Södermalm – hence, SoFo – and is full of cute cafés and postage stamp-sized fashion and design boutiques, often started by recent graduates of Beckmans School of Design.

If that sounds a little too bijou, then do as many locals do and hop on the free shuttle bus from Regeringsgatan 13 to **Ikea**'s gigantic warehouse store at Kungens Kurva (*see p155*). Ikea's products, though mass-produced and restricted at times by the flat-packing system, are design-savvy, and well-known designers work on its collections. Beware: this mega home-furnishing palace is so vast that once you enter, you may never find your way out.

A good place to get a sense of Swedish design through the years is the **National Museum** (*see p66*), which has a permanent exhibition on Scandinavian design from 1900 to 2000. It is also home to an impressive collection of applied art, design and industrial design from the 14th century to the present day.

For the contemporary scene, pay a visit to **Svensk Form** (Swedish Society of Crafts and Design; Holmamiralens väg 2, Skeppsholmen) – located just around the corner from the recently reopened Moderna Museet – which hosts cutting-edge exhibitions of products ranging from plastic household items and ceramic ovens through to maternity clothes. Established by Nils Månsson Mandelgren in 1845, Svensk Form claims to be the oldest organisation of its kind in the world. Its magazine, *Form*, has been published since 1932, and since 1983 the society has presented the annual Utmärkt Svensk Form awards to the creators of the best-designed new Swedish products of the year.

Svensk Form can take plenty of credit for the continued vibrancy of Swedish design. It was one of the main forces behind the successful 2005 Year of Swedish Design, which boosted the profile of design in the public consciousness through exhibitions and public projects up and down the country.

It now has ambitious plans to create Stockholm's first full-time design centre. The organisation has drawn up a blueprint for a museum, with the working title of **Stockholm Design Centre**, in Telefonplan, a trendy suburb to the west of the city centre. Exhibitions will include a broad range of Swedish and international design, and give plenty of space to experimental concepts. It is also hoped to use the centre for seminars, conferences and research.

At the time of writing there was still some way to go in organising funding, but Svensk Form was aiming to open the centre in 2008.

Where to Stay

Where to Stay 34

Features

Hotel Rival. *See p43.*

Where to Stay

Standards are high, but cheap sleeps are few and far between.

Shipshape above and below decks at the nautical **Lord Nelson**. *See p36.*

No wonder Stockholm is a major conference destination: it's a compact city full of effortlessly multilingual people – and lots of mid-range hotels. In the past many of these lacked character, and a few recent disappointments – notably the closure of the Lydmar, one of Stockholm's most distinctive hotels, and the reopening of the charmlessly renovated Scandic Anglais – seemed to indicate an industry running low on imagination and verve.

But there are now some more positive signs. A new Lydmar is being created next door to the **Grand Hôtel** (*see p37*), itself enjoying a new lease of life following an extensive renovation. A giant **Clarion** (*see p37*) is being built near the central station, and judging by their

> ❶ Green numbers in this chapter correspond to the location of each hotel as marked on the street maps. *See pp238-251.*

Södermalm property it should be a business hotel with a twist. And the new **Hotel Stureplan** (www.hotelstureplan.se), currently under construction in Östermalm, looks set to be a welcome addition – a fashionable boutique hotel in a 19th-century building (retaining period features, natch), located just a stone's throw from some of Stockholm's most fashionable shopping and clubbing.

Sweden's Hotel & Restaurant Association oversees the star ratings for the country's hotels. Nine hotels in the country merit the full five-star rating; eight of them are in or near Stockholm. They are the **First Hotel Reisen** (*see p35*), the **Grand** (*see p37*), the **Hilton** (*see p43*), the **Radisson SAS Royal Viking**, the **Radisson SAS Strand** (*see p39*), the **Sheraton** (*see p39*) and the **Victory** (*see p36*), plus the **Sigtuna Stadshotell** (*see p47*) which is in the small town of Sigtuna, 40 kilometres (25 miles) from Stockholm.

Hotel standards are high in Stockholm, and wherever you stay staff will almost certainly speak excellent English. Breakfast is typically a buffet of cereals, fruit, cold cuts, fish, cheese, hot dishes, crispbread, juice, tea and coffee. Swedes value the quality of beds and bedding (some hotels even have a pillow menu); note that double beds tend to come with two single duvets rather than one double-sized one.

Stockholm is not cheap, but it has plenty of youth hostels. These aren't just scuzzy pads for backpackers, but clean lodgings ideal for families, often offering single and double rooms. Be aware that you may have to buy (usually cheap) membership if you are not a member of a recognised hostelling association, and bedlinen, towels and breakfast will cost extra.

PRICES AND RESERVATIONS

Since Stockholm is a business hub, hotel rates can drop by as much as half on weekends. This means you can often enjoy deluxe surroundings for much less than you might expect. Always ask about packages and special deals (you may have to book two nights to get a discounted rate). Rates in July, when most Swedes take the month off, are usually cheaper.

We've divided the hotels by area and then according to the average price of a weekday double room. The categories are: **deluxe** (from 2,300kr per room); **expensive** (1,900kr-2,300kr per room); **moderate** (800kr-1,900kr per room); and **budget** (under 800kr per room), which also includes youth hostels. Breakfast is included in the price unless stated otherwise.

The tourist office produces a free hotel brochure and runs a very good reservations service: book online (www.stockholmtown.com), by phone (50 82 85 08), by email (hotels@stoinfo.se), by email (info@svb.stockholm.se), or in person at the Hotellcentrallen office on the concourse of Central Station. If you visit the office in person, there's a 50kr fee for a hotel, or 20kr for a hostel (same-day hostel bookings only). Alternatively, you could try Destination Stockholm (663 00 80, www.destination-stockholm.com), which offers hotel and sightseeing packages off-season.

CHAIN HOTELS

When you're hotel hunting, don't ignore the chain option: they may have a corporate feel, but you can expect high standards and good service. The following chains have websites available in English: **Choice Hotels Scandinavia** (www.choicehotels.se), **First Hotels** (www.firsthotels.com), **Radisson SAS** (www.radisson.com), **Rica City Hotels** (www.rica.se) and **Scandic Hotels** (www.scandic-hotels.com).

B&B AGENCIES

One of the cheapest ways to stay in Stockholm is in a private home. The following agencies can arrange a room in a private home for you, usually in the range of 200kr-500kr per person: **Stockholm Guesthouse** (www.stockholmguesthouse.com); **Bed and Breakfast Service Stockholm** (www.bedbreakfast.a.se); and **Gästrummet** (www.gastrummet.com).

Gamla Stan

Deluxe

First Hotel Reisen

Skeppsbron 12, 111 30 Stockholm (22 32 60/ www.firsthotels.com). T-bana Gamla Stan/bus 2, 43, 55, 59, 76. **Rates** 1,500kr-2,600kr double. **Credit** AmEx, DC, MC, V. **Map** p241 H8 ❶
This 17th-century former coffee house became a hotel in 1819. Now run by the First Hotel chain, it fully exploits its waterside location, with each of the 144 handsomely decorated rooms enjoying some sort of water view. There's a sauna in the vaulted cellar, while the deluxe rooms have either a sauna or jacuzzi en suite. A good restaurant adjoins the lobby, but sadly, the decor is unexciting, and the five-star Reisen hasn't quite shaken off the chain-hotel feel – though the fantastic location and views make amends.
Bar. Business centre. Concierge. Disabled-adapted rooms. Internet (high-speed, shared terminal). No-smoking rooms. Parking (395kr/day). Pool (indoor). Restaurant. Room service. Sauna. TV: pay movies.

The best Hotels

For designer chic
Nordic Light Hotel. *See p39.*

For tight budgets
Hotel Tre Små Rum. *See p45.*

For peace and quiet
Villa Källhagen. *See p46.*

For sea views
Hotel J. *See p46.*

For shopping and nightlife
Scandic Hotel Sergel Plaza. *See p39.*

For sheer class
Grand Hôtel. *See p37.*

For submarine dreams
Victory Hotel. *See p36.*

Lady Hamilton Hotel

Storkyrkobrinken 5, 111 28 Stockholm (50 64 01 00/ www.lady-hamilton.se). T-bana Gamla Stan/bus 3, 43, 53, 55, 59. **Rates** *1,750kr-2,650kr double.* **Credit** AmEx, DC, MC, V. **Map** p241 H7 ②

The Lady Hamilton is perhaps the nicest of the three small hotels owned by the Bengtsson family (the others are the Lord Nelson and the Victory; for both, *see below*). As the names suggest, all have some connection with the British naval hero. A ship's figurehead and a portrait of Nelson's mistress dominate the lobby at the four-star Lady Hamilton, but the rest of this warren-like building (dating from 1470) is stuffed with antiques. The 34 rooms are each named after a regional wildflower, and there are also four apartments for rent. The mix of colourful painted cupboards, wall paintings, grandfather clocks and old-fashioned fabrics is charming. A 14th-century well in the basement is now a plunge pool for the sauna.

Bar. Business centre. Internet (high-speed, shared terminal). No-smoking rooms. Parking (395kr/day). Restaurant. Room service. Sauna. TV: pay movies.

Victory Hotel

Lilla Nygatan 5, 111 28 Stockholm (50 64 00 00/ www.victory-hotel.se). T-bana Gamla Stan/bus 3, 43, 53, 55, 59. **Credit** AmEx, DC, MC, V. **Map** p241 J7 ③

Named after Admiral Lord Nelson's flagship, the five-star Victory leads the line for the three-hotel Bengtsson chain. Inside, you can hardly move for the colourful figureheads, brass instruments, carved whalebone and model boats. A letter dated 1801 from Nelson to Lady Hamilton complaining of seasickness is proudly displayed in the lobby. The

45 rooms, including 22 doubles and four suites, are named after Swedish sea captains. Downstairs are the sauna, meeting rooms and the Leijontornet restaurant, where part of a medieval city tower was unearthed in the 1980s. The hotel also has four apartments for stays of two weeks or longer.

Bar. Business centre. Internet (high-speed, shared terminals). No-smoking rooms. Parking (395kr/day). Pool (indoor). Restaurant. Room service. Sauna. TV: pay movies.

Expensive

Lord Nelson Hotel

Västerlånggatan 22, 111 29 Stockholm (50 64 01 20/www.lord-nelson.se). T-bana Gamla Stan/bus 3, 43, 53, 55, 59. **Rates** *1,490kr-2,290kr double.* **Credit** AmEx, DC, MC, V. **Map** p241 J7 ④

The smallest and cheapest option in the Bengtsson family's hotel group, the three-star Nelson must also be Sweden's narrowest hotel, only 5m (16ft) wide. Located right on Gamla Stan's tourist strip, this tall, 17th-century building with its glass-and-brass entrance is pretty ship-shape itself. Add in the long mahogany reception desk, the portraits of Nelson, the names of the floors (Gun Deck, Quarter Deck and so on) and assorted naval antiques and you could be forgiven for thinking you were sailing the ocean blue. The 29 recently refurbished rooms are pleasant but, as on a ship, quite snug – 18 are singles. There's no restaurant, but a snack bar serves breakfast and light meals. *Photo p34.*

Business centre. Internet (high-speed, shared terminals). No-smoking rooms. Parking (395kr/day). Room service. Sauna. TV: pay movies.

Grand Hôtel.

Rica City Hotel Gamla Stan

Lilla Nygatan 25, 111 28 Stockholm (723 72 50/
www.rica.se). T-bana Gamla Stan/bus 2, 3, 53, 55.
Rates 1,220kr-2,340kr double. **Credit** AmEx, DC,
MC, V. **Map** p241 J7 ❺

Just down the street from the Lord Nelson, this 51-
room hotel in a 17th-century building is steps from
the waterfront, but none of the rooms has a view.
For 65 years it was owned by the Salvation Army,
which used it as a hostel until it was purchased by
a Norwegian hotel chain in 1998 and transformed
into a first-class property. Rooms are elegant, in an
understated way, but they aren't very large. If you
want to steep yourself in the Old Town, and if location matters more than space, this is the place.
Internet (high-speed). No-smoking rooms. Parking
(350kr/day). Sauna. TV: pay movies.

Norrmalm

Deluxe

Berns Hotel

Näckströmsgatan 8, 111 47 Stockholm (56 63 22
00/www.berns.se). T-bana Kungsträdgården or
Östermalmstorg/bus 2, 47, 62, 69, 76. **Rates**
2,950kr-4,500kr double. **Credit** AmEx, DC, MC, V.
Map p241 G8 ❻

This boutique hotel is fantastically located near
Kungsträdgården, the shops of Hamngatan and the
boats of Nybroviken, and is popular with visiting
pop stars and business executives. Top-floor rooms
have big windows overlooking Berzelii Park, and if
you really want to push the boat out, consider the
Parkview suite, whose private patio overlooks the
Dramaten Theatre and the boats of Nybroviken, or
the Clock Suite, situated behind the distinctive Berns
clock, with a private sauna. Service is first-class, and
guests also get to use some of the facilities at Berns'
sister hotel, the peerless Grand (*see below*).
Bars (7). Business centre. Concierge. Internet
(high-speed, shared terminal). No-smoking rooms.
Parking (395kr/day). Restaurant. Room service.
TV: pay movies.

Clarion Sign

Norra Bantorget, PO Box 310, 101 26 Stockholm
(651 39 00/www.clarionsign.com). T-bana
T-Centralen/bus 1, 47, 53, 59, 69. **Rates** call for
details. **Credit** AmEx, DC, MC, V. **Map** p240 F5 ❼

When it opens in February 2008, this will be the
largest hotel in the city. Located right next to
Central Station, it will have 558 hotel rooms on 11
floors, a spa, an outdoor pool and, if the plans and
sketches are anything to go by, a healthy dose of
Scandinavian attitude. There'll be furnishings by
Arne Jacobsen (yes, yet more Swan chairs), Norway
Says, Poul Kjærholm and Alvar Aalto, while Swedish
super-chef Marcus Samuelsson will be opening a
branch of his New York restaurant Aquavit.
Bar. Business centre. Concierge. Internet (high-
speed). No-smoking rooms. Parking. Pool (outdoor).
Restaurant. Room service. Spa. TV: pay movies.

Grand Hôtel

Södra Blasieholmshamnen 8, PO Box 16424, 103 27
Stockholm (679 35 60/www.grandhotel.se). T-bana
Kungsträdgården/bus 2, 55, 59, 62, 65. **Rates**
3,700kr-4,900kr double. **Credit** AmEx, DC, MC, V.
Map p241 G8 ❽

See p41 **Grand ambition**.

Bar. Business centre. Concierge. Disabled-adapted rooms. Gym. Internet (high-speed, shared terminal). No-smoking rooms/floor. Parking (395kr/day). Restaurants (2). Room service. Sauna. TV: pay movies.

Nordic Light Hotel

Vasaplan, PO Box 884, 101 37 Stockholm (50 56 34 20/www.nordichotels.se). T-bana T-Centralen/bus 1, 47, 53, 59, 69. **Rates** 1,690kr-3,100kr double. **Credit** AmEx, DC, MC, V. **Map** p240 G6 ❾

The Nordic Light is stylish in a very Scandinavian way: white walls, wooden floors, absurdly comfortable beds, hearty breakfasts and, the icing on the cake, a 'Light Manager' to oversee the hotel illumination. Sophisticated lighting effects are employed throughout the hotel, with pretty patterns projected on to the walls of the 175 bedrooms and a chandelier that slowly changes colour in the airy bar-restaurant. The hotel's location near the Arlanda Express means it's only 20 minutes from hotel check-out to airport check-in. *Photo p40.*
Bar. Business centre. Disabled-adapted rooms. Gym. Internet (high-speed, shared terminals). No-smoking rooms. Parking (245kr/day). Restaurant. Room service. Sauna. Spa. TV: pay movies.

Radisson SAS Strand Hotel

Nybrokajen 9, PO Box 16396, 103 27 Stockholm (50 66 40 00/www.radissonsas.com). T-bana Kungsträdgården or Östermalmstorg/bus 2, 47, 62, 69, 76. **Rates** 1,795kr-2,590kr double. **Credit** AmEx, DC, MC, V. **Map** p241 G8 ❿

Knock-out views of the boats and ferries moored along Nybrokajen and Strandvägen give this excellent business hotel a little something extra. The Radisson Strand was built in 1912 for the Stockholm Olympics, and all the 152 rooms are tastefully furnished in classic Swedish style. A real splurge is the Tower Suite, a two-floor apartment with rooftop terrace, dining room, sitting room and spiral staircase leading up to the bedroom.
Bar. Disabled-adapted rooms. Internet (high speed). No-smoking rooms. Parking (390kr/day). Restaurant. Room service. Sauna. TV: pay movies.

Scandic Hotel Sergel Plaza

Brunkebergstorgs 9, PO Box 16411, 103 27 Stockholm (51 72 63 00/www.scandic-hotels.com/sergelplaza). T-bana T-Centralen/bus 43, 47, 52, 56, 65. **Rates** 1,450kr-3,490kr double. **Credit** AmEx, DC, MC, V. **Map** p241 G7 ⓫

Location is the main draw at the Scandic Sergel Plaza: slap bang in the concrete heart of the city, it's a credit card's throw from the main shopping streets of Hamngatan and Drottninggatan. The 403 rooms are brightly furnished, though the lobby is a mishmash of styles that takes in red leather sofas, faux-Greek statues and gilt-edged mirrors. There's a Swedish *smörgåsbord* in the restaurant, but this place is so popular with Japanese tourists that a Japanese breakfast is also served. Families are made to feel welcome, with surprises for children at check-in.

Bars (2). Business centre. Disabled-adapted rooms. Internet (high-speed). No-smoking rooms. Parking (275kr/day). Restaurant. Room service. TV: pay movies.

Expensive

Adlon

Vasagatan 42, 112 20 Stockholm (402 65 00/www.adlon.se). T-bana T-Centralan/bus 3, 47, 59, 62, 69. **Rates** 1,150kr-2,295kr double. **Credit** AmEx, DC, MC, V. **Map** p240 F6 ⓬

Originally opened in 1944 in a late 19th-century building, the Adlon is a friendly family-run hotel close to Central Station on the main thoroughfare of Vasagatan. Unusually, more than 60 of its 83 subtly decorated rooms are singles, so it attracts a large proportion of solo travellers. The bedrooms are generally very small – request one of the recently renovated rooms on the first floor.
Business services. Internet (high-speed, shared terminal). No-smoking rooms. Parking (260kr/day). TV: pay movies.

Nordic Sea Hotel

Vasaplan, PO Box 884, 101 37 Stockholm (50 56 30 00/www.nordichotels.se). T-bana T-Centralen/bus 1, 47, 53, 59, 69. **Rates** 1,490kr-2,390kr double. **Credit** AmEx, DC, MC, V. **Map** p240 G6 ⓭

The first thing you notice when you enter the Nordic Sea is water: a vast aquarium dominates the lobby and a window opens on to the ultra-chilly Icebar (*see p119*), where the drinks are served up in sub-zero conditions. With 367 rooms, and a jaunty blue-and-white colour scheme throughout, the Nordic Sea Hotel is larger and more affordable than the Nordic Light (*see above*), but not nearly as cool (ice notwithstanding).
Bars (2). Business centre. Disabled-adapted rooms. Internet (high-speed, shared terminal). No-smoking rooms. Parking (245kr/day). Restaurant. Room service. Sauna. TV: pay movies.

Sheraton Stockholm Hotel & Towers

Tegelbacken 6, PO Box 195, 101 23 Stockholm (412 34 00/www.sheraton.com/stockholm). T-bana T-Centralen/bus 3, 43, 59, 62. **Rates** 1,945kr-3,200kr double. **Credit** AmEx, DC, MC, V. **Map** p241 H6 ⓮

The Sheraton is just what you expect it to be: a large, brightly decorated international hotel with friendly, efficient service that attracts business travellers and American tourists. Inside you could be in any city, but outside you're neatly placed between the Central Station and medieval Gamla Stan. There's a champagne-and-cigars bar, a German restaurant, a clubby lounge for light meals, and also a small casino. Opt for an executive room if you want an Old Town view.
Bar. Business centre. Concierge. Disabled-adapted rooms. Gym. Internet (high-speed, shared terminal). No-smoking rooms. Parking (280kr/day). Restaurants (2). Room service. Sauna.

Nordic Light: a shining example of boutique chic. *See p39.*

Moderate

Freys Hotel

*Bryggargatan 12, PO Box 594, 101 31 Stockholm
(50 62 13 00/www.freyshotel.se). T-bana T-Centralen/
bus 1, 47, 53, 59, 65.* **Rates** 1,290kr-2,350kr double.
Credit AmEx, DC, MC, V. **Map** p241 F6
The Freys Hotel is a likeable, idiosyncratic place,
with 118 cheerfully decorated rooms and a lobby
adorned with paintings of cats. The location, down
a car-free street close to Central Station and the shops
on Drottninggatan, is convenient if a little drab. Still,
you can always cheer yourself up by visiting the
adjoining continental-style bar, which serves up
Stockholm's largest selection of Belgian beer.
*Bar. Disabled-adapted rooms. Internet (shared
terminal). Parking (250kr/day, must be booked in
advance). Restaurant. Sauna. TV: pay movies.*

Hotel Bentleys

*Drottninggatan 77, 111 60 Stockholm (14 13 95/
www.bentleys.nu). T-bana Hötorget/bus 1, 47, 52,
56, 65.* **Rates** 1,100kr-1,800kr double. **Credit**
AmEx, MC, V. **Map** p245 E6
Like its near-neighbour, the Queen's, Bentleys is a
privately owned hotel in a converted townhouse,
with a beautiful marble staircase and old-fashioned
cage lift. The 60 rooms are simple, clean and pleasant. From the stained-glass panels in the front door
to the art nouveau patterns on the hallway ceiling,
there's real charm to be found here. Staff are welcoming and prices are great given the central location. Choose a room on a higher floor with views
over the inner courtyard to avoid being disturbed
by the street noise from Drottninggatan.
Internet (shared terminal). Sauna.

Queen's Hotel

*Drottninggatan 71A, 111 36 Stockholm (24 94 60/
www.queenshotel.se). T-bana Hötorget/bus 1, 47, 52,
53, 69.* **Rates** 800kr-1,490kr double. **Credit** AmEx,
DC, MC, V. **Map** p241 F6
On the main pedestrian street in the heart of the
shopping district, this hotel is a good bet if you like
hustle, bustle and a convenient location. Family-
owned, it has 32 clean, plain rooms (some en suite,
though only one has a bathtub). Most of the doubles
can accommodate an extra bed or sofa bed. A piano
beckons in the lounge for any guest with the urge to
strike up a tune.
*Internet (shared terminal). No-smoking rooms.
TV: pay movies.*

Budget/youth hostels

City Backpackers Inn

*Upplandsgatan 2A, 111 23 Stockholm (20 69 20/
www.citybackpackers.se). T-bana T-Centralen or
Hötorget/bus 1, 47, 53, 65, 69.* **Rates** 230kr-295kr
per person; 1,740kr 6-bed apartment. **Credit** MC, V.
Map p240 F5
Located in a 19th-century building on Norra
Bantorget square, this 82-bed hostel is convenient,
a ten-minute walk from Central Station, and near
Hötorget and the shopping district. Rooms sleep
from two to eight, and an apartment with a private
kitchen, shower and toilet sleeps up to seven.
Facilities include a comfy lounge with a TV, books
and games, kitchen, laundry, free internet access and
– this is Sweden after all – sauna. No curfew.
Breakfast not provided.
*Internet (high-speed, shared terminals). No-smoking
rooms. Sauna. TV room.*

Vasastaden

Expensive

Hotel Birger Jarl

*Tulegatan 8, 104 32 Stockholm (674 18 00/www.
birgerjarl.se). T-bana Rådmansgatan/bus 2, 42, 43,
52.* **Rates** 1,490kr-2,205kr double. **Credit** AmEx,
DC, MC, V. **Map** p245 D6

The Birger Jarl is a design-savvy business hotel – 16 of its 235 rooms are one-offs by some of Sweden's most idiosyncratic designers, and the rest have been designed in more conventional (but still very attractive) series of 15 or 20 rooms. Fans of genuine retro should check themselves into the Retro Room, which looks just as it did in 1974, having accidentally been overlooked during the hotel's renovation. The quiet location in fairly residential Vasastaden won't suit everyone, but it's only a short walk from the action.

Bar. Business centre. Disabled-adapted rooms. Gym. Internet (high-speed, shared terminals). No-smoking rooms. Parking (250kr/day). Restaurant. Room Service. Sauna. TV: pay movies.

Moderate

Clas på Hörnet

Surbrunnsgatan 20, 113 48 Stockholm (16 51 30/www.claspahornet.com). T-bana Tekniska Högskolan/bus 2, 4, 42, 53, 72. **Rates** 1,195kr-1,695kr double. **Credit** AmEx, DC, MC, V. **Map** p245 C6 ⑳

First opened as an inn in 1731, Clas på Hörnet is an old-fashioned oasis of peace and quiet on a tree-lined street a short walk from old Odenplan. It has only ten rooms (most with four-poster beds), as well as an elegant restaurant serving excellent Swedish food and a small courtyard with a bar serving food and drinks alfresco. Many guests come from Scandinavian countries, attracted by the historic atmosphere and the late 18th-century Gustavian furnishings, which have been overseen by the Stockholms Stadsmuseum.

Bar. Business centre. Disabled-adapted rooms. Internet (high-speed). No-smoking rooms. Parking (250kr/day). Restaurant. Room service. TV: pay movies.

Hotell August Strindberg

Tegnérgatan 38, 113 59 Stockholm (32 50 06/www. hotellstrindberg.se). T-bana Hötorget/bus 1, 47, 53, 65, 69. **Rates** 995kr-1,550kr double. **Credit** MC, V. **Map** p245 E5 ㉑

Near a small park containing a startling nude statue of Swedish dramatist August Strindberg, who once lived down the road, stands this small, welcoming hotel. In 2004 it expanded to 27 rooms and opened a new lobby (decorated, of course, with a mural of Strindberg, cleverly made from the first three chapters of one of his books). Rooms are simple but pleasant, and there's a tranquil courtyard garden with a few tables and a trickling birdbath. A fine hotel in a quiet, central neighbourhood.

Disabled-adapted room. No-smoking rooms. Internet (high-speed). TV.

Hotel Gustav Vasa

Västmannagatan 61, 113 25 Stockholm (34 38 01/ www.hotel.wineasy.se/gustav.vasa). T-bana Odenplan/ bus 2, 4, 40, 47, 53. **Rates** 850kr-1,550kr double. **Credit** AmEx, DC, MC, V. **Map** p244 D4 ㉒

At Odenplan, facing the majestic Gustav Vasa church, this hotel is a quiet, old-fashioned place. The 37 rooms (some with shared bathroom, all non-smoking) are clean and comfortable, if a bit small and stuffy, and prices are good value. Family rooms sleep four or five people, and an excellent breakfast is served in the sunny breakfast room. Convenient for buses to Arlanda airport.

Business centre. Internet (shared terminals). No-smoking throughout. Parking (125kr/day). Room service (breakfast only). TV.

Grand ambition

The location of the **Grand Hôtel** (*see p37*) could hardly be more perfect – or more symbolic. Built in 1874, it stands by the harbour, with splendid views of the Royal Palace. On one side of the water, a regal building crowned with fluttering flags that is owned by the country's most influential family; on the other side, the King's official residence.

The Grand is part of Investor, an investment company reckoned to be worth around €13 billion in 2006, which is controlled by the Wallenberg family. (The most famous member of the family was Raoul Wallenberg, who saved many Hungarian Jews from the Holocaust.)

Unlike so many grand hotels that simply let themselves go in old age, the Grand has got its groove back thanks to a dramatic refurbishment, reasserting itself as the classiest place to lay your head in Stockholm.

The stunning, revamped Cadier Bar is once again the hottest place in town on a Friday night, particularly around the time of the Nobel Banquet when visiting royals and rock stars rub shoulders with newly crowned Laureates, who traditionally stay here after the awards ceremony. The new restaurant, Mathias Dahlgren, is also a smash hit.

Each of the 304 rooms is decorated differently, and while the cheapest rooms are far from spacious, the suites have real wow factor. The Princess Lilian Suite (named after a Welsh-born member of the Swedish royal family) is perhaps the most sumptuous in the entire Nordic region, and includes its own 12-person cinema. You'll need a king's ransom to check in – it costs 55,000kr per night – but if quality and class are top of your list, and money is no object, then this is the place to be.

Hotel Oden

Karlbergsvägen 24, 102 34 Stockholm (457 97 00/ www.hoteloden.se). T-bana Odenplan/bus 2, 4, 40, 42, 47. **Rates** 1,080kr-1,790kr double. **Credit** AmEx, DC, MC, V. **Map** p244 D4 ㉓

Notable mostly for its low prices, the Oden will appeal to budget travellers looking to save money on meals, since doubles have a fridge and stove (no frying allowed). There's a basic solarium, sauna and exercise room in the basement.

Business centre. Gym. No-smoking rooms. Internet (shared terminal). Parking (130kr/day). Sauna. TV.

Budget/youth hostels

Hostel Bed & Breakfast

Rehnsgatan 21, 113 57 Stockholm (15 28 38/ www.hostelbedandbreakfast.com). T-bana Rådmansgatan/bus 2, 4, 42, 43, 52. **Rates** 240kr per person dormitory; 680kr double. **Credit** MC, V. **Map** p245 D6 ㉔

A basic youth hostel which is centrally located, handy and cheap. There are 36 beds in two-, four-, eight- and ten-bed rooms, plus a summer-only annexe that sleeps 40 in one dormitory (mostly used for school trips). All showers and toilets are shared, it's open all year and it has a kitchen and laundry room. It's a basement hostel, so don't expect a room with a window, let alone a view. Do expect a free breakfast, however.

Internet (shared terminal). No smoking. TV room.

Vanadis Hotell och Bad

Sveavägen 142, 113 46 Stockholm (30 12 11/ www.vanadishotel.com). T-bana Odenplan or Rådmansgatan/bus 2, 4, 40, 52, 70. **Rates** 700kr-1,000kr double. **Credit** AmEx, DC, MC, V. **Map** p245 B5 ㉕

The Vanadis is best described as a swimming pool with a hotel attached. It's certainly unique: 53 tiny and austere rooms (no wardrobe and, in cheaper rooms, no window) adjoin a large open-air public pool (May-Sept) adorned with murals, in a park close to the city centre. Guests can swim for free in the pool (*see p193*) and the adjacent aquatic amusement park. Breakfast is served at the poolside café. Rooms are small, but so are prices, and both rooms and shared bathrooms are kept scrupulously clean. Good for families with small children or budget travellers who might fancy a splash.

No-smoking rooms. Parking (150kr/day). Pool (outdoor). Restaurant.

Djurgården

Expensive

Scandic Hasselbacken

Hazeliusbacken 20, 100 55 Stockholm (51 73 43 00/www.scandic-hotels.se). Bus 44, 47. **Rates** 1,990kr-2,590kr double. **Credit** AmEx, DC, MC, V. **Map** p242 J11 ㉖

Flanked by the trees of Stockholm's greenest island, its small garden full of peonies, the Hasselbacken's setting is delightful. Typically Scandinavian in style, its 122 rooms are comfortable and unfussy. It's a popular wedding venue, and the terrace and elegant Restaurang Hasselbacken are busy all weekend. Note that there is no local subway, so access is by bus, tram or the small ferry from Slussen. But the Hasselbacken does put you just a short walk from the Vasamuseet and Skansen, Stockholm's most popular tourist attractions.

Bars (2). Business centre. Disabled-adapted rooms. Internet (dataport, shared terminal). No-smoking rooms. Parking (170kr/day). Restaurants (2). Room service. Sauna. TV (pay movies/VCR).

Södermalm

Deluxe

Clarion Hotel Stockholm

Ringvägen 98, 104 60 Stockholm (462 10 00/www. clarionstockholm.com). T-bana Skanstull/bus 3, 4, 55, 74. **Rates** 1,280kr-2,090kr double. **Credit** AmEx, DC, MC, V. **Map** p250 N8 ㉗

In 2003, Clarion opened this gleaming 532-room property on the southern edge of Södermalm. Despite its size, it is surprisingly classy. Bedrooms are airy and stylish, bathrooms are smart, the lobby is flooded with light and the staff are attentive. Because it's primarily a business hotel, room rates plummet in summer and on weekends. For tourists, the main drawback is the poor location: it's on the

In a rich man's world: the deluxe **Hotel Rival**, owned by Benny from Abba.

opposite side of town from Arlanda airport and a bit of a schlep from the city centre (but then nowhere is that far in Stockholm). The lounge bar, called Upstairs, has spectacular views towards Globen. *Bars (2). Business centre. Concierge. Disabled-adapted rooms. Gym. Internet (high-speed, wireless). No-smoking rooms. Parking (270kr/day). Pool (indoor). Restaurants (2). Room service. Sauna. TV: pay movies.*

Hilton Stockholm Slussen

Guldgränd 8, PO Box 15270, 104 65 Stockholm (51 73 53 00/www.hilton.com). T-bana Slussen/bus 2, 3, 43, 53, 76. **Rates** 2,300kr-3,190kr double. **Credit** AmEx, DC, MC, V. **Map** p250 K7 ㉘ Once a Scandic Hotel, the Stockholm Slussen reopened as Sweden's first Hilton in 2002 and, despite its five-star rating, there's something faintly depressing about its lack of personality. Still, it has what you expect from a high-quality chain: a white marble lobby, two executive floors with their own reception area, bar and breakfast room, plus the added bonus of sweeping views towards Gamla Stan. If you can't justify the cost of an executive double room you can still enjoy the same panorama from the Ekens bar and restaurant, the outdoor terrace, or the smaller lobby bar which is called, appropriately, Views. *Bars (2). Business centre. Concierge. Disabled-adapted rooms. Gym. Internet (high-speed). No-smoking rooms. Parking (360kr/day). Pool (indoor). Restaurants (2). Room service. Sauna. Spa (beauty treatments and massage). TV: DVD/pay movies.*

Hotel Rival

Mariatorget 3, PO box 17525, 118 91 Stockholm (54 57 89 00/www.rival.se). T-bana Mariatorget/bus 4, 43, 55, 66, 74. **Rates** 1,490kr-3,290kr double. **Credit** AmEx, DC, MC, V. **Map** p250 K7 ㉙ Owned by Benny from Abba, the Rival was created by combining the best parts of the 1930s hotel that once stood here with high-tech comforts: there are flatscreen TVs, DVD players and Sony PlayStations in every room. The old cocktail bar and plush red-velvet cinema are art deco treasures. Small rooms are comfortable and stylish, while the large rooms have great views over trendy Södermalm's rooftops. Weekend rates can be excellent (they include breakfast, which weekday rates do not). The next-door Rival café is one of the best in town and the Rival bakery sells superb bread. *Bars (2). Business centre. Disabled-adapted rooms. Internet (high-speed, wireless). No-smoking rooms. Parking (370kr/day). Restaurant. Room service. TV: DVD/pay movies.*

Moderate

Columbus Hotell

Tjärhovsgatan 11, 116 21 Stockholm (50 31 12 00/ www.columbus.se). T-bana Medborgarplatsen/bus 2, 3, 53, 59, 76. **Rates** 1,250kr-1,550kr double. **Credit** AmEx, DC, MC, V. **Map** p251 L9 ㉚ This 18th-century building has a colourful history, having been variously a brewery, a poorhouse, and a hospital. In 1976 it became a hostel and then

gradually evolved into a charming three-storey hotel, carefully restored with its original polished-wood floors and tasteful Gustavian furnishings. There are two price categories, and even cheaper rooms, with shared bathrooms, are comfortable. The courtyard is a pleasant place for breakfast or a drink, and there's a guests-only wine cellar.

Bar. Internet (high-speed). No-smoking rooms. Parking (150kr/day). TV: pay movies.

Ersta Konferens & Hotell

Erstagatan 1K, PO Box 4619, 116 91 Stockholm (714 61 00/www.ersta.se). Bus 2, 3, 53, 66, 76. **Rates** 950kr-1,420kr double. **Credit** MC, V. **Map** p251 L10 ③

This 22-room hotel is a quiet oasis perched at the tip of Södermalm, where tour buses deposit their riders for one of Stockholm's most phenomenal views. Constructed for the Deacons' Society in 1850, the building is in a square amid beautifully landscaped gardens and across from Ersta Café, overlooking the city. There are small guest kitchens on each floor, and when the weather's good you can eat breakfast in the garden.

Business centre. Disabled-adapted rooms. Internet (high-speed). No-smoking rooms. Parking (175kr/day). TV (some rooms).

Hotell Anno 1647

Mariagränd 3, 116 46 Stockholm (442 16 80/www.anno1647.se). T-bana Slussen/bus 2, 3, 43, 53, 59. **Rates** 1,085kr-2,195kr double. **Credit** AmEx, DC, MC, V. **Map** p250 K8 ②

As its name suggests, this is an old building dating back to the 17th century, and the interior tries earnestly to stay in sync with the historic exterior. The 42 rooms (including one family room sleeping up to six) are a little faded, but the traditional decor somehow makes this forgivable. Besides, the location is terrific: it's hidden down a cul de sac just off Södermalm's most fashionable shopping street Götgatan, and the cobbled alleys of the Old Town are just minutes away.

Bar. Internet (high-speed). Parking (150kr/day). Restaurant. Room service. TV: pay movies.

Budget/youth hostels

Hotel Tre Små Rum

Högbergsgatan 81, 118 54 Stockholm (641 23 71/www.tresmarum.se). T-bana Mariatorget/bus 4, 43, 55, 66, 74. **Rates** 695kr double. **Credit** AmEx, MC, V. **Map** p250 L6 ③

This tiny, likeable hotel in Söder had three small rooms (hence the name) when it opened in 1993 but now there are seven (six doubles and one single), sharing three shower rooms. Clean and simple, it's ideal for budget travellers who plan to spend most of their time out and about. It's run by the very friendly Jakob and Christian, and is just a few minutes' walk from Mariatorget T-bana station.

Internet (shared terminal). No-smoking rooms. TV. Bike rental (150kr/day).

Zinkensdamm Vandrarhem & Hotell

Zinkens Väg 20, 117 41 Stockholm (hotel 616 81 10/hostel 616 81 00/www.zinkensdamm.com). T-bana Hornstull or Zinkensdamm/bus 4, 40, 66, 74. **Rates** Hostel 210kr-260kr per person in dormitory; 490kr-790kr double. **Credit** AmEx, DC, MC, V. **Map** p249 L4 ③

This youth hostel and family-friendly hotel is tucked away in peaceful Tantolunden park, a few minutes' walk from busy Hornsgatan. Nearby are lots of *koloniträdgårdar* – lovely little allotment gardens with charming wooden houses where Stockholmers cultivate a bit of countryside in the city. The yellow wooden hostel has a large courtyard and a small pub where guests congregate. The reasonable prices also include a buffet breakfast.

Bar. Internet (high-speed). No-smoking throughout. Parking (110kr/day). Sauna. TV room.

Långholmen

Budget/youth hostels

Långholmen Hotel & Youth Hostel

Långholmsmuren 20, PO Box 9116, 102 72 Stockholm (720 85 00/www.langholmen.com). T-bana Hornstull/bus 4, 40, 66. **Rates** Hostel 210kr-260kr per person in dormitory; 520kr-730kr double. *Hotel* 1,370kr-1,740kr double. **Credit** AmEx, DC, MC, V. **Map** p249 K2 ③

A former prison has been converted to a far from grim property on this small, green island south of Kungsholmen. Run as a hotel in winter and youth hostel in summer, it has a pub (winter only), a café (summer only, in the former exercise yard) and a 17th-century Wärdshus serving Swedish cuisine. The yellow 19th-century building is still quite jail-like, with cells (yes, that's where you sleep) arranged around a light-filled central atrium. There's a prison museum on site (see p84). One of Stockholm's most arresting places to stay. *Photo p47.*

Bar. Business centre. Disabled-adapted rooms. Internet (high-speed, wireless). No-smoking rooms. Parking (free). Restaurant. Room service. TV (some rooms).

Östermalm

Deluxe

Hotel Diplomat

Strandvägen 7, 104 40 Stockholm (459 68 20/www.diplomathotel.com). T-bana Östermalmstorg/bus 47, 62, 69, 76. **Rates** 1,695kr-3,095kr double. **Credit** AmEx, DC, MC, V. **Map** p242 G9 ③

The Diplomat is one of Stockholm's best-preserved art nouveau buildings, and its glamourous Strandvägen site affords some stunning views. The hotel oozes old-fashioned charm, with its antique cage lift, spiral staircase and intricate stained-glass windows. More modern are the serene first-floor lounge and the trendy T-Bar restaurant and bar on the ground floor, which serves excellent brunch and afternoon tea.

Bars (2). Business centre. Internet (high-speed). No-smoking rooms. Parking (310kr/day). Restaurant. Room service. Sauna. TV: pay movies.

Expensive

Hotel Esplanade
Strandvägen 7A, 114 56 Stockholm (663 07 40/ www.hotelesplanade.se). T-bana Östermalmstorg/ bus 47, 62, 69, 76. **Rates** 1,695kr-2,295kr double. **Credit** AmEx, DC, MC, V. **Map** p242 G9 ③
The Esplanade is next door to the Diplomat, and has the same staggering water views and four-star rating. All 34 rooms are different, and even if some of them are a little frumpy, it's hard not to love this place for its charm and character, especially as it has retained some of its original art nouveau interior. Considering its top-class location, the prices are excellent.
Internet (shared terminal). No-smoking rooms. Room service (breakfast only). Sauna. TV.

Hotell Kung Carl
Birger Jarlsgatan 21, PO Box 1776, 111 87 Stockholm (463 50 00/www.hkchotels.se). T-bana Hötorget or Östermalmstorg/bus 1, 2, 55, 56. **Rates** 1,450kr-2,140kr double. **Credit** AmEx, DC, MC, V. **Map** p241 F8 ③
The Kung Carl has glamorous neighbours – the Versace store flanks the entrance and it's close to affluent Östermalm, home to some of the poshest shops in Stockholm. The hotel is far from fashionable in style, but full of character and neatly located. Each of the 112 rooms is uniquely decorated, and there's an oddly shaped central atrium housing a small bar and pleasant restaurant.
Bar. Disabled-adapted rooms. Internet (high-speed). No-smoking rooms. Parking (220kr/day). Restaurant. Room Service. TV: pay movies.

Scandic Anglais
Humlegårdsgatan 23 (51 73 40 00/www.scandic-hotels.com/anglais). T-bana Östermalmstorg/bus 1, 2, 55, 56. **Rates** 1,800kr-2,300kr double. **Credit** AmEx, DC, MC, V. **Map** p246 E8 ③
After an 18-month renovation, the Scandic Anglais reopened in 2006 and promptly disappointed people. The location is terrific, with park views to one side and all of Östermalm's shops, clubs and restaurants nearby, but the hotel doesn't live up to its swanky setting. However, it has rooms at decent rates – the (windowless) single cabin rooms are downright cheap – and also offers free bicycle hire. A good place if you want to be in the heart of town without paying a fortune.
Bars (2). Business centre. Concierge. Disabled-adapted rooms. Internet (wireless, shared terminal). No-smoking rooms. Parking (350kr/day). Restaurant. Room service. Sauna.

Gärdet

Deluxe

Villa Källhagen
Djurgårdsbrunnsvägen 10, 115 27 Stockholm (665 03 00/www.kallhagen.se). Bus 69. **Rates** 1,590kr-2,700kr double. **Credit** AmEx, DC, MC, V. **Map** p243 F14 ④
Villa Källhagen is a tranquil waterside retreat surrounded by rolling parkland, yet is just a short bus ride from Östermalm. The original Red Cottage inn, dating from 1810, is now in the garden behind the new hotel, which was built in 1990. The sunny rooms feature the best of Scandinavian design, with bright fabrics, and light fittings designed by Josef Frank of Svenskt Tenn (*see p156*) fame, although the lobby and café could do with sprucing up. An excellent restaurant serves classic Swedish food with continental influences. Just 20 rooms, so book well in advance.
Bar. Business centre. Disabled-adapted rooms. Internet (high-speed). No-smoking rooms. Parking (free). Restaurants (2). Room service. Sauna. TV: free movies.

Kungsholmen

Expensive

Hotel Amaranten
Kungsholmsgatan 31, 104 20 Stockholm (692 52 00/www.firsthotels.com). T-bana Rådhuset/bus 1, 40, 52, 56. **Rates** 1,400kr-2,500kr double. **Credit** AmEx, DC, MC, V. **Map** p240 G4 ④
Thanks to its swish decor and its location around the corner from Scheelegatan, one of the city's busiest restaurant rows, this hotel has become a hub of activity. The expansive lobby-bar-restaurant has been refurbished, with leather seats in rich, chocolate hues, walnut floors and low-level lighting. The luxury does not quite carry through upstairs: rooms are more basic, but good value. The hotel is an easy ten-minute walk from Central Station.
Bar. Business centre. Disabled-adapted rooms. Gym. Internet (high-speed, shared terminal). No-smoking rooms. Parking (300kr). Pool (indoor). Restaurants (2). Room service. Sauna. TV: pay movies.

Further afield

Deluxe

Hasseludden Konferens & Yasuragi
Hamndalsvägen 6, 132 81 Saltsjö-Boo (747 64 00/ www.hasseludden.com). Boat from Strömkajen/ bus 444 to Orminge Centrum then bus 417 to Hamndalsvägen then 10min walk. **Rates** *Yasuragi package* 2,800kr-4,000kr double. **Credit** AmEx, DC, MC, V.

For something unusual, try Hasseludden, Sweden's only Japanese spa, where you can ease travel-weary muscles with a traditional Japanese bath, a swim, or a soak in a steaming outdoor jacuzzi overlooking the sea. Refresh yourself at the fruit and juice buffet, try a session of qi gong or Zen meditation – or go to the sushi school. All 162 sparsely furnished rooms and suites have water views. The hotel is a 30-minute boat ride from central Stockholm.
Business centre. Internet (high-speed). No-smoking rooms. Parking (free). Pool (indoor, jacuzzi outside). Restaurant. Room service. Spa. TV: pay movies.

Expensive

Hotel J
Ellensviksvägen 1, 131 28 Nacka Strand (601 30 00/ www.hotelj.com). Boat from Nybrokajen or Slussen/ T-bana to Slussen then bus 404, 443. **Rates** 1,395kr-2,195kr double. **Credit** AmEx, DC, MC, V.
A 20-minute bus, boat or taxi ride from the city, this hotel is beautifully situated on the coast. A 1912 summer house and two modern extensions house 44 rooms. Rooms in the old building are smaller and without balconies. You can rent mini-catamarans and the hotel has its own motorboat. Restaurant J on the quayside has a reputation for indifferent service but the views ensure that it stays busy.
Bar. Business centre. Disabled-adapted rooms. Internet (high-speed). No-smoking rooms. Parking (90kr/day). Restaurants (2). Room service. TV: pay movies.

Sigtuna Stads Hotell
Stora Nygatan 3, 193 30 Sigtuna (59 25 01 00/ www.sigtunastadshotell.se). **Rates** 1,990kr-2,590kr double. **Credit** AmEx, DC, MC, V.
On the outside, it looks like a fairly ordinary small-town hotel. But inside, the Sigtuna Stads Hotell is impeccably stylish and utterly seductive. It's all very Scandinavian, with modern furniture, polished wooden floors and pale walls. About 40 kilometres (25 miles) from Stockholm but close to Arlanda airport, it's a perfect place to start or end a Swedish trip. The town of Sigtuna (*see p206*), on Lake Mälaren, is charming, with lots of cosy cafés to explore.
Bar. Business centre. Disabled-adapted rooms. Internet (wireless). No-smoking rooms. Parking (free). Restaurants. Room service. Sauna.

Camping

Stockholm's most central campsite is **Östermalms Citycamping** (Fiskartorpsvägen 2, 10 29 03), at the Östermalm sports ground behind Stockholms Stadion. Near woodlands, it's got 179 camping spaces, and is open from the end of June to mid August. There is also a site for campervans on **Långholmen** (669 18 90, open late June-late Aug). To camp in Sweden, you need a validated Camping Card (125kr), which you can buy at any campsite.

Långholmen Hotel & Youth Hostel. *See p45.*

Sightseeing

Features

Millesgården. *See p95.*

Introduction

Cool, calm and compact, the Swedish capital is made for walking.

Sightseeing

With more than 70 museums, covering everything from royal jewels to sunken ships and Scandinavian design, Stockholm is clearly a city that has invested in its cultural attractions. Since the change in government in 2006, the state-run museums are no longer free, though a few of the city-run museums still are. The most impressive sight of all, of course, is Stockholm itself; comprised of 14 islands, centred on medieval Gamla Stan, it guarantees visitors one breathtaking vista after another.

The city breaks down into quickly recognisable, well-defined areas. There's no lurching from one overlapping neighbourhood to another, never quite knowing where you are. This is mainly because most of the city's districts are on self-contained islands.

Stockholm is very compact; it's never more than a couple of metro stops from one sight to another – though often the best, and most pleasant, way to get around is to walk. It takes

about 30 minutes to cross the city, from Norrmalm to Södermalm, but many places are only a few minutes' walk apart.

If you'd prefer to take public transport, the Tunnelbana metro system is fast, clean and efficient, as are the numerous buses that criss-cross the capital. In addition there are ferries between Södermalm, Djurgården and Norrmalm, though not all year round. *See pp216-218* for detailed information on all the public transport options.

One of your first stops should be the **Stockholm Tourist Centre** (Sverigehuset, Hamngatan 27, Norrmalm, 50 82 85 08, www.stockholmtown.se, open 9am-7pm Mon-Fri, 10am-5pm Sat, 10am-4pm Sun).

Guided tours

Authorised Guides of Stockholm
50 82 85 09/www.guidestockholm.com.
This association has been around for 50 years and all its guides must complete lengthy training. Individual or group guided tours are given to most of the key sights in Stockholm.

City Sightseeing & Stockholm Sightseeing
58 71 40 20/www.citysightseeing.com.
Tours by bus and foot (City Sightseeing) or boat (Stockholm Sightseeing). The Stockholm Panorama bus tour (1.5hrs, 210kr) is very popular, but the boat tours are probably the most attractive way to see the city. These include the Royal Canal Tour (1hr, 130kr) around Djurgården, and the Under the Bridges Tour (2hrs, 180kr). Tours run all year round (no boat tours from January to March), but are most frequent from May to September. For more information, visit the City Sightseeing ticket booth on Gustav Adolfs Torg by the opera house, or the Stockholm Sightseeing booth on Strömkajen in front of the Grand Hôtel. Walking tours also run several times a day from the end of June to the end of August (1hr, 100kr), departing from Gustaf Adolfs Torg. The same company offers horse and carriage tours of Gamla Stan, departing from Mynttorget from June to mid August (120kr per person). The new Swedish Wilderness tour (4hrs, 395kr) offers walking tours in nearby Tyresta National Park.

Hot-air balloon flights
Unlike most capital cities, Stockholm allows hot-air balloons to fly over its centre. The season is May to September, and flights are generally in the early

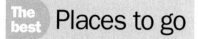

The best Places to go

For a history lesson
Witness royal power at **Kungliga Slottet** (*see p52*) and maritime disaster at the **Vasamuseet** (*see p75*).

With the kids
Be king of the jungle at the **Skansen Akvariet** (*see p74*) and take the wheel of a tram at the **Spårvägsmuseet** transport museum (*see p83*).

For culture vultures
Feast on contemporary art at the **Moderna Museet** (*see p78*) and gorge on historical treasures at the **National Museum** (*see p66*).

For a walk in the park
Relax in the beautiful **Bergianska Trädgården** botanical gardens (*see p95*).

To join the Nobelity
Visit the **Stadshuset** (*see p92*), Stockholm's iconic tower and host to the annual Nobel Prize banquet.

Watch the (water) world go by from **Stadshuset**'s terrace. *See p92.*

evening. You need to book at least two weeks in advance, and note that bad weather can result in cancellations. Try Scandinavia Balloons (55 64 04 65, www.balloons-sweden.se, 1,895kr per person for 1hr flight) or Far & Flyg (645 77 00, www.faroch flyg.se, 1,995kr for 1hr flight & champagne picnic on the ground afterwards).

RIB Sightseeing

20 22 60/www.ribsightseeing.se.

This company runs speedboat tours of Stockholm and the archipelago. Lifejackets and waterproof gear are provided. The 90-minute tours (from 295kr per person) take you to Djurgården and further out to Waxholm and Fjäderholmarna. Tours run from May to the beginning of September.

Tourist cards

If you're planning on doing a lot of sightseeing while in town, it may be worth buying a **Stockholm Card** (*Stockholmskortet*), a timed

pass that provides free admission to more than 70 of the city's museums and attractions, plus free travel on the Tunnelbana, city buses, trains and sightseeing boats (but not the city or archipelago ferries), and free street parking at official parking spots. Available for 24, 48 or 72 hours (the time starts from its first use), it costs 290kr, 420kr or 540kr for adults; 120kr, 160kr or 190kr for 7-17s. In the Sightseeing chapters, **Free with SC** indicates which museums provide free entry for Stockholm Card holders.

The less useful **SL Tourist Card** provides free travel, free admission to Kaknästornet, Gröna Lund and the Spårvägsmuseet, plus 50 per cent off entry to Skansen, but no other discounts. It costs 90kr for 24 hours, 190kr for 72 hours (55kr and 115kr for children).

You can purchase both cards from the **Stockholm Tourist Centre** (*see p50*) and **SL information centres** (*see p217*).

Gamla Stan & Riddarholmen

The city between the bridges is a tour guide's dream, from the Royal Palace to the Nobel Museum via a maze of medieval alleyways.

Sightseeing

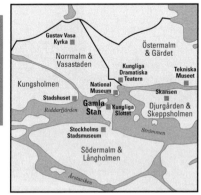

Gustav Vasa Kyrka

Norrmalm & Vasastaden

Kungsholmen

Stadshuset

Riddarfjärden

Stockholms Stadsmuseum

Gamla Stan

Kungliga Slottet

Östermalm & Gärdet

Kungliga Dramatiska Teatern

National Museum

Tekniska Museet

Skansen

Djurgården & Skeppsholmen

Strömmen

Södermalm & Långholmen

Årstaviken

Gamla Stan

Map p241

Gamla Stan is the living embryo of Stockholm's birth more than three-quarters of a millennium ago. The island straddles the crucial strategic gateway between the global reaches of the Baltic Sea and the expansive inland trade routes of Lake Mälaren. Many of its structures stand on foundations from the 17th and 18th centuries, packed tightly into the narrow, meandering streets which today echo with the footfalls of tourists and the lucky few who are permanent residents. The island's main drag, **Västerlånggatan**, offers the contemporary comforts of waffle cones, tourist treasures and kitsch craft boutiques.

Before Stockholm sprawled out on to neighbouring farmland and reclaimed lakebed, the whole city was once limited to this small island, referred to historically as 'the city between the bridges'. Some clever people built a fortress on the island's north-eastern shore around the 11th century, which enabled them to control the trade and traffic into Lake Mälaren, but there's no record of an actual city on Gamla Stan – which means 'the Old Town' – until Birger Jarl's famous letter of 1252, which

mentioned the name 'Stockholm' for the first time. The island city grew into a horrible mess of winding streets and ramshackle houses until most of the western half burned down in 1625. The city planners finally crafted a few right angles (today the streets traversing Stora Nygatan and Lilla Nygatan) and tore down the crumbling defensive wall around the island to make room for waterfront properties for the city council. The island has been home to the Swedish monarchy for hundreds of years, and the immense and splendid Kungliga Slottet (Royal Palace) is still the main sight.

Nowadays, walking around Gamla Stan's charming tangle of narrow streets and alleys lined with yellow, orange and red buildings is like taking an open-air history lesson. It can get very crowded, but you can avoid the bus-tour clusters by keeping off the main drags or ducking down side streets. The best approach is just to wander at will, soaking up the atmosphere.

Kungliga Slottet

The **Kungliga Slottet** (*photo p56*) sits on a hill at the highest point in Gamla Stan, where once stood the old fortress of Tre Kronor, which was almost completely destroyed – except for the north wing – by a fire in 1697. Royal architect Nicodemus Tessin the Younger designed the new palace, giving it a Roman baroque exterior. The architect Carl Hårleman completed Tessin's work in 1754.

The low, yellow-brown building is imposing rather than pretty; its northern façade looms menacingly as you approach Gamla Stan over the bridges from Norrmalm. The square central building around an open courtyard is flanked by two wings extending to the west and two more to the east. Between its eastern wings lie the gardens of Logården, and between the curved western wings is an outer courtyard; the ticket/information office and gift shop are in the south-western curve.

The southern façade with its triumphal central arch is the most attractive; it runs along

Get a feel for old Stockholm on the beautifully preserved streets of Gamla Stan.

Slottsbacken, the hill that leads up from **Skeppsbron** (*photo p57*) and the water to the back of **Storkyrkan** (*see p59*). This large space was kept open to make it easier to defend the palace. The obelisk in front of the church, designed by Louis Jean Desprez, was erected in 1799 as a memorial to those who fought in Gustav III's war against Russia in 1788-90.

Although the palace is the official residence of the royal family, the King, Queen and Heir Apparent, Princess Victoria, live on the island of Drottningholm (itself well worth a visit, *see p204*); Prince Carl-Philip has moved to the chic address of Slottsbacken 2, just across from the main entrance to the palace, and his sister Princess Madeleine has also flown the family coop to be nearer to the city's pulse. Visitors are welcome to explore the sumptuous **Representationsvåningarna** (Royal Apartments) and museums. The **Museet Tre Kronor** explores the history of the palace, while the **Skattkammaren** (Treasury), **Livrustkammaren** (Royal Armoury) and **Gustav III's Antikmuseum** (Museum of Antiquities) show off its prized possessions. If you plan on seeing most of the palace, buy the combined ticket (rather than individual tickets for each attraction), which provides admission to everything except the Livrustkammaren.

The limited opening hours and sheer size of the place mean that you'll probably have to visit a couple of times if you want to see it all.

Another royal museum, the **Kungliga Myntkabinettet** (*see below*) is located on Slottsbacken, opposite the entrance to the Royal Armoury. The **Högvakten** (Royal Guard; 402 63 17, www.hogvakten.mil.se) has been stationed at the palace since 1523, and is a popular tourist attraction. The guard changes posts every day in summer but less frequently in winter (June-Aug 12.15pm Mon-Sat, 1.15pm Sun, Sept-May 12.15pm Wed, Sat, 1.15pm Sun), to the sound of a marching band. Around 20 soldiers in full livery go through their paces in the palace's outer western courtyard. The whole thing lasts about 35 minutes.

Kungliga Myntkabinettet

Slottsbacken 6 (51 95 53 04/www.myntkabinettet.se). T-bana Gamla Stan/bus 2, 43, 55, 59, 76. **Open** *July-Sept* 9am-5pm daily. *Oct-June* 10am-4pm daily. **Admission** 50kr; 30kr concessions; free under-19s. Free Mon. **Free with SC**. **Credit** MC, V. **Map** p241 H8.

The Royal Coin Cabinet, a museum of rare coins and monetary history, is surprisingly large, filling three floors in a building directly south of the palace. The darkened ground floor displays numerous coins from around the world in different contexts, from the first coin made in Greece in 625 BC to what is claimed to be the world's biggest coin, which weighs in at a hefty 19.7kg (43lb).

Kungliga Slottet

Bordered by Slottsbacken, Skeppsbron, Lejonbacken & Högvaktsterassen (402 61 30/www.royalcourt.se). T-bana Gamla Stan/bus 2, 43, 55, 59, 76. **Open** *Representationsvåningarna, Museet Tre Kronor & Skattkammaren* June-Aug 10am-5pm daily. 1-14 Sept, last 2wks May 10am-4pm daily. 15 Sept-7 Jan, Feb-mid May noon-3pm Tue-Sun. Closed 3wks Jan. *Gustav III's Antikmuseum* 15 May-15 Sept 10am-4pm daily. **Admission** *Combination ticket* 130kr; 65kr concessions. *Individual tickets* 90kr; 35kr 7-18s; free under-7s. **Free with SC.** **Credit** AmEx, DC, MC, V. **Map** p241 H8.

Representationsvåningarna
Entrance in western courtyard.
The Royal Apartments occupy two floors of the palace and are entered by a grand staircase in the western wing. Since it's the stories behind the rooms and decorations that make the palace especially interesting – such as Gustav III's invitation to aristocrats to watch him wake up in the morning – taking a guided tour is highly recommended. Banquets are held several times a year in Karl XI's Gallery in the **State Apartments** on the second floor. Heads of state stay in the **Guest Apartments** during their visits to the capital, and for this reason parts or all of the palace may be occasionally closed. Downstairs in the Bernadotte Apartments, portraits of the current dynasty's ancestors hang in the

Walk Medieval Stockholm

Gamla Stan, previously known as Stadsholmen (Island City), has changed dramatically during its history. This walk will take you through the oldest part, though the buildings here represent nearly all periods, from the 13th to the 20th centuries.

   Start at the northern end of Västerlånggatan, at the corner of Myntgatan. As you walk south on Västerlånggatan, you are heading into the heart of Stockholm's earliest history. At the time of its founding in

the mid 1200s, the new city was confined to this small island, with defensive walls erected along Västerlånggatan and Österlånggatan. Västerlånggatan still has its winding medieval section, but during the last century it has become the area's busiest shopping street. The cast-iron shop windows, modelled on those of Paris, date from the 19th century.

   Continue on Västerlånggatan, turn left on Kåkbrinken and stop at corner of Prästgatan. The name Kåkbrinken dates from 1477 – *kåk* means 'pillory' and *brink* means 'steep hill' – referring to the fact that this hill once led up to the city's pillory at Stortorget. Traffic has always been a problem on these narrow streets, and to protect the buildings from damage by horses, carts and other traffic, a cannon, an iron grate and a Viking rune stone were strategically placed on the corners. In medieval times, Prästgatan (meaning Priest Street) ran just inside the first city wall.

Bernadotte Gallery. Medals and orders of various kinds are awarded in the **Apartments of the Orders of Chivalry**, and paintings of coats of arms decorate its walls. Until 1975, the monarch opened parliament each year in the impressive **Hall of State**, and directly across from this lies the **Royal Chapel** with pew ends made in the 1690s for the Tre Kronor castle. Services are held every Sunday and all are welcome to attend.

Museet Tre Kronor
Entrance on Lejonbacken.
A boardwalk built through the palace cellars, along with several models, enables visitors to see how war, fire and wealth have shaped the palace seen today. An old well from the former courtyard, a 13th-century defensive wall and the arched brick ceilings

are evidence of how the palace was built up around the fortress that was once there. Panels describe life within the castle, archaeological discoveries and building techniques.

Gustav III's Antikmuseum
Entrance on Lejonbacken.
This museum of Roman statues and busts, in two halls in the north-east wing of the palace, has been laid out to look exactly as it did in the 1790s when King Gustav III returned from Italy with the collection, which includes *Apollo and His Nine Muses* and the sleeping *Endymion*. The repairs and additions made to the statues at the time have been left intact, as well as the odd combinations of pieces, such as table legs on fountains. Nothing is labelled, in accordance with the period, so you should try and

Continue along Kåkbrinken to Stortorget.
To the medieval inhabitants of Stockholm, Stortorget was the central meeting place, the main market and the courthouse. On the north side of the square was the town hall (now the **Nobelmuseet**; *see p57*), where new laws and regulations were read to the public twice a year from an upstairs window. Penalties ranged from fines and flogging to hanging and beheading. Stortorget is also the site of the infamous Stockholm Bloodbath in 1520 (*see p14*).
Take Svartmangatan south from Stortorget to the corner of Kindstugatan.
Saint Gertrude's is the official name of what is commonly referred to as **Tyska Kyrkan** (German Church; *see p59*). In medieval times this was the guildhouse of the city's German merchants, and in the 1570s it was converted into a church; the building took its present form in the 1630s and after a fire in 1878 the spire was reconstructed. Note its frightening gargoyles.
Turn left on Kindstugatan and stop at the Fimmelstången bar at Kindstugatan 14.
This now tranquil street was once the scene of some infamous fights. One of them began at the Fimmelstången tavern, where the renowned poet Lasse 'Lucidor' Johansson was killed in 1674. After a long drinking session with his friends, Lucidor refused to answer a final toast from his companion. A fight broke out and he was subsequently stabbed to death. Lucidor was a brilliant linguist who earned his living writing poems on commission. In 1689, 15 years after his death, his poems were published in the book *Helicons Blomster* (*The Flowers of Helicon*).

Continue on Kindstugatan to Brända Tomten, the square with the tree, turn right and stop at Själagårdsgatan 13.
Started in the 1420s, **Själagården** was originally a combined hospital, poorhouse and old people's home run by Storkyrkan. In 1527, when Sweden became a Protestant country, King Gustav Vasa seized the Catholic church's gold and silver, and converted the building into a printing house to help spread the new religious teachings. Over the centuries the building has also been used as a school and a warehouse. In 1935 a functionalist building was erected on the site above the old medieval cellar, and today it is once again a senior citizens' home operated by Storkyrkan.
Continue on Själagårdsgatan to Tyska Brunnsplan, and turn left on Svartmangatan. Follow Svartmangatan as it becomes Södra Benickebrinken. Walk to Österlånggatan and stop outside restaurant Den Gyldene Freden at No.51.
Österlånggatan, running north from busy Järntorget, marks the eastern section of the first city wall. The Restaurant **Den Gyldene Freden** (*see p100*) opened on this street in 1722 and soon became one of the most popular taverns in town. It was nearly closed in 1919 but famous Swedish artist Anders Zorn bought the building and had the restaurant completely renovated. When Zorn passed away he bequeathed the building to the Swedish Academy and in 1922 the restaurant reopened, to the delight of many Stockholmers. It's famed for its traditional, yet creative Swedish dishes, and its historic interior will transport you to another time.

Sightseeing

Kungliga Slottet. *See p53.*

take the 20-minute tour (conducted in English) or borrow a pamphlet if you want to make the most of your visit.

Skattkammaren
Entrance on Slottsbacken.
The regalia of past Swedish royal families sparkles behind glass, with orbs, sceptres and crowns in adults' and children's sizes. The crowns are still in use for the monarch's inauguration and were present at the wedding of Carl Gustav and Silvia. The museum also contains Gustav Vasa's etched sword of state from 1541, the coronation cloak of Oscar II and the ornate silver baptismal font of Karl XI.

Livrustkammaren
Entrance on Slottsbacken (51 95 55 44/www.lsh.se/ livrustkammaren). T-bana Gamla Stan/bus 2, 43, 55, 62, 76. **Open** *June-Aug* 10am-5pm daily. *Sept-May* 11am-5pm Tue, Wed, Fri-Sun; 11am-8pm Thur. **Admission** 50kr; free under-19s. **Free with SC**. **Credit** AmEx, DC, MC, V. **Map** p241 H8.
The Royal Armoury is one of the palace's best museums – don't miss it. Sweden's oldest museum, which was founded in 1633, is stuffed full with armour, weapons and clothes from the 16th century onwards, and is housed in the palace's former cellars, which were used for storing potatoes and firewood. With wonderfully descriptive texts, the museum's first room shows what a bloody and dangerous business being a king once was. It contains the masked costume King Gustav III wore when he was assassinated in 1792, and the stuffed body of

Streiff, the horse that Gustav II Adolf was riding when he was killed in battle in 1632. Don't overlook the glass jar preserving the stomach contents of one of the conspirators to Gustav III's murder. Other rooms display splendid mounted knights, suits of armour, swords and muskets. Two rooms of clothes and toys – including a miniature carriage – describe the lost childhoods and early responsibilities of the royal children. The ceremonial coaches of the nobility lie beneath the main floor, in another hall. Guided tours in English are no longer given, but audio guides in English are provided for 20kr.

Other sights

There are plenty of other sights on Gamla Stan apart from the Royal Palace. At the top of Slottsbacken stands the imposing yellow bulk of Stockholm's de facto cathedral, **Storkyrkan** (*see p59*), the scene of royal weddings and coronations. Trångsund, the street at the front of the church, leads down to Gamla Stan's main square, **Stortorget** (*photo p60*). A former marketplace, it's surrounded by handsome, colourful 18th-century buildings, many containing cafés: the two located at the western end of the square, **Chokladkoppen** and **Kaffekoppen** (for both, *see p126*), are by far the best.

The large white building is the former Stock Exchange, designed by Erik Lallerstedt (not to be confused with one of Sweden's most famous chefs by the same name); it now houses the high-tech **Nobelmuseet** (*see p57*), telling the history of the esteemed Nobel Prizes. The Swedish Academy of Sciences permanently occupies the upper floor. Lallerstedt also designed the 1778 well in the centre of the square. Due to the land rising, the well dried up in the 19th century and was moved to Brunkebergstorg in Norrmalm, but it was then moved back again in the 20th century.

The notorious **Stockholm Bloodbath** – in which more than 80 noblemen, priests and burghers were hanged or decapitated at the command of the Danish king, Christian II – occurred in Stortorget in 1520. You can see a cannonball in the façade of the building at Stortorget 7, on the corner with Skomakargatan. It is said to have been fired at Christian II at the time of the Bloodbath, but in fact was placed much later as a joke, probably in 1795 by a furniture dealer named Grevesmühl.

Gamla Stan's main thoroughfares of **Västerlånggatan**, **Österlånggatan**, **Stora Nygatan** and **Lilla Nygatan** run north–south along the island. Crowded Västerlånggatan draws tourists to its many small shops, while the parallel street – narrow, curving **Prästgatan** – is a quiet alternative to the hubbub and far more atmospheric, giving you a much better idea of life in the crowded medieval city. At the southern end of Västerlånggatan is **Mårten Trotzigs Gränd**, the city's narrowest street at only 90 centimetres (three feet) wide. A bit further south is Järntorget, where you can sit outdoors and enjoy the excellent cakes and pastries of **Sundbergs Konditori** (*see p128*).

There are five hotels on Gamla Stan; two of them – the **Victory Hotel** (*see p36*) and the **Rica City Hotel Gamla Stan** (*see p37*) – are on Lilla Nygatan, as is the surprisingly interesting **Postmuseum** (*see 59*). On nearby Stora Nygatan 10-12 you can visit the **Forum för Levande Historia** (Living History Forum; 723 87 50, www.levandehistoria.org, open noon-5pm Tue-Sat). Opened in 2004, it's a government exhibition centre and library on human rights, prejudice and genocide.

The island's churches include the **Tyska Kyrkan** (German Church; *see p59*) and the **Finska Kyrkan** (Finnish Church) – proof of Sweden's long connections with its European neighbours. The latter is housed in a 1640s building opposite the Kungliga Slottet; originally a ball games court for the palace, it has been the religious centre of the Finnish community since 1725. Down the hill from the Finnish Church is the Swedish Institute's excellent **Sweden Bookshop** (*see p139*), a great place to pick up books about Sweden in English.

Gamla Stan also contains a number of beautiful palaces, former homes of the aristocracy. On the island's north-western tip on Riddarhustorget is **Bondeska Palatset**, designed by Tessin the Elder and the seat of the Supreme Court since 1949, and the lovely **Riddarhuset** (723 39 90, www.riddarhuset.se). The nobility governed from here until parliamentary reforms in 1866 knocked them down a notch or two. They still own the place, though, and will let you visit during lunch hour (11.30am-12.30pm Mon-Fri, admission 50kr, 25kr concessions) to admire their coats of arms (more than 2,000 in all), signet collection and early 17th-century chair with ivory engravings. Another way to see inside is to attend a concert by the **Stockholm Sinfonietta** (*see p188*).

Nobelmuseet

Börshuset, Stortorget (53 48 18 00/www.nobel museum.se). T-bana Gamla Stan/bus 2, 3, 43, 53, 55, 59, 76. **Open** *Mid May-mid Sept* 10am-5pm Mon, Wed-Sun; 10am-8pm Tue. *Mid Sept-mid May* 11am-8pm Tue; 11am-5pm Wed-Sun. **Guided tours** (in English) *Mid May-mid Sept* 11am, 3pm Mon, Wed-Sun; 11am, 2pm, 4pm, 5pm Tue. *Mid Sept-mid May* 11am, 4pm Tue-Sun. **Admission** 60kr; 40kr concessions; 20kr 7-18s; 120kr family ticket; free under-7s. **Free with SC**. **Credit** AmEx, MC, V. **Map** p241 J7.

The Nobel Museum opened in 2001 to commemorate the centenary of the Nobel Prizes. Although the museum is not that large, its two theatres showing short films about the laureates, television clips about

Skeppsbron. *See p53.*

the prizes and a computer room with an 'e-museum' bombard you with enough information to keep you entertained for a while. You can also listen to acceptance speeches over the years in audio booths, including that of Martin Luther King in 1964. Alfred Nobel's books, lab equipment and two packs of dynamite are displayed in a side room, along with his death mask and a copy of the first page of his four-page will, which called for the creation of the prizes. An exhibit on the Nobel banquet includes a glassed-in table setting and videos of the event. *See also below* **Nobel or ignoble?**

Postmuseum
Lilla Nygatan 6 (781 17 55/www.postmuseum. posten.se). T-bana Gamla Stan/bus 3, 53. **Open** *May-Aug* 11am-4pm Tue-Sun. *Sept-Apr* 11am-4pm

Nobel or ignoble?

At the time of his death in 1896, Alfred Nobel bequeathed his entire fortune as an endowment to humanity. His last will and testament specified that the generated interest 'shall be annually distributed in the form of prizes to those who, during the preceding year, shall have conferred the greatest benefit on mankind.' He specified five categories; physics, chemistry, medicine, literature and peace. The first prizes, set at 150,782 Swedish kronor, were awarded in 1901.

Despite the noble intent, it's difficult to measure up to 'greatest benefit on mankind' and perhaps more difficult to select worthy candidates. While the Nobel Museum (*see p57*) proudly displays its eminent laureates and their achievements, we've lined up four controversial winners.

Günter Grass
The most recent controversy came with the 1999 literature award to Günter Grass, which stirred conflict after Grass confessed that he had served in Nazi Germany's notorious Waffen SS elite force during World War II. Grass explained that he had been drafted as a teen and managed to never fire a shot while serving, and calls for the Nobel committee to revoke the award were dismissed. Grass is now known as both a leftist and pacifist.

Fritz Haber
The most notorious Nobel Prize recipient is Fritz Haber, popularly dubbed the 'father of chemical warfare'. Haber received the 1918 prize in chemistry at the end of World War I, during which he had developed a new weapon for warfare. The poisonous gas he invented, and whose production and distribution he oversaw, was chlorine gas, which killed thousands in the trenches in Belgium. His wife, who was a fellow chemist, committed suicide over her husband's 'success'.

Arthur Kornberg
Dr Arthur Kornberg received the 1959 Nobel prize for having apparently discovered the enzyme that copies DNA. As it turned out, he had in fact discovered the wrong enzyme. Despite this scientific blunder, Dr Kornberg retained his prize and his newfound stature overshadowed the efforts of ensuing scientists to disprove him. His own son, Thomas Kornberg, eventually isolated the true enzyme in 1970 – though he did not receive a Nobel nomination for his efforts.

Egas Moniz
More than half a century later, people continue to lobby for the posthumous revocation of Egas Moniz's 1949 prize in medicine, awarded for his discovery of the leucotomy – better known as the lobotomy. More lobotomies were performed in the three years following his award than in the 13 years since his original discovery. Opponents cite the misuse of the procedure, which condemns patients to a near zombie-like existence. Ken Kesey immortalised this misuse in *One Flew Over the Cuckoo's Nest*.

Nobel by numbers
Nobel Laureates 787 individuals, 19 organisations

Female Laureates 33

Youngest Laureate Lawrence Bragg (25yrs; Physics 1915)

Oldest Laureate Raymond Davis Jnr (88yrs; Physics 2002)

Multiple Winners John Bardeen (Physics 1956 & 1972); Marie Curie (Physics 1903, Chemistry 1911); Linus Pauling (Chemistry 1954, Peace 1962); Frederick Sanger (Chemistry 1958 & 1980); International Committee of the Red Cross (Peace 1917, 1944 & 1963); United Nations HIgh Commission for Refugees (Peace 1954 & 1981)

Tue, Thur-Sun; 11am-7pm Wed. **Admission** 50kr; 40kr concessions; free under-18s. **Free with SC**. **Credit** MC, V. **Map** p241 J7.

Life-size scenes depicting more than 360 years of the Swedish postal service make the main exhibit of this museum unexpectedly enjoyable. A mounted postal carrier, a farm boy running with the mail and a postal train wagon, among other tableaux, illustrate the effect of the postal service on people's lives over the centuries. From 1720 until 1869, the city's only post office was housed on this spot. Lilla Posten downstairs includes a miniature post office for kids and the gift shop sells stationery and, of course, stamps.

Nobelmuseet. See p57.

Storkyrkan

Storkyrkobrinken, Trångsund 1 (723 30 16/www. stockholmsdomkyrkoforsamling.se). T-bana Gamla Stan/bus 2, 3, 43, 53, 55, 59, 76. **Open** *21 May-29 Sept* 9am-6pm daily. *30 Sept-20 May* 9am-4pm daily. **Admission** 25kr; free under-16s; free Sun. **No credit cards**. **Map** p241 H7.

Dating from the mid 13th century, 'the Great Church' is the oldest congregational church in Stockholm and the site of past coronations and royal weddings. A huge brick church with a rectangular plan, it's been extended and rebuilt numerous times. Between 1736 and 1742, its exterior was renovated from medieval to baroque to match the neighbouring palace, and in 1743 the tower was raised to its current height of 66m (216ft). Inside, the style is primarily Gothic with baroque additions – such as the extravagant golden booths designed for the royal family by the palace architect Tessin the Younger. The main attraction is Bernt Notke's intricately carved wooden statue, *St George and the Dragon*, which is decorated with authentic elk antlers. The statue symbolises Sten Sture's victory over the Danes in a battle in 1471, and was given to the church by Sture himself in 1489. (A bronze copy of the statue can also be found in Köpmantorget, not far from the church.) Don't miss the famous *Parhelion Painting*, which shows an unusual light phenomenon – six sparkling halos – that appeared over Stockholm on 20 April 1535. It's one of the oldest depictions of the capital, though the painting is a 1630s copy of the earlier original. From July to mid August, theology students give guided tours (in Swedish and English) of the church's tower (2pm & 3pm, 40kr which includes entry fee to church), which involves climbing 200 steps on narrow wooden staircases for an amazing view of the black roofs of Gamla Stan.

Tyska Kyrkan

Svartmangatan 16A (411 11 88/www.st-gertrud.se). T-bana Gamla Stan/bus 3, 53. **Open** *July-Aug* 11am-5pm daily. *Sept-June* 11am-4pm daily. **Admission** free. **Map** p241 J8.

At the height of the Hanseatic League, when Stockholm had strong trade links with Germany, many German merchants settled in this area of Gamla Stan. They originally worshipped at the monastery on what is now Riddarholmen, but moved

Stortorget, scene of the infamous Stockholm Bloodbath. *See p56.*

to St Gertrude's guildhouse after its expansion in the 1580s. Baroque renovations in 1638-42 gave the German Church its present appearance; its tower was rebuilt after a fire in 1878. Tessin the Elder designed the royal pews, and Jost Henner created the richly decorated ornaments and figures on the portal. The church is best viewed from Tyska Brinken, where the tower rises up 96m (315ft) from the narrow street. At the church's summer concerts you can listen to a replica of a 17th-century organ, constructed for the church in 2004 at a cost of ten million kronor.

Riddarholmen

Map p241

Cut off from Gamla Stan by several lanes of traffic and a narrow canal, the tiny island of Riddarholmen is a gorgeous sanctuary of cobblestoned streets, 17th-century palaces and spectacular watery views. Most of the buildings now house government offices, and no one actually lives permanently on the island.

The main attraction is the medieval brick church, **Riddarholmskyrkan** (*see p61*). Next to the church is **Birger Jarls Torg**, the site of an 1854 statue of Stockholm's founder, Birger Jarl, dressed in a helmet and chainmail. The huge white **Wrangelska Palatset** stands to the west of the statue. Constructed as a nobleman's residence in the mid 17th century,

it was extensively rebuilt a few decades later by Tessin the Elder, under its new owner, Field Marshal Carl Gustaf Wrangel. The palace became the home of the royal family for several years after the Tre Kronor fire of 1697.

On the other side of the square is the well-preserved, pink-coloured **Stenbockska Palatset**, built in the 1640s by state councillor Fredrik Stenbock, and extended and renovated in succeeding centuries. Several of the palaces of Riddarholmen are today used by the Swedish courts and government authorities. They are seldom open to the public, but taking a walk around them is highly recommended.

Down by the water on **Evert Taubes Terrass**, you'll find one of the best views in Stockholm, looking out across the choppy water of Riddarfjärden and towards the shores of Lake Mälaren. The terrace is named after the much-loved Swedish poet and troubadour Evert Taube (who died in 1976) and there's a bronze sculpture of him, lute in hand, near the water. It's also a prime spot to celebrate the arrival of spring on **Walpurgis Night** (*see p159*), with a bonfire by the water and communal singing. Author and dramatist **August Strindberg** was born here in 1849. Although Strindberg's building has long since been torn down, a plaque in Swedish on a nearby wall commemorates the site of his birth.

North along the waterfront, on Norra Riddarholmshamnen, is the distinctive circular **Birger Jarls Torn**. The only remnant of the defensive fortifications built by Gustav Vasa around 1530 (along with part of the Wrangelska Palatset), it was given its name in the 19th century when it was mistakenly thought to have been built under Birger Jarl 600 years earlier. It's not open to the public.

Riddarholmskyrkan

Birger Jarls Torg (Royal Palace 402 61 30/www. royalcourt.se). T-bana Gamla Stan/bus 3, 53. **Open** *Mid May-mid Sept* 10am-4pm daily. Closed mid Sept-mid May. Tours in English 2pm & 4pm June-Aug. **Admission** 30kr; 10kr concessions, 7-18s; free under-7s. **Free with SC. No credit cards. Map** p241 J7.
The black, lattice-work spire of Riddarholmskyrkan is one of Stockholm's most distinctive sights, visible from all over the city. Construction on the church started in the late 13th century as a monastery for Franciscan monks. The church's benefactor, King Magnus Ladulås, is buried in the church along with 16 other monarchs, including Gustav III, Gustav II Adolf and, the last to be buried here in 1950, Gustav V. Since the 17th century, only two Swedish monarchs have not been buried here. Additions have been made to the church over time, in part to make room for more graves, since an estimated 500-1,000 people are buried in its floors and vaults – the floor consists almost entirely of grave-covering stone slabs. The southern wall was moved back in the 15th century, the tower was added in the late 16th century, and work began in 1838 on the current cast-iron spire after lightning struck the original. Colourful plaques of the Serafim order, which are awarded to Swedish nobility and visiting heads of state, decorate the walls of the church.

Helgeandsholmen

Map p241

This tiny oval-shaped island is connected to Norrmalm and Gamla Stan by two bridges: a pedestrian one at the western end and a car/pedestrian one at the eastern end. The **Riksdagshuset** (Parliament Building; *see below*) dominates the whole western half of the island. As you walk north, the new parliament building is to your left and the old one to your right, joined by two stone arches. The older section, completed in 1905, was designed by Aron Johansson, with two chambers for a bicameral parliament, baroque motifs and a grand staircase. At the same time he also designed a curved stone building across the street for the Bank of Sweden. After the country changed to a unicameral system in 1971, the bank moved out, the roof was flattened and the parliament's new glass-fronted debating chamber built on top.

This being Sweden, it's a pretty open system of government. There's a very detailed website (in Swedish and English) and an information centre (Storkyrkobrinken 7, www.riksdagen.se), and the parliament building is open for guided tours year-round (for information call 786 48 62). You can also visit the public gallery when parliament is in session and listen to debates.

Riksdagshuset

Riksgatan 3A (786 40 00/www.riksdagen.se). T-bana Kungsträdgården/bus 43, 62. **Open** (guided tours only) *End June-Aug* 11am, 3pm (Swedish), 12.30pm, 2pm (Swedish & English) Mon-Fri. *Sept-end June* noon (Swedish), 1.30pm (Swedish & English) Sat, Sun. **Admission** free. **Map** p241 H7.
Free 50-minute guided tours of the Riksdagshuset are given in Swedish, English and German. The guides are exceptionally well informed and the tour is interesting enough – if you don't mind a little education. You'll see the modern semicircular main chamber; at the front is a large tapestry, *Memory of a Landscape* by Elisabet Hasselberg Olsson, woven in 200 shades of grey. Beneath the chamber lies the former bank hall, now a lobby for the parliamentarians. In the old buildin°g, where the tour begins and ends, visitors are shown the grand former main entrance with its marble columns and busts of prime ministers, as well as the old dual chambers (now used as meeting rooms).

Riddarholmen.

Sightseeing

Norrmalm & Vasastaden

Ransacked by bulldozers in the 1960s, downtown Stockholm is now rebuilding for a better future.

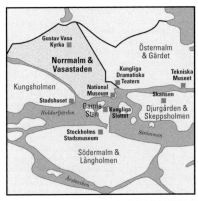

Norrmalm

Map p240 & p241

Most of the downtown, commercial centre of Norrmalm – also known as City – resulted from a massive 'renewal' campaign in the 1960s, in which nearly all of the district's older buildings were torn down in favour of boxy office space. The area continues to develop today, this time decidedly for the better, with renovated shopping centres, new designer boutiques and ultramodern hotels under construction on its western border. Aside from all the hotels and shopping opportunities, Norrmalm is also known for its restaurants, nightclubs and some key museums and sights.

In Stockholm's early years, city government discouraged construction on Norrmalm out of fear that an enemy attacking Gamla Stan would take shelter in the buildings. It seems the area has always been under threat from something – even in the early 16th century Gustav Vasa tore down many of Norrmalm's structures. By 1602, though, the district had grown to the extent that it was declared a separate city. This competition with Stockholm lasted just three and a half decades – in 1637 Normalm lost its indepedence and was absorbed into its larger neighbour.

Most visitors to Stockholm arrive in Norrmalm, zoomed in on the Arlanda Express to its terminal next to **Central Station** on busy Vasagatan, or by bus to its northern neighbour **Cityterminalen**. Both stations are linked to T-Centralen, the main Tunnelbana station, where all three lines of the metro network converge. Stepping out from Central Station, you immediately see the kind of functionalist concrete and steel buildings that dominate the area. Behind them can be seen the brick tower of the late 16th-century **St Clara Kyrka** (*see p66*), one of the area's oldest churches.

Those wanting to head straight into the heart of the shopping district should take **Klarabergsgatan** from Central Station, which ends at Sergels Torg. To see the water and the more picturesque areas of Norrmalm, head south on the eastern side of Vasagatan. Swing round the corner when you reach the **Sheraton Stockholm Hotel** (*see p39*) and walk one block up Jakobsgatan to avoid the horrible tangle of highways and viaducts. The nearby **Konstakademien** (Royal Academy of Art, www.konstakademien.se), on parallel Fredsgatan, occupies a renovated palace designed by Tessin the Elder in the 1670s. The academy was founded by King Gustav III in 1773 and moved into its current premises in 1780. In 1978 it was separated from the Royal University College of Fine Arts, which is today on Skeppsholmen. The academy's terrace bar (*see p119*) is very popular in summer, as is the restaurant **F12** (*see p101*). The academy's art exhibitions are closed during the summer.

Many of Sweden's government departments are nearby, such as the two buildings – one light orange and the other red – called **Rosenbad**, which house the offices of the prime minister. A stone walkway and bicycle path follow the northern shore of **Norrström** – from Rosenbad to the tip of the Blasieholmen peninsula. East on Fredsgatan is **Gustav Adolfs Torg**, named after King Gustav II Adolf, who greatly expanded the city in the early 17th century; a statue of the king stands in the centre of the square. Not far away there are Mediterranean antiquities in the **Medelhavsmuseet** (*see p66*) and dance costumes in the **Dansmuseet** (*see p65*).

On the square's eastern flank is the grand **Kungliga Operan** (*see p188*), styled after the Royal Palace in the late 19th century, with a splendid chandelier-strewn gold foyer 28 metres (92 feet) long. The original opera building, where King Gustav III was assassinated in 1792, looked exactly like **Arvfurstens Palats**, the building across from it, which was constructed in the 1780s and is now used by the Ministry for Foreign Affairs. The opera house contains four restaurants, varying in splendour and price; the fanciest, and one of Sweden's best, is **Operakällaren** (*see p103*). From the front of the opera house you get a beautiful view across the water towards the Kungliga Slottet; behind it is the earthy red Gothic structure of **St Jacobs Kyrka** (*see p66*).

The long rectangular park of **Kungsträdgården** (King's Garden) stretches north from here. This is a popular venue for open-air events and fairs. Originally a vegetable garden for the royal castle in the 15th century, the park later developed into a pleasure garden and opened to the public in the 18th century. A century later the French-born King Karl XIV Johan tore out the trees, erected a statue of his adoptive father, Karl XIII, and converted the garden into a field for military exercises. After his death it was quietly turned back into a park. The statue of Karl XII – his finger pointing east to his old battlegrounds in Russia – was added in 1868 near the water.

Two tree-lined avenues shade the restaurants and glassed-in cafés along the park's western and eastern edges. At the top end of the park, in front of a shallow pool with three fountains, is the touristy Friday's American Bar, while Volvo's newest and oldest cars are displayed in a showroom nearby. In winter there's skating on the park's ice rink.

The crowded thoroughfare of **Hamngatan** crosses the top of the park. At No.27 is **Sverigehuset**, the city's main tourist office (*see p50*). Bang opposite is **NK** (*see p137*), Sweden's first and most exclusive department store. For cheaper shops try the **Gallerian** mall (*see p137*) just up the street.

A couple of blocks west along from NK is **Sergels Torg**. This two-level area of glass, concrete and underground shops was built after the bulldozer extravaganza of the 1960s. The sunken modernistic square of black and white triangles is a popular spot for political demonstrations; the rather grubby, tall glass

Arlanda Express.

Kulturhuset.

tower surrounded by fountains in the middle of the traffic island was designed by sculptor Edvin Öhrström in 1972.

Architect Peter Celsing was responsible for **Kulturhuset** (*see p197*), the seven-storey structure that stands behind Sergels Torg like a great glass wall, which he built in the early 1970s. Today it's home to Sweden's only comic book library, **Serieteket**, while next door is one of Stockholm's biggest theatres, **Stadsteatern** (*see p198*). Take the escalators up to the one of the galleries on the upper floors to check out one of the many temporary art exhibitions. The top floor **Café Panorama** (*see p129*) has a great view of the square below. There's also a library, an internet café and a branch of **DesignTorget** (*see p150*).

Several main streets converge on Sergels Torg, including Klarabergsgatan and Sveavägen. The block-long, windowless **Åhléns** department store (*see p136*) occupies the north-west corner of the former, and is one of scores of shopping options. The pedestrian street of **Drottninggatan** (*photo p66*) is lined with shops from its start at the water's edge all the way north to Tegnérgatan, and is permanently packed with shoppers.

North from Sergels Torg five glass office buildings stand in a row towards the open space of Hötorget; built in the 1950s, they're city landmarks – whether people want them to be or not. **Hötorget** is home to the **PUB** department store (*see p137*) and an outdoor market selling fruit, flowers and a bit of everything. The indoor, international food hall, **Hötorgshallen** (*see p149*), bustles beneath the **Filmstaden Sergel** multiplex (*see p172*). On another side stands the **Konserthuset** (*see p187*). Stockholm's main concert hall is apparently a prime example of Swedish neo-classical style, but to the untrained eye the 1926 building looks suspiciously like a bright blue box with ten grey pillars attached to it.

Ivar Tengbom modelled the hall on the temples of ancient Greece, and the artworks inside depict figures and scenes from Greek mythology. Tengbom's son, Anders, renovated the building in 1972 to improve the acoustics. Einar Forseth (who also decorated the Golden Hall at the Stadshuset) created the floor mosaics in the entrance hall and main foyer, and Carl Milles sculpted the bronze statue of Orpheus near the front steps. There are guided tours (50kr) on Saturdays when there is a concert, but it's more fun to attend a performance.

Further north on Drottninggatan, **Centralbadet** (*see p153*) is a lovely, art nouveau bathhouse built in 1905, with café tables in its pretty front courtyard. Nearby, **Dansens Hus** (*see p200*) is the capital's main venue for modern dance and, just to the east, on Sveavägen, stands classical **Adolf Fredriks Kyrka**. It has a Greek cross plan and a beautifully painted ceiling; assassinated prime minister Olof Palme is buried in the cemetery here. On the corner of Drottninggatan and Tengnérgatan is the building in which August Strindberg spent the last four years of his life. His apartment is now the **Strindbergsmuseet** (*see p67*) – a must for fans of Sweden's greatest author. On Drottninggatan near the museum a few of Strindberg's famous quotes have been printed on the street in Swedish.

Down at the southern tip of Norrmalm the **Blasieholmen** peninsula pokes out into the water towards Skeppsholmen. At the end of this spur of land stands the imposing limestone façade of Sweden's largest art museum, the **National Museum** (*see p66*). North along the waterfront, on Strömkajen, in front of the five-starred **Grand Hôtel** (*see p39*), is the boarding point for sightseeing boats and ferries to the archipelago. Another wharf for ferries (to the archipelago and in the summer to Djurgården and Slussen) is across the peninsula at the small harbour of **Nybroviken**.

Overlooking the lawns of Berzelii Park is **Berns Salonger**, a legendary venue since the 1860s. It's still a nightlife favourite, and its magnificent salons, gilded and topped with crystal chandeliers, now house one of Stockholm's largest restaurants (*see p100*) and numerous bars (*see p167*). The adjoining boutique hotel (*see p37*) is a fine choice.

Dansmuseet

Gustav Adolfs Torg 22-24 (441 76 50/www. dansmuseet.se). T-bana Kungsträdgården/bus 2, 3, 43, 59, 62, 65. **Open** *May-Aug* 11am-4pm Mon-Fri; noon-4pm Sat, Sun. *Sept-Apr* 11am-4pm Tue-Fri; noon-4pm Sat, Sun. **Admission** 40kr; 30kr concessions; free under-18s. **Credit** AmEx, MC, V. **Map** p241 G7.

The Dance Museum displays costumes from Swedish and Russian ballets, paintings and sketches related to dance, and traditional masks and costumes from Africa, Thailand, China, Japan and Tibet. Rolf de Maré, who managed the Swedish Ballet in Paris in the 1920s, opened the museum in the French capital in 1933. When the museum closed in the 1940s the contents relating to Swedish and non-European dance were relocated to Stockholm. The collection is small but well presented, and now has free admission. Be sure to visit the well-stocked café.

My Stockholm Elin af Klintberg

Elin af Klintberg is the editor-in-chief of Plaza, an award-winning Stockholm-based magazine that focuses on art, architecture, fashion and design. She was raised on Lidingö, just outside central Stockholm, and currently lives in an apartment overlooking Vasastan.
My perfect day would begin with breakfast at a little Italian café, **Caffé Nero** (*Roslagsgatan 4, 22 19 35*), in Vasastan. Here you'll find the city's best coffee and great breakfast sandwiches. It attracts a cool crowd, and ever since it got a licence to serve wine it's jam-packed for lunch and dinner too.

Next I'd head over to the street that's become the heart of Stockholm's art scene, Hudiksvallsgatan, to see what Stockholm's best galleries have on show. My favourite is the **Natalia Goldin Gallery** (*see p176*), which specialises in the work of emerging Scandinavian artists.

Afterwards I'd walk another five minutes to Stockholm's loveliest park, Hagaparken. Sometimes I'll have a game of tennis at **Pelles Tennis School** (*Haga Kungspark,* 33 70 77, www.hagatennis.se). Other times I just like to sit in one of the enormous meadows and take in the views over the lake.

For lunch, I'd eat at **Haga Forum** (*Annerovägen 4, 33 48 44*), a glass pavilion at the city end of the park where both the food and wine list are excellent. Then in the afternoon I'd catch a film at the **Grand** on Sveavägen (*see p172*), which is the city's most beautiful cinema.

I'd eat dinner with friends at **Teatergrillen** (*Nybrogatan 3, 54 50 36 65*) and then, using the passageway that cuts through the kitchen, pop through to **Riche** (*see p169*) and go to the Lilla Baren club night, where you can hear some of Stockholm's best DJs.

When Lilla Baren closes at 2am I'd head over to Stockholm's smallest and best nightclub, which is located in the basement of the **Berns Hotel** (*see p37*). Here I'd try to grab one of the armchairs and check out the video installations on the walls and the great mix of people. When it closes at 4am, it's time to call a cab and head home.

Wall-to-wall shops: **Drottninggatan**. See p64.

Medelhavsmuseet

Fredsgatan 2 (51 95 50 50/www.medelhavsmuseet.
se). T-bana Kungsträdgården/bus 3, 43, 62, 65.
Open noon-8pm Tue, Wed; noon-5pm Thur-Sun.
Admission 60kr; free under-19s. **Free with SC.**
Map p241 G7.
Artefacts from Greece, Rome, Egypt and Cyprus
are housed in the Museum of Mediterranean
Antiquities. Displayed in the main hall are a variety of busts and statues, while other rooms contain
Islamic art, early medical instruments, ancient
sarcophagi and a reconstruction of an Egyptian
tomb. The Gold Room, a vault holding ancient
wreaths of gold, is open between 12.30pm and 1pm
or 2.30pm and 3pm. The second-floor Bagdad café
serves Mediterranean specialities for lunch. The
museum is worth a visit once you've seen the city's
major attractions.

National Museum

Södra Blasieholmshamnen (51 95 43 00/www.
nationalmuseum.se). T-bana Kungsträdgården/
bus 2, 55, 59, 62, 65, 76. **Open** *June-Aug* 11am-
8pm Tue; 11am-5pm Wed-Sun. *Sept-May* 11am-
8pm Tue, Thur; 11am-5pm Wed, Fri-Sun.
Admission 80kr; 60kr concessions; free
under-19s. **Free with SC. Credit** AmEx, MC, V.
Map p241 H8.

Paintings, sculptures, drawings and decorative arts,
dating from the Middle Ages to the present, are
displayed here, in Sweden's largest art museum.
The National Museum is not as impressive as some
of Europe's big art museums, but there are works
by the likes of Rembrandt, Rubens, Goya and Degas,
and substantial collections of 17th-century Dutch,
18th-century French and 18th- and 19th-century
Swedish art. The building, designed in 1866 to look
like a northern Italian Renaissance palace, is grand
and awe-inspiring. The central staircase is adorned
with colourful frescoes by Carl Larsson, including
two large and wonderful works at the top: *Gustav*
Vasa's Entry into Stockholm 1523 and *Midwinter*
Sacrifice. Owing to the enormous size of the
collection, temporary exhibitions are arranged
throughout the year based around historical and
national perspectives. Guided tours are available in
English in summer. The permanent exhibition on
the first floor, 'Design 19002000', showcases
20th-century Scandinavian design, including
porcelain, glassware and chairs made of every
material known to man. The indoor, courtyard-like
Atrium café/restaurant (*see p128*) is perfect for
cold winter days.

St Clara Kyrka

Klara Östra Kyrkogata 7 (723 30 31). T-bana
T-Centralen/bus 47, 52, 56, 59. **Open** 10am-5pm
daily. **Admission** free. **Map** p241 G6.
The copper spire of this brick 16th-century church
across from Central Station rises from a cluster
of dull, box-like 1960s buildings. St Clara Kyrka
was one of many churches built in the late 16th
century during the reign of Johan III, who had
a Catholic wife and a love of architecture.
He decided to build here in the 1570s since it was
the site of a former convent torn down in the
Reformation. Dutch architect Willem Boy designed
the church, and Carl Hårleman, who also completed
the interior of the Kungliga Slottet (*see p62*),
redesigned its roof and spire after a fire in the mid
18th century. Inside the sunlit church the ceiling is
painted with biblical scenes. The congregation gives
out bread and coffee to the homeless, so the
graveyard and nearby steps are often occupied by
homeless people. Classical concerts are held at
midday. Check here for daily listings of church
concerts around the city.

St Jacobs Kyrka

Västra Trädgårdsgatan 2 (723 30 38). T-bana
Kungsträdgården/bus 2, 43, 55, 59, 65. **Open**
24hrs daily. **Admission** free. **Map** p241 G7.
This newly renovated, red church overlooking
Kungsträdgården was commissioned in 1588 by
King Johan III. The project was abandoned four
years later when Johan died, but was resumed in
1630 and completed in 1643. The church is named
after the patron saint of pilgrims, who is depicted in
the sandstone sculpture above the southern entrance
carrying a walking staff. The church underwent
several interior renovations in the 19th century,

including the addition of five stained-glass panels behind the altar, depicting scenes from the New Testament. Sunday services are held in English at 6pm courtesy of the International Church in Stockholm.

Strindbergsmuseet

Drottninggatan 85 (411 53 54/www.strindbergs museet.se). T-bana Rådmansgatan/bus 52, 69. **Open** *Mar-Oct* noon-7pm Tue; noon-4pm Wed-Sun. *Oct-Feb* noon-4pm Tue-Sun. **Admission** 40kr; 25kr concessions; free under-19s. **Free with SC**. **No credit cards**. **Map** p245 E6.

August Strindberg moved into an apartment in the Blå Tornet (Blue Tower) in 1908; it was his last home and is now a museum. Much of it is taken up with temporary exhibits on Strindberg as a writer, dramatist, photographer and painter, but his tiny apartment is the main reason for visiting. An air of reverence dominates: you have to put white slippers on over your shoes to protect the floor, and his bedroom, study and sitting room are preserved as they were at the time of his death, his pens still neatly lined up on his writing desk. It's an atmospheric and moving place: you can just imagine the ailing playwright standing on the balcony to greet a procession of well-wishers on his last birthday, 22 January 1912. He died just a few months later, on 14 May, aged 63.

Vasastaden

Map p244 & p245

Much of the area of Vasastaden (commonly known as Vasastan), which lies to the north of Norrmalm, was built towards the end of the 1800s to accommodate Stockholm's rapidly growing population. Aside from its main thoroughfares of Sveavägen, Odengatan and St Eriksgatan, the area has remained primarily residential, although it does have a number of worthwhile sights, several beautiful parks and a sprinkling of restaurants, bars and hotels. The street blocks can be rather long, so you might want to jump on the T-bana.

In southern Vasastaden lies the small, rectangular park of **Tegnérlunden**. At one end a man-made stream flows out of a gazebo; at the other there's a statue of a beefy, naked August Strindberg sitting on a rock. The **Strindbergsmuseet** (*see above*) is on the corner of Drottninggatan and Tegnérgatan, and further east on Tegnérgatan you'll find a good selection of pubs, restaurants and antique shops. From here, turn left on broad, tree-lined **Sveavägen** – designed to look like a Parisian boulevard – and walk two blocks to the north.

Sightseeing

Ferries to the archipelago leave from **Blasieholmen**. *See p65.*

Gustaf Vasa Kyrka.

The south-east corner of the hillside park, **Observatorielunden**, is dominated by the grand **Handelshögskolan** (Stockholm School of Economics), designed by Ivar Tengbom, architect of the Konserthuset. Up the steep steps on top of the hill is the **Observatorie Museet** (*see p69*), overlooking a reflecting pool. Standing at the park's north-east corner, Gunnar Asplund's bright orange **Stadsbiblioteket** (Stockholm Public Library), is one of Sweden's best-known architectural works, instantly identifiable by its round central building. Several blocks north on Sveavägen is the kid-friendly, indoor water adventure park, **Vilda Vanadis** (*see p193*), in the quiet, hilly park of Vanadislunden.

If you head west from the library along busy Odengatan, you'll reach the triangle-shaped **Odenplan** square, bordered by the beautiful baroque **Gustaf Vasa Kyrka** (*see below*) and surrounded by the rumble of passing buses. Several budget hotels are located in this area.

Two blocks further west is the green retreat of **Vasaparken**, with outdoor summer cafés and a new football field/ice-skating rink, depending on the season. The easternmost section of the park was recently renamed **Astrid Lindgren's Terrace** after the author of the *Pippi Longstocking* children's

book series, who died in 2002; she lived across the street (*see p164* **The politics of Pippi**). The small **Judiska Museet** (*see p69*) – the only Jewish museum in Scandinavia – is nearby, and at the end of the park there's the bustling intersection of St Eriksplan.

The neighbourhood of Birkastan, west of St Eriksplan, was originally built in the early 20th century for the working classes, but the charming cafés and restaurants around **Rörstrandsgatan** are becoming increasingly fashionable. If you take St Eriksgatan south, you'll end up on Kungsholmen; if you head north, you'll arrive at the fascinating **Vin & Sprithistoriska Museet** (*see p69*).

Gustaf Vasa Kyrka

Odenplan (50 88 86 00/www.gustafvasa.nu). T-bana Odenplan/bus 2, 4, 40, 42, 47, 53. **Open** usually 11am-6pm Mon-Thur; 10am-3pm Fri; 11am-3pm Sat, Sun. **Admission** free (concerts & activities cost around 100kr). **Map** p244 D4.

The striking 60m-high (200ft) dome of Gustaf Vasa Kyrka rises far above Odenplan and its decidedly less impressive neighbouring buildings. This white church in the Italian baroque style is, without doubt, Vasastaden's most beautiful building. Completed in 1906, Gustaf Vasa Kyrka stands on a triangular island near the intersection of two busy streets.

The spectacular 1731 altarpiece is Sweden's largest baroque sculpture, originally created for the Uppsala cathedral. It depicts Jesus on the cross in front of a relief of Jerusalem. The ceiling frescoes in the dome, by Vicke Andrén, show scenes from the New Testament.

Judiska Museet

Hälsingegatan 2 (31 01 43/www.judiska-museet.se). T-bana Odenplan/bus 4, 42, 47, 53, 72. **Open** noon-4pm Mon-Fri, Sun. **Admission** 50kr; 20kr-40kr concessions; free under-12s. *Guided tours* 1.30pm Wed, Sun. **Free with SC**. **Credit** AmEx. **Map** p244 D4.

Across the street from Vasaparken, this small museum contains venerable religious objects and a permanant exhibit on the Holocaust. A Torah, an 18th-century menorah and a variety of yarmulkes (skullcaps) are displayed, plus a wooden Mizrach plaque from the first synagogue in Stockholm, dating from 1795. The museum's temporary exhibitions can be quite good, so it's worth checking what's on.

Observatorie Museet

Drottninggatan 120 (54 54 83 90/www. observatoriet.kva.se). T-bana Rådmansgatan/bus 40, 52, 53, 69. **Open** (guided tours only) *Apr-mid June, mid Aug-Oct* noon, 1pm, 2pm Sun. *Oct-Mar* 6-9pm Tue; noon, 1pm, 2pm Sun. *15 June-15 Aug* pre-booked group tours only. **Admission** 50kr; 25kr 7-18s; free under-7s. **Free with SC. No credit cards.** **Map** p245 D6.

The Royal Swedish Academy of Sciences built this hilltop observatory in the late 1740s. Now a museum dedicated to science, it's open for guided tours of the observation rooms and the 18th-century instruments of Pehr Wargentin, an astronomer and statistician who lived and worked here for 30 years. The guide describes how scientists tried to solve the pressing problems of their day, from calculating the distances between planets, to determining navigational longitude at sea. A narrow staircase leads to the dome, where you get a wonderful, unobstructed view of the Stockholm skyline. This is one of the city's lesser-known museums, but it is well worth a visit. On Tuesday evenings between October and March, you can stargaze through the museum's early 20th-century telescope.

Vin & Sprithistoriska Museet

Dalagatan 100 (744 70 70/www.vinosprithistoriska. se). Bus 2, 3, 40, 65, 70. **Open** 10am-7pm Tue; 10am-4pm Wed-Fri; noon-4pm Sat, Sun. **Admission** 40kr; 30kr concessions; free under-18s. **Free with SC. Credit** MC, V. **Map** p244 B3.

Between the 1920s and 1960s, all the imported wine and alcohol consumed in Sweden was processed through this warehouse, now the Historical Museum of Wines and Spirits. A path takes you past re-created environments from Sweden's history of alcohol production and consumption – a home distillery from the 1830s and a wine merchant's store from the early 1900s. You can press buttons to activate some of the machinery and pump a 'spice organ' to test your sense of smell. The excellent free audio tour in English really brings the exhibits to life – it's just a shame that this unique museum isn't nearer the centre of town. Call ahead to book a schnapps or wine tasting.

Crowd puller: Swedish design on display at the **National Museum**. *See p66.*

Djurgården & Skeppsholmen

Cultures high and low in Stockholm's green oasis.

Djurgården

Map p242 & p243

If you begin to feel cramped by the narrow streets and tourist crowds of the Old Town, or have had your fill of shopping and traffic on Norrmalm, do like the Stockholmers and head for the green oasis of Djurgården (pronounced 'your-gore-den'). The island, a short walk from downtown, has many of Stockholm's, if not Sweden's, best museums and attractions, as well as waterfront cafés and picnic spots, tranquil walking and cycling paths, and some of the best views in the city.

On the island's western half stand the world-class Vasamuseet, the open-air Skansen museum and Gröna Lund amusement park, which draw more than a million visitors a year. The rest of the island, with its leafy green trees and quiet meadows, is part of Ekoparken, the National City Park. Closed to traffic (except for buses and residents) at the weekend, its acres of undeveloped land are a much-loved green retreat from the rest of the city.

Swedish monarchs have owned the island since it was acquired by King Karl Knutsson in 1452. First developed for agriculture, it later became the private hunting grounds of royalty. King Karl XI established a series of manned gates in the 1680s to protect the park from

wolves, bears and poverty-stricken peasants looking for food. A branch of the royal court continues to administer the island and uses all the rents and fees it collects for Djurgården's preservation.

Crossing to the island from Strandvägen, over Djurgårdsbron – where you can rent bicycles, paddleboats and canoes – you'll see the magnificent **Nordiska Museet** (*see p73*) directly in front of you. This city landmark was designed in the style of a Nordic Renaissance palace and holds historical and cultural objects from all over Scandinavia. The path to the right of the bridge leads to **Junibacken** (*see p163*), a children's fantasy land with a train ride through the stories of Astrid Lindgren's books.

Further on lies the don't-miss **Vasamuseet** (*see p75*), home of the vast warship *Vasa*, which sank just off the island of Beckholmen on her maiden voyage in 1628. Fittingly, the purpose-built museum occupies the site of the former naval dockyard. If you're going to visit just one museum in Stockholm – and there are plenty – make it this one.

Djurgårdsvägen, the main route into and around the island, passes by the vast Nordiska Museet, the western entrance to Skansen and the quaint, old-fashioned **Biologiska Museet** (*see p72*), devoted to Scandinavian wildlife. Further south, the beautiful **Liljevalchs Konsthall** (*see p176*) stands on the corner of Djurgården's most developed area. It was set up with a donation of 500,000 kronor in the will of the enormously rich industrialist Carl Fredrik Liljevalch. After the artist Prince Eugen persuaded the state to donate the land, the gallery opened in 1916, with sculptures by Carl Milles over the door and on top of the tall black pillar nearby. It's now one of the best exhibition spaces in Sweden, with contemporary shows that change every three months. Next to the building is the lovely café **Blå Porten** (*see p131*), named after the 19th-century gate near Djurgårdsbron.

Next door the fascinating **Aquaria Vattenmuseum** (*see p72*) sits on the water next to the depot for the island's old-fashioned trams. Its waterfront café has spectacular

Gustav Vasa greets visitors to the **Nordiska Museet**. *See p73.*

views towards Skeppsholmen. Squeals, laughter and live music can be heard coming from the summer-only **Gröna Lund** amusement park (*see p73*), one block to the south. There are several hamburger and pizza places here, as well as the 1920s Hasselbacken restaurant on the hill across the street, next to the **Cirkus** concert/theatre venue (*see p184*).

East of Gröna Lund, Djurgårdsstaden is the island's only real residential area. Most of the houses and cottages along this district's narrow streets were built between the mid 1700s and the early 1800s as housing for shipyard workers. About 200 people live here today and the apartments are much sought after. This residential area is often overlooked by tourists, which makes a walk through its well-preserved, historic streets all the more charming. Whipping posts like the one in the district's tiny square, Skampålens Torg, once stood in public places around the city.

Continuing along Djurgårdsvägen, you soon arrive at the main entrance to **Skansen** (*see p74*). Stockholm's number one attraction with 1.4 million visitors a year, it's a mix of open-air history museum, amusement park and zoo,

covering almost the entire width of Djurgården – you shouldn't leave Stockholm without seeing it. It includes the **Skansen Akvariet** (*see p74*), which houses monkeys, crocodiles and bats, but you'll have to pay a separate entrance fee to see this.

The 47 bus route ends at the cove of Ryssviken, from where you can walk south to the palatial mansion of **Prins Eugens Waldemarsudde** (*see p73*), which has amazing views of the water, or walk north for about ten minutes to the café at **Rosendals Trädgård** (*see p131*), which is a great spot for a bite to eat. Nearby is **Rosendals Slott** (*see p73*), the summer retreat of Karl XIV Johan, the French marshal who was elected as Sweden's crown prince in 1810 and later went on to be crowned king.

To explore further east, be prepared to walk, cycle or drive. To reach the eastern half of Djurgården by bus, you'll need to plan ahead and take line 69 from the northern side of Djurgårdsbron. The bus takes you to the south-eastern tip of the island, where a Nordic art collection is displayed at swanky **Thielska Galleriet** (*see p74*) and waterfront

Skansen. *See p74.*

cafés at Blockhusudden look out on the **Fjäderholmarna** islands (*see p209*). The southern shore of this area of Djurgården is lined with the homes and estates of the extremely wealthy.

Most of eastern Djurgården is a nature reserve with a marsh, old oak trees and paths for horses, bikes and hikers. The narrow canal, **Djurgårdsbrunnskanalen**, which opened in 1834, is a pleasant place for a stroll, lined with trees and ending with a small footbridge near the sea.

Transport note: there's no Tunnelbana station on or near Djurgården. Bus 44 runs along Djurgårdsvägen as far as Skansen; bus 47, which passes by Central Station, goes further to Ryssviken, as does the historic tram line 7 (660 77 00, daily June to August, weekends only the rest of the year, departing from Norrmalmstorg). Alternatively, you can catch the Djurgårdsfärjan ferry, run by Waxholmsbolaget (614 64 50) from Slussen (free with an SL card), which stops at a jetty near Gröna Lund and then sails on to Skeppsholmen. Between May and August an alternative route stops at the Vasamuseet and then at Nybroplan on Norrmalm.

Aquaria Vattenmuseum

Falkenbergsgatan 2 (660 90 89/www.aquaria.se). Bus 44, 47/tram 7/ferry from Slussen or Nybroviken. **Open** *Mid June-mid Aug* 10am-6pm daily. *Mid Aug-mid June* 10am-4.30pm Tue-Sat. **Admission** 70kr; 60kr concessions; 35kr 6-15s; free under-6s. **Free with SC. Credit** AmEx, DC, MC, V. **Map** p242 J11.
A waterfall cascades over the entrance to this unusual aquarium, which is next to the *Vasa*. In the rainforest exhibit, you can go eyeball to eyeball with 1.5m-long (5ft) catfish, then step into a realistic jungle, with dripping plants, chirping insects and rain showers every ten minutes. Elsewhere, tropical fish swim in a long aquarium, and a mountain waterfall splashes down into a pool of trout. Environmental concerns are highlighted; a sign next to an open manhole encourages you to climb down for a 'sewer adventure', where you see the effects of pollution and acid rain. The water views from the café make it a good pit stop.

Biologiska Museet

Lejonslätten (442 82 15/tours 442 82 70/www. biologiskamuseet.com). Bus 44, 47/tram 7/ferry from Slussen or Nybroviken. **Open** *Apr-Sept* 11am-4pm daily, *Oct-Mar* noon-3pm Tue-Fri; 10am-3pm Sat, Sun. **Admission** 30kr; 10kr 6-15s; free under-6s. **Free with SC. Credit** AmEx, DC, MC, V. **Map** p242 H11.

Sightseeing

Designed after a medieval Norwegian church, the dark brown, shingled Biological Museum is a sanctuary of quiet in this otherwise bustling section of Djurgården. Beneath its A-framed roof, three dioramas depict Scandinavian wildlife. The ground floor features a valley in east Greenland and an Arctic cave, as well as a box containing a '*skvader*' – a fantasy hybrid of a hare and a grouse. Up the double-helix staircase lies the main attraction, a 360° diorama viewable from two platforms of the Swedish outdoors, including a coastline, cliff and forest, where you can spot bears, birds, deer and other immobile critters. Artist Bruno Liljefors (whose depictions of nature hang in the National Museet) painted the detailed backdrop. Except for replacing a few of its stuffed animals, the museum has remained unchanged since it opened in 1893. The museum is worth poking your head into for a few minutes, but no more.

Gröna Lund

Lilla Allmänna Gränd 9 (58 75 01 00/www.grona lund.com). Bus 44, 47/tram 7/ferry from Slussen or Nybroviken. **Open** *End Apr-mid Sept times vary.* **Admission** 60kr; 40kr 4-12s; free under-4s, over-65s. **Free with SC. Credit** AmEx, DC, MC, V. **Map** p242 J11.

Perched on the edge of Djurgården, with great views across the water, Gröna Lund ('the Green Grove') is Sweden's oldest amusement park. Built in 1883 and owned by the same family ever since, its historic buildings and well-preserved rides retain an old-world charm. You can even travel here by boat the way people did more than 100 years ago. Among the older favourites are carousels, bumper cars and Ferris wheels, while the newer fairground thrills come from two rollercoasters intertwined, and the free-fall 'power tower', Europe's highest at (gulp) 80m (264ft), with four of its seats modified to tilt forward. The rollercoaster *Kvasten* ('The Broom') opened in 2007, speeding ridegoers at 55km/h (35mph) over the park with their feet dangling in the air. You can buy multi-ride booklets or pay for each ride separately. Stick around for an evening pop concert, held about once a week. For more information on children's activities at the park, *see p163*.

Nordiska Museet

Djurgårdsvägen 6-16 (51 95 46 00/info 457 06 60/ www.nordiskamuseet.se). Bus 44, 47/tram 7/ferry from Slussen or Nybroplan. **Open** *June-Aug 10am-5pm daily; Sept-May 10am-4pm Mon, Wed-Fri; 10am-8pm Tue; 11am-5pm Sat, Sun.* **Admission** 60kr; free Tue 4pm-8pm; free under-18s. **Free with SC. Credit** AmEx, MC. **Map** p242 G11.

The Nordiska Museet, Sweden's national museum of cultural history, was the brainchild of Artur Hazelius, who also created Skansen. Everything about the place is big: the building itself, designed by Isak Clason and completed in 1907, is massive, though only a quarter of the originally intended size. On entering the aptly named Great Hall visitors are greeted by Carl Milles' colossal pink statue of a seated Gustav Vasa. (In his forehead is a chunk of oak from a tree planted by the king himself, so legend has it.) The museum's collection of artefacts is immense. Permanent exhibitions include Swedish traditions, manners and customs, fashion and folk costumes, re-created table settings from the 16th to the 20th centuries, and the Sami people. There are also marvellously detailed doll's houses and a collection of doom-laden paintings and photos by Strindberg that do nothing to dispel his madman image. The Textile Gallery features 500 textiles, hidden from sunlight in birch cabinets, dating from the 1600s onwards. The museum is quite old-fashioned in presentation, but no less fascinating for that. Lekstugan, the play area aimed at kids aged five to 12, is always popular. *Photo p71.*

Prins Eugens Waldemarsudde

Prins Eugens Väg 6 (54 58 37 00/www. waldemarsudde.com). Bus 47/tram 7/ferry from Slussen or Norrmalmstorg. **Open** 11am-5pm Tue, Wed, Fri-Sun; 11am-8pm Thur. **Admission** 85kr; 65kr concessions; free under-18s. **Credit** AmEx, DC, MC, V. **Map** p243 K13.

This beautiful waterfront property, comprising a grand three-storey mansion and an art gallery, was owned by Prince Eugen from 1899 until his death in 1947. The prince, a well-known Swedish landscape painter and the brother of King Gustav V, moved into the mansion upon its completion in 1904. The house's architect, Ferdinand Boberg, later designed the NK department store (*see p137*). The light, simply decorated rooms on the ground floor are furnished as the prince left them. Temporary art exhibitions, featuring the likes of Anders Zorn, Ernst Josephson, Isaac Grünewald and Carl Larsson, as well as the prince's wonderful landscape paintings, are displayed upstairs and in the gallery next door. The gallery was built in 1913 when Prince Eugen ran out of display space for his art collection. The prince himself designed the classical white flowerpots for sale in the gift shop. The mansion and artwork are impressive, but the grounds and views are even more so. Sculptures by Auguste Rodin and Carl Milles adorn the park, which is a great spot to relax, and a path leads us on to an 18th-century windmill.

Rosendals Slott

Rosendalsvägen (402 61 30/www.royalcourt.se). Bus 44, 47, 69. **Open** (by guided tour only) *June-Aug noon, 1pm, 2pm, 3pm Tue-Sun.* **Admission** 60kr; 25kr concessions; free under-7s. **Free with SC. No credit cards. Map** p243 H14.

King Karl XIV Johan's summer retreat, this light yellow building with grey pillars is designed in the Empire style, its wall paintings and decorative scheme reflecting the king's military background. The cotton fabric around the dining room is pleated to resemble an officer's tent, and the frieze in the Red Salon shows the Norse god Odin's victory over the frost giants. The fable of Eros and Psyche is told on the beautifully painted domed ceiling in the Lantern Room. The palace was designed by Fredrik Blom, who also created the Historiska Museet (see p87) and Skeppsholm church; it was prefabricated in Norrmalm then shipped out to Djurgården in pieces. Karl Johan always remained a Frenchman at heart: he never ate Swedish food and sometimes forced his less fragrant guests to wash their hands in cologne. The 45-minute tour offered in summer is the only way to see the inside of the palace.

Skansen

Djurgårdsslätten 49-51 (442 80 00/www.skansen.se). Bus 44, 47/tram 7/ferry from Slussen or Nybroviken. **Open** *Jan, Feb, Nov, Dec* 10am-3pm Mon-Fri; 10am-4pm Sat, Sun; *Mar, Apr, Oct* 10am-4pm daily; *May-mid June* 10am-8pm daily; *mid June-Aug* 10am-10pm daily; *Sept* 10am-5pm daily. Special opening hours during Christmas; call for details. **Admission** 30kr-90kr; free under-6s. **Free with SC**. **Credit** AmEx, DC, MC, V. **Map** p243 H-J12.

Founded in 1891 by Artur Hazelius, also responsible for the Nordiska Museet (see p73), Skansen is a one-stop cultural tour of Sweden. The 150-plus traditional buildings – homes, shops, churches, barns and workshops – are organised as a miniature Sweden, with buildings from the north of the country at the north, those from the middle in the middle, and so on. Most of the structures, situated along paths lined with elm, oak and maple trees, date from the 18th and 19th centuries. The striking 13th-century Norwegian storage hut that overlooks Djurgårdsbrunnsviken is the oldest; newest is the ironmonger's shop and the co-op grocery store from the 1930s. Most complete is the 1850s quarter, with cobblestoned streets and artisans' workshops, including a baker, glass-blower and potter. Watch them work, then buy the proceeds. Nearly all of the buildings are original and were moved here whole or piece by piece from all over Sweden. Skansen's staff – dressed in folk costumes – spin wool, tend fires and perform traditional tasks (Oct-Apr 11am-3pm; May-Sept 11am-5pm).

Animals from all over Scandinavia, including brown bears, moose and wolves, are kept along the northern cliff in natural habitats. There's also a petting zoo with goats, hedgehogs and kittens, and an aquarium/zoo, Skansen Akvariet (see below), near the southern entrance. An old-fashioned marketplace sits at the centre of the park, and folk-dancing demonstrations – with foot-stamping and fiddle-playing – take place in summer on the Tingsvallen stage.

Hunger pangs can be satisfied at a variety of eating places; the cafeteria-style Restaurang Solliden serves classic Swedish dishes and has a wonderful view of Djurgården and southern Stockholm. The 19th-century Gubbhyllan building to the left of the main entrance houses a Tobacco and Match Museum – it was a Swede who invented the safety match – and an old-fashioned café that serves simple dishes. Skansen is a popular destination on Sweden's national holidays since most of them, including Midsummer and Lucia, are celebrated here in traditional style – for more information, see p159 & p161. The Christmas market is a big draw too.

Don't miss the shop by the main gate, which is packed with traditional arts and crafts. In the summer on Tuesdays, be sure to stick around for 'Allsång på Skansen', a singalong concert on the Solliden stage that is broadcast nationally at 8pm (see p161 **Singing for Sweden**). *Photo p72.*

Skansen Akvariet

Djurgårdsslätten 49-51 (660 10 10/www.skansen-akvariet.se). Bus 44, 47/tram 7/ferry from Slussen or Nybroviken. **Open** *May* 10am-5pm Mon-Fri; 10am-6pm Sat, Sun. *1st 3wks June* 10am-6pm Mon-Fri; 10am-7pm Sat, Sun. *Midsummer-end July* 10am-8pm daily. *1st 2wks Aug* 10am-7pm daily. *Last 2wks Aug* 10am-6pm Mon-Fri; 10am-7pm Sat, Sun. *Sept-Apr* 10am-4pm Mon-Fri; 10am-5pm Sat, Sun. **Admission** 75kr; 40kr 7-15s, over-64s; free under-6s. **Free with SC**. **Credit** AmEx, DC, MC, V. **Map** p243 J12.

Some of the smallest monkeys you've ever seen are on show in this zoo and aquarium inside Skansen. Bright orange tamarins and pygmy marmosets hang from trees behind glass, and you can walk up the steps of a giant tree house where more than three dozen striped lemurs hop around while chewing on fresh vegetables. The less friendly-looking baboons crawl around a steep hill in another exhibit, complete with a crashed jungle jeep hanging from a branch. You can even pet a boa constrictor and a tarantula. There's lots to see – snakes, a nocturnal room full of bats, and two crocodiles (given by Fidel Castro to a Russian cosmonaut before ending up here). If you don't want to pay the separate entrance fee, you can watch the baboons and lemurs from outside.

Thielska Galleriet

Sjötullsbacken 6 (662 58 84/www.thielska-galleriet.se). Bus 69. **Open** noon-4pm Mon-Sat; 1-4pm Sun. **Admission** 50kr; 30kr concession; free under-16s. **No credit cards.**

Wealthy banker and art collector Ernest Thiel built this palatial waterside home on the eastern tip of Djurgården in the early 1900s. The eclectically styled building, with influences from the Italian Renaissance and the Orient, was designed by Ferdinand Boberg, who built Prins Eugens Waldemarsudde (see p73) at roughly the same time. Thiel lost most of his fortune after World War I, and the state acquired the property in 1924. Two years later this museum opened, displaying his collection of turn-of-the-20th-century Nordic art, including works by Carl Larsson, Bruno Liljefors and Edvard Munch (a close friend of Thiel). Although six works by some of these artists – valued at 24 million kronor – were stolen in the middle of the night on 20 June 2000, a crime that remains unsolved, there are still plenty of paintings to see. Thiel's bathroom has been turned into a small café serving cinnamon rolls and meat pies, and the urn containing his ashes lies beneath a statue by Auguste Rodin in the park. If you haven't seen enough Scandinavian art at the National Museet, this gallery should contain enough to satisfy you.

Vasamuseet

Galärvarvsvägen 14 (51 95 48 00/Museifartygen 51 95 48 91/www.vasamuseet.se). Bus 44, 47.
Open *Sept-May* 10am-5pm Mon, Tue, Thur-Sun; 10am-8pm Wed. *June-Aug* 8.30am-6pm daily.
Admission 80kr; 40kr concessions; free under-17s.
Free with SC. Credit AmEx, DC, MC, V.
Map p242 H10.

Entering the Vasa Museum for the first time is a jaw-dropping experience, as your eyes adjust to the gloom and you realise the monstrous size of the *Vasa* – the largest and best-preserved ship of its kind in the world. Built in the 1620s when Sweden was at war with Poland, the *Vasa* had two gun decks and 64 cannons, making it the mightiest ship in the fleet. Unfortunately, the gun decks and heavy

Voyage of discovery

Stockholm's most prized heirloom, the *Vasa* warship, continues to be a living legend rather than a dusty artefact catalogued into Sweden's maritime archives. She made waves at the time of her discovery in 1956, she returned to the surface to royal fanfare in 1961 and she was ceremonially installed in her stunning, custom-designed museum in 1991. And true to her diva status, she was diagnosed with a near fatal disease in 2000 when she became her own worst enemy, producing sulphuric acid. The acid began dissolving her mighty timbers from the inside out. But true to all great drama queens, the *Vasa* has beaten her affliction and currently enjoys an indefinite remission.

Keeping herself in the public eye, the mighty warship has begun to slowly reveal her 'true story'. Guides at the museum used to spin the tale that the instability of the ship

was caused by the orders of the King, Gustav II Adolf. The King was blamed for meddling with the design by adding a supposedly unplanned second gun deck, rendering her too top-heavy for her ballast load. The colourful yarn was corroborated by historical records demonstrating that no one was ever held accountable for the sudden sinking of the *Vasa* 20 minutes into her maiden voyage in 1628.

However, these and other myths have now been debunked. In 2007, *The Archaeology of a Swedish Warship of 1628*, the first volume in a multiple series, was published. It clears up former misunderstandings and popular myths about the doomed fate of the mighty ship on its maiden voyage. The book proves that, contrary to popular myth, the ship was built to its original specifications and not modified in the middle of construction. It also busts the fallacy that the *Vasa* was lost and forgotten during her 333-year sojourn in Stockholm Harbour, showing that there were several salvage attempts long before the successful raising of the ship in 1961, and several historical references to the wreck on Stockholm sea charts.

But the intrigue has not been completely cleared away. According to the primary researcher for the collected volumes, if a naval tribunal were held today, the captain would be made to walk the plank. However, it's still unclear which captain would have been on the plank. The sea captain went down honourably with his ship. The official captain-in-charge pointed his finger to the watery depths.
Volume I is on sale at the Vasa bookshop.

Vasa in figures

Max length	69m
Max width	11.7m
Max height	52.5m
Number of sails	10
Armament	64 guns
Crew	445 men

Sightseeing

The world famous museum

Living history, animals, traditions and handicraft

SKANSEN

Breaking the mould: the future's bright at the renovated **Moderna Museet**. *See p78.*

cannon made the ship top-heavy. During a stability test, in which 30 men ran back and forth across the deck, she nearly toppled over. Still, the king needed his ship and the maiden voyage went ahead. But only a few minutes after the *Vasa* set sail from near present-day Slussen on 10 August 1628, she began to list to one side. The gun ports filled with water and the ship sank after a voyage of only 1,300m (1,400yds). Of the 150 people on board as many as 50 died – the number would have been much higher if the ship had reached Älvsnabben in the archipelago, where 300 soldiers were waiting to board, before it went down. The reason the *Vasa* was so well preserved at her recovery in 1961 – 95% of the ship is original – is because the Baltic Sea is insufficiently saline to contain the tiny shipworm, which destroys wood in saltier seas.

Head first for the theatre to watch a short film about the *Vasa* and her discovery by amateur naval historian Anders Franzén, who spent five years searching for her with a home-made sampler device. On your own or with a tour (there are several daily in English) you can walk around the exterior of the 69m-long (225ft) warship and view the upper deck and keel from six different levels. The ornate stern is covered with sculptures intended to express the glory of the Swedish king and frighten enemies. No one's allowed on board, but you can walk through a re-creation of one of the gun decks. Although the ship is obviously the main attraction, the museum has expanded over the years to include exhibits on 17th-century life and shipbuilding, and features numerous models and dioramas, as well as computers that enable you to design ships and test

their seaworthiness. In a fascinating, eerie exhibit down by the keel, the skeletons of ten people who died aboard the *Vasa* are on display, as are reconstructed models of how they would have looked alive. The museum's restaurant has a dockside view of Skeppsholmen, and its gift shop is stocked with everything the *Vasa* enthusiast might need. *See also p76* **Voyage of discovery**.

Museifartygen

Open *June, mid Aug-end Aug* noon-5pm daily. *July-mid Aug* noon-7pm daily.

The entrance fee to the Vasamuseet also lets you on to two ships docked nearby: the lightship *Finngrundet* (1903), which was anchored in the ice-free part of Sweden's Gulf of Bothnia before lightships were replaced by lighthouses; and the *St Erik* (1915), which was Sweden's first ice-breaker, and was used to keep the archipelago channels clear. The torpedo boat *T121 Spica* (611 31 60, www.t121spica.se/uk), built in 1966, is also here in summer, and guided tours (by donation) are given by former crew members.

Skeppsholmen

Map p242

Once an important naval base and shipyard, the small island of Skeppsholmen is now primarily known for its museums and cultural institutions, many housed in ex-naval buildings. It's also a pleasant place for an amble, either along the tree-lined western shore with views of Gamla Stan, or along the wooden boardwalk of the eastern shore, where private and historic boats are docked. The island's museums, which had free entrance prior to 2007, are now only free for youths.

Crossing the narrow bridge from Blasieholmen, you'll see the **Östasiatiska Museet** (*see below*) on the hill to your left, housed in a long yellow building designed by Kungliga Slottet architect Nicodemus Tessin the Younger in 1700. The round, white, empire-style **Skeppsholmskyrkan** – officially known as Karl Johans Kyrka – stands nearby; designed for the navy by Fredrik Blom, it was completed in 1842 but has now been deconsecrated. The three-masted schooner **Af Chapman**, now a youth hostel, is normally docked to your right, but at press time it was scheduled to undergo renovation until January 2008. Behind the church stands the **Moderna Museet** (*see below*), occupying an earth-toned building designed by Spanish architect Rafael Moneo and completed in 1998; the adjoining **Arkitekturmuseet** (*see below*) is housed in a former naval drill hall.

On the north-east corner of Skeppsholmen, **Fotografins Hus** (*see p176*) exhibits contemporary photography in a long hall where the navy previously manufactured mines and torpedoes. The annual **Stockholm Jazz Festival** (*see p160*) is held further south on the eastern shore, and docked on the southern shore is the wooden ship **Tre Kronor** (Östra Brobänken, 54 50 24 10, www.stockholmsbriggen.se, open noon-4pm Sun, prices vary), recently built according to a mid 19th-century design. On the western corner of Skeppsholmen are the **Kungliga Konsthögskolan** (Royal University College of Fine Arts), housed in beautifully restored 18th-century naval barracks, and the headquarters of the Swedish Society of Crafts and Design, Svensk Form.

South of Skeppsholmen, and connected to it by a bridge, the tiny granite island of **Kastellholmen** is named after a castle built here in the 1660s. The castle was blown up in 1845 after an accident in a cartridge-manufacturing laboratory. A year later, Fredrik Blom designed a new, medieval-style castle with two red towers, one tall and one squat (not open to the public); the castle's cannons are fired on Sweden's national day on 6 June, as well as on the birthdays of the king, queen and crown princess.

Arkitekturmuseet

Exercisplan, Skeppsholmen (58 72 70 00/www. arkitekturmuseet.se). Bus 65. **Open** 10am-8pm Tue; 10am-6pm Wed-Sun. **Admission** 50kr; free 4-6pm Fri; free under-16s. **Credit** AmEx, DC, MC, V. **Map** p242 H9.

The Museum of Architecture, in a long hall linked to Moderna Museet (*see below*), displays some of Sweden's most famous buildings and architectural projects, including Stockholm's Stadshuset (City Hall), the Royal Palace and the five office buildings at Hötorget. Other models depict Swedish dwellings from 1,000 years ago to the present, and famous buildings outside Sweden. There's a glassed-in craft and play room for children at one end of the hall, and at the other a spacious room for temporary exhibitions on subjects such as national styles and globalisation. Worth a quick look for the finely detailed models, but try to come on Friday afternoon when the museum is free.

Moderna Museet

Skeppsholmen (51 95 52 00/www.modernamuseet. se). Bus 65/ferry from Slussen. **Open** *Museum* 10am-8pm Tue; 10am-6pm Wed-Sun. *Photograph library* noon-4pm Tue-Fri. **Admission** 80kr; 60kr concessions; free under-18s. **Credit** AmEx, MC, V. **Map** p242 H9.

When it opened in 1958, Moderna Museet soon gained a reputation as one of the world's most ground-breaking contemporary art venues. Housed originally in an old, disused naval exercise building, the museum's heyday came in the 1960s and '70s when it introduced Andy Warhol, Jean Tinguely, Robert Rauschenberg, Niki de Saint Phalle and many more to an astonished Swedish audience. The construction of Moneo's new museum building was completed in 1998, but it closed four years later owing to structural problems, including a mould infestation. The museum reopened in 2004 with a brighter interior, a more open floor plan, an espresso bar and – most importantly – no mould. Its collection of 20th-century art, featuring works by greats such as Picasso, Dali, Pollock and de Chirico, is arranged in reverse chronological order on the main floor. The terrace of the museum's restaurant offers beautiful views towards Östermalm. Though admission to the museum is no longer free, the '1st at Moderna' series on the first of every month offers a free look at a new exhibition. *Photo p77.*

Östasiatiska Museet

Tyghusplan, Skeppsholmen (51 95 57 50/www. mfea.se). Bus 65. **Open** 11am-8pm Tue; 11am-5pm Wed-Sun. **Admission** 60kr; free under-19s. **Credit** AmEx, MC, V. **Map** p242 H9.

The main focus of the Museum of Far Eastern Antiquities is a permanent exhibition on prehistoric China, presenting artefacts unearthed in the 1920s in a Chinese village by the museum's founder, Johan Gunnar Andersson. The exhibit, displayed in a dimly lit room echoing with sounds and voices, includes tools and pottery 3,000 to 4,000 years old, descriptions of burial traditions, and the symbols, as well as patterns, of prehistoric earthenware. The museum also has a large collection of far-eastern Buddhist sculptures. The gift shop sells Japanese tea sets, books on Asian art, religions and design, and kimonos.

Södermalm & Långholmen

Head south for stunning views and boho chic.

Sightseeing

Södermalm

Map p249, p250 & p251

Södermalm's working-class heritage no longer deters the posh folk from crossing the water locks at Slussen to eat, drink, live and be merry in the city's most diverse and colourful district. While museums are few, the stunning views of the city from the rocky northern heights outclass many other Stockholm sights. Trendy restaurants, cafés, bars and clubs continue to mushroom on the island known more affectionately and simply as Söder. The district's main focal points are Slussen and Medborgarplatsen, connected by Götgatan – a pedestrian shopping street that runs right through the middle of the island.

The first place you'll arrive at from Gamla Stan is the transport interchange of Slussen – a busy Tunnelbana and bus station. Structural reinforcements and redirection of heavy traffic have bought the area a few more years before politicians must find a costly permanent replacement for the complex clover intersection. While Slussen is not the most attractive introduction to Söder's charms, it does contain two of the island's main sights: the **Stockholms Stadsmuseum** (*see p83*), where you can learn about the city's history

since it was founded back in 1252, and **Katarinahissen** (*see p82*), the lift that elevates you to one of the best views in the capital. You can make a meal (or drink) of the view at **Eriks Gondolen** restaurant (*see p109*).

Splendid panoramic views across the water to the city centre are also available from the cliffs along the island's northern edge, particularly on **Monteliusvägen** and **Fjällgatan**. The former rises above Söder Mälarstrand, along which a string of pleasure and commercial boats are moored, including some boat hotels; the latter, to the east of Slussen, is a parade of 18th-century houses.

Head south from Slussen up the climb of the pedestrian section of Götgatan, past some fashionable boutiques and classic Söder mainstays – including late-night beer hall **Kvarnen** (*see p121*) – to the lively **Medborgarplatsen** (*photo p80*), where there's a small galleria, an indoor farmers' market and two cinema complexes. This large square has undergone a renaissance, adding expansive outdoor seating to the stylish restaurants facing Medborgarhuset. Built in 1939, the building houses a library, swimming pool, and concert venue, **Debaser** (*see p184*). A memorial to assassinated Swedish Foreign Minister Anna Lindh, who gave her last speech on the steps of Medborgarhuset, was inaugurated hastily near the steps on 10 September 2004, the first anniversary of her death.

Across the street, the minaret of the city's mosque (**Stockholmsmoskén**; *see p83*) rises over Björns Trädgard park, a welcoming park for all ages recently renovated to include a skate park.

Further south lies the quirkily trendy shopping area dubbed **SoFo**, standing for the grid of streets south of Folkungatan, which have a high concentration of independent artists and designers.

Although the residents of Södermalm are today as well off as other Stockholmers, the district is traditionally associated with the working class. Functionalist apartment buildings have replaced nearly all the small wooden houses that once covered the island.

However, if you walk west up Bastugatan from Slussen, you pass a charming neighbourhood on adjoining **Lilla Skinnarviksgränd**, with its few remaining 17th- and 18th-century wooden houses. Continue along to the cliffside boardwalk of **Monteliusvägen** for a truly spectacular view of the bay of Riddarfjärden and **Skinnarviksberget**, Stockholm's highest point at 53 metres (174 feet).

South of here, crossing the busy thoroughfare of Hornsgatan, is **Mariatorget**, an enjoyable square that is home to the stylish **Rival** hotel complex, which comprises hotel (*see p43*), restaurant (*see p107*), café and cinema (*see p173*), with original art deco features. One block to the east of Mariatorget is **Maria Magdalena Kyrka** (*see p82*), the oldest church on Söder.

Heading east from Götgatan, walk up Urvädersgränd past the rarely open **Bellmanhuset** (*see p81*), former home of 18th-century balladeer Carl Michael Bellman, to **Mosebacketorg**. This busy cobblestoned square has been Söder's entertainment centre since the mid 19th century, and is bordered by two of Stockholm's most popular and lively nightlife venues, **Södra Teatern** (*see p185*) and the adjoining **Mosebacke Etablissement** (*see p122*). Together they'll cover all your nightlife needs, from clubbing to drinking, cutting-edge performance to live music; in summer Mosebacke's outdoor terrace provides a fantastic view of Stockholm's

harbour. Further south is the landmark **Katarina Kyrka** (*see p81*), masterfully restored in the 1990s to its original baroque splendour, as well as a preserved early 18th-century neighbourhood on **Mäster Mikaels Gata**, which was named after the city's first paid executioner. Mäster Mikaels Gata and **Fjällgatan** were connected before the hill was blasted away at the turn of the 20th century in order to create main road **Renstiernas Gata**.

Södermalm is an expansive district and taking the T-bana or the bus is recommended for those who wish to see the sights but are on a time budget. Devotees of old-fashioned to modern forms of public transport should visit the entertaining (and child-friendly) **Spårvägsmuseet** (*see p83*) located over in the eastern reaches of the island, near nothing but residential apartments. For those who would prefer to see the district on foot, Södermalm can be explored via some excellent walking paths.

The wide street of Ringvägen curves round the southern border of Södermalm, passing through a shopping centre at Götgatan. The island's biggest and best park, **Tantolunden**, sits near the south-western shore, while the large red-brick church of **Högalidskyrkan**, designed by Ivar Tengbom in the National Romantic style and completed in 1923, stands on a hill to the north. Its octagonal twin towers are a striking landmark visible from many parts of the city.

Medborgarplatsen. See p79.

Towards the western end of Hornsgatan is the residential neighbourhood of **Hornstull**, thoroughly enjoying its continuing 'up-and-coming' status. Check out **Street** (*see p148* **Street talk**), an indoor and outdoor arts and crafts market, plus a mushrooming café and restaurant scene. Also on Hornstulls Strand is the small local **Kvartersbion** cinema (*see p173*), recently rescued by the Swedish Church when the city snubbed the one-man show and refused to continue to subsidise its rent. Residents of Hornstull are proud of their left-leaning neighbourhood, despite the creeping signs of affluence, and cult 'People's Republic of Hornstull' T-shirts are still occasionally spotted.

South of Södermalm is another of the city's best-known landmarks, the huge white sphere of sports arena **Globen** (*see p193*), which hosts major competitions and concerts.

Bellmanhuset

Urvädersgränd 3 (640 22 29/www.bellmanshuset.se). *T-bana Slussen/bus 2, 3, 53, 59, 76.* **Open** (guided tours only) 1pm 1st Sun of the mth. Check website for extra tours. **Admission** 60kr. **No credit cards**. **Map** p250 K8.

This small house just off Götgatan is the only remaining home of legendary Swedish songwriter Carl Michael Bellman. During his tenancy, between 1770 and 1774, he wrote much of his *Fredmans Epistlar*, a book of songs about Stockholm's drunks and prostitutes that parodies the letters of the apostle Paul in the New Testament. If the monthly tour (in Swedish) fits your schedule and you are a Bellman enthusiast, it can be quite entertaining.

KA Almgren Sidenväveri Museum

Repslagargatan 15 (642 56 16/www.kasiden.se). *T-bana Slussen/bus 2, 3, 43, 53, 55, 59, 76.* **Open** 10am-4pm Mon-Fri; 11am-3pm Sat, Sun. Guided tours 1pm Mon, Wed, Sat & Sun. **Admission** 65kr. **Free with SC**. **Map** p250 L7.

Knut August Almgren stole the technology for this former silk-weaving factory back in the late 1820s. While recovering from tuberculosis in France, he posed as a German-speaking Frenchman and gained access to factories where the innovative Jacquard looms were being used. He took notes, smuggled machinery out of the country and opened a factory in Sweden in 1833. The factory here closed down in 1974, but was then reopened as a working museum in 1991 by a fifth-generation Almgren. It reproduces silk fabrics for stately homes around Scandinavia, including the Royal Palace. The recently renovated additional floor houses an exhibition on the history of silk weaving in Sweden, along with a collection of silk portraits, landscapes and fabrics. You can watch its 160-year-old looms in action; they produce 2m (6.5ft) of fabric per day. Silk scarves and other handwoven fabrics are on sale in the gift shop.

Katarinahissen

Stadsgården 6 (642 47 86). *T-bana Slussen/bus 2, 3, 43, 53, 55, 59, 76.* **Open** *Jan-mid May, Sept-Dec* 10am-6pm daily; *mid May-Aug* 8am-10pm daily. **Admission** 10kr; 5kr 7-15s; free under-7s. **Free with SC**. **No credit cards**. **Map** p250 K8.

Katarinahissen.

The 38m-tall (125ft) black steel Katarina Lift stands beside the intersection at Slussen. Its observation platform and walkway gives pedestrians access to the Katarinaberget district and Mosebacketorg, a favourite Söder square, and it also serves as an entrance to Eriks Gondolen restaurant (*see p109*), housed beneath the walkway. But the main function of the lift is to provide tourists with a stunning view of the bay of Riddarfjärden, Gamla Stan and Djurgården (particularly good at sunset). If you're thrifty (and fit), you can also reach the platform by climbing the wooden hillside staircase or by walking up Götgatan and then turning left on to Urvädersgränd. *Photo p81.*

Katarina Kyrka

Högbergsgatan 15 (743 68 00/www.svkyrkan katarina.com). T-bana Medborgarplatsen or Slussen/bus 2, 3, 43, 53, 55, 59, 76. **Open** 11am-5pm Mon-Fri; 10am-5pm Sat, Sun. **Admission** free. **Map** p251 L8.

As Södermalm's population grew, it was agreed in the mid 17th century to split Maria Magdalena parish and build a new church. Katarina Kyrka, completed in 1695, was designed by Jean de la Vallé in baroque style with a central plan. A huge fire in 1723 destroyed the church's cupola and half the buildings in the parish. A more recent fire in 1990 burned down all but the church's walls and side vaults. Architect Ove Hildemark reconstructed the church (based on photos and drawings) using 17th-century building techniques. The yellow church with flat white pillars now looks much as it did before, but with a distinctly modern interior. Many victims of the Stockholm Bloodbath of 1520 were buried in the church's large cemetery. Organ music is played at noon on Tuesdays and Thursdays.

Maria Magdalena Kyrka

St Paulsgatan 10 (462 29 40/www.mariamagdalena. se). T-bana Slussen/bus 2, 3, 43, 53, 55, 59, 76. **Open** 11am-5pm Mon, Tue, Thur-Sun; 11am-7.30pm Wed. **Admission** free. **Map** p250 K7.

During his church-destroying spree after the Reformation in 1527, Gustav Vasa tore down the chapel that had stood on this site since the 1300s. His son, Johan III, methodically rebuilt most of the churches in the late 1500s. Construction on this yellowish-orange church with white corners began in 1580, but was not completed for about 40 years. It's Söder's oldest church and the first in Stockholm to be built with a central plan rather than a cross plan. Tessin the Elder designed the transept in the late 17th century and his son, the Younger, created the French-inspired stonework of the entrance portal in 1716. The church's rococo interior – with its depiction of Maria Magdalena on the golden pulpit and Carl Fredrik Adelcrantz's elaborate organ screen – was created after a fire in 1759. Several of Sweden's eminent poets are buried here, including beloved troubadour Evert Taube. Stop by for the organ music on Thursdays at 12.15pm.

Prison break: do some time at **Långholmens Fängelsemuseum**. *See p84.*

Thank you for the music

When Björn Ulvaeus and Benny Andersson met on a June night in 1966 in the town of Linköping, southern Sweden, 21-year-old Björn was on tour with the Hootenanny Singers and 20-year-old Benny was touring with the Hep Stars. Eight years later, on 6 April 1974, Abba won the Eurovision Song Contest in Brighton with 'Waterloo'. The rest, as they say, is history, and Abba have now sold around 370 million records across the world, surpassed only by Elvis and The Beatles. It may be 40 years since the band was born, but they still flog more than two million albums a year, and *Mamma Mia!* has played to more than 27 million people since its 1999 London opening. A Swedish cultural treasure to cherish and be proud of, and an untapped market for a museum… until now.

Stockholm's newest museum, **Abba the Museum** (www.abbamuseum.com), entirely dedicated to the legendary foursome, is due to open to visitors in spring 2009. Located at Slussen, in a former customs house, the museum will tell the story of the Swedish superstars through interactive and multimedia exhibits spread over three floors. A mock-up of the band's recording studio, Polar Studios, will even allow visitors to record their own rendition of Abba classics. The former band members have approved the project and will make material available to the museum, but are otherwise not involved, although the on-site 'largest Abba shop in the world' will undoubtedly keep Björn, Benny, Agnetha and Anni-Frid's retirement plan healthy for another 40 years.

Spårvägsmuseet

Tegelviksgatan 22 (686 17 60/www.sparvags museet.sl.se). Bus 2, 53, 55, 66. **Open** 10am-5pm Mon-Fri; 11am-4pm Sat, Sun. **Admission** 30kr; 15kr concessions, 7-18s; free under-7s; 75kr family ticket. **Free with SC. Credit** AmEx, MC, V. **Map** p251 M11.

What the Transport Museum lacks in descriptive texts and focused exhibits, it makes up for in quantity – more than 60 vehicles are stored in this former bus station in eastern Söder. Rows of carriages, trams and buses from the late 1800s to the present cover the development of Stockholm's transport system. For 1kr you can stand in a tramcar from the 1960s and pretend to drive as a grainy film of city streets flashes before you. Children can try on a ticket collector's uniform and ride a miniature Tunnelbana train (tickets cost 10kr). There's a café and a shop selling transport-related paraphernalia, including an excellent selection of Brio trains. The museum is perfect for a rainy-day visit – borrow a guidebook in English from the cashier, since most of the exhibits are labelled in Swedish.

Stockholmsmoskén

Kapellgränd 10 (50 91 09 00). T-bana Medborgarplatsen/bus 55, 59, 66. **Visiting hours** 10am-6pm daily. Guided tours in English available on request. **Prayers** 5 times daily; call for details. **Admission** free. **Map** p251 L8.

The conversion of Katarinastation, a former power station, into Stockholm's first mosque led to heated architectural debates. Prior to its inauguration in 2000, Stockholm's Muslim community worshipped in cellars and other cramped spaces, jokingly claiming to be Sweden's biggest underground movement. Ferdinand Boberg, the architect behind Rosenbad

(*see p62*) and the NK department store (*see p137*), designed Katarinastation. Inspired by Andalusian Moorish architecture, he decorated the lofty main hall in mosaic brick, with floor-to-ceiling vaulted windows. Fittingly, the original structure faces Mecca. As long as shoes are removed and women covered up (robes provided), visitors may view the prayer hall and lecture hall. Before you leave take a look at the massive copper doors facing Östgötagatan embedded with numerous mundane objects by the process of blast-moulding.

Stockholms Stadsmuseum

Ryssgården (50 83 16 20/www.stadsmuseum. stockholm.se). T-bana Slussen/bus 2, 3, 43, 53, 55, 59, 76. **Open** 11am-5pm Tue, Wed, Fri-Sun; 11am-7pm Thur. **Admission** free. **Map** p250 K8.

Nicodemus Tessin the Elder designed this building in the 1670s. After a fire in 1680, the renovations were supervised by his son, Tessin the Younger – architect of the Royal Palace. Renovations in 2003 spruced up the entrance and the peaceful courtyard, where you can sit and enjoy goodies from the café, which is decorated with fixings from an early 20th-century bakery. Temporary exhibitions are on the ground floor. A series of rooms on the floor named Stockholm Through All Times is a journey through the growth of the city from medieval times to the 17th century. The third floor takes you through the realistic models of a Stockholm factory from 1897, plus a city registrar's office and schoolroom from the same period. Don't miss peeking into the two reconstructed flats from the 1940s; one of these tiny rooms housed a family, plus additional lodgers. On the ground floor, Torget, a children's play area, re-creates a city market square and is open at weekends. This is Söder's best museum and a great place to learn about the city.

Sightseeing

Långholmen

Map p249

Just off the north-west tip of Södermalm near Hornstull lies the long, narrow island of **Långholmen** (Long Island). For 250 years this beautiful green island, almost a mile long, was home to a prison, in operation from 1724 to 1975. Thanks largely to the presence of the jail, Långholmen has remained undeveloped and, as a result, is something of a green retreat, complete with tree-shaded paths, cliffs dotted with nest-like nooks and two sandy beaches pefect for swimming. Today, the remaining part of the prison is run as a very pleasant budget hotel/hostel (*see p45*), with a café, conference centre and museum (**Långholmens Fängelsemusuem**; *see below*).

You can walk on to the island across Långholmsbron (which provides closest access to the former prison from Hornstull), or via Pålsundsbron to the east, located near a shipyard dating back to the 1680s. To access the middle of the island directly, walk across the enormous Västerbron bridge (worth crossing to take in the view of the city) and then take the newly renovated ramp or stairs down.

A walking/cycling path leads from the south of the island to the cliffs and beach in the north. **Bellmanmuseet** (*see below*) and the former

prison complex lie behind the beach – one of the most popular swimming spots in the city. For outdoor swimming without the hordes, head east to **Klippbadet**, a tiny, sandy cove. To the west of the prison stands **Karlshäll**, the previous residence of the prison warden, now a conference centre and restaurant. Curving back round to the south, take in the grace of the lovingly cared-for wooden sailboats lining the picture-perfect canal. Prisoners used to walk across a bridge to work at the factories on **Reimersholme**, a tiny island. Best known historically for the production of aquavit, the island is now residential.

Bellmanmuseet

Stora Henriksvik (669 69 69/www.bellman.nu). *T-bana Hornstull/bus 4, 40, 66, 77.* **Open** *March-mid May, Sept, Oct* noon-4pm Sat, Sun. *Mid May-mid June* noon-4pm Tue-Sun. *Mid June-Aug* noon-4pm daily. **Admission** 30kr; free under-15s. **No credit cards. Map** p249 J2.

The oldest part of this attractive two-storey house was built in the late 17th century as the toll office for boats travelling into Stockholm. The ground floor is divided up between a pleasant café and a museum devoted to celebrated 18th-century troubadour/songwriter Carl Michael Bellman (1740-1795), who used to sing in the taverns of the city. In the late 18th century, Bellman would visit Långholmen to see an opera singer friend who worked at the prison. Copies of portraits, text in Bellman's handwriting and a replica of his death mask and lute are on display. The café staff, if they aren't too busy, are happy to answer questions in English. The café and gardens are popular with the bathers using the beach in front of the house, and concerts take place here in summer.

Långholmens Fängelsemuseum

Långholmen Hotel, Långholmsmuren 20 (720 85 00/ tour bookings 720 85 77/www.langholmen.com). *T-bana Hornstull/bus 4, 40, 66, 77.* **Open** 11am-4pm daily. **Admission** 25kr; 10kr 7-14s; free under-7s. **Credit** AmEx, DC, MC, V. **Map** p249 K2.

This small museum describes the history of the Swedish penal system and gives a flavour of life inside Kronohäktet prison before it was turned into a hotel/hostel. You can visit a typical cell used between 1845 and 1930, read about Sweden's last executioner, Anders Gustaf Dalman, and see a scale model of the guillotine imported from France and used only once, in 1910 (the actual guillotine used is stored at the Nordiska Museet, though not on display). Visitors can view an assortment of prison paraphernalia, including the sinister hoods worn to hide an accused person's identity until sentenced (used until 1935). Nowadays, the Swedish government tries to avoid incarceration and a quarter of the 12,000 criminals sentenced each year are electronically tagged rather than imprisoned. Book in advance if you want a guided tour in English. *Photo p82.*

Långholmen.

Östermalm & Gärdet

Money makes this world go round.

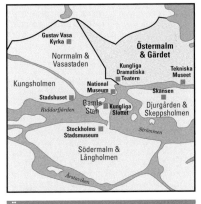

Gustav Vasa Kyrka
Norrmalm & Vasastaden
Östermalm & Gärdet
Kungliga Dramatiska Teatern
Tekniska Museet
Kungsholmen
National Museum
Stadshuset
Gamla Stan
Kungliga Slottet
Djurgården & Skeppsholmen
Skansen
Riddarfjärden
Stockholms Stadsmuseum
Strömmen
Södermalm & Långholmen
Årstaviken

Östermalm

Map p241, p242 & p246

This urban playground for the rich, beautiful and, often, famous is a shopper's paradise by day and a clubber's paradise by night. The main focus is the bustling square of **Stureplan**, at the centre of which stands the concrete rain shelter known as **Svampen** (the mushroom). Formerly a rather run-down area, Stureplan was revamped at the end of the 1980s and is now party central for glamour-seeking, fashion-conscious Stockholmers.

The clubs near here close around 5am at the weekend – later than the capital's other party spots – so you'll often see hordes of clubbers queuing in the small hours, in all weathers, to get into the most fashionable places.

Aside from the nightlife, Stureplan is also the city's most upmarket shopping area. The ultra-posh shopping mall **Sturegallerian** (*see p137*) borders the square; as well as designer boutiques, it also houses the exclusive art nouveau bath house **Sturebadet** (*see p154*). Shopaholics can spend a few happy hours trawling the surrounding streets, notably the lower end of **Birger Jarlsgatan** (which extends from the north of the city all the way to the water at Nybroviken), **Mäster Samuelsgatan**, **Biblioteksgatan** and **Grev Turegatan**. This is where you'll find international designer fashion boutiques, classy jewellery, fancy cosmetics and posh chocolates. But don't expect cutting-edge anything in

conventional Östermalm – the upper classes, both young and old, come here to reconfirm their status in that time-honoured way: by spending lots of money.

At the bottom end of Birger Jarlsgatan is **Nybroviken**, where the Cinderella and Strömma Kanalbolaget ferries depart for destinations in Lake Mälaren and the archipelago. Classics by Strindberg and Shakespeare are performed in the ornate white marble building facing Nybroplan square, the **Kungliga Dramatiska Teatern** (*see p87*) – one of Stockholm's leading theatres. Nearby is the idiosyncratic **Hallwylska Museet** museum (*see p86*).

If you walk up Sibyllegatan to the right of the theatre, you'll pass three buildings constructed by royal commission. Bread for the soldiers of the royal army was baked at the Kronobageriet, which today houses the charming and child-friendly **Musikmuseet** (*see p88*). The royal family's horses and cars are still kept in the **Kungliga Hovstallet** (*see p87*), the huge brick building to the right of the bakery. Further up is the unusual **Armémuseum** (*see p86*), where the royal arsenal used to be stored. Behind this lies 17th-century **Hedvig Eleonora Kyrka**, the former place of worship for the royal navy, which now holds regular classical music concerts.

To catch a glimpse of the Östermalm upper classes, head to **Östermalmstorg** opposite the church. When the first plans for Östermalm were drawn up back in the 1640s, sailors and craftsmen lived around this square. Nowadays, expensive boutiques sell clothes and home accessories, and the pavements are teeming with mink-clad elderly women walking small dogs. On the corner of the square is **Östermalms Saluhall** (*see p149*), a dark red-brick building constructed in 1888 and the flagship of the city's market halls. You can buy all sorts of gourmet delicacies, from fresh Baltic fish to wild rabbit – but it's pricey, so you could just stroll around the magnificent interior.

Östermalm's main green space is the **Humlegården**, the site of the king's hop gardens back in the 16th century and today a pleasant and very popular park with the **Kungliga Bibliotek** (Royal Library) on its southern bank. Theatre performances are held in the park in summer. Further up Karlavägen,

Kungliga Dramatiska Teatern.

on a hill overlooking the city, looms the tall brick tower of **Engelbrektskyrkan**. Designed by the leading Jugendstil architect Lars Israel Wahlman and opened in 1914, the church has an amazingly high nave – supposedly the tallest in Scandinavia.

For another kind of high life, follow the water's edge from Nybroplan along grand **Strandvägen**, lined with luxurious late 19th-century residences and still among the city's most prestigious addresses. Until the 1940s sailing boats carrying firewood from the archipelago islands used to dock on the quayside at Strandvägen; some of these vintage boats – with labels by each one – are now docked on its southern edge.

At the end of Strandvägen is the bridge leading over to leafy Djurgården, and north from there, on Narvavägen, is the imposing **Historiska Museet** (*see p87*); it's Sweden's largest archaeological museum, with an exceptional collection of Viking artefacts.

Strandvägen is part of an esplanade system mapped out for Östermalm in the late 1800s by city planner Albert Lindhagen. The project was only partially implemented, but includes the broad boulevards of Valhallavägen, Narvavägen and Karlavägen – the latter two radiating out from the fountain and circular pond (added in 1929) at **Karlaplan**. The central section of Karlavägen is dotted with sculptures by various international artists, and at its eastern end are the headquarters of Swedish radio and television. The buildings were designed by Erik Ahnborg and Sune

Lindström, who were also responsible for the **Berwaldhallen** concert hall (*see p187*) next door, home of the Swedish Radio Symphony Orchestra and Radio Choir.

Beyond the TV and radio buildings, on the border with Gärdet, is **Diplomatstaden**, a complex of grand mansions that houses most of the city's foreign embassies, including those of the UK and US. The adjacent park next to the water is named after Alfred Nobel, scientist, inventor and founder of the famous prizes.

Armémuseum

Riddargatan 13 (788 95 60/www.armemuseum.org). T-bana Östermalmstorg/bus 2, 47, 55, 62, 69, 76. **Open** (guided tours only) *English* July, Aug 1pm Tue-Sun. *Swedish* July, Aug noon, 1pm, 2pm, 3pm, 4pm Tue-Sun. **Admission** 60kr; free under-18s. **Free with SC. Credit** MC, V. **Map** p242 F9.
The story of Sweden at war, rather than its military infrastructure, is the museum's dominant theme, which may seem odd since Sweden has avoided conflict for the last 200 years. But with 1,000 years of history on show, you soon learn that the Swedes were once a bloody and gruesome lot. The Army Museum – housed since 1879 in the former arsenal, an impressive white pile built in the 18th century – reopened in May 2000 after seven years of renovation. Exhibited over three floors, it's not all uniforms and gleaming weaponry. Life-size (and lifelike) tableaux, such as a woman scavenging meat from a dead horse and doctors performing an amputation, show the horrific effects of war on both soldiers and civilians. The main exhibition begins on the top floor with the Viking age and the Thirty Years War, and continues below with the 20th century. The ground floor area houses an artillery exhibit and a restaurant. If you miss the highly recommended guided tour in English, the front desk provides a detailed pamphlet, also in English. The Royal Guard marches off from the museum (summer only) for the changing of the guard (*see p53*) at the Kungliga Slottet.

Hallwylska Museet

Hamngatan 4 (51 95 55 99/www.hallwylska museet.se). T-bana Östermalmstorg/bus 2, 47, 55, 62, 69, 76. **Open** (guided tours only) *English* July, Aug 1pm Tue-Sun. *Swedish* July, Aug noon, 1pm, 2pm, 3pm, 4pm Tue-Sun. **Admission** 60kr; free under-18s. **Free with SC. Credit** AmEx, MC, V. **Map** p241 F8.
Enter the opulent world of Count and Countess Walther and Wilhelmina von Hallwyl in one of Stockholm's most eccentric and engaging museums. This palatial residence was built as a winter home for the immensely rich couple in 1898. Designed by Isak Gustav Clason (architect of the Nordiska Museet), it was very modern for its time, with electricity, central heating, lifts, bathrooms and phones. The Countess was an avid collector of almost everything, from paintings and furniture to silverware and armoury that she picked up on her travels

around Europe, the Middle East and Africa. She always planned that the house should become a museum and donated the building and its collections to the Swedish state in 1920. Her vision became a reality in 1938 when the Hallwyl Museum was first opened to the public, eight years after her death. The house has been preserved exactly as it was left, and situated among the objets d'art are personal peculiarities, including a chunk of the Count's beard and a slice of their wedding cake. For a taste of how the other half used to live, the tour takes you through an assortment of 40 incredibly lavish rooms and is led by extremely well-spoken guides dressed up as butlers and maids.

Historiska Museet

Narvavägen 13-17 (51 95 56 00/www.historiska.se).
T-bana Karlaplan/bus 42, 44, 47, 56, 69, 76.
Open *May-Sept* 10am-5pm daily. *Sept-Apr* 11am-5pm Tue, Wed-Sun; 11am-8pm Thur. **Guided tours** *English* June-Aug 2pm daily. **Admission** 50kr; 40kr concessions; free under-18s. **Free with SC**. **Credit** AmEx, DC, MC, V. **Map** p242 F10.
Objects from the Stone Age to the 16th century are displayed in the Museum of National Antiquities, Sweden's largest archaeological museum. The plain design of this 1940 building – the façade looks like a tall brick wall with a door – gives no indication of the treasures within. To see the best exhibit, enter the darkened hall on the ground floor, where an impressive collection of Viking rune stones, swords, skeletons and jewellery is displayed. Detailed texts

Musikmuseet. *See p88.*

(in English) and maps describe the Vikings' economy, class structure, travels and methods of punishment. In the large halls upstairs, you'll find beautiful wooden church altarpieces, textiles and other medieval ecclesiastical artworks. Don't miss the basement, where the circular Guldrummet (Gold Room) displays more than 3,000 artefacts in gold and silver, from the Bronze to the Middle Ages. This collection was made possible by a unique Swedish law, more than 300 years old, which entitles the finders of such treasures to payment equal to their market value. In the foyer there's a copy of an Athenian marble lion statue – check out the Viking graffiti on its side. In 2004 the museum hit the headlines in connection with an installation about suicide bombers by an Israeli-born artist. On a visit to the museum, the Israeli ambassador to Sweden intentionally knocked over a lighting stand into the red pool designed to represent blood, shorting the electricity and causing a huge stir.

Kungliga Dramatiska Teatern

Nybrogatan 2 (tour information 665 61 15 or 665 61 75/www.dramaten.se). T-bana Kungsträdgården or Östermalmstorg/bus 2, 47, 55, 62, 69, 76, 91. **Guided tours** call for details. **Tickets** 50kr; 25kr under-18s. **Free with SC**. **Credit** AmEx, DC, MC, V. **Map** p241 F8.
Entrusted with the task of performing the classics, as well as staging new Swedish and foreign drama, the Royal Dramatic Theatre, or Dramaten, is Stockholm's number one theatre. It played host to a pre-Hollywood Greta Garbo and was a home from home for Ingmar Bergman, who directed plays here for over four decades. The lavish structure was built between 1902 and 1908 in Jugendstil style, with a white marble façade and gilded bronzework. Paintings and sculptures by Sweden's most famous artists decorate the building: Theodor Lundberg created the golden statues of *Poetry* and *Drama* at the front; Carl Milles was responsible for the large sculptural group below the raised central section of the façade; and Carl Larsson painted the foyer ceiling. The theatre's architect, Fredrik Liljekvist, wanted to create a grand and imposing structure and added the domed attic to give the building more prominence. It worked – it's one of Stockholm's most striking structures, particularly when the setting sun hits the golden lamp-posts and statues. The auditorium is equally stunning. A guided tour (call in advance if you want it in English) covers the main stage, smaller stages and rehearsal rooms (July tours only take place if there's a show on). For a wonderful view over Nybroviken, visit the outdoor café on the second-floor balcony. *See also p197.*

Kungliga Hovstallet

Väpnargatan 1 (402 60 00/www.royalcourt.se).
T-bana Östermalmstorg/bus 2, 47, 55, 62, 69, 76.
Open (guided tours only; in Swedish) *Mid Aug-mid Dec, mid Jan-May* 2pm Sat, Sun; *June-mid Aug* 2pm Mon-Fri. **Admission** 50kr; 20kr under-18s.
No credit cards. **Map** p242 F9.

Walk On the waterfront

In the summer, bus 47 is forever packed with tourists on the way to Djurgården, yet the green island can be easily and pleasantly reached on foot. This walk starts in Norrmalm, heads through Östermalm, continues along the water out to Djurgården, takes you to Skansen and ends with a ferry trip back to Slussen, just south of Gamla Stan and two stops on the T-bana back to Central Station.

Start in front of Sverigehuset at Hamngatan 27, home to the Stockholm Tourist Centre (see p50).

Directly across busy Hamngatan stands the handsome **Nordiska Kompaniet** (**NK**; see p137), Stockholm's most exclusive department store, which has been serving the city's smarter shoppers since 1915. As you head west on Hamngatan you pass pretty **Kungsträdgården** park (*see p63*) on your right. After half a block you reach Norrmalmstorg. The building located in the south-east corner of the square, at Norrmalmstorg 2, was the site of a famous bank robbery in August 1973, in which the sympathies of the hostages for their captors gave birth to the term 'Stockholm syndrome'. It's now home to Acne jeans' flagship store.

Cut through Berzelii Park to end up at Nybroplan.

Upon exiting this small park, with its central statue of Swedish chemist Jöns Jacob Berzelius, the imposing marble façade of the **Kungliga Dramatiska Teatern** (*see p87*) stands directly in front of you. Built between 1902 and 1908, the stunning Jugendstil structure is Stockholm's number one theatre. The statue of actress Margareta Krook in front of the building is kept heated at body temperature.

Head south-east on the waterside path along Strandvägen.

This recently rebuilt path, laid with slabs of granite, is one of the city's most scenic routes. Follow the path around the corner, where Strandvägen widens into the grand, tree-lined boulevard it became in the 1890s. Buy an ice-cream and gaze out at the islands of Skeppsholmen and Södermalm.

Take a right at Djurgårdsbron to enter Djurgården.

The Djurgårdsbron bridge, decorated with statues of Norse gods, was built for the Stockholm Exhibition of 1897. Cross the bridge and continue along the eastern side of Djurgårdsvägen past the **Nordiska**

The royal family's own horses, carriages and cars are still taken care of in this late 19th-century striped brick building designed by architect Fritz Eckert. The building is so vast that it occupies almost the entire block next to the Kungliga Dramatiska Teatern (*see p87*). A collection of 40 carriages from the 19th and 20th centuries (some still used for ceremonial occasions) stands in a long hall above the garage. Inside the garage are 11 cars, including a 1950 Daimler and a 1969 Cadillac Fleetwood. The stalls and riding arena may be empty if you visit in the summer, as this is when the horses are 'on vacation'. This place may be a hit for equestrian enthusiasts, but otherwise the tour is not particularly thrilling.

Musikmuseet

Sibyllegatan 2 (51 95 54 90/http://stockholm.music. museum). T-bana Östermalmstorg/bus 2, 47, 55, 62, 69, 76. **Open** 10am-5pm Tue-Sun. **Admission** 40kr; 20kr concessions; free under-19s. **Free with SC**. **Credit** MC, V. **Map** p241 F8.
Home to around 6,000 musical instruments, this fun, child-friendly museum echoes with a spontaneous symphony of noise. The hands-on exhibitions allow you to play an eclectic selection of instruments, from the electric guitar to the Swedish cow horn. With its

stucco walls and wood-beamed ceilings, the building still looks much like the Crown Bakery it was from the 1640s to 1958, when it was supplying bread to the Swedish armed forces. The Music Museum has a large collection of Swedish folk instruments, plus instruments from Africa, Asia and elsewhere in Europe. Wannabe rock stars should head downstairs to Lirum where a mocked-up stage allows you to belt out Abba's greatest hits. There are regular weekend concerts (call for a programme), and the upper floor is reserved for temporary exhibitions, which are always worth a look.

Gärdet

Map p243 & p247

The whole area to the east of Norrmalm was previously called Ladugårdsgärdet, which roughly translates as 'the field of barns'. As more affluent people moved in, the association with cattle became less desirable, and in 1885 the name was changed to Östermalm. Today, the district north of Valhallavägen and the open parkland to its south-east are known as **Gärdet**, although the undeveloped grassy area is still officially called **Ladugårdsgärdet**.

Sightseeing

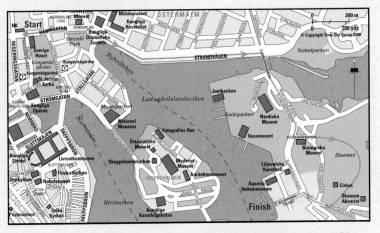

Museet (see p73), behind which lies the impressive **Vasamuseet** (see p75), containing the Vasa warship, raised up from the deep in 1961 after centuries on the seabed. To your left across the water is the broadcasting tower of **Kaknästornet** (see p90), the second tallest building in Sweden after the Turning Tower in Malmö.

Turn left on Hazeliusporten to arrive at the western entrance of Skansen.

Once you have seen **Skansen** (see p74), an excellent outdoor museum on Swedish culture and wildlife, leave via the main entrance in the south and walk north on Djurgårdsvägen to Allmänna Gränd, where you take a left. The terminal for ferries to Slussen lies at the end of this small street, with the **Gröna Lund** amusement park to your left (see p73). Ferries run every 15 minutes in summer (www.waxholmsbolaget.com).

Functionalist apartment complexes were built for working people in Gärdet and its northern neighbour, **Hjorthagen**, in the 1930s. The apartments are now mainly inhabited by middle-class residents and students. The stately complexes of the **Försvarshögskolan** (Swedish National Defence College) and the **Kungliga Musikhögskolan** (Royal College of Music) are located next to each other on the northern side of Valhallavägen. Just across Lidingövägen (the main road that heads north-east to the island of Lidingö) stands the historic **Stockholms Stadion** (see p194), built for the 1912 Olympic Games. It was designed by architect Torben Grut in National Romantic style to resemble the walls surrounding a medieval city, and its twin brick towers are a striking landmark.

Ladugårdsgärdet is part of **Ekoparken** (58 71 40 41, www.ekoparken.com), the world's first national city park, which also includes Djurgården, Hagaparken, Norra Djurgården and the Fjäderholmarna islands. Mainly open grassland and woods, with a few scattered buildings, this portion of the park stretches

for about two and a half kilometres (four miles) to the waters of **Lilla Värtan**, on the other side of which lies the island of **Lidingö** (see p95). Stockholmers come here to picnic, jog, ride horses or just get a taste of the countryside.

Nearer Östermalm is the 'Museum Park', a cluster of three museums: the **Sjöhistoriska Museet**, **Etnografiska Museet** and **Tekniska Museet** (for all, see p90). Keen sightseers with a lot of stamina could try to visit the lot in one day.

Further east is the **Kaknästornet** broadcasting tower (see p90), rising up from the forest like a giant concrete spear. Ascend to the observation deck at the top of the tower for a fantastic view right across the city; high-altitude refreshments are available in the tower's restaurant and café.

If you follow Kaknäsvägen, the road that runs past the Kaknäs tower, north-east towards the water you will come to a dirt trail in the forest to your right that winds around the scenic shoreline of **Lilla Värtan**. A 100-year-old pet cemetery with dogs, cats and a circus horse lies to the right of the trail.

Etnografiska Museet

*Djurgårdsbrunnsvägen 34 (51 95 50 00/www.
etnografiska.se). Bus 69.* **Open** 10am-5pm Mon,
Tue, Thur, Fri; 10am-8pm Wed; 11am-5pm Sat, Sun.
Guided tours & workshops call or check the website
for details. **Admission** 60kr; free under-20s. **Free
with SC. Credit** MC, V. **Map** p243 F14.

The dimly lit ground floor of the exotic-looking
National Museum of Ethnography features masks,
musical instruments and religious objects from seven
holy cities (Auroville, Benin, Benares, Jerusalem,
Yogyakarta, Beijing and Teotihuacan). Traveller's
Trunk is a collection of artefacts brought home by
Swedish explorers, the oldest of which were seized
by the pupils of famous Swedish botanist Carl
Linnaeus on their travels with Captain Cook. There's
a wide variety of colourful exhibits, beautifully
displayed, but some more explanations in English
wouldn't hurt. When you're tired of feeling thought-
ful, beers and teas of the world are served at the
museum's mellow Babjan restaurant. In the summer,
the restaurant lends bamboo mats for sitting outside.
You can also reserve a place for a tea ceremony in
the authentic Japanese tea house. Situated in the garden, the tea house was a gift from Japan to promote
friendship and cultural exchange between the two
nations. There's also a small museum shop selling
ethnic toys, trinkets and books.

Kaknästornet

*Mörka Kroken 28-30 (789 24 35/restaurant 667
21 80). Bus 69.* **Open** *Tower* July, Aug 9am-10pm
daily. Sept 10am-9pm daily. Oct-Dec 10am-9pm
Mon-Sat; 10am-5pm Sun. Jan-May 10am-5pm
Mon-Wed; 10am-9pm Thur-Sat; 10am-6pm Sun.
Restaurant opens approximately same times as
tower (check website for details). **Admission**
30kr; 15kr 7-15s; free under-7s. **Free with SC.**
Credit AmEx, DC, MC, V.

For an utterly spectacular aerial view of Stockholm
and its surroundings, visit this 155m-tall (510ft)
tower – one of Scandinavia's tallest buildings. On a
clear day you can see up to 60km (37 miles) from its
observation points up on the 30th and 31st floors.
Nearer to hand are the island of Djurgården to the
south, Gamla Stan and downtown to the west and
the beginning of the archipelago out to the east.
Designed by Bengt Lindroos and Hans Borgström,
the rather ugly concrete structure (itself visible
from all over the city) was completed in 1967 and
still transmits radio and TV broadcasts. On the
ground floor, the Stockholm Information Service
operates a busy visitor centre and gift shop. Lunch
and dinner are served in the restaurant and café on
the 28th floor.

Sjöhistoriska Museet

*Djurgårdsbrunnsvägen 24 (51 95 49 00/www.
sjohistoriska.nu). Bus 69.* **Open** *June-Aug* 10am-
5pm daily. *Sept-May* 10am-5pm Tue-Sun. **Guided
tours** 1pm daily (English tours must be pre-
booked). **Admission** 50kr; 40kr concessions;
free under-18s. Free Mon. **Free with SC. Credit**
MC, V. **Map** p243 F13.

Enquiring minds at **Tekniska Museet**.

Hundreds of model ships are displayed within
the long, curved National Maritime Museum,
designed in 1936 by Ragnar Östberg, the architect
behind Stockholm's famous Stadshuset (*see p92*). It's
an extensive and thorough survey – as it should
be, considering Sweden's long and dramatic maritime history. Two floors of minutely detailed
models are grouped in permanent exhibitions on
merchant shipping, battleships and ocean liners.
Ship figureheads depicting monsters and bare-
breasted women decorate the museum walls, and the
upper floor displays two ships' cabins from the
1870s and 1970s. But unless you're a nautical or
miniatures enthusiast, the temporary exhibitions are
probably the main reason for coming. In the basement, the children's room Saltkråkan offers ships
and a lighthouse to play in and, aside from a short
summer break, a kids' workshop is open on
Saturdays and Sundays (noon-4pm).

Tekniska Museet

*Museivägen 7 (450 56 00/www.tekniskamuseet.se).
Bus 69.* **Open** 10am-5pm Mon, Tue, Thur, Fri; 10am-
8pm Wed; 11am-5pm Sat, Sun. **Guided tours** daily
(call for details). **Admission** 60kr; 40kr concessions;
30kr 6-19s; 120kr family; free under-6s. Free 5-8pm
Wed. *Cino 4* 60kr; 30kr 4-19s. **Free with SC**
(museum only). **Credit** MC, V. **Map** p243 G14.

Inquisitive kids and adults alike can roam for hours
at the Museum of Science and Technology, which has
exhibits and activities intended to entertain and
educate – and they do. This huge house of learning
covers about 18,000sq m (60,000sq ft). Sweden's
oldest steam engine, built in 1832, dominates the large
Machine Hall, where aeroplanes – including one of
Sweden's first commercial aircraft from 1924 – hang
from the ceiling above bicycles, engines and cars. You
can also take a break in the cafeteria and pick up a
Star Trek uniform in the gift shop on your way out.
Cino 4 (Sweden's only 4-D movie theatre) has daily
shows in English.

Kungsholmen

Keep your eyes on the Prize.

Map p239 & p240
The majestic **Stadshuset** (City Hall), an
architectural gem visible from far and wide,
faces visitors as they cross Stadshusbron from
Norrmalm, and the city's famous landmark
tends to leave the rest of the island in its
shadow. But while what lies beyond is a fairly
nondescript mix of apartments, shops and
offices, Kungsholmen does also have a
sprinkling of tranquil parks and some good
neighbourhood restaurants, plus a few hip
outposts worth the trek. The island is within
a whisker of a Swedish mile (6.2 miles/ten
kilometres) in circumference, and the island's
waterside walkways are popular with joggers
seeking a run with a view.

During the 1640s, craftsmen, labourers and
factory owners were lured to Kungsholmen, then
mostly fields, by the promise of a ten-year tax
break. The island soon became home to all of
the smelly, fire-prone and dangerous businesses
that nobody else wanted. Unsurprisingly, given
the conditions, many residents became ill, and
Sweden's first hospital, the Serafimerlasarettet,
was built here in the 1750s. During the
Industrial Revolution, conditions hit an all-time
low – its diseased, starving inhabitants earned
Kungsholmen the nickname 'Starvation Island'.
The factories finally left the island in the early
1900s, to be replaced by government agencies,
offices and apartment buildings.

The quickest way to get to **Stadshuset**
(*see p92*) is to walk across Stadshusbron bridge
from Norrmalm – though navigating the roads
and railway lines leading from Central Station
can be a bit of a nightmare. The Stadshuset is
on your left – it's gigantic and hard to miss –
and the former Serafimerlasarettet hospital on
your right. Continue on down Hantverkargatan
and you'll reach **Kungsholms Kyrka**, a 17th-
century church with a Greek cross plan and a
park-like cemetery. Two blocks further on, a
right on to **Scheelegatan** puts you on one of
Kungsholmen's major thoroughfares, packed
with restaurants and bars.

Further down Scheelegatan, at the corner
of Bergsgatan, squats the city's gigantic,
majestic **Rådhuset** (courthouse), designed
by Carl Westman (1866-1936), a leading
architect of the National Romantic School.
Completed in 1915, it was designed to look
like 16th-century Vadstena castle in southern
Sweden, but also has art nouveau touches.
There are no guided tours, but you can take
a look around the public areas, including the
pleasant cloister-like garden.

Continuing west on Bergsgatan, you arrive at
Kronobergsparken, a pleasant hillside park
with Stockholm's oldest cemetery in its
north-west corner. To the north of the island the
Tullmuseet (Customs Museum; *see p93*) is
inside the Customs Office on Alströmergatan.
Nearby is one of Stockholm's trendiest interior
design shops, **R.O.O.M.** (*see p155*).

Kungsholmen's shops tend to offer a
fairly bland retail diet, but there is an
increasing number of individual treats of late.
Kungsholmen's main shopping streets are
St Eriksgatan and **Fleminggatan**, at their
most plentiful around the Fridhemsplan
Tunnelbana station. Music lovers head to the
former for its second-hand CD and vinyl shops.
If you work up an appetite, stop for coffee and
cakes at **Thelins** (*see p135*), an excellent
konditori. Alternatively, the bright and airy
shopping mall **Västermalmsgallerian**
(*see p137*), on the corner of St Eriksgatan
and Fleminggatan, offers a decent array of
Sweden's favourite brand names.

The huge but oddly elegant double-
spanned **Västerbron** bridge (1935) connects
Kungsholmen with Södermalm across
the expanse of Lake Mälaren. It's heavily
trafficked, but you'll get a spectacular view
of Stockholm from the centre of the bridge.

Sightseeing

Marieberg, the area on Kungsholmen just to the north of the bridge, once contained military installations and a porcelain factory, but is now the city's newspaper district. Two of the four Stockholm dailies – *Dagens Nyheter* and *Expressen* – have offices here. The Expressen building, designed by Paul Hedqvist, is prominent, soaring to 82 metres (270 feet).

The flat green lawns of adjoining **Rålambshovparken** were created in 1935, at the same time as Västerbron; the sculpture-studded park is popular with runners and picnickers, and there's a small sandy beach just along the shore at Smedsuddsbadet.

Walking and cycling paths line the northern and southern shores of Kungsholmen. For a beautiful view across the water, stroll from the Stadshuset along tree-lined **Mälarpromenaden**. Vintage boats and yachts moor here, and there are a couple of well-placed cafés en route. **Norr Mälarstrand**, the road that runs alongside the promenade, is lined with grand apartment blocks, built in the early 20th century when the factories had finally departed. Look out particularly for No.76, designed by Ragnar Östberg, architect of Stadshuset.

Stadshuset

Hantverkargatan 1 (50 82 90 59/www.stockholm. se/stadshuset). T-bana T-Centralen/bus 3, 62. **Open** *Stadshuset* (guided tours only; tours are in Swedish and English) *June-Sept* 10am, noon, 2pm daily; *Oct-May* 10am, noon daily. *Tower July-Aug* 10am-5pm daily; *Sept* 10am-4pm daily. Closed Oct-May. **Admission** Guided tour 60kr; tower 20kr; free under-12s. **Free with SC**. **Credit** AmEx, DC, MC, V. **Map** p240 H5.

The City Hall (1923), Stockholm's most prominent landmark, stands imposingly on the northern shore of the bay of Riddarfjärden. A massive red-brick building, it was designed by Ragnar Östberg (1866-1945) in the National Romantic style, with two inner courtyards and a 106m (348ft) tower. It's most famous for hosting the 1,300 or so guests who are lucky enough to be invited along to the annual Nobel Prize banquet, an event held in the Blue Hall on 10 December after the prizes have been awarded at Konserthuset (*see also p58* **Nobel or ignoble?**). The hall – which is designed to look like an Italian Renaissance piazza – was meant to be painted blue, but Östberg liked the way the sun hit the red bricks and changed his mind. The hall is also the home of an immense organ, with more than 10,000 pipes and 138 stops.

My Stockholm Jesper Waldersten

Artist and illustrator Jesper Waldersten has published seven books in Sweden and his work regularly appears in Dagens Nyheter, *one of the country's major newspapers. Current projects include a hand-printed book of poetry in collaboration with French poet Michel Gravil.*

If I had a friend in town on a warm day, I'd head straight to my favourite food shop, **Cajsa Warg** (*see p149*) on Södermalm, to buy all sorts of ingredients for a picnic. Then we'd head to the subway – probably pausing at two great record shops on the way, **Pet Sounds** (*see p156*) and **Skivfönstret** (*Gotgatan 132, 702 21 40, www.skivfonstret. com*), to see what's new – and take the train out to Skogskyrkogården. This woodland cemetery was created between 1917 and 1920 by two famous Swedish architects, Gunnar Asplund and Sigurd Lewerentz. We'd find a nice spot near Greta Garbo's grave and have our picnic.

Alternatively, if we wanted to have a picnic without leaving the city centre, we could simply grab a bottle of rosé from the **Systembolaget** (*Klarabergsgatan 62, 21 47 44, www.systembolaget.se*), pick up something ready-made from some of the food stalls in Hötorgshallen, and take a cab to Riddarholmen. This is the small island next to Gamla Stan. It's just as beautiful as the Old Town but much less crowded. Here we could sit right by the water and discuss the current hot topic in town – should the city build a floating hotel on the water near Stadshuset?

Afterwards we'd take the train to Rådmansgatan for a quick coffee at **Sosta Espresso Bar** (*see p130*), before visiting the Stadsbiblioteket, the main library in Stockholm. Also designed by Gunnar Asplund, it's famous for its spectacular rotunda. At the moment there's a competition underway to design an extension to the library. A winner will be picked from the six short-listed designs in 2007, and the building should be completed by 2013. After that, time to pick up some new clothes at **Filippa K** (the Grev Turegatan shop is best for men's clothes; *see p141*) or **Hugo** on St Eriksgatan (*see p143*), before a drink at **Gondolen** (*see p121*) and then some food at **Göteborg** in Hammarby Sjöstad (*Midskeppsgatan 31, 031 12 99 33*). It sits right on the water, so you can have dinner watching the boats go by.

Magnificent **Stadshuset**, home to city councils, Nobel niceties and whirlwind weddings.

In the astonishing Golden Hall upstairs, scenes from Swedish history are depicted on the walls in 18 million mosaic pieces in gold leaf. The artist, Einar Forseth (1892-1988), covered the northern wall with a mosaic known as the 'Queen of Lake Mälaren', representing Stockholm being honoured from all sides. The beamed ceiling of the Council Chamber, where the city council meets every other Monday, resembles the open roof of a Viking longhouse. The furniture was designed by Carl Malmsten. The opulent Oval Room, which is part of the guided tour, is a popular place for Swedish nuptials. Such is the demand, it's a speedy marriage merry-go-round as couples tie the knot in a no-frills 40-second ceremony. The extended version is three minutes.

You can only visit the interior of the Stadshuset by guided tour, but you can climb the tower independently. Follow a series of winding red-brick slopes then wooden stairs for a fantastic view over Gamla Stan. Three gold crowns – the Tre Kronor, Sweden's heraldic symbol – top the tower. At the edge of the outdoor terrace below the tower, by the waters of Riddarfjärden, are two statues by famous Swedish sculptor Carl Eldh (1873-1954): the female *Dansen* (Dance) and the male *Sången* (Song).

For refreshments, a cafeteria-style restaurant serves up classic Swedish dishes at lunchtime, while the Stadshuskällaren cellar restaurant offers the previous year's menu from the Nobel banquet.

Tullmuseet

Alströmergatan 39 (653 05 03/www.tullverket.se/ museum). T-bana Fridhemsplan/bus 1, 3, 4, 57. **Open** 11am-4pm Tue, Wed, Sun. **Admission** free. **Map** p239 F2.

The most interesting part of the Customs Museum is its section on smuggling. The oldest exhibits date from the 1920s and 1930s when alcohol was smuggled in from Estonia and Finland. One of the oldest pieces is a pair of XXL knickers dating from the 1920s, with secret pockets to conceal cannisters filled with 96% proof spirit, home-made by a lady caught by Swedish customs (a gurgling noise was heard by customs officers). Other methods for concealing contraband included bread, sofas and teddy bears. In 1622 a fence and toll (*tull*) booths were built around Stockholm to raise money for the wars of King Gustav II Adolf, and the museum displays a copy of one of these, as well as an early 20th-century customs office. Though it's a bit off the beaten track, the Customs Museum is free, so take a peek if you're in the area.

Further Afield

Plan your urban escape.

Haga & around

Rolling green lawns, cool woodlands and imposing 18th-century architecture make **Hagaparken** a popular outdoor destination. One of its biggest draws is the fact that it's within easy reach of the city centre, just north-west of Vasastaden on the western edge of Brunnsviken Bay. The legacy of King Gustav III and architect Fredrik Magnus Piper, this romantic English-style park with wandering paths, scenic views and assorted pavilions forms part of a broader national park in Stockholm, which was christened **Ekoparken** (58 71 40 41, www.ekoparken.com) in 1995 by the Swedish parliament. Tagged as the world's first national park within a city, Ekoparken consists of 27 square kilometres (ten square miles) of land and water, cutting a diagonal green swathe across the city from the island of Djurgården in the south-east to Ulriksdals Palace in the north-west.

In Haga's northern section, the lush **Fjärilshuset conservatory** (*see p163*) is full of exotic butterflies and tropical rainforest vegetation. To the south, three colourful copper tents form **Koppartälten**. Built as Gustav III's stables and guards' quarters, it now houses a restaurant, café and the **Haga Park Museum** (58 71 40 41, free admission), which contains an interesting pictorial history (all text is in Swedish) of the park and its buildings. The 'ruins' of a palace left incomplete after Gustav III's assassination in 1792 are east of the tents. Sweden's current king, Carl XVI Gustaf, was born in nearby **Haga Slott** (171 41 47 00, www.hagaslott.se), a castle now converted into a hotel and conference centre. Other buildings include the waterfront **Gustav III's Paviljong** (402 61 30, www.royalcourt.se), with Pompeii-style interiors by 18th-century interior decorator Louis Masreliéz. It's open for guided tours in summer (June-Aug noon, 1pm, 2pm, 3pm Tue-Sun, 50kr). You can also test the acoustics in the outdoor **Ekotemplet**, originally used as a summer dining room.

The 18th-century obsession with the exotic is evident in the Chinese pagoda and Turkish pavilion in the south of the park. A small island nearby (May 1-3pm Sun, June-Aug 9am-3pm Thur) has been the burial place of Swedish royalty since the 1910s.

On the southern tip of Hagaparken, enjoy a meal or Sunday brunch at **Haga Forum** (Annerovägen 4, 833 48 44, www.vilja gruppen.se/eng/rest/haga), a bus-terminal-turned-modern-restaurant with a terrace overlooking the park and water.

Sculptures by Swedish artists stand in **Norra begravningsplats** (Northern Cemetery), an elaborate 19th-century cemetery to the west across the E4 highway and north of Karolinska Sjukhuset hospital. Alfred Nobel, August Strindberg and Ingrid Bergman lie amid its hedges and landscaped hills.

Bus 3 or 52 will take you to Karolinska Sjukhuset from where you can walk to southern Hagaparken. For northern Haga, take the T-bana to Odenplan then catch bus 515 to the Haga Norra stop.

Northern Frescati

You'll know you're in Frescati, a cluster of scientific and academic institutions on the eastern shore of Brunnsviken, by the sound of Roslagsvägen, a thoroughfare that cuts through northern Frescati and connects to the E18 to the north. On the west side of the highway (cross under the viaduct) is the Royal Swedish Academy of Sciences, and beyond that, the lovely gardens and conservatories of **Bergianska Trädgården** (*see p95*), which borders Brunnsviken. On the east side stands the **Naturhistoriska Riksmuseet** (*see p95*), while to the south, in Frescati, lies the sprawling campus of **Stockholm University**, relocated from cramped city quarters to this site in 1970. From the campus, head east to Ekoparken's **Norra Djurgården** for hiking, horse riding or bird watching, or take a ten-minute walk west to **Brunnsviksbadet**, a local beach, where you can swim or rent canoes.

You can get to northern Frescati on the T-bana to Universitetet, then walk north for about seven minutes. Alternatively, take the Roslagsbanan commuter train, which leaves from Stockholm's Östra station near the Tekniska Högskolan. Get off at Frescati station: the gardens and museum are directly to the west and east, respectively. If you continue on the Roslagsbanan for 15 minutes, you'll reach **Djursholm**, one of Sweden's wealthiest neighbourhoods.

Suburban sculpture at **Millesgården**.

Swedish wildlife. Visitors enter the dinosaur exhibit through a dark volcanic room to find sharp-toothed birds sitting in trees above a skeletal T-Rex. The hands-on exhibits about space and the human body include a red Martian landscape, a spaceship's cockpit and a walk-through mouth. Many exhibits are labelled in Swedish only, so borrow a booklet in English from the information desk.

Sweden's only IMAX cinema, the Cosmonova (*see p173*), shows movies about the natural world on its huge screen – which also functions as a planetarium. Under-5s are not admitted. The gift shop sells science books, plastic animals and polished rocks.

Lidingö

Lidingö is an island of suburban tranquillity, just north-east of the city centre, and is largely populated by Stockholm's wealthier classes. The main attraction is **Millesgården** (*see below*), the former home and studio of the sculptor Carl Milles. Lidingö is also the birthplace of Raoul Wallenberg, the World War II Swedish diplomat who disappeared mysteriously in 1945 while in Soviet custody. Sculptures around the island have been erected in his honour.

Understandably, Lidingö is popular with outdoor enthusiasts: there's golf near Sticklinge and at Ekholmsnäs; cycling and jogging paths, which become cross-country ski trails in winter, at Stockby Motionsgård; and one of the nearest downhill ski slopes to Stockholm at the 70-metre high (230-foot) Ekholmsnäsbacken, south of the Hustegafjärden inlet. The beach at Fågelöuddebadet, in Lidingö's north-east corner, has a café and miniature golf course, as do the Breviksbadet outdoor pools in the south.

Bergianska Trädgården

Frescati (545 917 00/www.bergianska.se). T-bana Universitetet/bus 40, 540. **Open** *Gardens 9am-8pm daily. Edvard Andersons Växthus 11am-5pm daily. Victoriahuset May-Sept 11am-4pm Mon-Fri; 11am-5pm Sat, Sun. Closed Oct-Apr.* **Admission** *Gardens free. Edvard Andersons Växthus 50kr. Victoriahuset 20kr. Free under-15s.* **Free with SC. Credit** MC, V.

Amateur botanists and picnickers alike will find this idyllic botanical garden on a hilly peninsula by Brunnsviken. The Royal Swedish Academy of Sciences, which still conducts research here, moved the garden from Vasastaden to this waterfront area in 1885. Orchids and vines fill Victoriahuset, a small conservatory (1900); its pond contains giant water lilies, measuring up to 2.5m (8ft) across. The more recent Edvard Andersons Växthus, an all-glass conservatory, contains Mediterranean plants and trees in its central room, and flora from Australia, South Africa, California.

Naturhistoriska Riksmuseet

Frescativägen 40 (51 95 40 00/www.nrm.se). T-bana Universitetet/bus 40, 540. **Open** *Museum 10am-7pm Tue, Wed, Fri; 10am-8pm Thur; 11am-7pm Sat, Sun. Open Mon during holiday periods; call for details.* **Admission** *Museum 50kr; 40kr concessions; free under-18s. IMAX 85kr; 60kr concessions; 50kr 5-18s. Museum & IMAX 100kr; 80kr concessions.* **Museum free with SC. Credit** AmEx, MC, V.

Founded in 1739, the National Museum of Natural History is the largest museum complex in Sweden. More than nine million biological and mineral samples are stored in this monolithic brick building designed in 1907 by Axel Anderberg, architect of the Royal Opera. Beneath the black-shingled roof and light-filled cupola stands an exceptionally well-made tableaux of extinct creatures, prehistoric man and

Millesgården

Heserudsvägen 32 (446 75 90/www.millesgarden.se). T-bana Ropsten then bus 207 or bus 201, 202, 204, 205, 206, 207, 212 to Torsvik then walk. **Open** *Mid May-Aug 11am-5pm daily. Sept-mid May noon-5pm Tue-Sun.* **Admission** *80kr; 60kr concessions; free under-19s.* **Free with SC. Credit** AmEx, MC, V.

Works by sculptor Carl Milles (1875-1955) are displayed at his home and studio, which he donated to the state in 1936. His bronze statues stand alongside works by other artists on wide stone terraces, and its hilltop setting provides a dramatic backdrop of sky, land and water. The house is decorated with paintings, drawings and antiques purchased by Milles on his travels – he amassed the largest private collection of Greek and Roman statues in Sweden. The studio was not as tranquil as it appears today during three days in 1917, when Milles decided to destroy all his work and start again from scratch. After emigrating to the USA in 1931, he became a professor of art in Michigan, where he created more than 70 sculptures – the nudes often had to be fitted with fig leaves. An adjacent exhibition hall, which houses the gift shop, features contemporary and classic modern art.

Sightseeing

adult toys sexy lingerie accesoaries

Ooups
WWW.OOUPS.SE

Eat, Drink, Shop

Prinsen. *See p112.*

Restaurants

Meatballs are still on the menu, but Stockholm's smörgåsbord is growing ever more sophisticated.

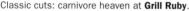

Classic cuts: carnivore heaven at **Grill Ruby**.

How exasperating it must be for the many talented chefs working in Stockholm that when you Google 'Swedish chef', the first thing that pops up is an incompetent Muppet with an unintelligible accent. The fact is that the dining scene in Stockholm is thriving. Choices for a night out range from traditional places serving classic Swedish dishes – herring or meatballs, with lots of potatoes, dill and lingonberries – up to the handful of world-class restaurants that offer extraordinarily innovative cuisine in ultra-hip surroundings.

The city has had some catching up to do over the last couple of decades. Thirtysomething Stockholmers still remember a time when a

> ❶ Purple numbers in this chapter correspond to the location of each restaurant as marked on the street maps. *See pp238-251.*

cappuccino was considered to be the height of sophistication. But Swedes as a nation travel a great deal, and all those trips abroad have broadened their horizons and raised their expectations. There's still plenty of room for improvement, though. At many restaurants the quality of service is disappointingly inattentive (though rarely unfriendly) – employment costs are so high in Sweden that places often feel like they are slightly understaffed.

EATING BY AREA

With some exceptions, such as **Mistral** (*see p99*), **Gamla Stan** is a wilderness when it comes to getting a good meal. Instead, head to **Södermalm** or **Kungsholmen** if you want to discover a charming little neighbourhood place, or make a beeline for **Stureplan** if you're after something fashionable and stylish. **Vasastaden** isn't as much fun to explore on foot, but has some of the most reliable restaurant choices. If you can't decide what you want, head to **Scheelegatan** on Kungsholmen or **Rörstrandsgatan** in Vasastaden. These two streets are packed with restaurants and bars and you're bound to find something to suit your taste buds.

A FEW TIPS

The restaurants of the moment are always packed, so it can sometimes be a battle to find a free table, even on weekdays. For popular places, you should always book in advance, especially for Fridays and Saturdays. Locals are also driven by pay day, which is usually the 25th of each month; in the preceding days restaurants can be less busy, only to be mobbed on the weekend after the cash comes in. Be aware too that many restaurants close in July for summer holidays.

Children are welcome everywhere, even in the smartest restaurants, and many places provide high chairs and kids' menus. All restaurants are smoke-free. Many restaurants will have a version of the menu in English, but at the ones that don't, staff will be happy to translate. For food terms, *see p228* **Vocabulary**.

PRICES, TIMING AND TIPPING

It is expensive to eat out in Stockholm, partly because people tend to go to a restaurant to have a whole new food experience rather than for just a simple, well-cooked meal in an informal environment. This, of course, has an effect on the atmosphere, as well as the prices – places can often be more pretentious than cosy. In addition, don't expect restaurants serving Swedish food to be automatically cheaper; local cuisine appears at the upper end of the price scale, alongside French or Italian. If you're looking for a budget meal, your best bet is Indian, Thai or Turkish.

If you're after cheap, fast food on the go, burgers, kebabs, hot dogs and paninis can be bought in most neighbourhoods. More traditional but rarer are the Swedish *strömming* stands, which serve delicious fried fish on a piece of bread.

For something fancy at a reasonable price, it's a good idea to have your main meal at lunchtime when many restaurants swap their à la carte menu for a fixed-price menu at a considerably lower price – look out for signs offering '*Dagens Lunch*' or '*Dagens Rätt*'.

Bear in mind that the Swedes are a highly punctual lot: they go for lunch bang on noon. To avoid this lunchtime crush, come a bit earlier or after 1pm. In the evening, people tend to eat early, around 7-8pm. Be aware that most kitchens close by 11pm, even if the restaurant's bar stays open later.

Service is always included in the bill, but it's still quite common to tip up to ten per cent on top. However, if the food or service is in any way substandard, it's acceptable to leave no tip at all. Tipping is not expected at lunchtime.

Gamla Stan

Contemporary

Mistral

Lilla Nygatan 21 (10 12 24). T-bana Gamla Stan/bus 3, 53, 59. **Open** 6pm-1am Tue-Fri. **Set menu** 615kr-815kr. **Credit** AmEx, DC, MC, V. **Map** p241 J7 ❶
One of Stockholm's best – and tiniest – restaurants, Mistral offers an entertaining and slightly peculiar dining experience. It is the creation of two young restaurateurs, chef Fredrik Andersson and maître d' Björn Vasseur, both of whom are a constant presence in the open kitchen and 18-seat dining room. The cooking is eccentric and always very good, the wine pairings are chosen with care, and while the bill ends on a high note (around 1,500kr per person), the whole experience feels worth it. A culinary experience of the highest order. Reserve several weeks in advance.

French/American

Bistro Ruby & Grill Ruby

Österlånggatan 14 (20 60 15/57 76/www.bistroruby. com). T-bana Gamla Stan/bus 2, 43, 55, 59, 76. **Open** *Restaurant* 5-11pm daily. *Brunch* 1-3pm Sat.

The best Restaurants

For a taste of the high life
Operakällaren (*see p103*), **Mathias Dahlgren** (*see p101*), **Mistral** (*see p99*) and **Edsbacka Krog** (*see p115*).

For a touch of jazz
Glenn Miller Café (*see p101*) and **Nalen** (*see p103*).

For Swedish classics
Bakfickan (*see p103*), **Pelikan** (*see p109*), **Lisa Elmqvist** (*see p112*) and **Prinsen** (*see p112*).

For dinner with the kids
Chutney (*see p109*) and **Sabai-Soong** (*see p110*).

For eating on the cheap
Lao Wai (*see p105*), **Crêperie Fyra Knop** (*see p109*) and **Halv Grek plus Turk** (*see p110*).

Mathias Dahlgren.

Bar 5pm-1am daily. Closed 2wks July. **Main courses** *Bistro Ruby* 175kr-395kr. *Grill Ruby* 179kr-420kr. **Credit** AmEx, DC, MC, V. **Map** p241 J8 ❷

These two sister restaurants set out to combine Paris and Texas. Bistro Ruby offers European formality in a classically pleasant environment ideal for a quiet chat. The menu goes from classic French to more modern Mediterranean influences, and it's all well cooked, tasty and not overworked. Next door, Grill Ruby is noisier and more fun, and it's all about the meat, so vegetarians should steer clear. With each cut you get a wide choice of tapas, salsas, and other accompaniments. The Saturday brunch is recommended.

Pontus by the Sea

Skeppsbronkajen Tullhus 2 (20 20 95/www.pontus frithiof.com). T-bana Kungsträdgården or Gamla Stan/bus 2, 43, 55, 71, 76. **Open** *Restaurant* 11.30am-2pm, 5-11pm Mon-Fri; 4-11pm Sat, Sun. *Bar* 11.30am-11pm Mon-Fri, Sun; noon-1am Sat. **Main courses** 205kr-345kr. **Credit** AmEx, DC, MC, V. **Map** p241 J8 ❸

Located in a huge, old customs building, this bustling quayside restaurant has one of Stockholm's best waterfront views (except when there's a cruise ship moored in front). When the sun shines, it's one of the city's most popular places for a beer and a bite to eat. The French food is good but priced slightly beyond its station.

Traditional Swedish

Den Gyldene Freden

Österlånggatan 51 (24 97 60/www.gyldenefreden.se). T-bana Gamla Stan/bus 2, 43, 55, 59, 76. **Open** 5-11pm Mon-Fri; 1pm-midnight Sat. **Main courses** 155kr-295kr. **Credit** AmEx, DC, MC, V. **Map** p241 J8 ❹

This first-class restaurant is housed in an 18th-century building owned by the Swedish Academy, and the dimly lit interior lends a suitably grandiose atmosphere to a meal here. Since it first opened in 1722, large sections of Stockholm's cultural elite have dined here – singer-poet Carl Michael Bellman, painter Anders Zorn and singer-composer Evert Taube were regular customers. As you'd expect, the menu is stocked with traditional Swedish dishes, including smoked reindeer, meatballs and plenty of herring and salmon.

Norrmalm

Contemporary

Berns Asia

Berzelii Park (56 63 22 22/www.berns.se). T-bana Kungsträdgården/bus 2, 47, 55, 62, 69, 76. **Open** *Sept-July* 11.30am-3pm Mon, Sun; 11.30am-3pm, 5-11pm Tue-Thur; 11.30am-3pm, 5-11.30pm Fri, Sat. *July-Sept* 11.30am-3pm Mon, Sun; 11.30am-3pm,

5-11pm Tue-Thur; 11.30am-11.30pm Fri; 1-11.30pm
Sat. **Main courses** 125kr-335kr. **Credit** AmEx, DC,
MC, V. **Map** p241 G8 ❺
Sir Terence Conran has done an admirable job in
transforming this jaw-droppingly grand ballroom
into a restaurant, and the kitchen does its best to be
industrious and innovative too, producing crossover
pan-Asian cuisine. The aims are ambitious but the
results can be uneven. The various bars are always
packed, and there's also a boutique hotel attached
(see p37).

Bistro Bern

Berzelii Park (56 63 25 15/www.bistroberns.se).
T-bana Kungsträdgården/bus 2, 47, 55, 62, 69,
76. **Open** 11am-midnight Mon-Fri; noon-midnight
Sat; 1-11pm Sun. **Main courses** 105kr-225kr.
Credit AmEx, DC, MC, V. **Map** p241 G8 ❻
Bistro Berns is a charming little place located in
Berzelii Park just in front of the hotel-restaurant.
Classic French dishes (coq au vin, liver anglaise,
croque monsieur) are served up in a cosy, elegant
space and the location, in the very heart of the city,
is perfect. The cramped interior just adds to the
overall charm.

Champenoise/Hälsingborg

Birger Jarlsgatan 101 (15 61 06/www.champenoise.
se) & 112 (673 34 20/www.restaurant-
halsingborg.se). T-bana Tekniska högskolan/bus
2, 4, 42, 53, 72. **Open** *Champenoise* 5.30-11pm
Tue-Sat. *Helsingborg* 5pm-1am Tue-Sat. Closed
July. **Set menu** *Champenoise* 325kr 2 courses.
Helsingborg 355kr 3 courses. **Credit** AmEx, DC,
MC, V. **Map** p245 B6 ❼❽
This pair of restaurants stand opposite each other
at the less well travelled end of Birger Jarlsgatan, far
removed from the bustle of Stureplan. Both are
gourmet places: Hälsingborg offers a selection of
three-course set menus (choose from the Sea, Farm
or Forest options) while Champenoise has two-
course menus for 325kr. Champenoise is, as you'd
expect, particularly well stocked with champagne.

F12

Konstakademien, Fredsgatan 12 (24 80 52/www.
fredsgatan12.com). T-bana T-Centralen/bus 3, 53,
59, 62, 65. **Open** 11.30am-2pm, 5pm-1am Mon-Fri;
5pm-1am Sat. Closed July. **Main courses** 270kr-
520kr. **Set menu** 1,095kr. **Credit** AmEx, DC, MC, V.
Map p241 H7 ❾
Consistently ranked as one of Sweden's best restaurants, F12 has a lot to live up to. There's no quib-
bling with the cuisine: the menu is divided into
'traditional' and 'innovative', with show-stealing
desserts to follow. But other aspects of the visit – the
tacky note in the menu advertising the owner's other
restaurants, the silly and awkward interior design,
wobbly service, the queue for the toilets – make you
wonder if it's worth it. A better bet would be to come
here on a summer's night for a drink at the terrace
bar and then head to Mathias Dahlgren at the Grand
Hôtel (see below) if you want a truly amazing blow-
your-budget meal.

Mathias Dahlgren

At the Grand Hôtel, Södra Blasieholmshamnen 6
(679 35 84/www.mathiasdahlgren.com). T-bana
Kungsträdgården/bus 2, 55, 59, 62, 65, 76. **Open**
Food Bar noon-2pm, 6pm-midnight Mon-Fri; 6pm-
midnight Sat. *Dining Room* 7pm-midnight Mon-Sat.
Main courses *Food Bar* 95kr-300kr. **Set menus**
Dining Room 800kr-2,000kr. **Credit** AmEx, DC,
MC, V. **Map** p241 G8 ❿
Mathias Dahlgren's previous restaurant, Bon Lloc,
was regularly listed as one of the best in the country, so it was a shock when he decided to close it and
temporarily vanished from the scene. Thankfully his
new place, located in the Grand Hôtel, lives up to
expectations. It's a two-room affair: the Food Bar is
a stripped-down room with bare wooden tables and
a steel bar, while the Dining Room is classy and elegant. The modern Scandinavian food is faultless:
smoked salmon from Tromsö, Norway; mussels
from New Bedford, USA; even oven-baked wild
chocolate from Bolivia. Head to the Dining Room for
a splurge dinner, or for a more affordable experience
perch in the Food Bar where dishes start at 95kr.

Moderna Museet

Slupskjulsvägen 7-9, Skeppsholmen (51 95 62 91/
www.momumat.se). Bus 65. **Open** 11.30am-2.30pm
Mon-Fri. *Brunch* 11.30am or 2pm Sat, Sun. **Main
courses** 115kr; *brunch* 235kr. **Credit** AmEx, DC, V.
Map p242 H9 ⓫
The Moderna Museet has an ordinary museum café,
of course, but also a dining room with white-cloth service and excellent food. It's only open for lunch but at
the weekend serves one of the city's best buffet
brunches. There are two sittings, one at 11.30am and
the other at 2pm, and reservations are necessary. The
food is (naturally) a modern take on Scandinavian
classics and desserts are particularly glorious.

Pontus!

Brunnsgatan 1 (54 52 73 00/www.pontusfrithiof.
com). T-bana Östermalmstorg/bus 1, 2, 55, 56.
Open 11.30am-2pm, 5pm-1am Mon-Fri; 5pm-1am
Sat. **Main courses** 170kr-295kr. **Set menu** 545kr.
Credit AmEx, DC, MC, V. **Map** p241 F7 ⓬
See p103 **Star quality**.

Mediterranean

Glenn Miller Café

Brunnsgatan 21A (10 03 22/www.glennmiller
cafe.com). T-bana Hötorget/bus 1, 43, 52, 56. **Open**
5pm-midnight Mon-Thur; 5pm-1am Fri, Sat. **Main
courses** 95kr-215kr. **Credit** MC, V. **Map** p241 E7 ⓭
This tiny place is a sympathetic bistro for anyone
on the lookout for reasonably priced food in a
relaxed environment, with jazz performances (see
p184) some nights as the perfect accompaniment. It
doesn't take much to pack the place, but the service
is personal and the rustic French food is well cooked.
Unpretentious restaurants like this are becoming
hard to find in Stockholm; we hope they don't
change a thing.

Operakällaren

Kungliga Operan, Karl XIIs Torg (676 58 01/
www.operakallaren.se). T-bana Kungsträdgården/
bus 2, 55, 59, 62, 76. **Open** 6pm-1am Tue-Sat.
Closed July. **Main courses** 260kr-420kr.
Set menu 795kr. **Credit** AmEx, DC, MC, V.
Map p241 G7 **⓮**
Operakällaren is without doubt one of Sweden's best
restaurants, with history and setting to match. As
the name (Opera Cellar) implies, this restaurant is
located in the Opera House, which has been open for
business since 1787 – although the present building
was erected in 1895. The present restaurant was created in the 1960s by legendary chef Tore Wretman,
who, more than any other person, is responsible for
turning the Swedes into foodies. Today you'll find
mouthwatering dishes such as black turbot with
potato and leek purée, or roast French pigeon with
hazelnuts, sweet and sour lentils and vegetable
ragoût. The desserts are sublime, particularly the
cloudberry gazpacho with almond milk sorbet. This
is a luxury establishment on all counts – food, service and wine. And make no mistake, the prices are
equally spectacular. Dress to impress.

Traditional Swedish

Bakfickan

Kungliga Operan, Karl XIIs Torg (676 58 09/
www.operakallaren.se). T-bana Kungsträdgården/
bus 2, 55, 59, 62, 65. **Open** 11.30am-11pm Mon-Fri;
noon-11.30pm Sat. **Main courses** 115kr-245kr.
Credit AmEx, DC, MC, V. **Map** p241 G7 **⓯**
In the opera house, alongside Operakällaren *(see*
above) and Operabaren *(see below)* you'll find
Bakfickan ('hip pocket'), the little brother of the trio
that shares the same giant kitchen. Head here for
quality traditional Swedish fare if you've been
turned away from the more upscale Opera establish-
ments for wearing trainers. *Photo p104.*

Nalen

Regeringsgatan 74 (50 52 92 01/www.nalen.com).
T-bana Hötorget/bus 1, 43, 52, 56. **Open** 11.30am-
11pm Mon-Fri; 5-11pm Sat. Closed July. **Main**
courses 225kr-255kr. **Set menu** 400kr. **Credit**
AmEx, DC, MC, V. **Map** p241 E7 **⓰**
This restaurant shares space with the old jazz haunt
Nalen *(see p184)*, and it's worth scouting out even
if you're not coming for the entertainment. Nalen
offers classic Swedish cuisine with the best of native
ingredients, like reindeer, pike-perch and herring,
at reasonable prices. The menu even highlights
dishes that are safe for those with food allergies, a
rare courtesy in Stockholm. Staff are attentive, and
the Irish coffee is the best in town.

Operabaren

Kungliga Operan, Karl XIIs Torg (676 58 08/
www.operakallaren.se). T-bana Kungsträdgården/
bus 2, 55, 59, 62, 65. **Open** 11.30am-3pm,
5pm-1am Mon-Wed; 11.30am-3pm, 5pm-2am

Star quality

Travellers arriving at Arlanda Airport are
greeted by the 'Hall of Fame', a series of
portraits of almost 80 famous Swedes.
It's a sign of the city's pride in its culinary
stars that alongside Abba, Björn Borg, the
Bergmans (Ingrid and Ingmar) and Sweden's
first astronaut, you'll also spot several of
Stockholm's most successful chefs. There's
Melker Andersson of F12, Henrik Norström
of Lux, and Pontus Frithiof, whose latest
venture opened in summer 2007.

While Swedes may, on the whole, be a
modest bunch, Frithiof has no such qualms.
First came Pontus in the Greenhouse (which
closed in 2007); followed by Pontus by the
Sea (*see p100*), a French brasserie in Gamla
Stan; and now it's simply Pontus! (*see p101*),
a huge three-floor eaterie close to Stureplan.
The newspaper *Svenska Dagbladet* compared
it to London's Quaglino's, gave it five stars
and said it was 'magnificent and like nothing
else in Stockholm'.

'The idea was to combine three different
concepts in one restaurant,' says Frithiof.

'There's an oyster bar with the best oysters in
Sweden; a cocktail bar where you can eat dim
sum, sashimi and sushi; and a dining room
with modern, fresh food.'

Decor leans towards the dramatic. In the
main dining room the walls are decorated
with custom-made wallpaper depicting many
of Pontus's favourite books – including,
of course, *Pontus by the Book*.

The main menu is divided into three parts:
Harvest, Catch and Season. Instead of
starters and main courses, dishes come
in three sizes so diners can structure their
meal as they wish. There's also a strong
emphasis on vegetables, which will please
diners exasperated by the paucity of
vegetarian options in Stockholm.

For people who just want to drop in for a
drink and eye up the stunning decor, the
must-try cocktail is the shizu martini, made
from OP Andersson aquavit and Japanese
shizu leaf. It's a delicious fusion of Swedish
and foreign influences – much like Frithiof
and his new restaurant.

Meatballs and music at **Bakfickan**, in the opera house. *See p103.*

Thur, Fri; 12.30pm-2am Sat. Closed last 3 wks July. **Main courses** 165kr-295kr. **Set menu** 360kr. **Credit** AmEx, DC, MC, V. **Map** p241 G7 ⑰
Operabaren is one of the city's true gems – and perhaps the finest place to come for traditional Swedish meatballs. Sitting on the old leather sofas and admiring the magnificent Jugendstil interior is like travelling back in time. Service from the white-jacketed waiters is impeccable, prices are fair and the food never disappoints. Particularly good on a Saturday lunchtime.

Wedholms Fisk
Nybrokajen 17 (611 78 74/www.wedholms fisk.se). T-bana Kungsträdgården/bus 2, 47, 62, 65, 69, 76. **Open** 11.30am-11pm Mon; 11.30am-11pm Tue-Fri; 5-11pm Sat. **Main courses** 265kr-535kr. **Credit** AmEx, DC, MC, V. **Map** p241 G8 ⑱
The standard of seafood in Stockholm is high, and it's at its highest at Wedholms Fisk. Located close to the waterfront in the heart of the city, this is a classic restaurant, both in terms of the decor and cuisine. Dishes are simple and unfussy: when the fish is this good, it needs little doing to it. Needless to say, quality like this doesn't come cheap; be prepared for the bill.

Vegetarian

Martins Gröna
Regeringsgatan 91 (411 5850). T-bana Hötorget/ bus 2, 43. **Open** lunchtimes only. Closed July. **Lunch** 75kr. **No credit cards. Map** p245 E7 ⑲

This small, unpretentious vegetarian restaurant is one of the most pleasant places to eat lunch in the city centre. Each day there's a choice of just two dishes (or you can have a mix of both), served with home-baked bread and tea and coffee for 75kr. It's far from sophisticated fare – hearty stews are popular – but it's tasty and filling. Try to avoid the noon rush when local office workers descend en masse.

Vasastaden

African

Abyssinia
Vanadisvägen 20 (33 08 40). T-bana St Eriksplan/ bus 2, 40, 69. **Open** 11am-11pm Mon-Fri; 2-11pm Sat. **Main courses** 85kr-165kr. **Credit** MC, V. **Map** p244 C4 ⑳
This is one of the few places in Stockholm offering *injera*, the pancake-like bread that serves as the base for most Ethiopian and Eritrean food. The Ethiopian food here is unpretentious and delicious. You eat with your hands and, if you so wish, you can wash it down with Ethiopian wine. The Abyssinia special, a selection of almost 15 dishes, is well worth trying.

Asian

Ki Mama
Observatoriegatan 13 (33 34 82). T-bana Odenplan/ bus 2, 3, 4, 40, 47, 53. **Open** 11.30am-9pm Mon-Fri; 3-9pm Sat, Sun. **Main courses** 65kr-145kr. **Credit** MC, V. **Map** p245 D5 ㉑

Eat, Drink, Shop

Stockholm's best sushi, hands down. There's a good selection of fish, cut in the regular Swedish size (Swedish sushi tends to be too big to eat in one bite), and reasonable prices. Ki Mama is deservedly popular among locals.

Lao Wai

Luntmakargatan 74 (673 78 00). T-bana Rådmansgatan/bus 2, 4, 42, 52, 72. **Open** 11.30am-2pm, 5.30-10pm Tue-Sat. Closed July-mid Aug, 24 Dec-mid Jan. **Main courses** 85kr-175kr. **Credit** AmEx, DC, MC, V. **Map** p245 D6 ㉒
Stockholm's best vegetarian restaurant is a bit hidden away, but it's worth seeking out. The base is Chinese, but with influences from several other Asian cuisines. Try the Jian Chang tofu (smoked tofu with shiitake mushrooms, sugar peas and fresh spices). At lunchtime, the menu is reduced to just one option.

Lilla Pakistan

St Eriksgatan 66 (30 56 46/www.lillapakistan. com). T-bana St Eriksplan/bus 3, 4, 70, 72, 77. **Open** 5-10pm Tue-Thur; 5-11pm Fri, Sat. **Main courses** 175kr-285kr. **Credit** AmEx, DC, MC, V. **Map** p244 E3 ㉓
Little Pakistan offers authentic Pakistani and northern Indian dishes. Everything is tasty and well prepared, right down to the amuse-bouches. There are a couple of vegetarian options too. The slightly stuffy staff are aware that their restaurant is no ordinary curry house.

Malaysia

Luntmakargatan 98 (673 56 69). T-bana Rådmansgatan/bus 2, 4, 42, 43, 52, 72. **Open** 11am-3pm Mon-Thur; 11am-2pm, 5-11pm Fri, Sat; 5-9pm Sun. Closed 2wks July. **Main courses** 150kr-250kr. **Credit** AmEx, DC, MC, V. **Map** p245 C6 ㉔
This restaurant is an eye-opener. All the exotic ingredients – kelp, tapioca and curry leaves – are prepared with care and served with a friendly smile. It's not cheap, but it's worth the expense. There's an ambitious vegetarian selection too.

Narknoi

Odengatan 94 (30 70 70/www.narknoi.nu). T-bana St Eriksplan/bus 3, 4, 47, 53, 65, 72. **Open** 11am-3pm, 5-11pm Mon-Fri; 4-11pm Sat, Sun. **Main courses** 120kr-195kr. **Set menus** 215kr, 255kr. **Credit** AmEx, DC, MC, V. **Map** p244 D4 ㉕
Unremarkable but reliable Thai restaurant located between Odenplan and St Eriksplan. The menu has all the traditional favourites: green curry, lemongrass dishes, noodles. It may seem conventional, but at least Narknoi knows its stuff.

Zense

Kungstensgatan 9 (20 66 99/www.zense.se). T-bana Rådmansgatan/bus 2, 42, 43, 44, 52. **Open** 11am-1.45pm, 5-10.30pm Mon-Thur; 11am-1.45pm, 5-11.30pm Fri, Sat. **Main courses** 110kr-185kr. **Credit** AmEx, MC, V. **Map** p245 D7 ㉖

New York-style Asian noodles are cooked to perfection at elegant Zense. Try the delicate plum sauce with spring rolls or the zing of shrimp and egg noodle red curry, bathed in coconut milk. The food is fresh, innovative and satisfying, and the desserts are just as outstanding: coconut, lime and mango in soups, cookies or sorbets that melt on the tongue. The minimalist decor lends a certain Zen-like calm, as do the quietly attentive waiters. Open for lunch and for takeaways in the evenings.

Contemporary

Cliff Barnes

Norrtullsgatan 45 (31 80 70/www.cliff.se). T-bana Odenplan/bus 2, 40, 52, 69, 70. **Open** 11am-2pm, 5pm-1am Mon-Fri; 5-11pm Sat; noon-5pm Sun. **Main courses** 140kr-215kr. **Set menu** 280kr. **Credit** AmEx, MC, V. **Map** p244 C4 ㉗
If the cool, sleek side of Stockholm starts to get to you, come here to meet regular Swedes being after-work happy, drinking beer (lots of it) and eating good, well-priced US-inspired food. It's a cocktail-pitcher kind of place, so it gets loud as the night draws on. And yes, it's named after JR's rival in Dallas. *See also p119.*

Dining Club

Gästrikegatan 3 (34 15 15/www.diningclub.se). T-bana St Eriksplan/bus 3, 4, 47, 70, 72. **Open** 5pm-midnight Mon-Thur; 5pm-1am Fri, Sat. **Main courses** 170kr-245kr. **Credit** AmEx, DC, MC, V. **Map** p244 D3 ㉘
A small, likeable restaurant on a side street off Odengatan, Dining Club serves ambitious food at fair prices with great wine recommendations. It's often less crowded than the restaurants on nearby Rörstrandsgatan, and there's also a sleek lounge bar in the basement.

Grill

Drottninggatan 89 (31 45 30/www.grill.se). T-bana Rådmansgatan/bus 40, 47, 52, 65. **Open** 11.30am-1am Mon-Fri; 5pm-1am Sat; 4pm-midnight Sun. **Main courses** 185kr-340kr. **Credit** AmEx, DC, MC, V. **Map** p245 E6 ㉙
Grill is another creation of Melker Andersson, the man behind F12 (*see p101*) and Kungsholmen (*see p113*). With its deliberate jumble of interior styles and its focus on all sorts of grilled meat, it leans towards the crowd-pleasing rather than the innovative end of the spectrum. The meat-heavy food is good if rather expensive, and guests seem to enjoy themselves. Open for lunch, but far better for dinner.

Paus

Rörstrandsgatan 18 (34 44 05/www.restaurang paus.se). T-bana St Eriksplan/bus 3,4, 72, 77. **Open** 5pm-1am Mon-Sat. **Main courses** 220kr-270kr. **Credit** AmEx, DC, MC, V. **Map** p244 D3 ㉚
Paus is one of the best and most dependable restaurants on busy Rörstrandsgatan. It's not as cheap as some of its neighbours, but you get your money's

Eat, Drink, Shop

worth with delicious international cuisine, such as smoked duck with pumpkin or char with prawns and fennel cream. The bar and dining area are quintessentially modern Swedish in appearance: pale walls, white tablecloths and simple wooden chairs.

Rolfs Kök

Tegnérgatan 41 (10 16 96/www.rolfskok.se). T-bana Rådmansgatan/bus 40, 47, 52, 65. **Open** 11am-1am Mon-Fri; 5pm-1am Sat, Sun. Closed July. **Main courses** 155kr-315kr. **Credit** AmEx, DC, MC, V. **Map** p245 E6 **①**

A favourite haunt for lunching business executives, this Stockholm design classic is well worth a visit for both the interesting food and decor. Chairs hang on the grey concrete walls, to be quickly taken down if more diners arrive. Solo eaters are lined up at the long bar overlooking the open kitchen. Enjoy fresh fish with tender meat, as East Asian ideas combine with southern European tricks. The creative somersaults usually succeed, though sometimes aim too high. Even so, a visit to Rolfs Kök is always a treat.

Tranan

Karlbergsvägen 14 (52 72 81 00/www.tranan.se). T-bana Odenplan/bus 2, 4, 40, 69, 72. **Open** 11.30am-1am Mon-Fri; 5pm-1am Sat, Sun. **Main courses** 125kr-280kr. **Credit** AmEx, DC, MC, V. **Map** p245 D5 **②**

Once a working-class pub, Tranan has drastically changed to reach out to the professionals who now inhabit Vasastaden. The transformation has been managed well, and Tranan has become one of the city's new classics – though success has taken a toll on the less-than-impressive service. The *isterband* (lard sausage – much tastier than it sounds) is great, as is the *silltallrik* (herring plate). There's a trendy bar in the basement (*see p121*).

Eastern European

Piastowska

Tegnérgatan 5 (21 25 08). T-bana Rådmansgatan/bus 2, 42, 43, 52. **Open** 11.30am-2pm, 6-11pm Mon-Fri; 6-11pm Sat. **Main courses** 95kr-195kr. **Credit** MC, V. **Map** p245 D7 **③**

Behind a rather heavy door on the otherwise posh Tegnérgatan lies a re-creation of a Polish family restaurant, with lace tablecloths, photos of Polish soldiers on the walls and heavy but well-prepared Polish food. It's not a restaurant for bright summer evenings, but when the snow is falling outside it's just the ticket.

Mediterranean

Le Bistro de Wasahof

Dalagatan 46 (32 34 40/www.wasahof.se). T-bana Odenplan or St Eriksplan/bus 4, 40, 47, 53, 72. **Open** 5pm-1am Mon-Sat. **Main courses** 145kr-240kr. **Set menus** 355kr-395kr. **Credit** AmEx, DC, MC, V. **Map** p244 D4 **④**

This French restaurant acts as a second home to writers, actors, singers and well-dressed wannabes. A bar and bistro, its main contribution to the culinary scene is its seafood – it imports oysters from France and the Swedish west coast. Next door, hipper sibling Musslan (No.46, 34 64 10, www.musslan.nu) serves a younger crowd with the same menu.

Den Gamle och Havet

Tulegatan 27 (661 53 00/www.visomkanmat.se). T-bana Rådmansgatan/bus 2, 4, 42, 53, 72. **Open** 5.30pm-midnight Mon-Sat; 5.30-10pm Sun. **Main courses** 140kr-245kr. **Credit** DC, MC, V. **Map** p245 C6 **⑤**

Created and run by the same family behind Döden i Grytan (*see below*), the name of this excellent Italian means 'the Old Man and the Sea'. Service is personable, and portions are large; a big, steaming bowl of their fish soup (225kr) is particularly wonderful.

Döden i Grytan

Norrtullsgatan 61 (32 50 95/www.dodenigrytan.se). T-bana Odenplan/bus 2, 40, 52, 65. **Open** 5.30pm-midnight Mon-Sat; 5-11pm Sun. **Main courses** 110kr-295kr. **Credit** AmEx, DC, MC, V. **Map** p244 B4 **⑥**

Don't let the strange name (Death in the Pot) or dead-end street location put you off – this is a welcoming neighbourhood Italian with friendly service and great food. The focus is on first-class meat – bistecca Fiorentina, salsiccia in all shapes and sizes, and pasta all'amatriciana – and as with its sister restaurant, Den Gamle och Havet (*see above*), the portions are enormous, so don't even think of attempting the full four-course Italian dinner.

Djurgården

Traditional Swedish

Djurgårdsbrunn

Djurgårdsbrunnsvägen 68 (624 44 00/www.bockholmen.com). Bus 69. **Open** 11.30am-1am daily. Closed Sept-May. **Main courses** 145kr-265kr. **Credit** AmEx, DC, MC, V.

On a warm summer's day it's hard to beat Djurgården, the greenest of Stockholm's inner islands, and at Djurgårdsbrunn you can easily spend hours sitting outside eating, drinking and enjoying the view across the canal. The food and decor make it feel like a lodge in the archipelago or a traditional countryside inn. Either way, it's an easy, pleasant walk from the city centre.

Ulla Winbladh

Rosendalsvägen 8 (663 05 71/www.ullawinbladh.se). Tram 7/bus 44, 47. **Open** 11.30am-10pm Mon; 11.30am-11pm Tue-Fri; noon-11pm Sat; noon-10pm Sun. **Main courses** 135kr-235kr. **Credit** AmEx, DC, MC, V. **Map** p243 H11 **⑦**

Despite its picturesque setting, old-fashioned Ulla Winbladh (named after a much loved friend of Swedish national poet and composer Carl Michael

Native nosh: **Pelikan** is as Swedish as *smör, ost och sill*. *See p109*.

Bellman), does not quite live up to its reputation. The kitchen seems to cut corners a little too often, and the service can sometimes verge on arrogant. The safest bets are the classic meatballs or fried *strömming* (Baltic herring), eaten outdoors in summer or in the cosy dining room in winter.

Södermalm

Contemporary

Bistro Süd
Swedenborgsgatan 8 (640 41 11/www.bistrosud.se). T-bana Mariatorget/bus 4, 43, 55, 66, 74. **Open** 5-11pm Mon, Sun; 5pm-midnight Tue-Thur; 5pm-1am Fri, Sat. **Main courses** 160kr-245kr. **Credit** AmEx, DC, MC, V. **Map** p250 L7 ⏣
This is a friendly neighbourhood place for the Mariatorget crowd of well-to-do journalists and artists. Food is straightforward and usually very good, and it's a pleasant place to have a bite to eat and rub shoulders in the crowded but relaxed bar.

Folkoperan Bar & Kök
Hornsgatan 72 (84 50 92/www.fbk.se). T-bana Mariatorget/bus 4, 43, 55, 66, 74. **Open** 6pm-1am Mon-Sat. **Main courses** 139kr-205kr. **Credit** AmEx, DC, MC, V. **Map** p250 K6 ⏣
This might be the culinary annexe to the city's alternative opera scene (*see p188*), but most of the clientele are not just in for a pre-show drink. The

restaurant is an attraction in its own right – there's a bustling bar downstairs, a cosy lounge with a good menu upstairs and a main dining room, where ambitious modern food is served at reasonable prices. The T-bone steak is a generous piece of meat served with deep-fried new potatoes, while the poached cod with horseradish is a more subtle creation. The bars can get crowded later on.

Ljunggren
Götgatan 36 (640 75 65/www.restaurang ljunggren.se). T-bana Slussen/bus 2, 3, 43, 53, 55, 59. **Open** 11.30am-1am Mon-Fri; noon-1am Sat. **Main courses** 170kr-670kr. **Credit** AmEx, DC, MC, V. **Map** p250 L8 ⏣
If any restaurant epitomises 'new Söder' it's Ljunggren, housed in the chic Bruno shopping arcade on Götgatan. The ad agency clientele, chummy service, lounge music, communal table, open kitchen and pan-Asian menu all make one think of Stureplan seven years ago (or New York 15 years ago).

Rival
Mariatorget 3 (54 57 89 15/www.rival.se). T-bana Mariatorget/bus 4, 43, 55, 66, 74. **Open** noon-midnight Mon-Fri; 5pm-midnight Sat. **Main courses** 180kr-250kr. **Credit** AmEx, DC, MC, V. **Map** p250 K7 ⏣
Benny of Abba fame is the owner of this food and hotel emporium, which has all the components for a complete date under one roof: get dinner, catch a

Lisa Elmqvist. *See p112.*

movie, grab a late-night cocktail and, if you get lucky, go to bed in one of the boutique hotel rooms. However, the quality of the food is a bit up and down. After starting out very ambitiously, the owners seem to have reverted to tried and tested staples. Dishes such as *toast skagen* (shrimp salad on toast) or meatballs are your best bet. For reviews of the cinema and hotel, *see p173* and *p43* respectively.

Roxy

Nytorget 6 (640 96 55/www.roxysofo.se). T-bana Medborgarplatsen/bus 2, 3, 53, 55, 66. **Open** 5pm-midnight Tue-Thur, Sun; 5pm-1am Fri, Sat. **Main courses** 170kr-240kr. **Credit** AmEx, DC, MC, V. **Map** p251 M9 ㊷

Gay and straight Stockholm meets in the stylish, laid-back Roxy. It has a classy bar, a nice lounge and friendly staff. The modern, Mediterranean-influenced food is good and reasonably priced.

Sardin

Skånegatan 79 (644 97 00). Bus 2, 3, 59, 76. **Open** 5pm-midnight Tue-Sat; 5-10.30pm Sun. **Main courses** 95kr-210kr. **Credit** MC, V. **Map** p251 M9 ㊸

With just 18 seats, guests are tightly packed into this tiny restaurant where the walls are decorated with sardine tins. It's a cute and cosy place, serving good-value food and with warmer staff than most Stockholm restaurants.

Mediterranean

Crêperie Fyra Knop

Svartensgatan 4 (640 77 27). T-bana Slussen/bus 2, 3, 43, 55, 59. **Open** 5-11pm daily. **Main courses** 45kr-75kr. **Credit** AmEx, MC, V. **Map** p250 L8 ㊹

If you're French and homesick, or looking for an inexpensive but romantic meal, this could be the place. The decor in the two dark, cosy little rooms is kitsch, complete with old fishing nets and lifebelts. The savoury and sweet crêpes are delicious and cheap enough that you can go for a dance at nearby Mosebacke (*see p169*) afterwards.

Lo Scudetto

Åsögatan 163 (640 42 15/www.loscudetto.se). T-bana Medborgarplatsen/bus 2, 59, 66, 76, 53. **Open** 5pm-midnight Mon-Sat. Closed 4wks from Midsummer. **Main courses** 130kr-235kr. **Credit** AmEx, MC, V. **Map** p251 L9 ㊺

A culinary pioneer at the trendier end of Åsögatan, this local Italian (named after the Italian football league trophy) is not what it seems at first sight. It's rustically styled down, the walls sparsely decorated with portraits of Swedish footballers, and has an adjoining hole-in-the-wall bar with a TV always tuned to the local sports station. But don't expect simple spaghetti here – this is a marvellously subtle Italian kitchen, and the bresaola, ravioli and tiramisú are all prepared with a loving and skilful hand. One of the city's few genuinely top-class Italians. Reservations essential.

Middle Eastern

Matkultur

Erstagatan 21 (642 03 53). Bus 2, 3, 53, 66, 76. **Open** 5pm-midnight Mon-Sat. **Main courses** 130kr-200kr. **Credit** AmEx, DC, MC, V. **Map** p251 L10 ㊻

This crowded and friendly place is proud of its culinary crossover: Turkish and Lebanese specialities with a hint of Sweden. Prices are moderate, and the customers are young and arty. If you still have strength after a filling dinner, it's also close to the bars on Skånegatan.

Traditional Swedish

Eriks Gondolen

Stadsgården 6 (641 70 90/40/www.eriks.se). T-bana Slussen/bus 2, 3, 43, 55, 76. **Open** 11.30am-1am Mon-Fri; 4pm-1am Sat. **Main courses** 245kr-295kr. **Set menu** 650kr. **Credit** AmEx, DC, MC, V. **Map** p250 K8 ㊼

It's hard to imagine a restaurant with a more spectacular view. The bar and restaurant are both suspended over Slussen, underneath the Katarinahissen walkway, with views over Gamla Stan and the water. Enter via the bridge from Mosebacke Torg or take the lift up from the waterfront close to McDonald's. The menu offers both French and Swedish dishes. This is where locals bring their foreign friends or business associates to wow them on their arrival in town. The owner, Erik Lallerstedt, also runs Eriks Bakficka, a popular restaurant down at street level in Östermalm that's terrific for Swedish food surrounded by well-heeled locals (Fredrikshovsgatan 4, 660 15 99).

Pelikan

Blekingegatan 40 (55 60 90 90/www.pelikan.se). T-bana/bus 3, 55, 59, 74. **Open** 11.30am-1am Mon-Fri; 5pm-1am Sat, Sun. **Main courses** 145kr-190kr. **Credit** AmEx, MC, V. **Map** p251 M8 ㊽

Not many restaurants feel as genuinely Swedish as this beer hall in Södermalm. Its elegant painted ceilings and wood-panelled walls haven't changed since the days before Söder became trendy, back when restaurants served only *husmanskost*. Classics on offer here include *pytt i panna*, SOS (*smör, ost och sill* – butter, cheese and herring), and meatballs with lingonberries and pickled cucumber. Check dishes listed on the blackboard to find the real bargains (under 100kr), such as knuckle of pork with root vegetable mash, or fried salted herring with onion sauce. Ice-cold schnapps is compulsory. *Photo p107.*

Vegetarian

Chutney

Katarina Bangata 19 (640 30 10/www.chutney.se). T-bana Medborgarplatsen/bus 55, 59, 66. **Open** 11am-10pm Mon-Fri; noon-10pm Sat, Sun. **Main courses** 80kr-135kr. **Credit** MC, V. **Map** p251 M8 ㊾

Eat, Drink, Shop

A favourite with the alternative crowd, complete with environmentally conscious art on the walls and vegan food on the plates. The service is friendly, the portions huge and the prices decent. Good for lunch or early dinner after doing the SoFo shopping rounds, with tables outside for people-watching.

Östermalm & Gärdet

Asian

Sabai-Soong

Linnégatan 39B (663 12 77/www.sabai.se). T-bana Östermalmstorg/bus 1, 44, 55, 56, 62. **Open** 11am-10pm Mon; 11am-11pm Tue-Thur; 11am-midnight Fri; 4pm-midnight Sat; 3-10pm Sun. **Main courses** 115kr-210kr. **Credit** AmEx, DC, MC, V. **Map** p246 E9 ⑤⓪

The Thai food at Sabai-Soong is well prepared, diverse, and good value for money, the latter a rare commodity in this upmarket neighbourhood. The children's menu and modest prices explain the abundance of families and young people who keep this place busy most nights. Staff are brisk and efficient, and no one waits long for their food.
Other locations Kammakargatan 44, Norrmalm (790 09 13).

Contemporary

Babs Kök och Bar

Birger Jarlsgatan 37 (23 61 01/www.babsbar.se). T-bana Östermalmstorg/bus 1, 2, 55, 56. **Open** 5pm-midnight Tue, Wed; 5pm-1am Thur-Sat. Closed July. **Main courses** 165kr-185kr. **Credit** AmEx, DC, MC, V. **Map** p245 E7 ⑤①

You have to walk through the foyer of art-house cinema Zita (*see p173*) to find this down-to-earth bar and restaurant. Have a drink, eat a simple dish from the open kitchen, or sip a coffee before the film starts. It's one of the few places around Stureplan where it's possible to eat without ending up broke, and there's everything from steak to monkfish on the menu.

Elverket

Linnégatan 69 (661 25 62/www.restaurang elverket.se). T-bana Karlaplan/bus 42, 44, 56. **Open** 11am-midnight Mon-Thur; 11am-1am Fri, Sat; 11am-4pm Sun. **Main courses** 175kr-270kr. **Brunch** 200kr. **Credit** AmEx, DC, MC, V. **Map** p242 F10 ⑤②

This busy bar-restaurant is in an old electricity plant, together with the more experimental stage of the Dramaten theatre (*see p197*). The food is modern crossover and moderately priced, with a pre-theatre menu and a selection of tapas. It's closed for several weeks during the summer, when the owners retreat to the island of Gotland to run their restaurant there.

PA & Co

Riddargatan 8 (611 08 45). T-bana Östermalmstorg/bus 2, 47, 55, 62, 65. **Open** 5pm-midnight daily. **Main courses** 95kr-250kr. **Credit** AmEx, DC, MC, V. **Map** p241 F8 ⑤③

This restaurant has long been a favourite hangout for Stockholmers. And no wonder. The food – Swedish classic and international fare – is superb, and the service splendid: swift and friendly but with personality. Tables fill up fast so you can have a hard time getting in, but waiting at the bar is pleasant too. Serves one of the city's best burgers, and is particularly good for Saturday brunch.

Riche

Birger Jarlsgatan 4 (54 50 35 60/www.riche.se). T-bana Östermalmstorg/bus 2, 47, 55, 62, 65. **Open** 11.30am-1am Mon, Tue; 11.30am-2am Wed-Fri; noon-2am Sat. **Main courses** 100kr-325kr. **Credit** AmEx, DC, MC, V. **Map** p241 F8 ⑤④

Riche is one of the most popular places in town for an afterwork drink, but the menu – a fairly ambitious mix of traditional Swedish dishes with international classics – doesn't always succeed. For a more intimate and reliable experience, you may want to opt for adjacent Teatergrillen (Nybrogatan 3, 54 50 36 65), for some classic French cuisine.

Undici

Sturegatan 22 (661 66 17/www.undici.org). T-bana Östermalmstorg/bus 1, 2, 42, 55, 56. **Open** 6pm-1am Tue-Thur; 4pm-3am Fri; 6pm-3am Sat. Closed July-mid Aug. **Main courses** 155kr-295kr. **Set menu** 695kr. **Credit** AmEx, DC, MC, V. **Map** p246 E8 ⑤⑤

Owner Tomas Brolin grew up in northern Sweden and played football professionally in northern Italy, so Undici is a tribute to both regions. The space is neutral, but the menu is welcoming as Swedish classics mingle with Italian dishes and truly luxurious creations like roasted fillet of venison with artichoke, gnocchi di potata and truffle stock. A lounge and bar keep things hopping until the early hours of the morning.

Middle Eastern

Halv Grek plus Turk

Jungfrugatan 30 (665 94 22/www.halvgrekplus turk.com). T-bana Stadion/bus 1, 42, 44, 56, 62. **Open** 5.30pm-midnight Mon-Sat; 5.30-11pm Sun. **Meze** 50kr-95kr each. **Credit** AmEx, DC, MC, V. **Map** p246 E9 ⑤⑥

Slightly off the beaten track and with an entrance marked by an easy-to-miss sign, it's worth the extra effort to find this gem of a restaurant. Born of a friendship between Greek and Turkish restaurateurs, the decor at Halv Grek plus Turk is modern Middle Eastern, accented with elegant lounge sofas, bright colours and soft lighting. The clientele is a mixed urban set and the menu features small meze dishes, and an assortment of cold and hot dishes. Aside from the traditional classics (houmous, meatballs, baba ganoush), you'll find inspired dishes such as chicken liver terrine with metaxa. The spicy chicken wings are a delight, as are the 'Manti' dumplings (yoghurt and spiced lamb). Service is attentive, friendly and efficient.

Northern delights

Fish

Herring – called **sill** on the west coast and **strömming** in Stockholm – used to be the staple food of the Swedish diet. Today, this little fish is still much loved and always on the menu, in the cheapest lunch restaurant and the poshest luxury establishment. For lunch it's often blackened (*sotare*) and served with mashed potatoes, melted butter and perhaps lingonberry sauce. Don't be put off by the sweet lingonberries: all the savoury traditional foods are served with sweet preserves and sauces – and it tastes great.

Inlagd strömming (pickled herring) is prepared in almost as many different ways as there are Swedes. If you manage to find a traditional Swedish *smörgåsbord* (available in every single restaurant around Christmas), this is what you should start with, before moving on to the meats. A plate of pickled herring and fresh new potatoes with special soured cream (*gräddfil*) will make any Swede foggy-eyed, while **gravad strömming** (pickled herring cured with a mustard sauce) is indispensable for celebrating Midsummer. Served, of course, with some beer and aquavit, a strong liqueur distilled from potato or grain mash and flavoured with caraway seeds (*kalled snaps*).

Red **kråftor** (crayfish) are eaten everywhere when the season starts in August, when there are crayfish parties galore (preferably outside

under a full moon). Cooked with huge amounts of dill, they're an unmissable special treat.

Lax (salmon) needs no introduction: just remember that **gravlax** means cured with sugar and salt, not to be confused with the smoked variety. Fish from inland lakes and the Baltic are relatively rare, the most delicious being the **gös** (pike-perch). However, plenty of fish from the west coast lands on the plates of Stockholm's restaurants, and **torsk** (cod), although more and more scarce, is a vital part of Swedish culinary tradition and is served in many different ways. The most interesting is **lutfisk**, which is only served around Christmas. The cod is salted and air-dried, then soaked in lye, which transforms it into something that looks and tastes nothing like fish. It's served with peas, butter and a béchamel sauce.

Meat

Swedish **köttbullar** (meatballs) are, of course, a speciality, immortalised not least by the Swedish chef in *The Muppet Show*. They're eaten with pickled cucumber, a cream sauce and lingonberries.

Pytt i panna is regularly found in most restaurants: it consists of diced and fried meat and potatoes, adorned with a fried egg and pickled beetroots. **Rimmad oxbringa** (lightly salted brisket of beef) is beautifully tender. Anything with '*rimmad*' attached to it means that it is first salted and then boiled.

Kåldolmar (stuffed cabbage rolls) are made Swedish by wrapping cabbage leaves rather than vine leaves around minced pork. The concept was introduced when King Karl XII was stranded in Turkey after attempting, and failing, to invade Russia in 1708.

Game, such as **älg** (elk) and **rådjur** (roe deer), are popular in the autumn. They are mainly roasted and served with potatoes, lingonberries and a cream sauce.

Schnapps

Stockholmers use every possible excuse to drink a glass or more of *brännvin* (schnapps). It comes in many varieties, highly flavoured with native herbs and spices such as caraway, aniseed, coriander and fennel. The traditional way to drink *brännvin* is to fill the first glass to the brim, the second only halfway. Before downing the glasses, it's customary to sing a *snapsvisa* ('schnapps ditty').

Eat, Drink, Shop

Mediterranean

Divino

*Karlavägen 28 (611 02 69/611 12 04/www.divino.se).
Bus 1, 42, 44, 55, 56.* **Open** 6-11pm Mon-Sat. Closed
July. **Main courses** 275kr-295kr. **Set menu** 625kr.
Credit AmEx, DC, MC, V. **Map** p245 D7 ⓗ

Considered by many to be Stockholm's best Italian
restaurant, this is certainly one of its most elegant
and priciest, and the food usually lives up to the heav-
enly name. Try the olive-fried back of lamb with garlic cream, followed by panna cotta with rhubarb jelly.

Sturehof

*Stureplan 2 (440 57 30/www.sturehof.com). T-bana
Östermalmstorg/bus 1, 2, 55, 56.* **Open** 9am-2am
Mon-Fri; noon-2am Sat; 1pm-2am Sun. **Main
courses** 140kr-395kr. **Credit** AmEx, DC, MC, V.
Map p241 F8 ⓘ

Long opening hours make it possible to get a meal
in this classic Stockholm brasserie at almost any
time of day, a rare thing in this town. The massive
dining room is elegant, with white linen tablecloths,
uniformed waiters and nicely designed furniture, but
the atmosphere stays lively and cheerful. Service is
attentive, and the menu follows classic French bistro
tradition, with seafood and shellfish a speciality.
Among the starters are a few Swedish classics such
as smoked Baltic herring and *toast skagen*. After dinner, step into the lively O-baren *(see p124).*

Traditional Swedish

Lisa Elmqvist

*Östermalms Saluhall (55 34 04 00/www.lisaelmqvist.
se). T-bana Östermalmstorg/bus 56, 62.* **Open**
9.30am-6pm Mon-Thur; 9.30am-6.30pm Fri;
9.30am-4pm Sat. **Main courses** 125kr-289kr.
Credit AmEx, DC, MC, V. **Map** p242 F9 ⓙ

Lisa Elmqvist is one of three sister restaurants. The
main one, located inside the fabulous red-brick
indoor food market Östermalms Saluhall, is a perfect
place to sit and enjoy classic Swedish fish dishes
surrounded by the bustle of the market shoppers.
Outside on Östermalmstorg is an outdoor café, Lisa
på Torget, while over on Djurgården is a waterside
restaurant, Lisa på Udden (Biskopsvägen 7, 660 94
75, www.lisapaudden.se). *Photo p108.*

Prinsen

*Mäster Samuelsgatan 4 (611 13 31/www.restaurang
prinsen.se). T-bana Östermalmstorg/bus 2, 55, 56,
62, 69.* **Open** 11.30am-11.30pm Mon-Fri; 1-11.30pm
Sat; 5-10.30pm Sun. **Main courses** 175kr-295kr.
Credit AmEx, DC, MC, V. **Map** p241 F8 ⓚ

Artworks, many of them said to be payment to settle bills, crowd the walls of this legendary writers'
haunt. 'The Prince' can be relied upon to offer atmosphere and an excellent range of classic Swedish *husmanskost*. The herring platter and *biff rydberg* (beef
with fried potatoes and egg) are classics. When the
weather allows, try to bag one of the tables outside.

Villa Källhagen

*Djurgårdsbrunnsvägen 10 (665 03 10/www.
kallhagen.se). Bus 69.* **Open** 11.30am-2pm, 5-11pm
Mon-Fri; noon-11pm Sat; noon-5pm Sun. **Main
courses** 135kr-305kr. **Brunch** 210kr. **Set
menu** 595kr. **Credit** AmEx, DC, MC, V.
Map p243 G13 ⓛ

A dining experience of the first order is to be had
here, where typical Swedish dishes, with a European
twist, are transformed into works of art. In summer,
you can sit outdoors to eat and then stroll along the
water. In autumn and winter there's a fire blazing in
the hearth. The popular blends Asian treats
with a typical Swedish *smörgåsbord*. The restaurant
closes in July but the bistro is open.

Kungsholmen

Asian

Hong Kong

*Kungsbro Strand 23 (653 77 20/www.hongkong.
lunchinfo.com). T-bana Rådhuset/bus 1, 40, 59.*
Open 11am-10pm Mon-Fri; 1-10pm Sat, Sun.

Main courses 110kr-395kr. **Credit** AmEx, DC, MC, V. **Map** p240 G5 ⑫

This is one of only a few places in Stockholm serving authentic Chinese food. The owner, Sonny Li, delivers spicy Cantonese and Sichuanese dishes from the giant gas stove. Apart from the stir-fry dishes, there's an ambitious array of steam-cooked choices. The speciality is Peking duck – Chinese business folk (and the King no less) all come here for the red-glazed bird, which must be ordered two days in advance.

Roppongi

Hantverkargatan 76 (650 17 72/www.roppongi.se). T-bana Fridhemsplan/bus 3, 4, 40, 52, 62. **Open** 11am-10pm Mon-Fri; noon-10pm Sat; 1-9pm Sun. **Main courses** 145kr-220kr. **Credit** AmEx, DC, MC, V. **Map** p239 G2 ⑬

Roppongi serves the best sushi in this part of town, plus decent tempura and *gyoza* (pockets of fried dough stuffed with minced pork or shrimp), among other things. It's always crowded, especially the few tables that appear outside in the summer. You can always order takeaway sushi and walk down to the water at nearby Rålambshovsparken.

Prinsen.

Contemporary

Allmänna Galleriet 925

Kronobergsgatan 37 (41 06 81 00/www.ag925.se). T-bana Fridhemsplan/bus 1, 3, 4, 57, 77. **Open** 5pm-1am Tue-Sat. Closed mid June-mid Aug. **Main courses** 145kr-230kr. **Credit** AmEx, DC, MC, V. **Map** p239 F3 ⑭

Part of the charm of this restaurant/bar/lounge housed in a former silver workshop is the fun of finding the place. It's down a dull side street, through an unmarked door next to a sex shop and up two flights of stairs. Inside, the industrial setting feels more like a New York loft, with its white-tile walls often adorned with temporary art exhibitions, and it attracts a fashionable young crowd. The braised lamb leg with yellow beetroot and the fish stew are outstanding. Well worth seeking out. *Photo p114.*

Kungsholmen

Norr Mälarstrand, Kajplats 464 (50 52 44 50/www.kungsholmen.com). T-bana Rådhuset/bus 3, 40, 52, 62. **Open** 5pm-1am Mon-Wed, Sun; 5pm-2am Thur-Sat. **Main courses** 175kr-325kr. **Credit** AmEx, DC, MC, V. **Map** p240 H4 ⑮

One of the newer stars on the restaurant scene is this ultra-fashionable spot which takes its name from its island location. Even though it's a huge place, it's frequently packed and reservations are necessary. A sibling to F12 (*see p101*) and Grill (*see p105*), it's funkily decorated and also takes an unconventional approach to courses. The menu is built around six different bars – sushi bar, salad bar, bread bar, bistro bar, grill bar and ice cream bar. While this is good fun for diners, it means your dishes don't always arrive at the same time. Staff also struggle to cope with the number of diners. However the cocktails are first class, and in the summertime they open the bar on a floating pontoon in front of the restaurant.

Salzer

John Ericssonsgatan 6 (650 30 28/www.salzer.nu). T-bana Rådhuset/bus 3, 40, 52, 62. **Open** 5pm-1am Mon-Sat. **Main courses** 110kr-230kr. **Credit** AmEx, DC, MC, V. **Map** p240 H3 ⑯

Salzer's calm atmosphere makes the buzz of the city seem far away. Swedish dishes are mixed with French and Italian inspiration in traditional offerings like *isterband* (lard sausage), sole and fillet of lamb. The restaurant is housed in one of Stockholm's most beautiful functionalist houses and few places offer such a pleasing combination of good Swedish cosiness and good Swedish style.

Spisa Hos Helena

Scheelegatan 18 (654 49 26/654 50 26/www.spisa hoshelena.se). T-bana Rådhuset/bus 1, 3, 40, 52, 62. **Open** 11am-midnight Mon-Fri; 3pm-midnight Sat; 3-11pm Sun. Closed July. **Main courses** 175kr-230kr. **Credit** AmEx, DC, MC, V. **Map** p240 G4 ⑰

A home from home for many locals, serving straightforward, delicious modern European cuisine. The sesame-grilled tuna is lovely, but if you fancy some-

Eat, Drink, Shop

**Allmänna Galleriet
925.** *See p113.*

thing more basic, there's always a club sandwich or salad on the menu. Main courses are all less than 200kr, and the red walls make this as cosy and welcoming a place as you're likely to find.

Stockholm Taste

Wargentinsgatan 3 (654 56 10). T-bana Rådhuset/bus 1, 40, 52, 56. **Open** 11am-8pm Mon-Thur; 11am-6pm Fri. **Main courses** 55kr-70kr. **No credit cards. Map** p240 G4 ❻❽

This stylish soup café is one of the best-kept secrets on Kungsholmen. The soups are often exotic, using Indian or Asian spices and ingredients, and the fresh bread is delicious. Get here early for one of the few tables or a seat at the counter.

French

Absinth

Fleminggatan 62 (651 99 01/www.absinth.se). T-bana Fridhemsplan/bus 1, 3, 4, 57, 77. **Open** 11am-2pm, 5.30-10pm Mon; 11am-2pm, 5.30-11pm Tue-Fri; 5.30pm-midnight Sat; 3-9pm Sun. **Credit** AmEx, MC, V. **Map** p239 F2 ❻❾

This is a bistro serving classic French dishes: steak frites, moules frites, chèvre chaud, escargots. But what you don't expect is just how pleasant it all is. There aren't many good places to eat in this corner of Kungsholmen, which makes Absinth all the more enjoyable. Small, busy and well staffed, it's just what you want a small neighbourhood restaurant to be.

Middle Eastern

Tabbouli

Norra Agnegatan 39 (650 25 00/www.tabbouli. lunchinfo.com). T-bana Rådhuset/bus 1, 3, 40, 52, 62. **Open** 5-10pm Mon-Thur; 5pm-midnight Fri, Sat. **Main courses** 145kr-189kr. **Set menus** 235kr, 295kr. **Credit** AmEx, DC, MC, V. **Map** p240 G4 ❼⓿

The low tables in the cosy Tabbouli's labyrinthine dining area ensure that at least part of your meze lands in your lap, but the food is so good you won't mind picking up the crumbs. Aside from an expertly prepared meze buffet, the lamb dishes are notably good (the secret, the owner says, is marinating the meat in oil for two days).

Further afield

Contemporary

Edsbacka Krog

*Sollentunavägen 220, Sollentuna (96 33 00/www.
edsbackakrog.se). Commuter train to Sollentuna
Centrum then bus 525, 607, 627 to Edsbacka.* **Open**
5.30pm-midnight Mon-Fri; 2pm-midnight Sat. Closed
July. **Main courses** 370kr-420kr. **Set meals** 750kr-
1,200kr. **Credit** AmEx, DC, MC, V.

The easiest way to get here is by taxi, and it's a small
price to pay for the chance of food this good. The
menu is French-meets-Swedish and follows the seasons. The interior, surroundings and service are all
exquisite. Edsbacka Krog is the only restaurant in
Sweden with two Michelin stars.

Traditional Swedish

Fjäderholmarnas Krog

*Stora Fjäderholmen (718 33 55/www.
fjaderholmaskrog.se). Ferry from Nybroplan*
or Slussen. **Open** 11.30am-midnight Mon-Fri; noon-
midnight Sat; noon-11pm Sun. **Main courses**
195kr-335kr. **Set menus** 425kr-695kr. **Credit**
AmEx, DC, MC, V.

If you want the archipelago experience without taking a two-hour ferry then this island is the place to
come, just 25 minutes from the city by boat. Try for
a table outside on the wooden deck, where you can
sit and watch the boats go by, and order some of the
excellent fish dishes. Booking advisable.

Lux

*Primusgatan 116, Lilla Essingen (619 01 90/
www.luxstockholm.se). Bus 1, 57.* **Open** 11am-2pm,
5-11pm Tue-Fri; 5-11pm Sat. **Main courses** 315kr-
340kr. **Credit** AmEx, DC, MC, V.

On the small island of Lilla Essingen, close to
Kungsholmen, is one of the city's best restaurants.
Lux has magnificent views over the water with outdoor dining in the summer. The kitchen serves high-
quality Swedish food – such as fillet of venison with
spiced sausage, beetroot and pickled chanterelles –
without making a fuss about it. A sister shop in the
next street sells outstanding bread, pastries, chocolates and ready-made desserts.

Bars

Plenty of cracking krogar, as long as you've got enough kroner.

The land of socialism and equality? Far from it. When it comes to nightlife, Stockholm is famous for its trendy bars, membership cards, VIP rooms, long queues and fickle bouncers. But don't let the occasional 'regulars only' put you off. The city has plenty of variety and most places are accessible if you know when to arrive, what to wear and how to behave.

Nearly all the doormen likely to test your patience work at the bars and clubs around **Stureplan**, in the heart of the financial district. Although some locals may shun this area as a playground for bankers and local celebrities, it is still unchallenged as the number one party spot in Stockholm.

The most popular venues around Stureplan are recognisable by their sleek, MTV-inspired interiors. As mentioned, doormen are fussy, often rejecting would-be patrons solely on appearance while lifting the velvet ropes for TV celebrities, regulars and attractive young women. To avoid the hassle, dress fashionably and arrive before the crowds start building up at around 10pm.

If you like to sip your drinks in more down to earth places, the former workers' district of **Södermalm** (aka Söder) may be the place for you. Here attitudes are less superficial and doormen are friendlier.

Watering holes around **Vasastaden**, **Kungsholmen** and **Gamla Stan** are generally less happening at weekends – although we have listed many notable exceptions.

Live music venues and dance clubs have a place in Stockholm's nightlife, but they don't occupy centre stage. Instead, the scene is largely based around the *krog* – essentially a bar-cum-restaurant. (An explanation for this is that any establishment that serves alcohol must, by law, also serve food.) The popular *krogar* often take on club elements, with DJs, bouncers at the door and late-night dancing on whatever floor space is available. In fact, many of Stockholm's best bars also house its best clubs (*see pp167-169* **Clubs**). Opening hours can vary greatly, though most bars stay open on Friday and Saturday nights until either 1am or 3am. A small number of places around Stureplan shut at 5am, which is the latest closing time allowed by law.

While happy to queue for 30 minutes to get into a popular *krog*, most Stockholm twentysomethings, in their desperation to be seen in only the hippest bar, shun their second-rate counterparts (dubbed *b-krogar*), unwilling to stop in even for a single beer. These venues are recognised by their lack of attention to detail, cheap beer, pool tables and jukeboxes. Generally, the clientele is either too young to get into the trendier bars (18 to 20 or younger) or too old to want to (35 and up).

Stiff taxes make alcohol expensive in Sweden. A large glass of beer generally sets you back between 35kr and 50kr and cocktails start at around 80kr. To counterbalance this, a typical Stockholmer's weekend will start with a few drinks with friends at home. This tradition, called *värma* ('warming'), is particularly common among students. As a result, the bars don't begin to fill until around 9.30pm to 11pm.

Despite the relatively high prices, the selection of beer on offer is pretty lacklustre. Most Swedes are content to order a *stor stark* ('large strong'), which invariably results in a large glass of bland local lager, such as Pripps, Spendrups or Falcon. If your favourite beer is not on tap, ask for it in a bottle. Mixed drinks have enjoyed increased popularity recently, prompting bartenders to expand their repertoire.

The best Bars

For cheap(ish) beer
Dovas. *See p125.*

For a cold one
Icebar. *See p119.*

For guest-list glam
Riche. *See p125.*

For a heavy metal hangover
Medusa. *See p118.*

For killer views
Gondolen. *See p121.*

❶ Pink numbers in this chapter correspond to the location of each bar as marked on the street maps. *See pp238-251.*

Although the drinking age in Sweden is 18, bars are free to set higher limits and 20 or 23 is not unusual. We've mentioned age restriction only when it's 20 or over.

Sweden introduced a ban on smoking in 2005 and rules are strictly enforced. A few venues sport small, unfurnished smoking rooms, but the practice is less common than was expected before the law went into effect. Generally most Stockholmers have welcomed the smoking ban.

A particular quirk of Stockholm nightlife is the ubiquitous cloakrooms manned by authoritarian attendants who, it seems, will stop at nothing to get you to hand over your coat. Although the 10kr to 15kr fee is an annoying extra to the evening's expenses, it will at least prevent your jacket from being stolen. Huge, dripping winter coats are to blame for this mildly mercenary culture.

Baby, it's cold inside: the **Icebar** is kept at a positively chilly -4°C. *See p119.*

Eat, Drink, Shop

Gamla Stan

In the Old Town, most of the bars are situated around **Kornhamnstorg** or **Järntorget**. If you're a jazz fan, try the bar at **Stampen Jazzpub** (*see p183*), which is pretty lively.

Engelen

Kornhamnstorg 59 (50 55 60 90/www.wallmans. com). T-bana Gamla Stan/bus 3, 53, 55, 59, 76. **Open** *Bar* 4pm-3am Mon-Sat; 5pm-3am Sun. *Food served* until 11pm daily. **Minimum age** 23. **Admission** (after 8pm) 50kr Mon-Thur, Sun; 80kr Fri, Sat. **Credit** AmEx, DC, MC, V. **Map** p241 J8 ❶
Posing as a rustic tavern (both bar and restaurant), Engelen caters firmly to groups of passing tourists and middle-aged locals looking to get down and party. The main room has a stage where Sweden's top covers bands play familiar tunes from 8.30pm to midnight most days. When that's finished, guests move down to the vaulted nightclub in the 15th-century cellar, where Top 40 tracks are mixed with a selection of popular classics.

Flyt

Kajplats Kornhamnstorg (21 37 29/www.flyt.se). T-bana Gamla Stan/bus 3, 53. **Open** *Apr-Sept* 3pm-1am Mon-Thur; noon-1am Fri, Sat; noon-midnight Sun. *Food served* until 11pm Mon-Sat; 10pm Sun. **Minimum age** 23. **Credit** MC, V. **Map** p241 J8 ❷
See p120 **All aboard**.

Medusa

Kornhamnstorg 61 (21 87 00/www.medusabar.com). T-bana Gamla Stan/bus 3, 53, 55, 59, 76. **Open** *Bar* 2pm-3am daily. *Food served* until midnight daily. **Minimum age** 21. **Admission** (after 11pm) 60kr. **Credit** AmEx, MC, V. **Map** p241 J8 ❸
A small bar with a cavernous basement, Medusa is Gamla Stan's heavy-metal hangout. The upstairs bar plays basic rock music to a mixed crowd of tourists and local headbangers. Downstairs in the catacombs, the music is louder and harder. A small bar serves beer to guests whooping it up on the two tiny dancefloors. Mind your head.

Norrmalm

Café Opera

Operahuset, Karl XIIs Torg (676 58 07/www. cafeopera.se). T-bana Kungsträdgården/bus 2, 55, 59, 62, 76. **Open** *Bar* 6pm-3am daily. *Food served* until 2.30am daily. **Minimum age** 23. **Admission** (after 10pm) 140kr. **Credit** AmEx, DC, MC, V. **Map** p241 G7 ❹
In the back of the Stockholm Opera House, Café Opera is one of the most elegant and exclusive venues in town. A restaurant by day, in the evening it's an extravagant party bar with a big dancefloor. The interior is a luxurious mix of Scandinavian chic and remodelled baroque. The crowd ranges from twentysomething trend-followers to scantily clad women and older men in suits.

Sparkling cocktails and conversation at party favourite **Cliff Barnes**.

F12 Terrassen

Fredsgatan 12 (411 73 48/www.fredsgatan12.com).
T-bana Kungsträdgården/bus 3, 53, 62, 65.
Open *May-Aug* 9pm-3am Mon-Sat. Closed Sept-
Apr. **Minimum age** 20. **Credit** AmEx, DC, MC, V.
Map p241 H7 **❺**
In the historic Royal Academy of Arts building,
trendy F12 is best known for its outside terrace,
open during summer only. Hip types groove to the
music and take in the great views towards Gamla
Stan and the Riksdag. The restaurant inside is
equally stylish.

Icebar

Nordic Sea Hotel, Vasaplan 4 (50 56 31 24/www.
nordichotels.se). T-bana T-Centralen/bus 1, 47, 53,
59, 69. **Open** 3pm-midnight Mon-Sat; 3-9pm Sun.
Admission 160kr incl 1 vodka drink. **Credit**
AmEx, DC, MC, V. **Map** p241 G6 **❻**
You can be as cool as you like about this slightly
gimmicky attraction, designed by the people behind
the Icehotel in Jukkasjärvi in the far north of Sweden,
but the minute you don your silver high-tech pon-
cho and sip from your ice glass, you'll be giggling
and snapping photos with the rest of them. This tiny
sub-zero bar, maintained at a chilly -4°C (23°F), is in
a corner of the Nordic Sea Hotel (*see p39*) in
Norrmalm. With 20 minutes of chilling usually
enough for most, the turnover is high, and the
chances for socialising therefore slim. Loud music
and fine Absolut shooters (one included in the steep
entrance fee) keep spirits high. The bar's maximum
occupancy is 30. If you are part of a large group it's
wise to book in advance. *Photo p117.*

Karlsson & Co

Kungsgatan 56 (54 51 21 40/www.karlsson-co.
com). T-bana Hötorget/bus 1, 47, 52, 53, 56.
Open *Bar* 11am-3am Mon-Fri; noon-3am Sat.
Food served until 11.30pm Mon-Sat. **Minimum**
age 27. **Admission** (after 9pm) 90kr Wed, Fri,
Sat; 40kr Thur. **Credit** AmEx, DC, MC, V.
Map p241 F6 **❼**
Next door to Kicki's (*see below*), this bar and restaurant caters mainly to a crowd of older partygoers
and tourists. Faux mooseheads and nostalgic
American signs adorn the walls, and the usual
drinks are served up from three bars. Karlsson also
has a large dancefloor, blackjack and roulette tables,
and five slot machines.

Kicki's

Kungsgatan 54 (10 00 26/www.kickis.nu). T-bana
Hötorget/bus 1, 47, 52, 53, 56. **Open** *Bar* 10am-3am
Mon-Fri; 11am-3am Sat; noon-3am Sun. *Food served*
until 9.30pm daily. **Minimum age** women 18,
men 20. **Admission** (after 9pm) 60kr Fri, Sat.
Credit AmEx, DC, MC, V. **Map** p241 F6 **❽**
Local partygoers mix with tourists at this camp
dive-bar next to the pedestrian shopping street
Drottninggatan. Karaoke is on offer every night
(9.30pm-1.30am) except Mondays, Thursdays and
Sundays, when covers bands and 'model competi-
tions' are held. Other activities include soft-core male

strip acts and foam parties. Kicki's utterly unimpressive interior has three bars, two cramped dancefloors, a blackjack table and dozens of tacky framed
posters. Good fun… if you're under 25.

Vasastaden

Nightlife in Vasastaden is quite spread out,
with most of the bars on **Rörstrandsgatan**
or within a few blocks of the busy intersection
of **Odengatan** and **Sveavägan**.

Bagpipers Inn

Rörstrandsgatan 21 (31 18 55). T-bana St Eriksplan/
bus 3, 4, 42, 72. **Open** *Bar* 4pm-midnight Mon; 4pm-
1am Tue-Thur; 3pm-1am Fri; 2pm-1am Sat; 2-11pm
Sun. *Food served* until 10pm Mon, Sun; until 11pm
Tue-Sat. **Minimum age** 23. **Credit** AmEx, MC, V.
Map p244 D2 **❾**
The bartenders wear kilts at this Scottish-themed
pub decorated with dark wood, green walls and
knick-knacks from the Highlands. The beer is not
cheap (46kr-49kr for a pint), but there's a decent
selection of around a dozen brews on tap, many from
the UK and Ireland. The crowd consists mainly of
thirtysomethings and out-of-towners drawn by the
cosy atmosphere. The Bagpipers Inn is usually
packed at the weekends.

Cliff Barnes

Norrtullsgatan 45 (31 80 70/www.cliff.se). T-bana
Odenplan/bus 2, 40, 52, 69. **Open** *Bar* 11am-1am
Mon-Fri; 5pm-1am Sat; noon-5pm Sun. *Food served*
until 11pm Mon-Sat; until 4pm Sun. **Minimum age**
23. **Credit** AmEx, MC, V. **Map** p244 C4 **❿**
On the outskirts of Vasastaden, in what was once a
home for widows, Cliff Barnes is a down-to-earth
party bar/restaurant. The worn wooden floors, high
ceilings and large vaulted windows make it ideal for
enthusiastic beer drinking and loud conversation.
At 11pm on Fridays and Saturdays the lights are
turned down and the music (popular classics from
the 1960s and '70s) is turned up. Although several
large signs clearly forbid it, dancing on the tables is
not uncommon. Cliff Barnes takes its name from JR's
unlucky arch rival in Dallas, and a framed portrait
of Ken Kercheval (the actor who portrayed Barnes)
decorates the bar's main wall.

La Habana

Sveavägen 108 (16 64 65/www.lahabana.se). T-bana
Rådmansgatan/bus 2, 42, 52, 53. **Open** *Bar* 5pm-
1am daily. *Food served* until 10pm Mon-Wed, Sun;
until 10.30pm Thur-Sat. **Minimum age** 20. **Credit**
AmEx, DC, MC, V. **Map** p245 D6 **⓫**
As one of few Cuban bars in Stockholm, La Habana
makes a refreshing alternative to the otherwise
largely mainstream places in the area. The interior
is all dark wood and white walls, but the crowd, the
drinks and the music are much more colourful as
Latin Americans and Swedes meet and mix. The
small basement bar serves up great mojitos, and the
floor comes alive with salsa dancing later on.

Eat, Drink, Shop

All aboard

Eat, Drink, Shop

Be it a boat or a pontoon, Stockholm offers a plethora of bars on the water.

Flyt (*see p118*), located near the Slussen locks at the edge of Gamla Stan, is often packed to the gills in summer. The restaurant-bar is made to look like an old steamboat, but is in fact nothing more than a decked out pontoon. Ironically the old Flyt – meaning 'Float' – sank during a hurricane in January 2005 and has since been replaced. Flyt caters mainly to tourists and locals who drop by for a few drinks on their way elsewhere. Hang out and watch as boats gather waiting for the locks to open.

Mälarpaviljongen (*see p125*) was once a simple summer restaurant along Norrmalm's promenade, but has recently branched out with a vast pontoon with a walk-around bar.

The designer furniture, elevated sofa deck, flowers and olive trees bring together the best Scandinavian design has to offer. It's Miami Stockholm-style with heated floors to boot. The view of Riddarfjärden is great. On the downside drinks are steep, starting at 125kr.

M/S Gerda (*see p125*), located near the Preem gas station, was once the US barge 'Missouri' and was used in the Normandy Landings. Many lifetimes later it's been converted to the largest floating restaurant-bar in Stockholm with an add-on pontoon for extra space. The venue features an electrically controlled roof, outdoor heating and a boat dock. The palm trees and sleek furniture offer a luxurious Mediterranean feel and the view streaches from City Hall in the east to Västerbro in the west. Despite its size the place is packed during warm summer nights.

Kungsholmen (*see p125*) is another lavishly rebuilt pontoon with a boat dock, large bar, electric sunroof and walls that keep out the wind. The full view of Riddarfjärden is spectacular and the place is packed on warm summer nights. Outdoor heating keeps the place comfortable on chilly evenings.

Patricia (*see p122*), perhaps best known for its gay nights on Sundays, serves up a major party on summer nights and winter weekends. The boat was originally launched in 1938 from Smith's Shipyard in Middlesbrough, and once worked as a lightship in the English Channel. Winston Churchill spent time on the ship during the war and the 35-seat private room has been named in his honour. In its current state Patricia is a restaurant, bar and nightclub all fused into one. It features four dancefloors and as many as seven bars on four levels in summer. During the weekends, covers bands rock the boat from 8pm. Patricia is a campy and fun place for all ages.

Paus

Rörstrandsgatan 18 (34 44 05/www.restaurang paus.se). T-bana St Eriksplan/bus 3, 4, 42, 72. **Open** *Bar* 5pm-1am Mon-Sat. *Food served until* 11pm Mon-Sat. **Minimum age** 23. **Credit** AmEx, DC, MC, V. **Map** p244 D3 ⑫

Well placed on a quiet residential street of cafés and bars, Paus has a cream-coloured interior with large monochrome paintings and a giant mirror wall. It specialises in quality cocktails but doesn't take itself too seriously, with a laid-back, neighbourhood feel.

Storstad

Odengatan 41 (673 38 00/www.ahlbom.se). T-bana Rådmansgatan/bus 2, 4, 42, 53, 72. **Open** *Bar* 5pm-1am Mon-Thur; 4pm-3am Fri; 6pm-3am Sat. *Food served* until 11pm Mon-Sat. **Minimum age** 23. **Credit** AmEx, DC, MC, V. **Map** p245 C6 ⑬

The hip mix with the suit-and-tie brigade at the hottest bar in Vasastaden. Storstad (literally 'Big Town') has a chic white interior, huge windows and a large L-shaped bar that allows for a great deal of person-to-person interaction. This is a trendy spot and features the usual guest DJs playing all the right tunes, but it is not as reserved as similar venues – some might even call it a classy pick-up bar. For a darker version of the same thing, check out its sister bar, Olssons Video, next door.

Tranan

Karlbergsvägen 14 (52 72 81 00/www.tranan.se). T-bana Odenplan/bus 2, 4, 40, 69, 72. **Open** *Bar* 5pm-1am daily. *Food served* until 11.45pm daily. **Minimum age** 23. **Credit** AmEx, DC, MC, V. **Map** p245 D5 ⓮

Described as a 'modern classic' in the local entertainment guides, Tranan is the quintessential Stockholm bar. In the basement of the well-respected Tranan restaurant, it combines minimalist chic with the cosy feel of a cellar. A DJ spins the records as twentysomethings congregate around the sturdy wooden tables. Never too surprising, Tranan still manages to holds its own as one of the most enduring grade-A bars in Stockholm.

Södermalm

Nightlife hotspots on Söder are **Götgatan** and the area around **Medborgarplatsen**. Several small bars are also scattered south of **Folkungagatan**. The **Rival** (*see p43*) on Mariatorget has a cosy, art deco cocktail bar, and the **Clarion Hotel** (*see p42*) has two lively bars.

Akkurat

Hornsgatan 18 (644 00 15/www.akkurat.se). T-bana Mariatorget/bus 43, 55, 66, 74. **Open** *Bar* 11am-midnight Mon; 11am-1am Tue-Fri; 3pm-1am Sat; 6pm-1am Sun. *Food served* until 11pm daily. **Minimum age** 23. **Credit** AmEx, DC, MC, V. **Map** p250 K7 ⓯

Beer lovers frustrated with Stockholm's lack of good ale should head straight to Akkurat. Don't be put off by the run-of-the-mill pub interior, as this bar offers no less than 28 varieties of beer on tap, from fermented Belgian lambics to British cask conditioned ale. There are 600 varieties of bottled beer and 400 whiskies. True connoisseurs can book taste tests, starting at 270kr per person. Music every Sunday at 9pm includes anything from covers groups to indie rock.

Fenix

Götgatan 40 (640 45 06/www.fenixbar.nu). T-bana Slussen or Medborgarplatsen/bus 2, 3, 43, 53, 55. **Open** *Bar* 11am-1am Mon-Fri; noon-1am Sat; noon-midnight Sun. *Food served* until 11pm daily. **Minimum age** 23. **Credit** AmEx, DC, MC, V. **Map** p250 L8 ⓰

This gaudy party bar offers a refreshing alternative to the tasteful minimalism of many Stockholm drinking dens. With red walls, crazy artwork and mosaic decorations, it attracts a crowd of twenty- and thirtysomethings dressed for a night out. The cavernous basement has a dancefloor and lounge area.

Gondolen

Stadsgården 6 (641 70 90/www.eriks.se). T-bana Slussen/bus 2, 3, 43, 53, 55. **Open** *Bar* July 5.30pm-1am Mon-Sat. Aug-June 11.30am-1am Mon-Fri; 1pm-1am Sat. *Food served* July until 11pm Mon-Sat. Aug-June 11.30am-2.30pm Mon-Fri; 5-11pm Sat. **Credit** AmEx, DC, MC, V. **Map** p250 K8 ⓱

At the top of the historic Katarina lift, Gondolen is an ideal place for a tall drink. The bar sits under the walkway connecting the lift with Mosebacke, and provides a panoramic view of Djurgården to the east and Riddarfjärden to the west. Drinks are reasonably priced, despite the feeling of international luxury. You can get to the bar either from Mosebacke in the Katarinahissen (5kr) or via the restaurant's free lift at Stadsgården 6. *Photo p122.*

Kvarnen

Tjärhovsgatan 4 (643 03 80/www.kvarnen.com). T-bana Medborgarplatsen/bus 55, 59, 66. **Open** *Kvarnen* 11am-3am Mon-Fri; noon-3am Sat; 5pm-3am Sun. *H2O* 5pm-3am Mon-Fri; 7pm-3am Sat. *Eld* 10pm-3am Wed, Thur; 9pm-3am Fri, Sat. *Food served* until 11pm daily. **Minimum age** 21 (Mon-Thur), 23 (Fri, Sat). **Credit** AmEx, MC, V. **Map** p250 L8 ⓲

Originally a beer hall, Kvarnen ('Windmill') has evolved into one of the most popular late-night pubs on Söder. The lofty main room, filled with rows of tables and loud chatter, plays no music and retains the look and feel of a beer hall. It is flanked by two more recent additions: the small Mediterranean-themed H2O bar in what used to be a kitchen, and the flame-inspired Eld ('Hell') bar in the basement. Eld heats up in the wee hours, when dancing erupts. Kvarnen is also packed with Hammarby supporters before matches. Show up early at the weekend to avoid the horrific queue that winds down the block. Bouncers are strict but fair. *Photo p123.*

Ljunggrens

Götgatan 36 (640 75 65). T-bana Slussen/bus 2, 3, 43, 53, 55. **Open** *Bar* 5pm-midnight Mon, Tue; .5pm-1am Wed-Sat. *Food served* until 11pm Mon-Sat. **Minimum age** 23. **Credit** AmEx, MC, V. **Map** p250 L8 ⓳

One of the few bars on Götgatan that can compete with the clubs around Stureplan, Ljunggrens is a darkly sleek place for hip young things. The DJs favour hip hop and electronic music and the small bar area spills into a trendy, miniature shopping mall also equipped with an additional bar. Doormen can be fussy on busy nights.

Metro

Götgatan 93 (442 03 30). T-bana Skanstull/bus 3, 55, 74, 94. **Open** *Bar* 4pm-1am Mon-Thur; 4pm-2am Fri, Sat. *Food served* until 10pm Mon, Sun; until 11pm Tue-Sat. **Minimum age** 20. **Credit** AmEx, DC, MC, V. **Map** p251 N8 ⓴

Originally a cinema, Metro is now one of Södermalm's more popular nightspots. The rows of seats have been replaced with a large, circular bar around which twenty- and thirtysomethings rub

Gondolen. *See p121.*

elbows, mingle and flirt. Beyond the bar, under a fleet of bulbous lamps, is a sizeable lounge area. Another bar is in a separate room near the entrance. Yet another bar, in the restaurant, is open to non-dining guests from around midnight.

Mosebacke Etablissement

Mosebacke Torg 3 (55 60 98 90/www.mosebacke.se).
T-bana Slussen/bus 2, 3, 43, 53, 55. **Open** *Bar* Mid May-Aug 11am-1am Mon-Thur, Sun; 11am-2am Fri, Sat. Sept-mid May 4pm-1am Mon-Thur, Sun; 4pm-2am Fri, Sat. *Food served* Mid May-Aug until midnight daily. Sept-mid May until 9pm daily. **Minimum age** varies. **Admission** 60kr-80kr. **Credit** AmEx, DC, MC, V. **Map** p250 K8 ㉑
A definite winner among musicians and underground types, Mosebacke is Stockholm's hottest venue for cutting-edge performance acts and live music (*see p185*). The historic building features two bars and a dancefloor/stage area – check local papers for details or drop by for a surprise show. In the summer, two additional bars open on the large outdoor terrace, which offers a fantastic view of Stockholm harbour.

Nada

Åsögatan 140 (644 70 20). T-bana
Medborgarplatsen/bus 53, 59, 66, 76. **Open**
Bar 5pm-1am daily. *Food served* until 11pm daily.
Credit AmEx, DC, MC, V. **Map** p251 M9 ㉒
Locals congregate at this small two-room bar, known for its tapas menu and gold-adorned ceiling. Situated in the heart of the SoFo district, Nada is

low-key on weekdays, when patrons can be seen drinking beer and playing board games. DJs are on hand daily with anything from garage to Janis Joplin. At weekends Nada is filled to the brim with local partygoers making their first stop of the night. Outside seating in summer.

O'Learys

Götgatan 11 (644 69 01/www.olearys.se). T-bana
Slussen/bus 2, 3, 43, 53, 55. **Open** *Bar* 5-10pm Mon; 5-11pm Tue-Thur; 5pm-1am Fri; 1pm-1am Sat; 2-11pm Sun. *Food served* until 9pm Mon; until 10pm Tue-Sun. **Minimum age** 21. **Credit** AmEx, DC, MC, V. **Map** p250 K8 ㉓
This Boston-Irish sports bar is very popular with Anglophiles, American expats and die-hard sports fans. The green interior is covered with framed sports posters, neon beer signs and, above all, televisions: it's got three big-screen TVs and 35 regular televisions. There are 45 beers to choose from, most from the UK, Ireland and the US. Along with the obligatory slot machines, O'Learys also has a 'pop-a-shot' basketball game. Call in advance to reserve tables during major sporting events.
Other locations Kungsholmsgatan 31, Kungsholmen (654 52 10); Central Station, Norrmalm (613 62 60).

Patricia

Stadsgårdskajen 152 (743 05 70/www.lady
patricia.se). T-bana Slussen/bus 2, 3, 43, 53, 55.
Open 5pm-1am Wed, Thur; 6pm-5am Fri, Sat; 6pm-5am Sun (gay night). **Minimum age** 20 (Fri, Sat).
Admission (after 9pm) 90kr. **Credit** AmEx, MC, V.
Map p241 K8 ㉔
See p120 **All aboard**.

Pelikan

Blekingegatan 40 (55 60 90 90/www.pelikan.se).
T-bana Skanstull/bus 3, 55, 59, 74. **Open** *Bar*
3.30pm-1am Mon-Fri; 1pm-1am Sat, Sun. *Food served* 5-11pm daily. **Credit** AmEx, MC, V. **Map** p251 M8 ㉕
This charming beer hall is well away from the action in a mainly residential area in southern Södermalm. The clientele ranges from ageing regulars to young Southside hipsters in designer clothes. Drop in for a beer or visit the adjoining bar, Kristallen, adorned with oriental rugs and ornate chandeliers.

Pet Sounds Bar

Skånegatan 80 (643 82 25/www.petsoundsbar.se).
T-bana Medborgarplatsen/bus 3, 66. **Open** *Bar*
5pm-1am Mon-Sat. *Food served* until 10pm Mon-Sat. **Minimum age** 20. **Credit** AmEx, DC, MC, V.
Map p251 M9 ㉖
Home to Söder's large indie-rock crowd, Pet Sounds Bar is an extension of the legendary record store across the street. The Pet Sounds record store (*see p156*) used to host small concerts and was the first to book New Order in the 1980s. Nowadays the bar hosts these concerts in its basement, which features a stage, bar and DJ booth. The ground floor houses a restaurant. Both areas are decorated with concert and film posters on the black and red tiled walls.

Snaps

*Götgatan 48 (640 28 68). T-bana Medborgarplatsen/
bus 55, 59, 66.* **Open** *Bar* 5pm-1am Mon-Wed; 5pm-
3am Thur-Sat. *Food served* until 11pm Mon-Sat.
Minimum age 23. **Credit** AmEx, DC, MC, V.
Map p250 L8 ㉗

In the vaulted basement of a 17th-century mansion,
Snaps is one of Söder's most popular party bars,
second only to Kvarnen and Mosebacke (for both,
see p121). The main room features a dining area, bar
and blackjack table. For more action, venture downstairs, where there's a dancefloor/lounge in tones of
deep red. In summer, you can eat outside in a large
courtyard. Show up before 11pm to avoid queuing.

Snotty

*Skånegatan 90 (644 39 10). T-bana
Medborgarplatsen/bus 3, 66.* **Open** *Bar* 4pm-1am
daily. *Food served* until 10pm daily. **Credit** AmEx,
DC, MC, V. **Map** p251 M9 ㉘

Local hipsters and musicians love this tiny hole-in-
the-wall restaurant and bar. It was previously linked
to the Pet Sounds music store and the walls are decorated with images of rock and film stars. The bar
staff take their music selection seriously, playing the
latest underground cuts.

WC

*Skånegatan 51 (644 19 81). T-bana
Medborgarplatsen/bus 55, 59, 66.* **Open** *Bar*
5pm-1am daily. *Food served* until 11pm daily.
Brunch 11.30am-3.30pm Sat, Sun. **Minimum age**
20. **Credit** AmEx, MC, V. **Map** p251 M8 ㉙

A small, rectangular basement venue, WC is one of
the more popular of the many bars on Skånegatan.
The colourful interior, funky lighting and bar stools
with holes in the seats are self-consciously cool. On
the downside, it can get hopelessly crowded on
weekend nights. Claustrophobes, beware.

Östermalm

Most bars and nightclubs around Stureplan
are on or near one of the three main streets
intersecting the square: **Kungsgatan**, **Birger
Jarlsgatan** and **Sturegatan**.

Anglais

*Humlegårdsgatan 23 (51 73 40 00/www.scandic-
hotels.com). T-bana Östermalmstorg/bus 1, 2, 55,
56, 91.* **Open** *Lobby bar* 10am-2am Mon-Fri; noon-
2am Sat, Sun. *Champagne bar terrace* May-Sept
11.30am-11pm daily. **Credit** AmEx, DC, MC, V.
Map p246 E8 ㉚

One of the most famous hotel lounges around
Stureplan, the Anglais' sleek oval bar usually features a cool mix of business types, partygoers and
international hotel guests. In summer venture up to
the seventh floor Champagne Bar (open May-Sept).
The terrace offers an excellent view of Humlegården
park. A VIP room with its own private terrace can
be rented for 5,000kr, which includes five bottles of
champagne and an unlimited supply of strawberries.

Kvarnen. *See p121.*

Annakahn

*Riddargatan 12 (440 30 00). T-bana
Östermalmstorg/bus 1, 2, 47, 55, 62.* **Open** 5pm-
1am Mon-Wed; 5pm-2am Thur-Sat. *Food served* until
11pm Mon-Sat. **Minimum age** 23. **Credit** AmEx,
DC, MC, V. **Map** p241 F8 ㉚

An upmarket Indian restaurant by day, Annakahn
turns into a trendy low-key lounge bar at night. The
DJ spins hip hop, soul and house music while posh
twentysomethings start the evening off with a few
fancy drinks. The Indian artwork has been commissioned by local artist Jens Fränge. Don't miss the
green house drink, Annakahn, made with a mix of
basil and ginger (85kr).

Dubliner

*Smålandsgatan 8 (679 77 07/www.dubliner.se).
T-bana Östermalmstorg/bus 2, 47, 55, 62, 76.*
Open 4pm-1am Mon, Sun; 4pm-3am Tue-Fri; 1pm-
3am Sat. *Food served* until 11pm daily. **Minimum
age** 21. **Admission** (after 9pm) 80kr Fri, Sat.
Credit AmEx, DC, MC, V. **Map** p241 F8 ㉜

A sharp contrast to the trendy clubs surrounding
it, the Dubliner is as close as you'll come to a genuine Irish pub in Stockholm. It's fairly rowdy and
while the waitresses are Swedes, most of the bar
staff speak English only – a mix of Aussies, Brits
and Irishmen. The stage features covers bands and
traditional Irish acts. The Dubliner is also a good
place to catch major sporting events, with a big
screen. There are seven beers on tap including
Guinness, Kilkenny and John Smith's, as well as 25
bottled beers.

Solidaritet.

East

*Stureplan 13 (611 49 59/www.east.se). T-bana
Östermalstorg/bus 1, 2, 55, 56, 91.* **Open** *Bar*
11.30am-3am Mon-Sat; 5pm-3am Sun. *Food served*
until 11pm daily. **Minimum age** 23. **Credit** AmEx,
DC, MC, V. **Map** p241 F8 ❸

A sushi restaurant by day, East turns into
Stockholm's foremost hip hop and soul hangout by
night. Two bars serve beer and cocktails, while a DJ
plays hard-hitting beats for one of the most ethni-
cally diverse crowds in the city. A small section of
the first bar doubles as a dancefloor later. In summer, East offers an outdoor bar terrace area with a
view of Stureplan. It can be difficult to get past the
bouncers, so dress to impress and arrive before
10.30pm to avoid the hassle and the wait.

Hotellet

*Linnégatan 18 (442 89 00/www.hotellet.info).
T-bana Östermalstorg/bus 1, 42, 44, 55, 56.*
Open *Bar* 5pm-midnight Mon, Tue; 5pm-1am Wed,
Thur; 4pm-1am Fri; 6pm-1am Sat. *Food served* until
11pm Mon-Sat. **Minimum age** 25. **Credit** AmEx,
DC, MC, V. **Map** p246 E8 ❸

Featured in international design magazines such as
Wallpaper*, Hotellet has become the hotspot for
young urban professionals and posh partygoers
alike. Its two storeys, plus an extra level upstairs,
contain a total of four bars. The downstairs lounge
heats up at night as the DJ sorts out pop and house
music. In summer, Hotellet opens its Miami-style
outside patio, with a handsome lawn and two bars
(May-Sept, open until 10pm). Queues get long
around 11pm.

Laroy

*Birger Jarlsgatan 20 (54 50 37 00/www.stureplans
gruppen.se). T-bana Östermalstorg/bus 1, 2, 55, 56,
91.* **Open** *Bar* 10pm-3am Wed, Fri, Sat. **Minimum
age** 25. **Credit** AmEx, DC, MC, V. **Map** p246 E8 ❸

Rich kids in designer shirts flash platinum cards and
order bottles of champagne at this posh, two-storey
bar and restaurant. Although there's no dancefloor,
people let loose on all available floor space as Top
40 music pumps through the speakers. Dress smart
and arrive before 10.30pm to get in.

Nox

*Grev Turegatan 30 (54 58 24 00/www.nox.se).
T-bana Östermalstorg/bus 1, 42, 44, 55, 56.* **Open**
5pm-1am Tue-Thur; 4pm-1am Fri; 6pm-1am Sat.
Food served until 11pm Tue-Sat. **Minimum age**
23. **Credit** AmEx, DC, MC, V. **Map** p246 E8 ❸

Home to Stureplan's younger jet set, Nox's two
levels offer a darkly sleek atmosphere. The DJ spins
house music Thursdays to Saturdays to a posh
crowd dressed for a night on the town. In summer
Nox opens the doors to its popular back yard (May-
Sept). Queues are seldom a major problem.

O-baren

*Stureplan 2 (440 57 30). T-bana Östermalmstorg/
bus 1, 2, 55, 56.* **Open** 7pm-2am daily. **Minimum
age** 23. **Credit** AmEx, DC, MC, V. **Map** p241 F8 ❸

A dark rock, hip hop and soul den in a back room of the exclusive Sturehof restaurant, O-baren has a bar and large dancefloor bounded by bleacher-like seats. Although spontaneous dancing is common-place, the clientele never loses its cool.

Riche

Birger Jarlsgatan 4 (54 50 35 60/www.riche.se) *T-bana Östermalmstorg/bus 2, 47, 55, 62, 91.* **Open** 11.30am-midnight Mon; 11.30am-1am Tue; 11.30am-2am Wed-Fri; noon-2am Sat. *Food served* until 11pm Mon; until midnight Tue-Sat. **Minimum age** 23. **Credit** AmEx, DC, MC, V. **Map** p241 F8 ③⑧

A favourite bar for Stockholm's business, media and advertising professionals, Riche is more edgy and sophisticated than most Stureplan bars. Twenty and thirtysomethings hang out in the smaller bar (Lilla Baren) with loud DJ music and spontaneous danc-ing. The larger bar-and-dining area features an older crowd who remember when Riche was the coolest place in town in the 1980s. The two queues get bad around 11pm at weekends.

Solidaritet

Lästmakargatan 3 (678 10 50/www.solidaritet *stureplan.se). T-bana Östermalmstorg/bus 1, 2, 55, 56, 91.* **Open** *Bar* 10pm-5am Wed-Sat. **Minimum age** 25. **Admission** 100kr (until 3am), 200kr (after 3am) Sun. **Credit** AmEx, DC, MC, V. **Map** p241 F8 ③⑨

Don't let the name fool you. Solidaritet (Solidarity) is the quintessential Stureplan bar/club with a long queue, steep cover charge, sleek *Miami Vice*-inspired interior and plenty of reserved tables. Not to mention the best-looking people in town. The venue has two spacious levels and four bars, including one in a year-round covered patio that doubles as a dancefloor in the late hours. DJs play house and pop music. Dress to kill and arrive before 11pm to avoid the queue.

Undici

Sturegatan 22 (661 66 17/www.undici.se). T-bana *Östermalmstorg/bus 1, 2, 43, 55, 56.* **Open** 6pm-1am Tue-Thur; 4pm-3am Fri; 6pm-3am Sat. *Food served* until 11pm Mon-Sat. **Minimum age** 25. **Credit** AmEx, DC, MC, V. **Map** p246 E8 ④⓪

Founded and owned by Swedish football legend Tomas Brolin, Undici is one of Stureplan's more rowdy party spots. The spacious interior is stylish and darkly minimalistic with leather booths. Yet the place is distinctly low-brow and heats up on week-ends when the DJ spins pop music and campy Eurovision *Schlager* music. Dancing on the bar and the tables is common – and local celebrities can be spotted from time to time.

Kungsholmen

AG (Allmänna Galleriet 925)

Kronobergsgatan 37, 2nd floor of office building *(410 68 100/www.ag925.se). T-bana Fridhemsplan/* *bus 1, 3, 4, 57, 77.* **Open** 5pm-1am Tue-Sat. *Food* *served* until 11pm Tue-Sat. **Minimum age** 23. **Credit** AmEx, DC, MC, V. **Map** p239 F3 ④①

Often compared to a SoHo nightclub, Allmänna Galleriet 925 (AG for short) doubles as a restaurant, nightclub and occasional performing arts venue. Previously a silver smithy, AG does not have its own street entrance. Instead, patrons must pass through the door of a seedy office building (next to a porn shop) and climb two flights of stairs to reach the entrance. Inside, the look is very cool – tiled white walls offset by brown Chippendale couches and dark designer furniture. The clientele is a mix of trendy artist types and designer suits.

Dovas

St Eriksgatan 53A (650 80 49). T-bana Fridhemsplan/ *bus 1, 3, 4, 57, 77.* **Open** *Bar* 11am-1am daily. *Food served* until 11.30pm daily. **Minimum age** 20. **Credit** AmEx, MC, V. **Map** p239 F3 ④②

Dovas is easily one of the most unsettling dives in Fridhemsplan. Its darkened interior with wooden booths houses a bizarre mix of local drunks and oth-ers too young to get into trendier places with higher minimum ages. Tattoos and shaved heads are com-monplace, as are random conversations that start with an accusation and end with some inebriated barfly putting his arm round your shoulder. The beer is dirt cheap at 23kr for a half-litre glass.

Kungsholmen

Norr Mälarstrand 464 (50 52 44 50/www. *kungsholmen.com). T-bana Rådhuset/bus 3, 40,* *52, 62.* **Open** 5pm-midnight Mon-Wed; 5pm-2am Thur-Sat; 5-11pm Sun. *Food served* until 11pm Mon-Sat; 10pm Sun. **Credit** AmEx, DC, MC, V. **Map** p240 H4 ④③

See p120 **All aboard**.

Lokal

Scheelegatan 8 (650 98 09). T-bana Rådhuset/bus 3, *40, 52, 62.* **Open** *Bar* 4pm-1am Mon, Tue, Sun; 4pm-2am Wed, Thur; 4pm-3am Fri, Sat. *Food served* until 11pm daily. **Minimum age** 23. **Credit** AmEx, DC, MC, V. **Map** p240 G4 ④④

When Lokal first opened a few years back, everyone compared it to Storstad (*see p120*) in Vasastaden. Both have similarly stylish white interiors, enormous shopfront windows, L-shaped bars and guest DJs playing soul or house. However, Lokal is (as the name implies) more of a local venue.

Mälarpaviljongen

Norr Mälarstrand 63 (650 87 01/www. *malarpaviljongen.se). T-bana Rådhuset/bus 3, 40,* *52, 62.* **Open** *May-Sept* 11am-midnight daily. *Food served* until 11pm daily. **Credit** AmEx, MC, V. **Map** p239 H3 ④⑤

See p120 **All aboard**.

M/S Gerda

Norr Mälarstrand 466 (650 80 31/www. *restauranggerda.se). T-bana Rådhuset/bus 3, 40,* *52, 62.* **Open** *May-Sept* 11.30am-1am Mon-Fri; noon-1am Sat; noon-11pm Sun. *Food served* until 11pm Mon-Sat; 10pm Sun. **Credit** AmEx, DC, MC, V. **Map** p240 H4 ④⑥

See p120 **All aboard**.

Cafés

Coffee is a national pastime in Sweden, but just don't ask for decaf.

The Swedish café is a unique cultural institution that cannot be summed up as a mere pit stop for a hot drink and sticky bun. Indeed, the average Stockholm café is the place where people go to meet, chat and do business in an informal setting.

Coffee, largely as a result of Sweden's historical uneasiness regarding alcohol, is the national fix. If there were an Olympic gold medal for coffee drinking, the Swedes would win it every time. And it's not the instant stuff – they like it thick and strong.

Most cafés serve the usual range of lattes and cappuccinos. The exception to this is the more traditional style of *konditori*, which may be restricted to the filtered variety. Decaffeinated coffee is generally regarded with both suspicion and derision here, and you will also find it hard to get a cup of tea that the British would recognise as such. Strong coffee, weak tea sort of sums it up. But everywhere sells soft drinks and you may even find smoothies and freshly squeezed fruit juices on the menu.

And just as the British have afternoon tea, so the Swedes have their own tradition of *fika*, a cup of coffee served with a bun or cake, usually any time from about 2.30pm onwards. This laid-back tradition probably goes a long way to explaining why the city is mercifully free from US-style coffee chains. Generally speaking, the proprietor of the café is the person working behind the till, and this makes for a personable atmosphere among the city's many cafés.

All cafés serve a selection of biscuits, cakes and sandwiches. The *kanelbulle* (cinnamon bun) is a typical treat to have alongside your coffee. Watch out too for seasonal favourites – at Christmas time it is the *lussekatt* (a saffron flavoured bun) and at Easter it is the magnificent *semla*, a truly epic creation of pastry, almond paste and whipped cream.

Some places have branched out to take advantage of the Swedish lunch culture. Most people here will leave their desks and take time out to sit and eat a proper lunch, so cafés now tend to cater by providing a limited but reasonably priced *dagens* (daily) lunch menu.

The general rule is that you pay at the counter when you order. If you are ordering a meal, you will usually be given a ticket with a number that will be called out when the waiter comes out of the kitchen. There is no seating surcharge in Stockholm so feel free to sit inside, outside, at the bar area, wherever you wish. In a few places, usually the older style *konditori*, a waitress service still exists, but it is fairly rare. Tipping is not commonplace in Sweden.

Gamla Stan

For ice-cream and fresh waffles, stop at **Café Kåkbrinken** (Västerlånggatan 41, 411 61 74), near Sundbergs Konditori (*see p128*).

Chokladkoppen

Stortorget 20 (20 31 70/www.chokladkoppen.com). T-bana Gamla Stan/bus 2, 3, 43, 53, 55, 59, 71, 76. **Open** *Winter* 10am-10pm Mon-Thur, Sun; 9am-11pm Fri, Sat. *Summer* 9am-11pm Mon-Thur, Sun; 8am-midnight Fri, Sat. **No credit cards. Map** p241 J7 ❶
Just how good can a hot chocolate really be? To find out, skip Gamla Stan's tourist traps and head for this place on Stortorget, the charming square at the centre of Gamla Stan. Colourful Chokladkoppen has a trendy feel and loud music – dance and cheesy pop – and is popular with Stockholm's gay crowd. The laid-back service suffers at weekends when it gets ridiculously busy. In summer, the tables outside are a prime spot. Along with its famous hot chocolate, it serves fantastic cakes and snacks. *Photo p128*.

Grillska Husets Konditori

Stortorget 3 (787 86 05). T-bana Gamla Stan/bus 2, 3, 43, 53, 55, 59, 71, 76. **Open** 9am-6pm Mon-Fri; 11am-6pm Sat, Sun. **Credit** AmEx, MC, V. **Map** p241 J8 ❷
This café and bakery in a corner of Stortorget is run by a charitable group that works with the homeless. For a real treat, walk through the downstairs café and follow the signs through to the tranquil first-floor terrace, one of Gamla Stan's best-kept secrets. With good-value pastries and friendly service on offer, spend your change here and make a difference.

Kaffekoppen

Stortorget 18 (20 31 70). T-bana Gamla Stan/bus 2, 3, 43, 53, 55, 59, 71, 76. **Open** 8am-11pm Mon-Thur, Sun; 8am-midnight Fri, Sat. **No credit cards. Map** p241 J7 ❸
This sister café to neighbouring Chokladkoppen (*see above*) has old wooden tables and chairs and a tiny 13th-century interior, where it serves home-made

❶ Olive green numbers in this chapter correspond to the location of each café as marked on the street maps. *See pp238-251.*

Eat, Drink, Shop

Atrium. *See p128.*

delights – the white chocolate cheesecake is fantastic. Sit outside and you could land yourself a ringside seat for a concise history of Stockholm's Old Town, as Stortorget is a customary stop for guides taking their flocks to nearby Nobelmuseet (see p57).

Muren

Västerlånggatan 19 (10 80 70). T-bana Gamla Stan/bus 3, 53, 55, 59, 76. **Open** 10am-9pm Mon-Thur, Sun; 9am-10pm Fri, Sat. **No credit cards.** **Map** p241 H7 ❹

Navigate the cobblestones to this café, which transforms itself from a trendy café in winter into a popular ice-cream parlour in summer. Remnants of the building's 13th-century wall remain intact (though not visible), hence the name. This gay-friendly establishment serves the usual selection of sandwiches and pastries when in café mode; otherwise it dishes up one of the largest selections of ice-cream in the capital. The famously huge cones come in four flavours – vanilla, chocolate, cinnamon and saffron – and fill the air with a sweet aroma.

Sundbergs Konditori

Järntorget 83 (10 67 35). T-bana Gamla Stan/bus 2, 3, 43, 53, 55, 59, 71, 76. **Open** June-Aug 9am-9pm daily. Sept-May 9am-10pm Mon-Fri; 10am-10pm Sat, Sun. **Credit** MC, V. **Map** p241 J8 ❺

This place has served hot coffee from a copper samovar for more than 200 years. Believed to be Stockholm's oldest *konditori*, it was founded in 1785 by Johan Ludvig Sundberg. According to local lore, King Gustav III had a secret passageway from the Kungliga Slottet straight to the bakery. Don't expect newfangled frappuccinos and smoothies here: come to Sundbergs for traditional cakes and atmosphere. This is a good starting point for navigating the curiosities and cobbles of nearby Västerlånggatan, Gamla Stan's busiest street.

Norrmalm

In addition to the following, try old-fashioned **Vete-Katten** (Kungsgatan 55, 20 84 05), a tearoom with classic Swedish pastries.

Atrium

Nationalmuseet, Södra Blasieholmshamnen 2 (611 34 30/www.restaurangatrium.se). T-bana Kungsträdgården/bus 65. **Open** June-Aug 11am-8pm Tue; 11am-5pm Wed-Sun. Sept-May 11am-8pm Tue, Thur; 11am-5pm Wed, Fri-Sun. **Credit** AmEx, DC, MC, V. **Map** p241 H8 ❻

Many of Stockholm's museums have excellent cafés, especially the Dansmuseet (see p65) and Aquaria Vattenmuseum (see p72), but by far the best is this place. You can *fika* here without forking out the museum entrance fee, so contemplating the works of Carl Larsson isn't obligatory. Though the museum, opposite the Royal Palace, is a bit dark and moody, sitting in the glass-roofed courtyard café is like having coffee in Renaissance Florence. Atrium offers a

Hot chocolate heaven at **Chokladkoppen.** *See p126.*

bit more than your average café – the food, served buffet-style, is as exquisite as the surroundings. The café is often hired out for private functions on Tuesday and Thursday evenings. *Photo p127.*

Café Söderberg
Kungsträdgården 2:41 (21 74 75/www.cafe soderberg.se). T-bana Kunstragarden/bus 2, 47, 55, 62, 76. **Open** May-Sept 8am-11pm daily. Oct-Apr 10am-7pm daily. **Credit** AmEx, MC, V. **Map** p241 G7 ❼

This delightful café, situated at the base of St Jacobs Church on Kungsträdgården, was named after author Hjalmar Söderberg, whose novel *Doktor Glas* was set in the area. The café is a sweet, old-fashioned glasshouse, complete with stained glass and trees sprouting through the floor up to the ceiling. In the summer, you can sit outside and watch the world go by. For a more contemporary take on the glasshouse vernacular, head directly across Kungsträdgården to Piccolino (*see below*).

Piccolino
Kungsträdgården (611 78 08/www.kungstradgarden. nu). T-bana Kungsträdgården/bus 2, 47, 55, 62, 76. **Open** June-Aug 8am-10pm Mon-Fri; 10am-10pm Sat, Sun. Sept-May 10am-9pm daily. **Credit** MC, V. **Map** p241 G8 ❽

What once was a lone glasshouse structure in Kungsträdgården has duplicated five-fold into a row of cafés almost spanning the park's length. But Piccolino, Stockholm's first espresso bar, is the original and best. Opposite the winter ice-rink and summertime outdoor stage, and popular with Swedish celebs, this small café is good for people-watching. The elms surrounding it are important for many locals: 30 years ago they were saved after a sit-down protest against the decision to build a Tunnelbana station next door to Café Opera. *Photo p130.*

Tintarella di Luna
Drottninggatan 102 (10 79 55). T-bana Rådmansgatan/bus 1, 2, 4, 42, 72. **Open** 9am-7pm Mon-Fri; 10am-5pm Sat; 11am-5pm Sun. **No credit cards.** Map p245 E6 ❾

Tintarella di Luna is one of the city's more laid-back Italian cafés, but it's very small, so be prepared to wait for a table. The macchiato is amazing. Don't miss the quotes (in Swedish) of world-famous Swedish author/playwright August Strindberg that fill the pavement outside – if they whet your appetite, the Strindberg Museum (*see p67*) is just across the street.

World News Café
2nd Floor, Kulturhuset, Sergels Torg 3 (14 56 06/ www.kulturhuset.stockholm.se). T-bana T-Centralen/ bus 47, 56, 59, 69, 91. **Open** Mon-Sat; noon-4pm Sun. **Credit** MC, V. **Map** p241 G7 ❿

This café, set in Stockholm's famous Kulturhuset, allows you to sip your latte while flicking through newspapers from all over the world. There's a fantastic view of the fountain and glass structure at Sergels Torg too. If you are looking for something a

bit more substantial than a sandwich, try Café Panorama on the top floor, which does an excellent lunch menu.

Café Levinsky's
Rörstrandsgatan 9 (30 33 33). T-bana St Eriksplan/ bus 3, 4, 42, 47, 77. **Open** 7.30am-10pm Mon-Thur; 7.30am-8pm Fri; 9am-7pm Sat; 10am-9pm Sun. **Credit** MC, V. **Map** p244 E3 ⓫

Whenever you've got a smoothie craving, head to Levinsky's (try blueberry and banana). Alongside the usual café offerings, Levinsky's has a welcome Mexican twist; the enchiladas are highly recommended. The only mystery is the collection of Heinz soup cans on display, which, incidentally, don't feature on the menu. For dessert, pop round the corner to Stockholms Glasshus (Birkagatan 8, 30 32 37, www.glasspasta.com) for home-made ice-cream in flavours you had previously only dreamed about. **Other locations** Vallhallavägen 155, Östermalm (662 65 24); Götgatan 58, Södermalm (644 71 20).

Creem
Karlbergsvägen 23 (32 52 65). T-bana Odenplan/ bus 2, 4, 40, 42, 47, 72. **Open** 8am-9pm Mon-Thur; 8am-6pm Fri-Sun. **Credit** MC, V. **Map** p244 D4 ⓬

On first impressions this place looks frighteningly trendy, but don't let the designer interior put you off, as it is one of the city's cosiest cafés. The salami sandwiches are first-class, while the health-conscious can opt for the popular low-fat dishes (*hälsotallrik*). The sofas in the inner room guarantee relaxation. **Other locations** Flemminggatan 22, Kungsholmen (651 53 00); Folkungagatan 57, Södermalm (640 28 38).

Galento
Surbrunnsgatan 31 (612 00 45/www.galento.com). T-bana Rådmansgatan/bus 2, 4, 42, 72, 96. **Open** 10am-6pm Mon-Fri; 10.30am-6pm Sat, Sun. **No credit cards.** Map p245 C6 ⓭

Galento is the sort of place you might find bearded intellectuals grappling with the intricacies of existentialism over a cappuccino or two. The styling is

The best Cafés

For drinking in the views
Hermans Trädgårdcafé. *See p132.*

For seriously strong coffee
Lisas Café & Hembageri. *See p132.*

For taking the kids
Cookbook Café. *See p134.*

For the best *semla* in town
Thelins. *See p135.*

original beatnik, accompanied by jazz and world music on the stereo. However, with the generously portioned soup, which comes complete with filled baguette, you are unlikely to come across too many starving poets.

Gino's Coffee

Odengatan 47 (644 40 33/www.ginoscoffee.com). T-bana Rådmansgatan/bus 2, 4, 42, 72. **Open** 8am-9pm Mon-Fri; 10am-9pm Sat, Sun. **No credit cards. Map** p245 C6 ⓮
Eponymous owner Gino, a former hairdresser and self-styled entrepreneur, has opened his second café on the busiest street in Vasastaden (the original is on Gamla Stan). It's a cool joint, with discerning music and decent coffee.
Other locations Västerlånggatan 54, Gamla Stan (442 22 68).

Kafe Kompott

Karlbergsvägen 52 (31 51 77). T-bana St Eriksplan/ bus 3, 42, 47. **Open** 10am-8pm Mon-Fri; 10.30am-6pm Sat, Sun. Closed mid July-mid Aug. **Credit** MC, V. **Map** p244 D3 ⓯
Breakfast and brunch buffets are the main attractions at this café, where the British-style fry-up has a continental twist. It's an all-you-can-eat affair, with pancakes and jam for dessert. Despite being a tad pricey, it's hugely popular, especially on the weekends. There's an enclosed garden area at the front with seating outside during the summer months.

Ritorno

Odengatan 80-82 (32 01 06). T-bana Odenplan/bus 4, 47, 53, 72. **Open** 7am-10pm Mon-Thur; 7am-8pm Fri; 8am-6pm Sat; 10am-6pm Sun. **Credit** AmEx, MC, V. **Map** p244 D4 ⓰
Time stands still at this 1950s café, where beautiful old jukeboxes are still in working order. The regulars voiced a collective outcry when a revamp was recently suggested, so the battered leather sofas and kitsch decor remain. Ritorno offers everything from traditional shrimp sandwiches to calorie-dripping Danish pastries with funny names, such as 'one of those' and 'sumthing sweet'. If you don't drink coffee, try the apple soda Pommac. A local hangout for artists and writers, the café doubles as a gallery and the paintings on show are for sale.

Sosta

Sveavägen 84 (612 13 49/www.sostabar.com). T-bana Rådmansgatan/bus 52. **Open** 8am-6pm Mon-Fri; 10am-5pm Sat. **No credit cards. Map** p245 D6 ⓱
This is a standing room-only espresso bar known all over Sweden for its extraordinary coffee and low prices – although some say it's as famous for the well-dressed *baristas* making the *doppios* and serving cornettos. Try the focaccias or the home-made strawberry sorbet and you'll realise that Sosta is the closest you'll get to Italy in Scandinavia.
Other locations Jakobsbergsgatan 7, Norrmalm (611 71 07); Götgatan 30, Södermalm (505 259 70).

Piccolino. *See p129.*

Valand

*Surbrunnsgatan 48 (30 04 76). T-bana Odenplan
or Rådmansgatan/bus 2, 4, 42, 53, 72.* **Open** 8am-
7pm Mon-Fri; 9am-5pm Sat. **No credit cards.**
Map p245 C5 ⑱

Silence is golden at Valand, one of the city's most
peaceful cafés. This *konditori* is a throwback to the
1950s; the cranky old couple who run it have
refrained from updating the place, hence the original retro look. The service is fairly slow and down-
beat, but then again this isn't the place for a quick
coffee buzz. You head to Valand's vinyl couches for
traditional cakes (try the vanilla and almond bun)
and to feel like you're an extra in an old black-
and-white movie.

Vurma

*Gästrikegatan 2 (30 62 30). T-bana St Eriksplan/bus
3, 4, 42, 77.* **Open** 10am-6pm Mon-Fri; 11am-6pm
Sat, Sun. **Credit** AmEx, MC, V. **Map** p244 D4 ⑲

This retro hotspot comes highly recommended; even
the staff hang out here on their day off. The lengthy
menu adds an exotic twist to the usual sandwiches
and snacks, catering imaginatively for both veggies
and carnivores. The decor is a 1970s kaleidoscope
of colour, with swirls of oranges, browns and greens.
The service is good, as is the grub, and the soothing
tunes tone down the brash interior. If you fancy a
grassy retreat after brunch, Vasaparken is nearby.
Vurma's Kungsholmen branch has its own bakery.
Other locations Polhemsgatan 15,
Kungsholmen (650 93 50).

Xoko

*Rorstrandgatan 15 (31 84 87/www.xoko.se). T-bana
St Eriksplan/bus 3, 4, 42, 77.* **Open** 7.30am-6.30pm
Tue; 7.30am-11pm Wed-Fri; 9am-11pm Sat; 9am-6pm
Sun. **Credit** AmEx, MC, V. **Map** p244 E3 ⑳

This café and bakery is quite simply a visual and gastronomic feast. Situated in Birkastan, Stockholm's
most bohemian quarter, Xoco's quirky interior – all
illuminated sci-fi circles – is worth a visit in itself. But
as Xoco is owned by one of Sweden's leading *choco-
latiers*, there are plenty of other reasons to drop by.

Djurgården

In addition to those listed below, many of
Djurgården's museums have good cafés. Try
the café at the **Aquaria Vattenmuseum** (*see
p72*), with its waterfront view; Café Ektorpet,
set outside an 18th-century cottage on a hill
overlooking the water, at **Prins Eugens
Waldemarsudde** (*see p73*); or one of
Skansen's (*see p74*) numerous cafés and
eateries, the best of which is Café Petissan,
situated in the Town Quarter in a cosy building
from the late 17th century.

Blå Porten

*Djurgårdsvägen 64 (663 87 59). Bus 44, 47/
tram 7/ferry from Slussen or Nybrokajen.*
Open *May-Aug* 11am-10pm Mon-Fri; 11am-7pm

Sat, Sun. *Sept-Apr* 11am-7pm Mon, Wed, Fri-Sun;
11am-9pm Tue, Thur. **Credit** AmEx, MC, V.
Map p242 H11 ㉑

The 'Blue Door' is, without doubt, Stockholm's most
romantic café. Next door to prominent art gallery
Liljevalchs Konsthall (*see p176*), this beautiful
piazza-like garden is a secret hideaway in the heart
of the island. The interior isn't that exciting, so you
should probably choose somewhere else on a rainy
day. There's a medieval-style table inside laden with
a mouth-watering display of desserts. If you're visiting Vasamuseet, Skansen or Gröna Lund, then Blå
Porten is the perfect stop.

Rosendals Trädgård

*Rosendalsterrassen 12 (54 58 12 70/www.
rosendalstradgard.com). Bus 47/tram 7.* **Open**
Mid Jan-Mar, Oct-mid Nov 11am-4pm Tue-Sun.
Apr 11am-5pm Tue-Sun. *May-Sept* 11am-5pm
daily. Closed mid Nov-mid Jan. **Credit** MC, V.
Map p243 H13 ㉒

The green-fingered café located in this upmarket
garden centre offers some of the finest cakes and
sandwiches in town – all of it organic and grown
or baked on the premises. Rosendals Trädgård is
well known for its seasonal desserts, and its recipes
fill the pages of bestselling cookbook *Rosendals
trädgårdscafé*. In summer, people devour fruit pie
at picnic tables or on the grass under the apple trees;
in winter they keep warm with a mug of *glögg*
(mulled wine) in the greenhouses. There is a small
shop selling jam, bread and flowers (which you can
pick yourself). To get there, take bus 47 to the last
stop at Waldemarsudde then continue a few feet
in the same direction and you'll see a sign – the
place is a little tricky to find, so be prepared to ask
for directions.

Södermalm

Blooms Bageri

*St Paulsgatan 24 (640 90 36). T-bana Mariatorget/
bus 43, 55, 66.* **Open** 8am-6pm Mon-Fri; 10am-5pm
Sat, Sun. **Credit** MC, V. **Map** p250 K7 ㉓

This small café close to Södermalm's beautiful view-
point, Mariaberget, knows there's nothing more
relaxing than seeing other people work – only a window divides Blooms Bakery from its café. The bread
and buns are as fresh as can be – often still warm
from the oven.

Café dello Sport

*Pålsundsgatan 8 (668 74 88). T-bana Hornstull/
bus 4, 40, 66.* **Open** 9am-6pm daily. **Credit** MC, V.
Map p249 K3 ㉔

This soccer-mad café is fairly famous during cup
matches, when enthusiastic crowds assemble to
watch the game. The staff are an incredibly jolly
bunch and the café is situated at the foot of Högalids
Kyrka, opposite a pleasant play park, so it really is
worth a visit, even if you have absolutely no interest in sport. The focaccias, cappuccinos and Italian
soft drinks are all delicious.

Eat, Drink, Shop

Hermans Trädgårdcafé

Fjällgatan 23 (643 94 80/www.hermans.se). T-bana Slussen/bus 2, 3, 53, 76, 96. **Open** *Sept-May* 11am-9pm daily. *June-Aug* 11am-11pm daily. **Credit** MC, V. **Map** p251 L9 ㉕

This spectacular vegetarian café boasts amazing views over the Stockholm skyline – you can pick out nearly all the major landmarks, together with the cruise ships and tourist boats shuttling in and out of the harbour. The café offers a buffet menu at lunch and in the evening, and you can opt for just a main course or include one of the delicious fruit pies. It really is worth the short trudge up the hill from Slussen.

Lasse i Parken

Högalidsgatan 56 (658 33 95). T-bana Hornstull/bus 4, 40, 66. **Open** *May-Aug* 11am-5pm daily. *Sept-Apr* 11am-5pm Sat, Sun. **Credit** MC, V. **Map** p249 K2 ㉖

This charming café is set an 18th-century house, where many of the original features have been retained. Outside there is a large seating area complete with a stage, which is used for musical and theatrical performances during the summer months. As this is an extremely popular place at weekends, it can take a bit of time to queue up and get your refreshments – however, it is such a lovely location that it is worth the minor aggravation. To get there, take bus 4 or 40 over Västerbron to Högalidsgatan for an amazing view of Långholmen.

Lisas Café & Hembageri

Skånegatan 68 (640 36 36). T-bana Medborgarplatsen/bus 59. **Open** 6.30am-3pm Mon-Fri; 8am-3pm Sat. **No credit cards.** **Map** p251 M8 ㉗

Motherly Lisa has been getting up at 4am every morning for the last 13 years to serve the residents of Södermalm. She has around 250 photos of regulars gracing the walls of her café and claims she can tell you a story about each and every one of them. Cinnamon buns (*kanelbulle*) are the house speciality, but ask for a latte or a frappuccino at your peril, since any coffee with warmed-up milk is barred from her menu – she champions the survival of the plain coffee. Lisas Café & Hembageri is as local as they come and continues to weather the storm of competition from the slew of trendy new cafés sprouting up in the area.

Puck

Hornsgatan 32 (641 10 30). T-bana Slussen/bus 2, 3, 4, 43, 55, 66. **Open** 9am-7pm Mon-Fri; 10am-7pm Sat, Sun; *July* 10am-5pm daily. **Credit** MC, V. **Map** p250 K7 ㉘

A quiet retreat from the nearby hustle and bustle of Slussen, this small, cosy café is well frequented by locals. Puck is known for its good sandwiches and the kind of laid-back charm that people have come to expect from the south side of the city, and the staff are only too willing to have a chat. Vegetarians are also pretty well catered for, with a selection of

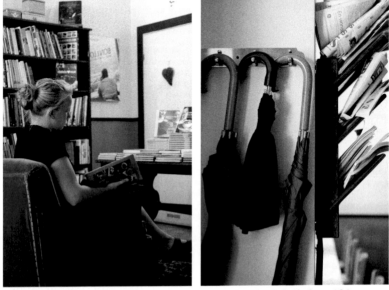

Come for coffee, stay for lunch and plan dinner at the **Cookbook Café**. *See p134.*

Coffee to stay

Café culture in Sweden is as rich as the coffee the natives consume by the gallon. As the pub is to the Brits, so the café is to the Swedes. Apart from the Finns, the Swedes drink more coffee per capita than any other nation, on average downing 4.5 cups each per day – and, unlike the take-out cup culture prevalent elsewhere, Swedes like to sit down with a classic white porcelain cup and saucer for their cup of java.

This caffeine society started with King Karl XII, who brought coffee to Sweden from Turkey in 1714. It fell from favour under the reign of King Gustav III, however, as he branded it poison in the latter half of the 18th century and banned its consumption. As part of an attempt to prove the toxic perils of coffee, he devised an experiment using a couple of convicted murderers: one he sentenced to coffee on a daily basis, the other to pint-sized doses of tea. But the experiment fizzled as the killers lived well into old age, with the coffee drinker – or so the story goes – outliving the tea drinker. And both of them outlived Gustav, who was murdered.

Coffee climbed back up the local charts in 1855, when the home-brewing of alcohol was criminalised as the country attempted to curb rampant alcohol abuse. Many Swedes turned to caffeine as a booze replacement. And in the 19th century, when sexuality was a taboo subject and spicy food was thought to arouse the desires of the Devil, coffee and biscuits were one of life's few pleasures.

At the beginning of the 20th century it was considered indecent for a woman to visit a restaurant unless she was accompanied by a man. So instead, women organised coffee parties or met up at cafés; today you will still sometimes hear the term *kaffekärring* ('coffeelady') used to describe a scandalmonger.

Getting a coffee fix, with a little something sweet on the side, is now a firmly established Swedish pastime. They call it *fika*, which loosely translates as 'indulge in coffee and chat at leisure'. For a marathon *fika*, it is wise to find a café offering endless refills (*påtår*) for free or a token charge. Most importantly, don't worry about overstaying your welcome. As long as you have even a sip of coffee left in your cup, nobody expects you to leave. You're supposed to be there for hours – that's what *fika* is all about.

pretty well catered for, with a selection of inventive recipes on offer. The opening hours can vary a bit at weekends.

South of Folkungagatan

Skånegatan 71 (702 06 60). T-bana Medborgarplatsen/bus 3, 59, 76. **Open** 9am-7pm Mon-Fri; 11am-7pm Sat, Sun. **Credit** AmEx, MC, V. **Map** p251 M9 ㉓

The area now ambitiously dubbed SoFo, short for South of Folkungagatan, has become something of a hub for independent fashion designers, small record shops and trend-conscious types. From young mums to middle-aged hippies, the eclectic mix of clientele at this café personifies the area's celebrated diversity. South of Folkungagatan is famed for its hot paninis, which are named after local streets – try the Folkungagatan, with cheese, ham, walnuts and honey.

String

Nytorgsgatan 38 (714 85 14). T-bana Medborgarplatsen/bus 3, 59, 66. **Open** 9.30am-9pm Mon-Fri; 10.30am-7pm Sat, Sun. **Credit** MC, V. **Map** p251 M9 ㉚

Once a furniture shop that served coffee to its customers, String is now a café that also sells furniture. Everything from the deckchair you sit on to the plate you eat off is for sale, and this is also the closest

you'll get to having your coffee in a shop window. String is as fun and hip as its young fan base, whose favourite hangover cure is the weekend breakfast buffet, and it has started offering live music in the basement on Sunday afternoons.

Wayne's Coffee

Götgatan 31 (644 45 90/www.waynescoffee.se). T-bana Slussen/bus 2, 3, 43, 53, 55, 59, 76. **Open** 8am-7pm Mon-Fri; 10am-7pm Sat; 11am-7pm Sun. **Credit** AmEx, MC, V. **Map** p250 L8 ㉛

No need to look for Wayne, he has a habit of popping up just about everywhere in town. Friendlier and more personal than other US-inspired cafés, Wayne's is deservedly popular among locals and you'll find branches all over the city. Wayne's caters, unusually in Sweden, for the decaf drinker and the weight-conscious – low-fat milk (*lätt mjölk*) is available on request. Everything on the menu, from the fruit smoothies and chocolate-chip cookies to the pitta bread rolls, is delicious. *Photo p135.*
Other locations Drottninggatan 31, Norrmalm (20 17 80); Kungsgatan 14, Kungsholmen (791 00 86); Odengatan 52, Vasastaden (34 56 88); Vasagatan 7, Norrmalm (24 59 70); SEB, Sergels Torg 2, Norrmalm (56 84 95 20); Mäster Samuelsgatan 28 (in Akademibokhandeln), Norrmalm (20 07 90).

Östermalm

Cookbook Café

Birger Jarlsgatan 76 (20 63 08/www.thecookbook cafe.com). T-bana Rådmansgatan or Tekniska Högskolan/bus 2, 4, 43, 53, 72. **Open** 8am-6pm Mon-Fri; 11am-5pm Sat. **Credit** MC, V. **Map** p245 C7 ②

Run by two Swedish-American sisters with a taste for wholesome goodness, the Cookbook Café has become a culinary institution in Stockholm and has even spawned a series of cookery books. It can feel like a mother and toddler group at times – prams are not allowed in the café, so you might have to negotiate a maze of parked-up buggies to get inside. If you do find a free seat, everything from the lunch dishes to dessert is delicious. No doubt they are inspired by the huge collection of cookery books on show from around the world, the most bizarre of which has to be *Cooking in the Nude for Golf Lovers*. *Photo p132.*

Depå

Smålandsgatan 10 (611 77 33/www.depa.se). T-bana Kungsträdgården/bus 2, 47, 55, 62. **Open** 8am-6pm Mon-Fri; noon-5pm Sat. **No credit cards.** **Map** p241 F8 ③

This chic little café is located in one of Stockholm's most exclusive shopping areas and is an excellent spot to take the weight off your feet for a while. Although Depå boasts a sushi and healthy lunch selection, it would be almost rude not to try the Snickers tart or strawberry pie.

Gateau

Sturegallerian, Stureplan (611 75 64/www.gateau. se). T-bana Östermalmstorg/bus 1, 2, 55, 56. **Open** 8am-7pm Mon-Fri; 9am-5pm Sat; 11am-5pm Sun. **Credit** AmEx, DC, MC, V. **Map** p241 F8 ②

Hold on to your purse strings – sweet-toothed tourists could blow their holiday budget at Gateau, purveyor of amazingly good cakes and pastries. Spaciously spread out on the first floor of luxurious shopping centre Sturegallerian, Gateau has several award-winning chefs on board. Prices are deservedly high but the afternoon tea special (warm scones, jam, marmalade and tea) won't break the bank. There is also a small shop in the mall, on the floor below, selling cakes and bread.

Saturnus

Eriksbergsgatan 6 (611 77 00). T-bana Östermalmstorg/bus 2, 42, 44. **Open** 8am-9pm Mon-Fri; 10am-midnight Sat, Sun. **Credit** AmEx, DC, MC, V. **Map** p245 D7 ③

Sweden's Crown Princess Victoria has been known to frequent this place, although the famous cinnamon buns hardly need the royal seal of approval; these gigantic pastries are out of this world and are big enough to feed a small family. You might have problems finding Saturnus, though – there isn't a proper sign, just a model of the planet hanging above the entrance. It's close to independent cinema Zita (*see p173*), so it's packed with cineastes during evenings and weekends.

Sturekatten

Riddargatan 4 (611 16 12). T-bana Östermalmstorg/bus 2, 55. **Open** May-Aug 9am-6pm Mon-Fri; 10am-5pm Sat. *Sept-Apr* 8am-8pm Mon-Fri; 9am-6pm Sat; 11am-6pm Sun. **Credit** MC, V. **Map** p241 F8 ③

If it ever stops serving fine coffee and cakes, Sturekatten should be delicately preserved forever. With two storeys of lace and antiques it's like an 18th-century doll's house. The house speciality is apple pie with meringue but it also serves delicious *semlor* (whipped cream and almond paste buns). The waitresses don old-style black and whites and, though it may sound like a pensioner's pleasure-dome, it's actually just as popular with teenagers. In the summer season, there is a pleasant little courtyard terrace to relax in. Free tables don't come easy here, so if the queue is too long, sister café Vete-Katten (Kungsgatan 55, 20 84 05) in nearby Norrmalm is also worth a try for a similar taste of old-fashioned hospitality.

Wienerkonditoriet

Biblioteksgatan 6-8 (611 21 16). T-bana Östermalmstorg/bus 2, 47, 55, 62. **Open** 7am-10pm Mon-Sat; 8am-10pm Sat; 10am-10pm Sun. **Credit** AmEx, DC, MC, V. **Map** p241 F8 ③

Located on one of Stockholm's most fashionable shopping streets, this is a good hangout for Ab Fab types. The downstairs area is fairly run of the mill in terms of decor, so try for a seat upstairs with its 1950s styling and views out over the street.

Kungsholmen

Bagel Deli

St Göransgatan 67 (716 11 40/www.bageldeli.net). T-bana Fridhemsplan/bus 3, 4, 40, 62. **Open** 7am-9pm Mon-Fri; 10am-9pm Sat, Sun. **Credit** AmEx, MC, V. **Map** p239 F2 ③

This school of bagel wizardry wouldn't look out of place on New York's Upper West Side. They are keen on cream cheese here, but there's a feast of fillings on the menu and you can't fail to pick a winner. Otherwise, the salads are stomach-stuffing – piled high with the best bits, you'll have to hunt for the boring lettuce leaves. There's always something typically Swedish and seasonal on the menu, and the lattes and freshly baked cakes are some of the best in town. No wonder this place is packed to bursting at weekends.

Café Julia

St Eriksgatan 15 (651 45 15). T-bana Fridhemsplan/bus 3, 4, 40, 52, 62. **Open** 10am-9pm Mon-Thur; 10am-7pm Fri-Sun. **Credit** DC, MC, V. **Map** p239 G2 ③

This haven for home-made soft cheese started out in a one-room apartment with a young couple making cheese in their bathtub. Now the bathroom has expanded to become one of Kungsholmen's most popular cafés. The soft cheese is churned in six flavours (try the horseradish), and any questions about the recipes are regarded as industrial espionage. The home-made cheesecake is, needless to say, the most popular dessert. Julia also sells picnic baskets filled with goodies.

Filibabba Coffee & Bakery

Parmmätargatan 7 (653 05 42/www.filibabbacafe. com). T-bana Radhuset/bus 3, 62. **Open** 7am-6pm Mon-Fri; 9.30am-5pm Sat, Sun. **Credit** AmEx, MC, V. **Map** p240 H4 ⓨ

This gorgeous little café is conveniently situated right beside the Tunnelbana exit and the rather more picturesque Kungsholms Kyrka. The entrance is a slightly perilous set of steps down into a cosy little cavern of a place. Boasting the best carrot cake in Stockholm, this is the perfect place to hole up on a winter's day.

Mälarpaviljongen

Norr Mälarstrand 64 (650 87 01/www. malarpaviljongen.se). T-bana Fridhemsplan/ Rådhuset/bus 3, 40, 52, 62. **Open** *May-Sept* 11am-midnight daily, weather permitting. **Credit** MC, V. **Map** p239 H3 ⓨ

This open-air café, situated right on the shore of Lake Mälaren, is the most picturesque spot in Stockholm to enjoy a latte. There's an excellent lunch menu, together with a choice of sandwiches, cakes and vanilla sauce-drizzled fruit pies. A new floating bar area has just been added if you fancy something a little stronger.

Muffin Bakery

Fridhemsgatan 3 (651 88 00). T-bana Fridhemsplan/ bus 4, 49, 57, 69. **Open** 9am-7pm Mon-Thur; 9am-5pm Fri-Sun. **Credit** MC, V. **Map** p239 G2 ⓨ

The Muffin Bakery's super-sized muffins are so famous that they even have their own cookery book. The café itself is a bit drab, so opt to sit outside on the grass instead. It's so popular with young parents on their way to Rålambshovsparken that it can be hard to find a seat. Stick to the sweet options, as the savoury muffins can be a bit too cheesy. Anyway, who needs other options when there are chocolate cheesecake muffins?

Thelins

St Eriksgatan 43 (651 19 00/www.thelinskonditori. se). T-bana Fridhemsplan/bus 1, 3, 4, 57. **Open** 7.30am-7pm Mon-Fri; 9am-6pm Sat, Sun. **Credit** MC, V. **Map** p239 F2 ⓨ

A traditional *konditori* and the place to sample the finest sweet Swedish delicacies, Thelins has more than 100 years of experience behind it. It's not exactly at the cutting edge of the city's café scene, but it does house the very best *semla* in Stockholm. Pick up a numbered ticket on your way in – it's a rather impersonal touch, but at peak times it's the only way to control the rush. Don't be afraid to ask the staff for advice on what to order – they might look bored but they are passionate about their cakes. **Other locations** Karlaplan 13, Ostermalm (663 6289); Odengatan 44, Vasastaden (612 6378).

Have a nice day: fast service and friendly smiles at US-style **Wayne's Coffee**. *See p133.*

Eat, Drink, Shop

Shops & Services

Chuck out the chintz.

Top of the shops: supremely elegant **NK**.

Shopping in Stockholm is a neatly arranged affair and certain streets are known for certain types of stores. It's not an exact science, but can give you some good starting points from which to begin a more wide-ranging exploration, credit card in hand.

For any visitor new to town, the best place to start is **Norrmalm**. On Hamngatan you'll find the heart of Stockholm shopping, the NK department store, as well as that world-famous Swedish success story, H&M. Drottninggatan, on the other hand, is rather like Oxford Street in London: always busy, full of chain stores, and best avoided at the weekend.

Östermalm is best for luxury goods and sophisticated fashion. Birger Jarlsgatan is home to some of the big names in the fashion world including Gucci, Mulberry, Versace and Louis Vuitton. For Scandinavian clothing, head to Grev Turegatan where you'll find Bruuns Bazaar, Filippa K, J Lindeberg and Anna Holtblad. Sibyllgatan is the street for new and vintage interior design, from Modernity, Pukeberg, Jacksons and Asplund, though down on Strandvägen there are two legendary Swedish stores selling interior design: Svenskt Tenn and Carl Malmsten.

Södermalm is the place to go for funkier fashion and other cool stuff. Start with the stores on Götgatan (the Bruno Götgatsbacken mini-mall, 10-Gruppen, Weekday) and then head off to rummage around the ever-so-trendy SoFo (South of Folkungagatan) area.

Vasastaden is the ideal hunting ground for second-hand treasures. St Eriksgatan has a run of second-hand record shops, while Upplandsgatan and Odengatan have a fine selection of antique shops.

Go to **Gamla Stan** only if you want a T-shirt with a moose on – Västerlånggatan is an awful line-up of tourist traps. Österlånggatan is nicer and has some charming shops, such as Kalikå for children's clothing and toys.

OPENING HOURS AND TAX REFUNDS

Most stores are usually open 10am to 6pm on weekdays. On Saturdays, smaller retailers may only open from 11am to 2pm and on Sundays many are closed. Department stores are usually open from 10am to 7pm on weekdays and 10am or 11am to 5pm or 6pm at the weekend.

In many shops, non-EU residents can ask for a Tax-Free Cheque when purchasing items costing more than 200kr (not including taxes). The cheque can be cashed at the airport when leaving the country (with a refund of 10 to 12 per cent). Look for the 'Tax-Free Shopping' sticker on shop doors, and be sure to get only one cheque for all your purchases in the department stores. For further information, call Global Refund on 0410 48 450 or visit www.globalrefund.com. Note that taxes are always included in the listed price in Sweden.

General

Department stores

Åhléns

Klarabergsgatan 50, Norrmalm (767 60 00/www.ahlens.se). T-bana T-Centralen/bus 47, 52, 56, 59, 65. **Open** 10am-8pm Mon-Fri; 10am-7pm Sat; 11am-6pm Sun. **Credit** AmEx, DC, MC, V. **Map** p241 G6.

You can't get much more central than Åhléns, which is located in a massive brick building next to Sergels Torg. It's an excellent mid-range department store with a good cosmetics and perfume section, a well-stocked homewares department and a large CD shop. The clothing department stocks threads by Swedish designers and international labels. You can get a luxurious facial in the Stockholm Day Spa and there's a big supermarket, Hemköp, in the basement.

NK

Hamngatan 18-20, Norrmalm (762 80 00/www.nk. se). T-bana Kungsträdgården or Östermalmstorg/ bus 2, 43, 47, 55, 59, 62, 69, 76. **Open** 10am-7pm Mon-Fri; 10am-6pm Sat; noon-5pm Sun (*June, July* noon-4pm Sun). **Credit** AmEx, DC, MC, V. **Map** p241 F7.

Eternally elegant, Nordiska Kompaniet is one of the city's most treasured institutions. The famous revolving sign on the roof – with the letters NK on one side and a clock on the other – is visible from all over town. A sort of Swedish Selfridges, it's a first-class store, particularly good for clothes, Swedish souvenirs (crafts and glassware in the basement) and gourmet food. You can get your photos developed while you have a coffee in Café Entrée, one of several great places to eat.

Malls

Bruno Götgatsbacken

Götgatan 36, Södermalm (757 76 00/www.bruno gallerian.se). T-bana Slussen or Medborgarplatsen/ bus 2, 3, 43, 53, 55, 59, 66, 76. **Open** *Shops* 10am-7pm Mon-Fri; 10am-5pm Sat; noon-4pm Sun. *Cafés & restaurants* call for details. **Credit** varies. **Map** p250 L8.

Sometimes called Galleria Bruno, this micro-mall, which opened up in 2004, consolidates Götgatan's status as one of Stockholm's hippest shopping streets. There's a café in the atrium, a cool bar (Ljunggrens; *see p121*) and several typically Swedish stores, including the likes of Filippa K, WE/JL and H&M. *Photo p138.*

Gallerian

Hamngatan 37, Norrmalm (www.gallerian.se). T-bana Kungsträdgården/bus 2, 47, 55, 59, 69. **Open** 10am-7pm Mon-Fri; 10am-6pm Sat; 11am-5pm Sun. **Credit** varies. **Map** p241 G7.

Located just down from Sergels Torg and just up from NK, Stockholm's first shopping mall is the place for everyday items rather than luxury goods. Among its 60 shops and cafés you'll find Foot Locker, BR-Leksaker for toys, DIY specialist Clas Ohlson, even TopShop. It's far from glamorous but packed every weekend.

PUB

Hötorget 13-15, Norrmalm (402 16 15/www.pub.se). T-bana Hötorget/bus 1, 52, 56. **Open** 10am-7pm Mon-Fri; 10am-5pm Sat, Sun. **Credit** AmEx, DC, MC, V. **Map** p241 F6.

Facing the bustling outdoor fruit and veg market at Hötorget, PUB is more of a mall than a department store, and a pretty boring one at that. Greta Garbo once worked in the millinery department and modelled hats for the store's catalogue.

Sturegallerian

Entrances at Grev Turegatan 9 & Stureplan, Östermalm (www.sturegallerian.se). T-bana Östermalmstorg/bus 1, 2, 55, 56, 62. **Open** 10am-7pm Mon-Fri; 10am-6pm Sat; noon-5pm Sun (*June, July* noon-4pm Sun). **Credit** varies. **Map** p241 F8.

If Sergels Torg is the people's centre of Stockholm, Sturegallerian and its environs are the centre for the jet set. As the city's most glamorous mall it has plenty of upmarket boutiques for picky customers, as well as super-spa Sturebadet (*see p154*), and the kind of ambience that comes only with a glass roof and marble floors. Café Pluto and Tures are excellent hangouts for post-retail refreshments, or there's the elegant Sturehof if you want to push the boat out. The bookshop Hedengrens (*see p138*) has a good collection of books in English about Stockholm.

Västermalmsgallerian

St Eriksgatan & Flemminggatan, Kungsholmen (737 20 00/www.vastermalmsgallerian.com). T-bana Fridhemsplan/bus 1, 3, 4, 57, 59. **Open** 10am-7pm Mon-Fri; 10am-5pm Sat; 11am-5pm Sun. **Credit** varies. **Map** p239 F2.

This pleasant shopping mall connected to the Fridhemsplan T-bana station kickstarted the revitalisation of Kungsholmen when it opened its doors a few years back. Shops include an ICA supermarket, Björn Borg, H&M, Face Stockholm, Granit, DesignTorget and many others. Café W in the entrance is busy all day long.

The best Streets

For chic antiques

Map p244 & p245.
Head for **Upplandsgatan** in Vasastaden to pick up some vintage souvenirs.

For luxury threads

Map p241.
Birger Jarlsgatan in Östermalm is dripping with haute couture.

For modern living

Map p250.
Kit out your home and body Söder-style on the southside's hip **Götgatan.**

For second-hand sounds

Map p239.
St Eriksgatan in Kungsholmen is the place to go for old records and CDs.

Specialist

Books & magazines

English-language

The books section at department store **NK** (*see p137*) has a good selection of fiction titles in English, plus guidebooks and maps.

Akademibokhandeln

Mäster Samuelsgatan 32, Norrmalm (613 61 00/ www.akademibokhandeln.se). T-bana T-Centralen or Hötorget/bus 43, 47, 52, 59, 69. **Open** 10am-7pm Mon-Fri; 10am-5pm Sat; noon-4pm Sun. **Credit** AmEx, DC, MC, V. **Map** p241 F7.

Akademibokhandeln has seven branches in the city and offers the best range of English paperbacks in Stockholm. The flagship store now has an excellent paperback department with an entire floor of books in English.

Other locations throughout the city.

Alfa Antikvariat

Drottninggatan 71A, Norrmalm (21 42 75). T-bana Hötorget. **Open** 10am-6pm Mon-Fri; 10am-4pm Sat. **Credit** AmEx, DC, MC, V. **Map** p241 F6.

This used bookshop on Drottninggatan has a good English department in the basement and lots of English paperbacks on the ground floor.

Hedengrens

Sturegallerian, Stureplan 4, Östermalm (611 51 28/www.hedengrens.se). T-bana Östermalmstorg/ bus 1, 2, 55, 56. **Open** 10am-7pm Mon-Fri; 10am-6pm Sat; noon-5pm Sun (*June, July* noon-4pm Sun). **Credit** AmEx, DC, MC, V. **Map** p241 F8.

Opened in 1898, Hedengrens is one of Stockholm's most famous bookshops. It specialises in novels and the arts, and half the stock is in English. Check out the English translations of Swedish authors such as Selma Lagerlöf, Torgny Lindgren and Astrid Lindgren. The fiction section also includes titles in Spanish, Italian, German, French, Danish and Norwegian. Ideal for browsing.

Pocketshop

Central Station, Norrmalm (24 27 05/www. pocketshop.se). T-bana T-Centralen/bus 47, 53, 69. **Open** 5.40am-10pm Mon-Fri; 7am-8pm Sat; 9am-10pm Sun. **Credit** AmEx, DC, MC, V. **Map** p241 G6.

Pocketshop has around 400 contemporary fiction titles in English. The two branches in Central Station (one in the main hall, the other downstairs by the commuter trains) are a great place to pick up a book for a long train ride.

Other locations: Götgatan 40, Södermalm (640 94 05); Kulturhuset, Sergels Torg, Norrmalm (22 05 15); Gallerian, Hamngatan 37, Norrmalm (406 08 18); Västermalmsgallerian, Kungsholmen (654 83 00).

Bruno Götgatsbacken. *See p137*.

Sweden Bookshop

*Slottsbacken 10, Gamla Stan (453 78 00/www.
swedenbookshop.com).* **Open** *Oct-July* 10am-6pm
Mon-Fri. *Aug-Sept* 10am-6pm Mon-Fri; 11am-4pm
Sat. **Credit** AmEx, DC, MC, V. **Map** p241 H8.
The Swedish Institute bookshop, opposite the Royal
Palace, is the best place to find books about Sweden
in more than 30 languages. These range from Astrid
Lindgren's children's books to Henning Mankell's
thrillers, as well as publications on Swedish food,
history, culture and language.

Specialist

Alvglans

*Folkungagatan 84, Södermalm (642 69 98/www.
alvglans.se). T-bana Medborgarplatsen/bus 2, 53,
59, 66.* **Open** 11am-6pm Mon-Fri; 11am-4pm Sat.
Credit MC, V. **Map** p251 L9.
The Spawn action figures alone are worth the trip
to the comics heaven of Alvglans. The shop stocks
bestsellers such as X-Men and Spiderman, as well
as rare anime movies and manga DVDs.

Kartcentrum

*Vasagatan 16, Norrmalm (411 16 97/www.kart
centrum.se). T-bana T-Centralen/bus 2, 3, 53, 62,
69.* **Open** 9.30am-6pm Mon-Fri; 10am-4pm Sat.
Credit AmEx, DC, MC, V. **Map** p241 G6.
Conveniently located just opposite Central Station,
this travel specialist has a good range of maps,

guidebooks and atlases, as well as CD-Rom maps
and marine charts for the more intrepid traveller.

Konst-ig

*Basement, Kulturhuset, Sergels Torg, Norrmalm (20
54 20/www.konstig.se). T-bana T-Centralen/bus 47,
52, 56, 59, 65.* **Open** 11am-7pm Mon; 10am-7pm
Tue-Fri; 10am-5pm Sat; noon-4pm Sun. **Credit**
AmEx, MC, V. **Map** p241 G7.
Stockholm's leading art bookshop, covering design,
architecture, photography, fashion and more.
Located in the basement of Kulturhuset, next to
DesignTorget (*see p150*).

Children

Fashion

H&M (*see p143*) is the most successful clothes
shop for both parents and children in Sweden.
You'll find kids' clothes at the larger H&M
stores, such as Hamngatan 22 (796 54 34),
Sergelgatan 1 (796 54 41) and Drottninggatan
56 (796 54 57), all situated in Norrmalm.
The **NK** (*see p137*) kids' department deals in
designer babies' and children's clothing.

Kalikå

*Österlånggatan 18, Gamla Stan (20 52 19/www.
kalika.se). T-bana Gamla Stan/bus 2, 43, 55, 59, 76.*
Open 10am-6pm Mon-Fri; 10am-4pm Sat; 11am-3pm
Sun. **Credit** AmEx, DC, MC, V. **Map** p241 J8.

Eat, Drink, Shop

Only the absence of incense reveals that this is not a time machine with the dial set to the 1970s. With clothes, hats, finger puppets and stuffed toys all in brightly coloured velour, you can reincarnate your youngster as a hippie kid.

Polarn o Pyret

Hamngatan 10, Norrmalm (411 41 40/www.polarn opyret.se). T-bana Östermalmstorg/bus 2, 47, 55, 59, 62, 69. **Open** 10am-7pm Mon-Fri; 10am-5pm Sat; noon-5pm Sun. **Credit** AmEx, DC, MC, V. **Map** p241 F8.

Polarn o Pyret (the Pal & the Tot) became famous in the 1970s when its striped, long-sleeved T-shirt dressed a generation of kids. With a retro revival in the new millennium, today grown-ups and children alike can be seen sporting Polarn o Pyret's soft fabrics and simple styles. And, of course, stripes. **Other locations** Gallerian, Hamngatan 37, Norrmalm (411 22 47); Västermalmsgallerian, Kungsholmen (653 57 30); Fältöversten, Karlavägen 13, Östermalm (660 62 75); Ringen, Götgatan/Ringvägen, Södermalm (642 03 62).

Toys

BR-Leksaker

Gallerian, Hamngatan 37, Norrmalm (54 51 54 40/ www.br-leksaker.se). T-bana Kungsträdgården or T-Centralen/bus 43, 47, 55, 62, 65. **Open** 10am-7pm Mon-Fri; 10am-6pm Sat; 11am-5pm Sun. **Credit** AmEx, DC, MC, V. **Map** p241 G7.

This large toy store is located in the Gallerian mall, opposite NK, and stocks all the usual suspects of the toy world, including Lego and Disney products.

Bulleribock

Sveavägen 104, Vasastaden (673 61 21). T-bana Rådmansgatan/bus 2, 4, 42, 43, 52, 72. **Open** 11am-6pm Mon-Fri; 11am-3pm Sat. **Credit** AmEx, MC, V. **Map** p245 D6.

It's no wonder that Swedish children seem content – and clever – when they spend their pocket money at places like Bulleribock, which specialises in colourful, traditional toys.

Krabat & Co

Folkungagatan 79, Södermalm (640 32 48/www. krabat.se). T-bana Medborgarplatsen/bus 2, 3, 53, 59, 66, 76. **Open** 10am-6pm Mon-Fri; 10am-4pm Sat. **Credit** AmEx, MC, V. **Map** p251 L9.

Who do you want to be? Krabat has great dressing-up outfits for wannabe knights, fairies, Indian chiefs, pirates, clowns and Robin Hoods. **Other locations** Kungsgatan 53, Norrmalm (24 94 20).

Electronics & photography

Fotoquick

Åhlens City, Norrmalm (411 99 15/www.foto quick.se). T-bana T-Centralen/bus 47, 52, 53, 56, 69. **Open** 10am-8pm Mon-Fri; 10am-7pm Sat; 11am-6pm Sun. **Credit** AmEx, DC, MC, V. **Map** p241 G7.

The cost of film developing in Stockholm can vary a great deal, sometimes by as much as 100kr per film. Fotoquick is a cheap option, developing a 36-print colour film in one hour for 179kr. **Other locations** Central Station, Norrmalm (21 29 55); Hamngatan 16, Norrmalm (21 40 42); Ringens Köpcentrum, Götgatan 100, Södermalm (640 98 10).

OnOff

Kungsgatan 29, Norrmalm (701 07 10/www. onoff.se). T-bana Hötorget/bus 1, 43, 52, 55, 56. **Open** 10am-7pm Mon-Fri; 10am-5pm Sat; noon-4pm Sun. **Credit** AmEx, MC, V. **Map** p241 F7.

Sweden's biggest retailer of electronic goods, including computers, cameras, audio-visual equipment and mobile phones. While the prices are certainly friendly, the shop is understaffed, so save valuable queuing time by calling in advance to check what you're looking for is in stock. **Other locations** Sveavägen 13-15, Norrmalm (54 51 12 00); Fältöversten, Karlavägen 19, Östermalm (701 06 20).

Fashion

Designer

Most of the designer shops are clustered around hotspot Stureplan: on the lower end of Birger Jarlsgatan and along swanky Biblioteksgatan. On Birger Jarlsgatan you'll find plenty of top-end international designers, including **Gucci** (No.1, 54 50 05 44), **Cerruti** (No.5, 678 45 00), **Max Mara** (No.12, 611 14 66), **Versace** (No.21, 611 91 90) and **Hugo Boss** (No.28, 611 42 40). **Emporio Armani**'s store can be found at Biblioteksgatan 3 (678 79 80).

Götgatsbacken (the northern part of Gotgatan) on Söder had a facelift about ten years ago and now houses various fashion boutiques, including **Filippa K**. The area of Södermalm known as SoFo, south of Folkungagatan, has a high concentration of independent fashion designers. The department stores **NK** (*see p137*) and **Åhléns** (*see p136*) also have good designer departments.

Acne

Hamngatan 10-14, Östermalm (20 34 55). T-bana Östermalmstorg/bus 2, 47, 55, 59, 62, 76. **Open** 10am-7pm Mon-Fri; 10am-5pm Sat. **Credit** AmEx, DC, MC, V. **Map** p241 F7.

The not-so-glamorously named Acne started out as an advertising agency, became a jeans manufacturer and is now an all-round designer, although it's still best known for its innovative denim.

Anna Holtblad

Grev Turegatan 13, Östermalm (54 50 22 20/ www.annaholtblad.se). T-bana Östermalmstorg/ bus 1, 2, 55, 56. **Open** 10.30am-6.30pm Mon-Fri; 10.30am-4pm Sat. **Credit** AmEx, DC, MC, V. **Map** p241 F8.

Anna Holtblad has been one of Sweden's top designers for the past 20 years. She is best known for her folklore-inspired knitwear.

Filippa K

Götgatan 23, Södermalm (55 69 85 85/www.
filippak.com). T-bana Slussen/bus 2, 3, 43, 53,
55, 59, 76. **Open** 10am-7pm Mon-Fri; 10am-4pm
Sat; noon-4pm Sun. **Credit** AmEx, DC, MC, V.
Map p250 L8.
Filippa K creates basic, good-quality clothes with clean Scandinavian lines for Swedish men and women wanting to dress fashionably without sticking out from the crowd. It has recently started making kitchenware as well.
Other locations Grev Turegatan 18,
Östermalm (54 58 88 88); Biblioteksgatan 2,
Östermalm (611 88 03).

J Lindeberg

Grev Turegatan 9, Östermalm (678 61 65/www.
jlindeberg.com). T-bana Östermalmstorg/bus 1, 2,
55, 56. **Open** 10am-7pm Mon-Fri; 10am-5pm
Sat; noon-5pm Sun. **Credit** AmEx, DC, MC, V.
Map p241 F8.
Johan Lindeberg first became a must-have name among the capital's media, fashion and PR types, but has now become more mainstream. The clothes are basic but with unexpected details; the staff are playful but professional.

Maria Westerlind

Drottninggatan 81A, Norrmalm (23 45 45/
www.mariawesterlind.com). T-bana Hötorget or
Rådmansgatan/bus 52, 69. **Open** 10.30am-6.30pm
Mon-Fri; 11am-4pm Sat. **Credit** AmEx, DC, MC, V.
Map p245 E6.
Traditional lines, mild colours and simple fabrics are what make Maria Westerlind one of Sweden's best young designers. The twentysomething women who get their striped dresses and floral skirts here are aware of style and quality, but prefer not to be too eye-catching.

Mrs H Stockholm

Inside Passagen mini mall, Birger Jarlsgatan 7
(678 02 00/www.mrsh.se). T-bana Östermalmstorg/
bus 1, 2, 47, 55, 62. **Open** 11am-6.30pm Mon-
Fri; noon-4pm Sat. **Credit** AmEx, DC, MC, V.
Map p245 E6.
Mrs H stocks bags, shoes, clothes and make-up for the true fashionista. Here you will find hand-picked items from Sonia Rykiel, Juicy Couture, Marc Jacobs, Alexander McQueen and the like.

Tiger of Sweden

Jakobsbergsgatan 8, Norrmalm (440 30 60/www.
tigerofsweden.com). T-bana Östermalmstorg/bus 2,
43, 59. **Open** 10.30am-6.30pm Mon-Fri; 11am-5pm
Sat; noon-4pm Sun. **Credit** AmEx, DC, MC, V.
Map p241 F8.
Tiger first became known for dressing Swedish pop phenomenon Kent, and suddenly it was dressing a whole generation of young males. Suits are still the trademark, but Tiger now also makes casualwear

H&M. *See p143.*

Eat, Drink, Shop

Local looks

No one could ever accuse Sweden of being a hotbed of individuality. Walk around Stockholm and you'll quickly notice that people like to dress, well, alike. Whenever something emerges as a fashion must-have, everyone has it. Another thing you'll notice is that the boys are as fashion-conscious as the girls. It's a city of people keen to join a trend as soon as it emerges, and were you to rummage through the closets of a handful of stylish Stockholmers, you'd be sure to find one or more of the following brands.

Acne

See p140

Best known for its jeans line, Acne is in fact a conglomerate of several different ventures, including a successful advertising company. But it's the jeans that people talk about – and copy. It seems appropriate that such an influential company should have a symbolic flagship store: the Acne store on Norrmalmstorg is housed in a converted bank. It was here, in 1973, that a robbery and hostage situation introduced the world to the concept of Stockholm Syndrome.

Björn Borg

See p146

Yes, it's the same Björn Borg who won Wimbledon, though reportedly he doesn't have much involvement in the company that bears his name. The thing to get hold of is the underwear. Some of the other pieces are great, but it's the knickers – for men and women – that are not only comfortable but make a perfect souvenir.

Filippa K

See p141

Filippa Knutsson is on her way to becoming the patron saint of young professional Swedes. For simple, reliable, stylish clothing, she's hard to beat. Most clothes stick to a simple palette of black, white or grey, with occasional splashes of colour. If you want to blend in, you come here.

Tiger of Sweden

See p141

This is a Tiger with a dual personality. Tiger suits are sharp, slim-fitting and great quality – the perfect outfit for professional Swedes. (Its 2007 collection was inspired, bizarrely, by Manhattan real estate agents.) Meanwhile the jeans line is much more trend-conscious and aimed at a younger audience.

WESC

www.wesc.com

The full name, We Are the Superlative Conspiracy, may be pompous and the mission statement pretentious – 'a street fashion brand for intellectual slackers' – but We, as WESC is also known, has taken its skateboard aesthetic and turned it into a global brand, with stores as far afield as Tokyo, Seoul and Beverly Hills.

and clothes for women. The look is classic with a contemporary twist. The shop also sells quality shoes and accessories.
Other locations PK-Huset, Hamngatan 10-14, Norrmalm (20 20 55).

General

Diesel has recently opened a larger and more modern store at Biblioteksgatan 9 (678 07 09) near Stureplan. You can also find **Oasis** just a few doors down at Nos.8-10 (660 69 51), as well as the newly opened **Urban Outfitters** at No.5 (54 50 65 90).

Boutique Sportif
Renstiernas Gata 26, Södermalm (411 12 13). Bus 2, 53, 59, 66, 76. **Open** noon-6pm Mon-Fri; noon-5pm Sat. **Credit** AmEx, MC, V. **Map** p251 M9.
Boutique Sportif has its own take on streetwear, with logo sweatpants, funky tees and baggy pants for him and her. The shop is well known for its tops with different parts of the city printed on the front. Do get your own hooded jacket with 'SoFo', 'Vasastan' or simply 'Stockholm' across the chest; don't worry about the staff, they won't bite.

Brothers
Drottninggatan 53, Norrmalm (411 12 01/www. brothers.se). T-bana T-Centralen/bus 47, 52, 56, 59, 65. **Open** 10am-7pm Mon-Fri; 10am-6pm Sat; noon-5pm Sun. **Credit** AmEx, DC, MC, V. **Map** p241 F6.
This nationwide chain provides Swedish men with everything from suits to socks. The shop is spacious and the staff are friendly and happy to sort you out with own label Riley or something slightly more costly from J Lindeberg or Lyle & Scott.

Cali
Brunnsgatan 9, Norrmalm (56 74 99 08/www. caliroots.se). T-bana Östermalmstorg/bus 1, 2, 55, 59. **Open** noon-6.30pm Mon-Fri; noon-5pm Sat. **Credit** MC, V. **Map** p241 E7.
Cali has a great selection of streetwear for men and women. You will find sneakers from Vans, vintage from Adidas and baggy pants from Fresh Jive, as well as jewellery.

H&M
Hamngatan 22, Norrmalm (52 46 35 30/www. hm.com). T-bana Kungsträdgården or T-Centralen/ bus 2, 43, 47, 59, 65. **Open** 10am-7pm Mon-Fri; 10am-6pm Sat; noon-5pm Sun. **Credit** AmEx, DC, MC, V. **Map** p241 F7.
International megastore H&M needs little introduction. By quickly designing copies of each new season's catwalk fashions, it has made itself almost as well known worldwide as Ikea. The clothes are trendy and cheap and mostly of surprisingly good quality. There are branches all over Stockholm but Hamngatan is the store where the latest clothes arrive first. *Photo p141.*
Other locations throughout the city.

Hugo
St Eriksgatan 39, Kungsholmen (652 49 90/www. hugo-sthlm.com). T-bana Fridhemsplan/bus 1, 3, 4, 40, 62. **Open** 10.30am-7pm Mon-Fri; 11am-4pm Sat; noon-4pm Sun. **Credit** AmEx, DC, MC, V. **Map** p239 F2.
Fashion-conscious men who don't worry about paying a little extra to look a little extra get everything from underwear to suits at Hugo. Staff hand-pick a few garments from different international labels every season, so this is the place to find something exclusive. Top Swedish designer labels Tiger and Filippa K are sold here.

Indiska Magasinet
Drottninggatan 53, Norrmalm (10 91 93/www. indiska.se). T-bana T-Centralen/bus 47, 52, 56, 59, 65. **Open** 10am-7pm Mon-Fri; 10am-6pm Sat; 11am-5pm Sun. **Credit** AmEx, DC, MC, V. **Map** p241 F6.
Once upon a time Indiska was associated with poor quality and design, dressing only backpackers coming home from eight months in Asia and missing the tie-dye scarves from those blurry nights in Goa. But these days it sells a range of fashionable but still orientally influenced clothes and accessories for women and children at nearly Asian prices. Their imported furniture and homeware have also become extremely popular.
Other locations throughout the city.

Lindex
Kungsgatan 48, Norrmalm (21 77 80/www. lindex.se). T-bana Hötorget/bus 1, 52, 56. **Open** 10am-7pm Mon-Fri; 10am-6pm Sat; noon-4pm Sun. **Credit** AmEx, DC, MC, V. **Map** p241 F7.
A very reasonably priced Swedish chain for women and children. The image is a little middle-aged, but a great amount of money and effort has been spent on supermodels and TV ads to brighten up the brand. The underwear and swimwear section is always worth checking out.
Other locations throughout the city.

Plagg
Odengatan 75, Vasastaden (31 90 04). T-bana Odenplan/bus 2, 4, 40, 53, 72. **Open** 10am-6.30pm Mon-Fri; 11am-4pm Sat, Sun. **Credit** AmEx, DC, MC, V. **Map** p245 D5.
At Plagg, the smart-looking 21st-century woman gets classy clothing from designers such as Denmark's DAY/Birger et Mikkelsen or Sweden's hugely successful Filippa K. The selection is larger than you think when you see the size of the shop.
Other locations St Eriksgatan 37, Kungsholmen (650 31 58); Rörstrandsgatan 8, Vasastaden (30 58 01); Götgatan 31, Södermalm (442 00 55).

Solo
Smålandsgatan 20, Östermalm (611 64 41/ www.solo.se). T-bana Östermalmstorg/bus 2, 47, 55, 59, 62, 76. **Open** 10am-7pm Mon-Fri; 10am-6pm Sat; noon-5pm Sun. **Credit** AmEx, DC, MC, V. **Map** p241 F8.

Melanders Blommor. *See p148.*

Solo has one of the best selections of jeans in the whole of Stockholm, featuring cool brands such as Acne, Cheap Monday and Nudie. The friendly and persuasive staff know how to flatter both you and your bottom.

Other locations Västermalmsgallerian, Kungsholmen (653 38 20).

Svea
Birger Jarlsgatan 7, Östermalm (679 60 13/www. sveasvea.se). T-bana Östermalmstorg/bus 2, 47, 55, 62, 65. **Open** 10am-8pm Mon-Fri; 10am-6pm Sat; 11am-5pm Sun. **Credit** AmEx, DC, MC, V. **Map** p241 F8.

This Swedish skate label with a crown logo produces modern casualwear with an emphasis on quality and often with a quirky twist. The first men's collection was released in spring 2007.

Other locations Souk mall, Drottninggatan 53, Norrmalm (50 57 41 11).

VeroModa
Hamngatan 37, Norrmalm (14 10 41/www. veromoda.com). T-bana Kungsträdgården or T-Centralen/bus 2, 43, 47, 59, 62. **Open** 10am-7pm Mon-Fri; 10am-6pm Sat; 11am-4pm Sun. **Credit** AmEx, DC, MC, V. **Map** p241 G7.

Danish VeroModa is the only chain of clothes shops that can compete with H&M when it comes to trendy, cheap women's clothing. But the selection is much smaller than its rival's.

Other locations throughout the city.

Used & vintage

59 Vintage Store
Hantverkargatan 59, Kungsholmen (652 37 27). T-bana Rådhuset/bus 3, 40, 52, 62. **Open** noon-7pm Mon-Fri; noon-4pm Sat. **Credit** AmEx, DC, MC, V. **Map** p240 G3.

'Retro with a feeling of now' is how owner Annette defines the clothes she packs into her small shop. Her carefully selected dresses, jackets, skirts, trousers and tops from the 1960s, '70s and '80s are definitely worth a detour.

Lisa Larssons Second Hand
Bondegatan 48, Södermalm (643 61 53). Bus 2, 53, 59, 66, 76. **Open** noon-6pm Tue-Fri; noon-3pm Sat. **No credit cards. Map** p251 M9.

Lisa Larssons is one of the most popular second-hand shops for Stockholm's trendy young things. Lots of leather jackets but also more dressy items for men and women.

Mormors Skattkista
Bondegatan 56, Södermalm (643 61 09). Bus 2, 53, 59, 66, 76. **Open** 1-6pm Mon-Fri. **No credit cards**. **Map** p251 M9.

Mormors Skattkista sells vintage clothes, bags and jewellery from as far back as the 1920s. The quality is good, since the owner has pre-selected the stock, not letting just any old thing into her shop. There are also vintage toys for sale.

Fashion accessories

Bags, gloves & hats

Mrs H Stockholm (*see p141*) is a fine stop for bags and shoes, and **Accessorize** has a shop at Biblioteksgatan 5 (611 04 05).

Östermalms Handskaffär

St Eriksgatan 31, Kungsholmen (650 06 02). T-bana Fridhemsplan/bus 1, 3, 4, 40, 62. **Open** 11am-6pm Mon-Fri; 11am-3pm Sat. **Credit** AmEx, DC, MC, V. **Map** p239 F2.

Even if the shop looks pretty empty from the outside, Östermalms Handskaffär is most definitely not. In a few square metres, you can find the most feminine jewellery from Holmquist & Co, pink suede or traditional black leather gloves, and colourful bags from Danish label Friis & Co. With its mid-range prices, this shop is a find.
Other locations Karlavägen 61, Östermalm (661 30 78).

Wedins Accent

Drottninggatan 66, Norrmalm (54 52 32 63). T-bana Hötorget/bus 1, 47, 53. **Open** 10am-7pm Mon-Fri; 10am-5pm Sat; noon-4pm Sun. **Credit** AmEx, MC, V. **Map** p241 F6.

Looking for soft suede gloves, large bags, a silk scarf or new leather wallet? Wedins Accent has it all, with price tags more suited to the hippie than the yuppie.

Other locations Drottninggatan 56, Norrmalm (56 84 91 18); Sergelgatan 11-15, Norrmalm (54 51 79 53); Kungsgatan 48, Norrmalm (21 30 06).

Jewellery

Antikt, Gammalt & Nytt

Mäster Samuelsgatan 11, Norrmalm (678 35 30). T-bana Östermalmstorg/bus 1, 2, 47, 59, 69. **Open** 11am-6pm Mon-Fri; 11am-4pm Sat. **Credit** AmEx, DC, MC, V. **Map** p241 F8.

This is the place to go when you need an antique rhinestone tiara or a glass brooch in any colour, size or price range. The shop was dreamed up by Tore and Mats Grundström when they discovered a warehouse full of long-forgotten 1940s gear. You will have to fight over all the best pieces with stylists and other dedicated followers of fashion.

Efva Attling

Hornsgatan 42, Södermalm (642 99 49/www. efvaattlingstockholm.com). T-bana Mariatorget/ bus 43, 55, 59, 66. **Open** 10.30am-6pm Mon-Fri; 11am-4pm Sat. **Credit** AmEx, DC, MC, V. **Map** p250 K6.

Efva Attling is the glamorous lady silversmith who first made it as an Eileen Ford model and pop star (with the band X-models), and then hit the headlines for marrying the gorgeous female musician Eva Dahlgren. She makes simply beautiful silver and gold jewellery with names such as 'Homo Sapiens'

and 'Divorced with Children'. Her international client list includes celebrities such as Madonna and Jennifer Aniston.
Other locations Birger Jarlsgatan 9, Östermalm (611 90 80).

Glitter
Gallerian, Hamngatan 37, Norrmalm (411 27 40/ www.glitter.se). T-Centralen/bus 43, 47, 59. **Open** 10am-7pm Mon-Fri; 10am-6pm Sat; 11am-4pm Sun. **Credit** AmEx, MC, V. **Map** p241 G7.
Glitter is a countrywide chain of budget jewellery shops, but this is the only one in Stockholm. It is the place to pick up a pair of dirt cheap plastic earrings or a bracelet of faux pearls. The prices somehow manage to compete with H&M.

WA Bolin
Stureplan 6, Östermalm (54 50 77 70/www.bolin.se). T-bana Östermalmstorg/bus 1, 2, 55, 56. **Open** 10am-6pm Mon-Fri; 11am-3pm Sat. **Credit** AmEx, DC, MC, V. **Map** p241 F8.
WA Bolin was established in 1791 and provides the royal family with jewellery. As well as vintage and classic pieces, it also sells trendier styles. Quality and service are exquisite.

Lingerie & underwear

Björn Borg
Sturegallerian, Stureplan, Östermalm (678 20 40/ www.bjornborg.se). T-bana Östermalmstorg/bus 1, 2, 55, 56. **Open** 10am-7pm Mon-Fri; 10am-6pm Sat; noon-5pm Sun (July 10am-5pm Sat; closed Sun). **Credit** AmEx, DC, MC, V. **Map** p241 F8.
Björn Borg, once the king of tennis, is now the king of Swedish smalls and his collection, from underwear to bags and shoes, is ace.
Other locations Västermalmsgallerian, Kungsholmen (652 12 40).

Gustaf Mellbin
Västerlånggatan 47, Gamla Stan (20 21 93). T-bana Gamla Stan/bus 3, 43, 53, 55, 76. **Open** 10.30am-6pm Mon-Fri; 10.30am-3pm Sat. **Credit** AmEx, DC, MC, V. **Map** p241 J7.
The shop assistants at stylish lingerie shop Gustaf Mellbin could become your new best friends if you're looking for good service and cups up to F, G and even H. Expensive but great quality.

Shoes

Don & Donna
Biblioteksgatan 9, Östermalm (611 01 32). T-bana Östermalm/bus 1, 2, 55, 56. **Open** 10am-7pm Mon-Fri; 10am-5pm Sat; noon-4pm Sun. **Credit** AmEx, DC, MC, V. **Map** p241 F8.
Don & Donna's handsome shoe shop has been popular for ages. They stock their own label (which is also sold at Wedins), as well as internationally known names.

Jerns Skor
Nybrogatan 9, Östermalm (611 20 32/www.jerns.se). T-bana Östermalmstorg/bus 2, 47, 62, 69, 76. **Open** 10am-7pm Mon-Fri; 10am-4pm Sat; noon-4pm Sun. **Credit** AmEx, DC, MC, V. **Map** p241 F8.
Chain store Jerns puts the emphasis on elegance when it comes to footwear, although you can still find a pair of beaded flip-flops. It's the place for bigfoots to find smart designs in larger sizes.
Other locations Sveavägen 44, Norrmalm (10 15 33); Drottninggatan 37, Norrmalm (40 20 72 09); Gallerian, Hamngatan 37, Norrmalm (20 97 50).

Nilson Skobutik
Biblioteksgatan 3, Östermalm (611 94 56/www. nilson.com). T-bana Östermalmstorg/bus 2, 47, 55, 59, 62. **Open** 10am-7pm Mon-Fri; 10am-5pm Sat; noon-4pm Sun. **Credit** AmEx, DC, MC, V. **Map** p241 F8.
Upmarket chain store Nilson can fit you out with a pair of high-quality leather boots, high-heeled slingbacks or smart loafers. Trendy styles at good prices.
Other locations Kungsgatan 7, Norrmalm (20 62 25); Gallerian, Hamngatan 37, Norrmalm (411 71 75); Sergelgatan 21, Norrmalm (406 04 40).

Rizzo
Biblioteksgatan 10, Östermalm (611 28 08/www. rizzo.se). T-bana Östermalmstorg/bus 1, 2, 55, 56. **Open** 10am-7pm Mon-Fri; 10am-5pm Sat; noon-4pm Sun. **Credit** AmEx, DC, MC, V. **Map** p241 F8.
A few years ago Rizzo made mostly sensible shoes. Now heels and strappy sandals are taking over the collection. The men's section includes cool labels such as Debut, Paul Smith and Boss.
Other locations Kungsgatan 26, Norrmalm (781 04 96); Gallerian, Hamngatan 37, Norrmalm (21 85 21).

SkoUno
Gamla Brogatan 34, Norrmalm (20 64 58). T-bana Hötorget or T-Centralen/bus 1, 47, 52, 53, 69. **Open** 10am-6pm Mon-Fri; 10am-4pm Sat. **Credit** AmEx, MC, V. **Map** p241 F6.
With Dr Martens and Spice Girls-style platform Buffalos, plus a great variety of other known brands, SkoUno is one of Stockholm's most vibrant boutiques.
Other locations: Drottninggatan 70, Norrmalm (21 98 89); Gamla Brogatan 23, Norrmalm (21 34 61).

Sneakersnstuff
Åsögatan 124, Södermalm (743 03 22/www. sneakersnstuff.com). T-bana Medborgarplatsen/bus 59, 66. **Open** 11am-6.30pm Mon-Fri; 11am-5pm Sat, noon-4pm Sun. **Credit** AmEx, MC, V. **Map** p251 M8.
Aimed at the clubgoer rather than the marathon man, twentysomethings come here to pick up the latest sneaker release from Nike. Streetwear also available.

Florists

You'll find excellent flower stalls in the city's open spaces, such as **Östermalmstorg**, **Norrmalmstorg**, **Hötorget**, **Odenplan**, **Medborgarplatsen** and **Södermalmstorg**.

Östermalms Saluhall.
See p149.

Christoffers Blommor

Kåkbrinken 10, Gamla Stan (24 00 75). T-bana Gamla Stan/bus 3, 53. **Open** 10am-6pm Mon-Fri; 10.30am-4pm Sat. **Credit** AmEx, MC, V. **Map** p241 J7.

Christoffer is charming and his small shop on one of the narrower streets in Gamla Stan is a good place to grab some flowers.

Melanders Blommor

Hamngatan 2, Norrmalm (611 28 59/www. melandersblommor.se). T-bana Östermalstorg/bus 2, 47, 62, 69, 76. **Open** 10am-6pm Mon-Fri; 10am-4pm Sat. **Credit** AmEx, DC, MC, V. **Map** p241 F8.

Established in 1894, this small shop is probably the poshest florist in Stockholm, supplier to the king and various other well-heeled Swedes. *Photo p144.*

Food & drink

Bakeries & pâtisseries

Riddarbageriet

Riddargatan 15, Östermalm (660 33 75). T-bana Östermalmstorg/bus 2, 47, 62, 69, 76. **Open** 8am-6pm Mon-Fri; 8am-3pm Sat. **Credit** MC, V. **Map** p242 F9.

Street talk

An Englishman started **Street** (Hornstulls Strand 4, Södermalm) with the aim of bringing a London-style street market buzz to Stockholm. Founder John Higson said Street should be 'a stage where inventiveness, drama, discovery and new meetings can take place'. It certainly took inventiveness to take a totally nondescript street in Södermalm, decorate it with a mosaic of mirror shards and turn it into a lively weekend destination. There's a restaurant with a large alfresco dining area that uses ingredients sourced from local farmers; a lounge bar with a lengthy DJ line-up that serves organic wine; a stage that hosts everything from poetry slams to comedy shows; and, outside by the water, a smaller

stage where you might catch a bit of interpretive dance on a sunny afternoon.

The only trouble with the place is that the stalls themselves can be slightly underwhelming. Expect lots of beaded jewellery, second-hand clothes and extremely bad art. The best of the bunch are the stalls selling colourful Scandinavian children's clothes. If the Street restaurant is too busy, continue under the bridge to Café Loopin Marin, a likeable little place with a smashing waterfront location at the end of the jetty.

● *Street normally takes place on alternate weekends from March until Christmas. The bar is open Friday and Saturday, and the restaurant opens daily. For details, check the website at www.streetinstockholm.se.*

The best bread in Stockholm. The cakes are outstanding too, but it's Johan Sörberg's sourdough loaves that the locals love. There are a handful of small tables inside and it's one of the few places in town that serves tea in a pot. Sister property to the bakery at the Hotel Rival (*see p43*).

Vete-Katten

Kungsgatan 55, Norrmalm (20 84 05/www. vetekatten.se). T-bana Hötorget or T-Centralen/bus 1, 47, 53, 69. **Open** 7.30am-8pm Mon-Fri; 9.30am-5pm Sat. **Credit** AmEx, DC, MC, V. **Map** p241 F6.
This old-fashioned tearoom serves classic Swedish pâtisseries such as *prinsesstårta* ('princess tart' – a cream-filled cake encased in green marzipan). You can also buy biscuits, bread, cinnamon, vanilla and cardamom rolls, plus home-made ice-cream.

Drinks

All forms of strong alcohol (over 3.5 per cent) may only be purchased at state-owned **Systembolaget** shops. The largest store in Stockholm is at Klarabergsgatan 62, Norrmalm (21 47 44, www.systembolaget.se, open 10am-8pm Mon-Fri, 10am-3pm Sat). Check the website for other stores.

Sibyllans Kaffe & Tehandel

Sibyllegatan 35, Östermalm (662 06 63/www. sibyllanskaffetehandel.com). T-bana Östermalmstorg/ bus 1, 42, 44, 56, 62. **Open** 9.30am-6pm Mon-Fri. **No credit cards. Map** p242 E9.
When the wind comes from the south you can smell the heady fragrance of Sibyllans ten blocks away. This family-run shop dates back to World War I and the interior, with its old-fashioned tea and coffee jars, hasn't changed much since. There's a vast range of teas from all over the world. Sibyllans' own blend, Sir Williams, is a mix of Chinese green teas.

General

Food is expensive in Sweden, particularly in Stockholm. **ICA** and **Coop Konsum** are probably the biggest supermarket chains. In fancy Östermalm (around Östermalmstorg) you will find more delicatessen-style supermarkets. Both **NK** (*see p137*) and **Åhléns** (*see p136*) have excellent, though pricey, supermarkets in their basements.

Cajsa Warg

Renstiernas Gata 20, Södermalm (642 23 50/ www.cajsawarg.se). Bus 2, 3, 55, 66, 76. **Open** 8am-9pm Mon-Fri; 10am-9pm Sat, Sun. **Credit** AmEx, DC, MC, V. **Map** p251 L9.
Cajsa Warg was a famous Swedish chef at the beginning of the 20th century, known for her creative cooking. This shop, which has a large takeaway menu, uses her name to sell everyday groceries and deli items (Swedish, Mediterranean and Asian). A great place to stock up for a picnic.

Markets

Hötorgshallen

Hötorget, Norrmalm (www.hotorgshallen.se). T-bana Hötorget/bus 1, 52, 53, 69. **Open** *Indoor market* May-Aug 10am-6pm Mon-Fri; 10am-3pm Sat. Sept-Apr 10am-6pm Mon-Thur; 10am-6.30pm Fri; 10am-4pm Sat. *Outdoor market* usually 10am-7pm Mon-Fri; 10am-5pm Sat; noon-5pm Sun. **Map** p241 F6.
A visit to Hötorgshallen is a culinary trip around the world. Built in the 1950s, the hall was renovated in the 1990s and its international character has grown along with immigration to Stockholm. You can buy everything from Middle Eastern falafel to Indian spices, as well as fantastic fish and meat, and there are several good places to grab lunch. Outside there's a bustling fruit, vegetable and flower market on Hötorget, which first opened as a market in the 1640s.

Östermalms Saluhall

Östermalmstorg, Östermalm (www.ostermalms hallen.se). T-bana Östermalmstorg/bus 1, 55, 56, 62. **Open** 9.30am-6pm Mon-Thur; 9.30am-6.30pm Fri; 9.30am-4pm Sat (*June-Aug* 9.30am-2pm). **Map** p241 F8.
This gastronomic temple has been serving the city's gourmets since 1888. Get tempted by a wide variety of fresh bread from Amandas Brödbod, delicious chocolate from Betsy Sandbergs Choklad, excellent fish and seafood from Melanders Fisk, vegetables from Lisa Janssons and more. The numerous well-reputed restaurants and cafés are filled with well-heeled Östermalm ladies who lunch. The large square outside has a handsome flower stall and an open-air café, Lisapåtorget, which is a sibling to Lisa Elmqvist's excellent fish restaurant inside the hall. Expensive but worth it. *Photo p147.*

Söderhallarna

Medborgarplatsen 3, Södermalm (714 09 84/www. soderhallarna.com). T-bana Medborgarplatsen/bus 55, 59, 66. **Open** 10am-6pm Mon-Wed; 10am-7pm Thur, Fri; 10am-4pm Sat. **Map** p250 L8.
Söderhallarna, which is a rather unsightly construction, is Stockholm's newest indoor market. It's handy for a great selection of fresh produce – if you can endure its soulless, mall-like atmosphere.

Specialist

Stockholm is blessed with many small health food shops, and most of the major supermarkets have sections devoted to various nut-free, gluten-free and fat-free foods. **Skanstulls Hälsokost** (Ringvägen 106, Södermalm, 641 52 79) sells everything from organic vegetables to aromatherapy oils and vitamin pills.

Androuët Ostaffär

Sibyllegatan 19, Östermalm (660 58 33/www. androuet.nu). T-bana Östermalmstorg/bus 1, 47, 62, 69, 76. **Open** 10.30am-6pm Mon-Fri; 10.30am-3pm Sat. **Credit** AmEx, DC, MC, V. **Map** p242 F9.

In 1909 Henri Androuët set up his first cheese store in Paris; in 1997 the Stockholm shop opened. In this excellent shop you'll find more than 100 different cheeses from all over France. Many are fairly obscure, but all are outstanding.

Ejes Chokladfabrik

Erik Dahlbergsgatan 25, Gärdet (664 27 09/www. ejeschoklad.se). T-bana Karlaplan/bus 1, 4, 62, 72. **Open** *Late Aug-late July* 10am-6pm Mon-Fri; 10am-3pm Sat. Closed late July-late Aug. **Credit** MC, V. **Map** p246 D10.

The mocha nougat and Irish coffee truffles alone are worth the trip to this traditional *chocolatier*, which was established in 1923. Everything is made by hand without preservatives. Just going into the shop, crammed with chocolates, is an experience. Call to book a tasting.

English Shop

Söderhallarna 134, Södermalm (640 44 04/www. englishshop.se). T-bana Medborgarplatsen/bus 55, 59, 66. **Open** 10am-6pm Mon-Wed; 10am-7pm Thur, Fri; 10am-4pm Sat; noon-4pm Sun. **Credit** AmEx, DC, MC, V. **Map** p250 L8.

All the tea (Tetley, Twinings, Typhoo), biscuits (Ginger Snaps, Digestives, Jaffa Cakes) and other British treats you could ever want. Decent prices, and handily located inside Söderhallarna.

Hong Kong Trading

Kungsgatan 74, Norrmalm (21 79 76). T-bana T-Centralen/bus 1, 47, 53, 59, 69. **Open** 10am-6.30pm Mon-Fri; 10am-5pm Sat. **Credit** AmEx, MC, V. **Map** p240 F5.

There are quite a few Asian food shops nearby and friendly Hong Kong Trading is one of the biggest. It has a well-assorted stock of noodles and herbs and a great range of fresh Asian vegetables and fruits. Staff are helpful.

Taj Mahal Livs

Kammakargatan 40, Norrmalm (21 22 81). T-bana Rådmansgatan/bus 43, 46, 52. **Open** 10am-4pm Mon-Fri; 10am-4pm Sat. **Credit** MC, V. **Map** p245 E6.

Asian, Indian and African foodstuffs are sold in this kitschy shop. There's everything from huge sacks of rice and lentils to shelves stacked with African hairstyling products and Asian herbs and spices. It's a family-run place and sometimes closes for family events and holidays.

Gifts & stationery

Bookbinders

Norrlandsgatan 20, Norrmalm (611 18 80/www. bookbindersdesign.com). T-bana Östermalmstorg/bus 1, 2, 55, 56. **Open** 10am-6.30pm Mon-Fri; 11am-3pm Sat. **Credit** AmEx, DC, MC, V. **Map** p241 F8.

Originally opened in 1927, Bookbinders sells some of the best stationery in Stockholm. Prices are high, but so is the quality of the vividly coloured paper, books, linen-covered boxes and folders.

Other locations NK, Hamngatan 18-20, Norrmalm (762 88 81); Åhléns, Klarabergsgatan 50, Norrmalm (676 60 00).

Bungalow Porslin

Kungsholmsgatan 15, Kungsholmen (654 48 40/ www.bungalow.se). T-bana Rådhuset/bus 1, 40, 52, 59. **Open** noon-6pm Mon-Fri; 10am-3pm Sat. **Credit** MC, V. **Map** p240 G4.

Bungalow specialises in 20th-century Swedish ceramics and has masses of stuff from major companies such as Gustavsberg piled high on the shelves. The store is a good place to find affordable and distinctive crockery.

Coctail & Coctail Deluxe

Coctail: Skånegatan 71, Södermalm (642 07 40/ www.coctail.nu). Coctail Deluxe: Bondegatan 34, Södermalm (642 07 41). Bus 2, 53, 59, 66, 76. **Open** *Both* 11am-6pm Mon-Fri; 11am-4pm Sat; noon-4pm Sun. **Credit** MC, V. **Map** p251 M9.

Coctail and Coctail Deluxe are a pair of kitsch emporia selling all the funky furniture, unusual jewellery, colourful homewares and retro clothing you could ever want, not to mention garden gnomes and Elvis bead curtains.

DesignTorget

Kulturhuset, Sergels Torg, Norrmalm (50 83 15 20/ www.designtorget.se). T-bana T-Centralen/bus 47, 52, 56, 59, 65. **Open** 10am-7pm Mon-Fri; 10am-5pm Sat; noon-4pm Sun. **Credit** AmEx, MC, V. **Map** p241 G7.

The concept of DesignTorget is that promising new designers can sell their work on a commission basis alongside established companies. You'll find an assortment of jewellery, household goods, ceramics, textiles and furniture, as well as some original gifts and amusing gadgets.

Other locations: Götgatan 31, Södermalm (462 35 20); Birger Jarlsgatan 18, Östermalm (611 53 03); Västermalmsgallerian, Kungsholmen (33 11 53).

Ordning & Reda

Götgatan 32, Södermalm (714 96 01/www.ordning-reda.com). T-bana Medborgarplatsen or Slussen/bus 2, 3, 43, 53, 55, 59, 66, 76. **Open** 10am-7pm Mon-Fri; 10am-5pm Sat; noon-5pm Sun. **Credit** AmEx, DC, MC, V. **Map** p250 L8.

A heaven for stationery addicts, Ordning & Reda was established by the same family that owns Bookbinders (*see above*), and sells all sorts of fun and brightly coloured stationery.

Other locations: Drottninggatan 82, Norrmalm (10 84 96); NK, Hamngatan 18-20, Norrmalm (762 84 62); Åhléns, Klarabergsgatan 50, Norrmalm (676 60 00); Sturegallerian, Stureplan, Östermalm (611 12 00); Fältöversten, Karlaplan 13, Östermalm (667 84 40).

Stockhome

Kungsgatan 25, Norrmalm (662 52 84/www. stockhome.se). T-bana Hötorget. **Open** 10am-6.30pm Mon-Fri; 10am-5pm Sat; noon-4pm Sun. **Credit** AmEx, MC, V. **Map** p241 F7.

Eat, Drink, Shop

Eat, Drink, Shop

10 Swedish Designers – they're bound to have it in your colour. *See p152.*

The city has so many small shops selling utterly tasteful, utterly humourless monochromatic *objets*, that it comes as a relief to find somewhere as big, vibrant and good fun as Stockhome. Located under the Regeringsgatan bridge, it's full of unusual household stuff, much of it made from brightly coloured plastic. There are things for every room in the house, plus an excellent range of children's products. Ideal for one-stop gift shopping.

10 Swedish Designers

Götgatan 25, Södermalm (643 25 04/www. tiogruppen.com). T-bana Slussen/bus 2, 3, 43, 53, 55, 59, 66, 76. **Open** 10am-6pm Mon-Fri; 11am-4pm Sat; noon-4pm Sun. **Credit** MC, V. **Map** p250 L8.

Tiogruppen was set up by ten young textile artists back in 1970 and since then their creations have become design classics. The colourful, bold geometric designs – available as bags, cushions, oven gloves, trays, ironing board covers or just fabric – are a must-have. *Photo p151.*

Health & beauty

Complementary medicine

Inspira Handelsbod

Rörstrandsgatan 42, Vasastaden (34 54 23/ www.inspira.cc). T-bana St Eriksplan/bus 3, 4, 47, 72. **Open** noon-6.30pm Mon-Fri. Closed 4wks in summer. **No credit cards. Map** p244 D2.

Fresh herbs, natural cough mixtures and other herbal medicines and hygiene products are all on sale at Inspira Handelsbod. You can simply browse through the books, or why not try some 'heart wine' or 'nerve cookies'?

Hairdressers

Toni & Guy (Götgatan 10, Södermalm, 714 56 56, www.toniandguy.se) has its largest European branch in Stockholm.

Björn Axén

Norrlandsgatan 7, Norrmalm (54 52 73 50/www. axens.se). T-bana Östermalmstorg/bus 2, 47, 55, 59, 62, 76. **Open** 9am-6pm Mon, Tue, Fri; 9am-7pm Wed, Thur; 9am-3.30pm Sat. **Credit** AmEx, DC, MC, V. **Map** p241 F8.

Queen Sylvia is among the well-heeled customers at Stockholm's smartest hair salon. A cut costs around 610kr, but it's half that if you're willing to let a trainee loose on your locks.

Other locations Åhléns City, Klarabergsgatan 50, Norrmalm (54 52 73 50).

Hair & Face

Gamla Brogatan 21 & 25, Norrmalm (406 07 07/ 20 42 22/www.hair-facestockholm.se). T-bana Hötorget or T-Centralen/bus 1, 47, 52, 53, 56, 65. **Open** 10am-7pm Mon-Fri; 10am-5pm Sat. **Credit** MC, V. **Map** p241 F6.

These two small, pleasant Hair & Face salons near T-Centralen are good places to pop into if you want a trendy Swedish hairdo at a fair price.

Other locations Regeringsgatan 27, Norrmalm (677 00 33); PUB, Hörtorget, Norrmalm (21 88 81).

Opticians

Synsam

Norrlandsgatan 10, Norrmalm (679 85 15/ www.synsam.se). T-bana Kungsträdgården or Östermalmstorg/bus 1, 2, 47, 55, 59, 62, 69, 76. **Open** 9am-6pm Mon-Fri; 10am-3pm Sat. **Credit** AmEx, DC, MC, V. **Map** p241 F8.

Scandinavia's largest group of opticians has around a dozen branches in Stockholm. A good place to buy sunglasses, contact lens supplies or, if you want to look totally Scandic, a pair of Danish-designed Lindberg spectacles.

Other locations throughout the city.

Pharmacies

Access to medication is strictly controlled in Sweden and in most cases you need a doctor's prescription. However, you can buy painkillers and other simple medicines in state-run pharmacies all over town. For more information on prescription medicines, call **Läkemedelsupplysningen** (medicine information office) toll-free on 020 66 77 66.

Apoteket CW Scheele

Klarabergsgatan 64, Norrmalm (454 81 30/www. apoteket.se). T-bana T-Centralen/bus 47, 52, 56, 59, 69. **Open** 24hrs daily. **Credit** AmEx, MC, V. **Map** p241 G6.

Apotek Enhörningen

Krukmakargatan 13, Södermalm (0771 45 04 50). T-bana Mariatorget/bus 43, 55, 66, 74. **Open** 8.30am-10pm daily. **Credit** AmEx, MC, V. **Map** p250 L6.

Shops

Cow Parfymeri

Mäster Samuelsgatan 9, Östermalm (611 15 04/ www.cowparfymeri.se). T-bana Östermalmstorg/bus 2, 43, 55, 59, 62, 69. **Open** 11am-6pm Mon-Fri; 11am-4pm Sat. **Credit** AmEx, DC, MC, V. **Map** p241 F8.

This small boutique sells top-line cosmetics, such as Commes des Garçons, Philosophy and Vincent Longo. The staff is made up of professional make-up artists and although it's all a bit elitist, the products and service are well worth the extra pennies.

Face Stockholm

Biblioteksgatan 1, Östermalm (611 00 74/www.face stockholm.com). T-bana Östermalmstorg/bus 2, 55, 59, 62, 69. **Open** 10am-7pm Mon-Fri; 10am-5pm Sat; noon-4pm Sun. **Credit** AmEx, DC, MC, V. **Map** p241 F8.

Great for high-quality, no-nonsense cosmetics in streamlined packaging, though some of the stores are starting to show their age. There are around a dozen branches dotted throughout the city. **Other locations** throughout the city.

Spas

In addition to those listed below, the **Stockholm Day Spa** on the fourth floor of Åhléns (*see p136*) offers massages, hydrotherapy and facial treatments.

Centralbadet

Drottninggatan 88, Norrmalm (54 52 13 00/www. centralbadet.se). T-bana Hötorget/bus 1, 47, 52, 53. **Open** 6am-8pm Mon-Fri; 8am-8pm Sat; 8am-5pm Sun (changing rooms close 9pm daily). **Admission** 110kr-150kr. **Minimum age** women 18; men 23. **Credit** AmEx, DC, MC, V. **Map** p241 F6.

In 1904 Jugendstil architect Wilhelm Klemming realised a dream about an 'open window to nature' when he designed Centralbadet. Set back from the street in a pretty garden, it has beautiful art nouveau interiors and a fairly inexpensive café. Take a dip in the pool or jacuzzi, experience different types of sauna, have a massage (one-hour Swedish massage costs 550kr) or a treatment (herbal bath costs 300kr). Friendly staff and a delightful air of faded grandeur make it more appealing than fashionable Sturebadet (*see p154*).

Hasseludden Yasuragi

Hamndalsvägen 6, Saltsjö-boo (747 64 00/www. hasseludden.com). Bus 417 to Hamndalsvägen then 10mins walk/Vaxholmsbolaget boat from Strömkajen. **Open** 8am-10pm daily. **Admission** 8am-4pm Mon-Thur 890kr; 4-10pm Mon-Thur 1,090kr; Fri-Sun 1,190kr. **Credit** AmEx, DC, MC, V.

My Stockholm Andrew Duncanson

Andrew Duncanson moved from Scotland to Stockholm in 1998 and opened Modernity (see p155), a store devoted to 20th-century design. For anyone interested in the big names of mid-century modern furnishing – Wegner, Wirkkala, Juhl, Aalto, Jacobsen et al – it's unmissable.

I live in Östermalm and for me the best way to start the day is with a brisk walk – or even a jog – round Djurgården. Afterwards you can get breakfast at **Rosendahls Trädgård** (*see p131*), a lovely café and plant nursery. It's great for fresh food and you can get something healthy, or indulge with one of the cakes that are freshly baked on the premises. While I'm on Djurgården I'd visit the **Thielska Galleriet** (*see p74*). It's a Jugundstil building that was commissioned by a Swedish banker, Ernest Thiel, in 1904. He wanted a place to display his art collection, which contains several works by Edvard Munch. Because the house was built around the collection, it feels very integrated.

For lunch, I love Nybroe Smørrebrød in the **Östermalms Saluhall** market (*see p149*). They do these great Danish open sandwiches, which is maybe a strange thing to eat in Stockholm but you don't see them anywhere else and they are excellent. After that, I might visit **Georg Jensen Damask** (*Birger Jarlsgatan 2, 86 11 28 89, www.damask.dk*) for another Danish product – high-quality table linens. They stock everything from typically Scandinavian geometric designs to more modern patterns. I often buy wedding

presents here. I also like the contemporary Swedish silver at **Nutida Svenskt Silver** (*Arsenalgatan 3, 611 67 18, www.nutida.nu*), the paper at **Ljunggrens** in Gamla Stan (*Kopmangatan 3, 676 03 83, www. ljunggrenspapper.se*) and, on Södermalm, the pottery, jewellery and glass at **Konsthantverkarna** (*Södermalmstorg 4, 611 03 70, www.konsthantverkarna.se*). This is a place that promotes contemporary handicrafts, but not in a macramé-and-knitwear sense. They help young designers continue traditional crafts.

It's always nice to visit the **National Museum** (*see p66*). The first floor design department is the closest thing there is in Stockholm to a proper design museum. Afterwards I might continue over the bridge to Skeppsholmen and spend a couple of hours at the **Moderna Museet** (*see p78*).

To round off the day: dinner at **PA & Co** (*Riddargatan 8, 611 08 45*). There are posher restaurants in town, and more expensive ones, but PA is small, informal and always bustling. You don't have to go wild – you can eat traditional Swedish husmanskost for just over a hundred kronor or have something special for 300kr. They don't take reservations, but if you pop in after lunchtime they will hold a table for you for that evening. I eat there at least once a week, and it's consistently good. You'll see everyone here – models, actors, sportsmen, authors – so it's great for a bit of people-watching.

Eat, Drink, Shop

The renovation of the run-down 1970s premises of Hasseludden into a Japanese spa hotel, including a pool, outdoor hot bath, sauna and restaurant, was a masterstroke. Massages and beauty treatments are also available. Located on the edge of the Stockholm archipelago, it makes for a brilliant day trip. For a review of the Hasseludden hotel, *see p47*.

Sturebadet

Sturegallerian, Stureplan, Östermalm (54 50 15 00/www.sturebadet.se). T-bana Östermalmstorg/ bus 1, 2, 55, 56, 62. **Open** *Sept-June* 6.30am-10pm Mon-Fri; 9am-7pm Sat, Sun. Closed 2wks July. **Admission** annual membership 16,700kr; day membership 295kr. **Minimum age** 18. **Credit** AmEx, DC, MC, V. **Map** p241 F8.

Dating from 1885, swanky Sturebadet is the traditional upper-class and celeb favourite, next to the hub of their universe, Stureplan. It offers a gym with personal trainers, assorted massages, treatments and cures, a beautiful art nouveau pool, plus an extraordinary Turkish bath that can be rented for meetings with up to 20 people (3,500kr for two hours). This doesn't all come cheap: the Breakfast Club deal, which includes breakfast each weekday, costs 14,500kr a year.

Interiors

For more on Swedish design, *see pp28-31*.

Antiques & second-hand

There are several branches of **Stadsmissionen** (www.stadsmissionen.se), a not-for-profit organisation that sells people's cast-off clothing, books and household items to raise money for the homeless and other needy Swedes. They can be found at Stortorget 5, Gamla Stan (787 86 61); Bondegatan 46, Södermalm (642 19 41); and Hantverkargatan 78, Kungsholmen (652 74 75).

For antiques, there's a terrific cluster of shops on Upplandsgatan in Vasastaden, near the Odenplan T-bana station. These include **Domino Antik** (No.25, 33 78 58) for 20th-century furniture and lights; **Old Touch** (No.43, 34 90 05) for lace and crystal; **Jerner Antik** (No.36, 30 92 40) for rustic pieces; **Carléns** (No.40, 31 34 01) for glass pieces; and **Bacchus** (No.46, 30 54 80) for china and 20th-century pieces.

Jacksons

Sibyllegatan 53, Östermalm (665 33 50/www. jacksons.se). T-bana Östermalmstorg/bus 1, 43, 44, 56, 62. **Open** noon-6pm Mon-Fri; 11am-3pm Sat. **Credit** AmEx, DC, MC, V. **Map** p241 F8.

Jacksons has been selling top-quality international and Scandinavian design for more than 20 years. Well worth a visit for its glass, ceramics, furniture and other decorative arts.

Lagerhaus.

Kurt Ribbhagen
Birger Jarlsgatan 13, Östermalm (54 50 78 60).
T-bana Östermalmstorg/bus 1, 2, 55, 56. **Open**
9am-6pm Mon-Fri. **Credit** AmEx, DC, MC, V.
Map p241 F8.
Kurt Ribbhagen is the best antique silver shop in the
city and is also handily located next door to the
Stockholm branch of renowned Danish silversmith
Georg Jensen.

Modernity
Sibyllegatan 6, Östermalm (20 80 25/www.
modernity.se). T-bana Östermalmstorg/bus 2, 47,
62, 69, 76. **Open** noon-6pm Mon-Fri; 11am-3pm Sat.
Credit AmEx, DC, MC, V. **Map** p242 F9.
Scotsman Andrew Duncanson specialises in
Scandinavian 20th-century design, including furni-
ture, ceramics, glass and jewellery. If you're a fan of
Alvar Aalto and Arne Jacobsen, then this place is an
absolute must. *See also p153* **My Stockholm**.

General

Stockholm is heaving with shops devoted
to interior design. Essential pit stops include
DesignTorget (*see p150*) and **10 Swedish
Designers** (*see p152*).

Asplund
Sibyllegatan 31, Östermalm (662 52 84/www.
asplund.org). T-bana Östermalmstorg/bus 56, 62.
Open 11am-6pm Mon-Fri; 11am-4pm Sat. **Credit**
AmEx, MC, V. **Map** p242 F9.
The airy Asplund showroom is a good source of
newly designed design classics, including furniture,
rugs, glasswares and lighting, by Scandinavian and
international designers.

Carl Malmsten
Strandvägen 5B, Östermalm (23 33 80/www.
c.malmsten.se). T-bana Östermalmstorg/bus 47, 55,
62, 69, 76. **Open** 10am-6pm Mon-Fri; 10am-4pm Sat.
Credit MC, V. **Map** p242 G9.
High-quality furniture, textiles and light fittings by
legendary Swedish designer Carl Malmsten. The
shop, which is now run by his grandson Jerk
Malmsten, sells classics from the 1950s and 1960s,
as well as rugs and books.

Granit
Götgatan 31, Södermalm (642 10 68/www.
granit.com). T-bana Medborgarplatsen or Slussen/
bus 43, 55, 59, 66. **Open** 10am-7pm Mon-Fri;
10am-5pm Sat; noon-4pm Sun. **Credit** AmEx, DC,
MC, V. **Map** p250 L8.
Granit sells lots of simple things at low prices: storage boxes, unadorned glassware and crockery,
spices, coffee, notebooks and photo albums, plus
hundreds of other plain but pleasant items. Be
warned: it's almost impossible to go into Granit
without finding something you want to buy.
Other locations Kungsgatan 42, Normalm
(21 92 85); Västermalmsgallerien, Kungsholmen
(650 73 25).

Ikea
Kungens Kurva, Skärholmen (020 43 90 50/www.
ikea.se). Bus 173, 707, 710, 748/free Ikea bus from
Regeringsgatan 13 on the hr 11am-5pm daily and
from Ikea on the half-hr 11.30am-5.30pm daily.
Open 10am-8pm Mon-Fri; 10am-6pm Sat, Sun.
Credit AmEx, DC, MC, V.
In Sweden Ikea is more than just a furniture store,
it's a way of life. It's well worth visiting even if
you're not after any flat-pack, just to see how the
Swedes spend their weekends. The on-site restau-
rant sells excellent meatballs with lingonberries.
Other locations Barkarby, Barkarby Handelsplats,
Järfälla (020 43 90 50).

Lagerhaus
Drottninggatan 31-37, Normalm (23 72 00/www.
lagerhaus.se). T-bana T-Centralen/bus 47, 52, 56,
59, 69. **Open** 10am-7pm Mon-Fri; 10am-5pm Sat;
noon-4pm Sun. **Credit** AmEx, DC, MC, V. **Map** p241 G7.
Huge candles, absurd kitchen implements, cheap
minimalist porcelain and paperback fiction – all
under the same roof. It's a bit chaotic, but if you're
lucky you might find something that looks more
expensive than it really is.
Other locations Birger Jarlsgatan 18, Östermalm
(611 80 40).

Nordiska Galleriet
Nybrogatan 11, Östermalm (442 83 60/www.
nordiskagalleriet.se). T-bana Östermalmstorg/
bus 2, 47, 55, 62, 69, 76. **Open** 10am-6pm
Mon-Sat; noon-4pm Sun. **Credit** AmEx, DC, MC, V.
Map p241 F8.
In its large, fashionable home on Nybrogatan,
Nordiska Galleriet sells furniture, lights and gifts
from Nordic and international designers. Both past
masters (Alvar Aalto, Arne Jacobsen) and contemporary names (Philippe Starck, Jonas Bohlin) feature.

Norrgavel
Birger Jarlsgatan 27, Östermalm (54 52 20 50/www.
norrgavel.se). T-bana Östermalmstorg/bus 2, 3, 43,
55, 56. **Open** 10am-6pm Mon-Fri; 10am-4pm Sat;
noon-4pm Sun (closed Sun May-Aug). **Credit** AmEx,
DC, MC, V. **Map** p246 E8.
Functionalist furniture – with supremely elegant
beds, chairs and shelves – and a wealth of home
accessories, inspired both by Japanese minimalism
and 1950s Scandinavian design.

R.O.O.M.
Alströmergatan 20, Kungsholmen (692 50 00/www.
room.se). T-bana Fridhemsplan/bus 1, 3, 4, 57, 59.
Open *June-Aug* 10am-6pm Mon-Fri; 10am-4pm
Sat. *Sept-May* 10am-6.30pm Mon-Fri; 10am-5pm
Sat; 11am-5pm Sun. **Credit** AmEx, DC, MC, V.
Map p239 F2.
R.O.O.M. sells beautiful, expensive furniture and
furnishings, all so perfectly displayed that it's an
excellent source of ideas even if you can't afford to
buy anything. It also sells lots of tableware, books
and small gift-sized items. It's particularly popular
for a weekend browse followed by a *fika* in the
adjoining café.

Svenskt Tenn

Strandvägen 5, Östermalm (670 16 00/www.svenskt tenn.se). T-bana Östermalmstorg/bus 47, 55, 62, 69, 76. **Open** 10am-6pm Mon-Fri; 10am-4pm Sat; noon-4pm Sun (closed Sun June-Aug). **Credit** AmEx, DC, MC, V. **Map** p242 G9.

A Stockholm classic that should not be missed. Founded by Estrid Ericson in 1924, Svenskt Tenn is best known for the furniture and, in particular, the textiles created by Josef Frank, who worked for the company for 30 years after joining in 1934. His designs are still the mainstay of the shop's products, which are not cheap but exquisite.

Music & entertainment

CDs & records

Bashment

Bondegatan 6, Södermalm (640 05 84/www. bashmentmusic.com). T-bana Medborgarplatsen/ bus 2, 55, 59, 66, 76. **Open** 10am-8pm Mon-Fri; 11am-8pm Sat; noon-5pm Sun. **Credit** MC, V. **Map** p251 M8.

Bashment sells Jamaican reggae and dancehall in a laid-back manner. This is one of the few shops in Stockholm for obscure Afro-Caribbean music, and a good source of gig tickets too.

Multi Kulti

St Paulsgatan 3, Södermalm (643 61 29/www. multikulti.se). T-bana Slussen/bus 2, 3, 43, 53, 55, 59, 76. **Open** 11am-6.30pm Mon, Tue; 11am-7pm Wed-Fri; 11am-4pm Sat. **Credit** MC, V. **Map** p250 K7.

The smell of incense fills this tiny, classic shop which has just about every style of world music you could possibly imagine. It also stocks a small range of books and videos. Staff are both committed and knowledgeable.

Pet Sounds

Skånegatan 53, Södermalm (702 97 98/www.pet sounds.se). T-bana Medborgarplatsen/bus 2, 55, 59, 66, 76. **Open** 11am-7pm Mon-Fri; 11am-5pm Sat; 1-5pm Sun. **Credit** AmEx, MC, V. **Map** p251 M8.

Pet Sounds is the oldest and still the best indie shop in Stockholm. There's a lot of 1960s music and soundtracks, plus a decent range of soul music.

Musical instruments

Halkan's Rockhouse

Noe Arksgränden 2, Södermalm (641 49 70/www. halkans.com). T-bana Medborgarplatsen/bus 55, 59, 66. **Open** 11am-6pm Mon-Fri; 11am-4pm Sat. **Credit** (over 100kr) AmEx, MC, V. **Map** p250 K8.

Just off Götgatan, Halkan's is the place to head if you're looking for old guitars or professional repairs. Other good instrument shops nearby include Vintage Guitars (Götgatan 28, 643 10 83) and Estrad (Folkungagatan 54, 640 12 60) for keyboards and assorted studio equipment.

Sport & fitness

Fiskarnas Redskapshandel

St Paulsgatan 2, Södermalm (55 60 96 50/ www.abfiskarnas.se). T-bana Slussen/bus 2, 3, 43, 53, 55, 59, 76. **Open** 10am-6pm Mon-Fri; 10am-2pm Sat. **Credit** AmEx, DC, MC, V. **Map** p250 K7.

You can fish in the middle of the city (popular spots include the bridges by the parliament building and the eastern side of the Royal Palace). From angling to professional fly-fishing gear, Fiskarnas has the lot.

Friluftsbolaget

Sveavägen 62, Norrmalm (24 30 02/www.frilufts bolaget.se). T-bana Rådmansgatan/bus 43, 52. **Open** 10am-7pm Mon-Fri; 10am-5pm Sat; noon-4pm Sun. **Credit** DC, MC, V. **Map** p245 E6.

Everything you need for that outdoors or camping weekend. Friluftsbolaget specialises in the Swedish brand Fjällräven, famous both for its outstanding quality and timeless 1970s cut.

Tickets

You can also book tickets for major events through **Ticnet** (0771 70 70 70, www. ticnet.se) and the **tourist office** (*see p50*).

Box Office

Norrmalmstorg, Norrmalm (10 88 00/www. boxoffice.se). T-bana Östermalmstorg or Kungsträdgården/bus 2, 47, 55, 59, 62, 69, 76. **Open** *June-mid Sept* 10am-6pm Mon-Fri. *Mid Sept-May* 10am-6pm Mon-Fri; 10am-4pm Sat. **Credit** AmEx, DC, MC, V. **Map** p241 F8.

Tickets for opera and major theatre shows, concerts and sporting events in both Stockholm and abroad. You have to visit the shop in person to buy tickets for Stockholm venues. Expect to incur 5% commission if you pay with a foreign credit card.

Travel

On Sveavägen, between Kungsgatan and Sergels Torg, there is a crowd of travel agencies, including **STS, Resevaruhuset, Apollo, Flygvaruhuset, Ticket, Ving, Resia, Always** and **Fritidsresor**.

Kilroy Travels

Kungsgatan 4, Norrmalm (0771 54 57 69/www. kilroytravels.com). T-bana Östermalmstorg or Hötorget/bus 1, 2, 43, 55, 56. **Open** *Shop* 10am-6pm Mon-Fri. *Phone enquiries* 9am-6pm Mon-Fri. **Credit** MC, V. **Map** p241 F7.

There are Kilroy branches in Sweden, Denmark, Norway, Finland and the Netherlands. Originally focusing on cheap tickets for students and young people, they now offer tickets for all ages. Be prepared to queue.

Other locations Allhuset, Stockholm University, Frescati (0771 54 57 69).

Arts & Entertainment

Features

Festivals & Events

From Nobel Day to the noble game of boules.

Swedes hold hard to traditions and the calendar is dotted with beloved, quintessentially Swedish events such as **Valborgsmässoafton** (Walpurgis Night; *see p159*) and **Luciadagen** (Lucia Day; *see p161*); both great opportunities for visitors to dabble in Swedishness. The calendar isn't all age-old tradition, though; there are plenty of events with a more contemporary flavour – for example the **Pride** celebrations *(see p160)*, and the culturally diverse **Re:Orientfestivalen** *(see p159)* – and the festival calendar continues to diversify. There are also plenty of sports events, and not just for spectators: if you're feeling fit you might want to enter the **Midnattsloppen** *(see p160)*, or even the **Stockholm Marathon** *(see p159)*.

For general information on seasonal events and festivals, contact the **tourist office** *(see p50)*. For information on the seasons and weather in Sweden, and the dates of public holidays, *see pp219-227*.

Spring

Påsk (Easter)

Date Mar/Apr.

For many Swedes, Easter's greatest significance is getting a four-day weekend, well timed to polish up the boat or tidy up the garden. Still, the painting and eating of eggs is a hallowed tradition at the Easter *smörgåsbord*, along with salmon and pickled herring prepared in endlessly creative ways. On Maundy Thursday or Easter Saturday, young girls dress up and paint themselves as Easter witches, and then go around begging sweets from generous neighbours, handing over home-made Easter cards in exchange.

Stockholm Art Fair

Sollentunamässan, Sollentuna (www.sollentuna expo.se). Pendeltåg train to Sollentuna. **Date** 4 days in early Apr.

At the beginning of April, the Swedish art industry gets together for four intense days. Everyone's there – students, artists, gallery owners, dealers, curators,

All the world's a stage at the **Parkteatern** festival.

critics and visitors – and events include seminars, talks and meetings, as well as the opportunity just to enjoy the art.

Valborgsmässoafton (Walpurgis Night)

Thoughout the city. **Date** 30 Apr.

Though they once protected Swedes from witches, the bonfires of Valborgsmässoafton now mark the end of winter and the coming of spring. Walpurgis Night is celebrated all over Sweden, but for visitors to Stockholm the place to be is either the open-air Skansen museum *(see p163)*, where fireworks add extra sparkle to the evening's festivities, or Evert Taubes Terras on Riddarholmen.

Första Maj (May Day)

Date 1 May.

If you happen to be in Stockholm on May Day, you'll probably run into marchers waving banners in Sergels Torg and other large squares throughout the city. The first of May has been celebrated in various ways since 1890. In the early 19th century, May Day was a hugely popular festival in Djurgården park and featured a royal procession. By the late 19th century, though, it had turned into a rally of industrial workers. It's a lot more low-key these days, but it's still an important event for left-wing Stockholmers. Due to the cold weather, there's no maypole dancing – that's saved for Midsummer *(see below)*.

Tjejtrampet

Location varies; check website for details. (450 26 10/ www.tjejtrampet.com). **Map** p247. **Date** May.

Given that Stockholm is such a bicycle-friendly city, it makes sense that it should host the world's largest women-only bicycle race. Since the first race in 1990, some 80,000 women have cycled the 42km (26-mile) course. It is open to cyclists of all levels. Teenage girls and grandmothers pedal side-by-side in a show of female unity and a spirit of friendly competition.

Summer

Parkteatern (Park Theatre)

Parks throughout the city (506 20 284/www. stadsteatern.stockholm.se). **Date** June-Aug daily.

There's been free outdoor theatre in Stockholm's parks since 1942, and many performances can be enjoyed by non-Swedish speakers, such as circus shows, music concerts, and dance. There are workshops on everything from playing steel drums to klezmer or Swedish folk dance.

Stockholm Early Music Festival

Tyska Brinken 13, Gamla Stan (070 460 03 90/ www.semf.se). T-bana Gamla Stan/bus 3, 53. **Map** p241 J7. **Date** early June.

This four-day event attracts an impressive roster of established and new artistic talent from Sweden and Europe performing a programme of music from the Middle Ages, Renaissance and baroque periods. The festival takes place in Gamla Stan.

Stockholm Marathon

Start point: Lidingövägen, Hjorthagen. Finish point: Stockholms Stadion, Hjorthagen (54 56 64 40/www. marathon.se). **Map** p246 C9. **Date** Sat in early June.

Few cities can match the beauty of this marathon route, which takes runners along waterside Strandvägen, Norrmälarstränd and Skeppsbron. Head for Lidingövägen to watch the runners take off, or if you want to be ready to glimpse the winner at the finish line, position yourself at Stockholms Stadion on Vallhallavägen.

Skärgårdsbåtens Dag (Archipelago Boat Day)

Strömkajen, Norrmalm (662 89 02). T-bana Kungsträdgården/bus 2,55,59,62,65,76. **Map** p241 G8/H8. **Date** 1st Wed in June.

If the idea of travelling on one of Stockholm's old-fashioned steamboats appeals, there's no better day to do it than Archipelago Boat Day. A parade of vessels make their way from Strömkajen to Vaxholm in the early evening. For those who don't catch a ride, good places to view the boats are Strömkajen, Skeppsholmen, Kastellholmen and Fåfängen. The boats arriving in Vaxholm are greeted by live music and an outdoor market; visitors have a couple of hours to explore Vaxholm before returning to Stockholm. *Photo p160.*

Nationaldag (National Day)

Date 6 June.

Sweden's National Day celebrates Gustav Vasa's election as King of Sweden on 6 June 1523 and the adoption of a new constitution on the same date in 1809. If you want a glimpse of the royal family in their traditional blue-and-yellow folk costumes, visit the open-air Skansen museum *(see p163)*, where, since 1916, the King of Sweden has presented flags on this day to representatives of various organisations and charities.

Mayo Boules Festival

Rålambshovsparken, Kungsholmen (714 04 20/ www.mayo.se). T-bana Fridhemsplan/bus 3, 40 52, 62. **Map** p241 G8. **Date** mid June.

Boules, or pétanques as aficionados call it, has a long history in Sweden, particularly with upper-class seniors, but a group of boules-crazy folk breathed new life into the sport by launching northern Europe's largest boules festival in 1994. The name, La Mayonnaise (or Mayo for short), is a jibe at the world's largest boules festival, La Marseillaise, in France. But there's nothing stuffy about this crowd-pleasing festival, which organises friendly competitions for work colleagues, seniors and rookies, as well as more serious contests between the official international teams.

Midsommarafton (Midsummer Eve)

Date Friday closest to 24 June.

The longest day of the year has been revered in Scandinavia since the days of pagan ritual. Modern Swedes flock to summer cottages and Stockholmers

Archipelago Boat Day. *See p159.*

set sail for quiet coves in the archipelago to commemorate this festive feast to fertility. Women and men in traditional dress dance around the flower-decorated maypole. It's said that if an unmarried girl picks seven different flower types and puts them under her pillow on Midsummer Eve, she will dream of her future husband.

Stockholm Jazz Festival

Skeppsholmen (55 61 45 64/55 69 24 40/tickets 07 71 70 70 70/www.stockholmjazz.com). Bus 65. **Tickets** 450kr 1 day; 1695kr 5 days. **Map** p242 H9. **Date** 1wk mid July.

The Stockholm Jazz Festival, which takes place in July, is one of Sweden's premier live music festivals, and it's prestigious enough to pull in some top-rate international artists (Steely Dan in 2007). The main site on the island of Skeppsholmen couldn't be more picturesque; other venues include Konserthuset *(see p187)*, and stages in Kungsträdgården, Mosebacke Etablissement *(see p185)* and Fasching *(see p183)*. Some 30,000 spectators come to listen to more than 40 concerts featuring jazz, soul, blues and more.

Stockholm Pride Week

Tantolunden, Södermalm (www.stockholmpride.org). T-bana Zinkensdamm or Hornstull/bus 4, 40, 66, 74. **Map** p249 M4. **Date** 1wk in July/Aug.

Since its birth in 1998, Stockholm Pride Week has grown into the biggest gay Pride celebration in Scandinavia, with five days of partying, plus debates and entertainment. The heart of the action is the large open space of Tantolunden park on Södermalm. The festival includes art exhibitions, films, parties and, on the Saturday, the big parade. *See also p179.*

Re:Orientfestivalen

Södra Teatern, Mosebacketorg 1-3, Södermalm (702 15 99/www.reorient.se). T-bana Slussen/bus 2, 3, 43, 53, 55, 59, 76. **Map** p250 K8. **Date** 2nd wk in Aug.

Stockholm takes on a multicultural flavour during this annual festival, bringing together artists from the Middle East, northern Africa, India and Europe to perform at Södra Teatern *(see p185)* on Södermalm. During the four-day festival, there's a bazaar selling crafts, clothes and food and, in the evenings, festivalgoers can sit back and smoke a Turkish water pipe at the Oum bar or dance at the Re:Orient Club. A lecture series adds some intellectual weight to this laid-back festival.

Midnattsloppet (Midnight Race)

Start: Ringvägen. Finish: Hornsgatan (649 71 71/ www.midnattsloppet.com). **Map** Start & finish p249 L5. **Date** mid Aug.

This popular night-time race could only be possible in the land of the midnight sun. More than 16,000 runners of all ages navigate a 10km (six-mile) course around the island of Södermalm. But it's much more than a race – and some 200,000 spectators get in on the act with cheering, music and partying. To catch the starting gun, position yourself at Ringvägen, just south of the Zinkensdamm athletics field, at 10pm and then wait for the first runners to cross the finish line at Hornsgatan, not far from the starting point.

Autumn

Lidingöloppet

Around Lidingö (765 26 15/www.lidingoloppet.se). **Date** weekend in late Sept-early Oct.

The world's biggest cross-country race has become a tradition for Swedes, and the challenging course attracts runners from all over the world. The first Lidingöloppet was held in 1965, and every year thousands of runners from some 30 different countries pass the finish line on Grönsta Gärde.

Stockholm Open

Kungliga Tennishallen, Lidingövägen 75, Norra Djurgården (450 26 25/www.stockholmopen.se). Bus 73, 291, 293. **Tickets** 150kr-450kr adult; around 70kr concessions. **Map** p247 B11. **Date** Oct.

In 1969 veteran tennis star Sven Davidson received a letter from American colleagues asking him to arrange a competition in Sweden with tennis pros and amateurs from all over the world. The event now draws around 40,000 spectators each year, and has earned accolades as one of the most well-organised tournaments in Europe.

Stockholm International Film Festival

Various venues around Stockholm (677 50 00/ www.filmfestivalen.se). **Date** mid Nov.

The ten-day Stockholm Film Festival aims at launching young filmmakers and broadening the forum for innovative high-quality films in Scandinavia. It may not be Cannes, but it can still attract some big names: past guests have included Quentin Tarantino, the Coen brothers and Lars von Trier.

Arts & Entertainment

Winter

Advent
Date Dec.
You can tell Christmas is approaching when you start to spot the Advent candles or Advent stars hanging in the windows of homes, shops and offices. Nearly every home has an Advent candlestick, usually a little box with four candle-holders nestled in moss and lingonberry sprigs. The first candle is lit on the First Sunday of Advent and allowed to burn down only one quarter, so that it won't burn out before the fourth candle is lit.

Christmas markets
Date early-end Dec.
Skansen's Christmas market is held at weekends throughout December until Christmas Eve (the only day Skansen is closed). Look out for Swedish craft products, traditional Christmas ornaments made of straw, hand-dipped candle and Christmas fare such as smoked sausage, eel, salmon, *pepparkakor* (gingersnaps), *glögg* (mulled wine) and saffron buns.

Nobeldagen (Nobel Day)
Konserthuset, Hötorget, Norrmalm & Stadshuset, Hantverkargatan 1, Kungsholmen (Nobel Foundation 663 09 20/www.nobel.se). **Date** 10 Dec.
The year's Nobel Prize laureates are honoured in a ceremony at Konserthuset (*see p187*). In the evening, the royal family attends a banquet at Stadshuset (City Hall; *see p92*). Tickets for this glittering affair are usually only granted to the privileged few, though 250 of the 1,300 seats are reserved for lucky students. The rest have to be content with watching the proceedings on television and sighing over the fabulous menu.

Luciadagen (Lucia Day)
Date 13 Dec.
Among the best-known of Sweden's festivals, Lucia is celebrated in mid-December, in the heart of the winter darkness. The Lutheran Swedes adopted the Sicilian St Lucia because Lucia is connected with lux, the Latin for light. All over Sweden, a procession of singers, dressed in white, full-length chemises with red ribbons around their waists, are led by a woman dressed as Lucia, with a crown of lit candles on her head.

Jul (Christmas Day)
Date 24-26 Dec.
The main celebration is at home, held on Christmas Eve (though restaurants all over the city offer the traditional, overflowing *Julbord* or *smörgåsbord* for most of December). A traditional *Julbord* ('Christmas table') is typically eaten in three stages. You start with various types of herring and salmon, then move on to the meats (meatballs, sausages and ham), accompanied by 'Jansson's Temptation' – an anchovy, potato and cream casserole. You polish it all off with a sweet berry-filled pastry. Christmas Day itself is usually a quiet day.

Nyårsafton (New Year's Eve)
Date 31 Dec.
The New Year's Eve celebration in Sweden is a public and raucous contrast to the quiet and private Christmas festivities. Visitors can join the crowds at Skansen (*see p163*), where New Year's Eve has been celebrated every year since 1895. At the stroke of midnight, a well-known Swede reads Tennyson's 'Ring Out, Wild Bells'. Throughout the city, crowds fill the streets, feasting on seafood at various restaurants and moving from one club or bar to another.

Singing for Sweden

Sweden is a nation filled with people who love to sing, and not exclusively in the shower. It's estimated that between 600,000 and 700,000 Swedes sing weekly in choirs, and that fondness for choral singing goes some way towards explaining the enduring popularity of **Allsång på Skansen** (www.skansen.se), a sing-along tradition at Skansen reminiscent of the BBC's *The Good Old Days*.

Attending Allsång på Skansen is an annual pilgrimage for some Swedes. For many others it's the 'must-do' of a Stockholm summer visit. The long-running sing-along show was an instant success in May 1935, when the audience was invited to sing along with its musical director, Sven Lilja. Televised since 1979, the show now has two million viewers for its summer broadcasts, as dedicated families all over Sweden devote Tuesday evenings (from 24 June 2008) to belting out oldies-but-goodies in front of the TV.

In the early years, the musical selection always remained the same mixture of popular numbers. But by the time of Sven Lilja's death in 1951 tastes had changed, and the songs changed with them. Traditions die hard, though, and the repertoire remains classically Swedish, although the artists performing are as likely to be today's teenage heart-throbs as stars of yesteryear. This strategy of appealing to young and old alike has been a win-win for both pop music artists and die-hard fanatics, and the Allsång tradition, which could so easily have become fodder for fuddy-duddies, is currently enjoying über pop cult status.

Children

Europe's cuddliest capital.

Children – and parents – will find themselves very well looked after in Stockholm, one of the most child-friendly cities in the world. A 2007 UNICEF report on the well-being of children in industrialised countries ranked Sweden as second-best overall, and thanks to a healthy attitude towards children and an extensive social welfare policy, the young are generally taken care of and respected within society.

The city is especially convenient for parents of babies and younger kids. All new buses graciously bow to street level, giving parents with prams easy access; bus travel is also free for one adult with a child in a pram. If you've left your pram at home, you can rent one for 225kr per week at **Bonti** (Norrtullsgatan 33, 30 69 16). Under-sevens travel free on buses, the Tunnelbana and commuter trains, and at weekends (noon on Friday to midnight on Sunday) up to six children under the age of 12 ride for free with an accompanying adult.

Although there are no restaurants specifically aimed at kids, most restaurants and cafés provide highchairs, children's menus and help with warming baby food.

If your family likes to spend time outdoors, as the Swedes do, Stockholm offers wide pavements, plenty of open green spaces and a beautiful location on the water. In winter, when the lakes are frozen, you'll see parents skating across the ice pushing prams. But if you're not that adventurous, the centrally located ice-rink at **Kungsträdgården** (20 01 77) is a popular choice. Skating there is free; skate rental costs 40kr per hour for adults, 20kr per hour for kids.

In the warmer months, head out to the island of Djurgården, an urban national park. As well as acres of grass to run around on, it contains most of the city's best kids' attractions. It's also mostly traffic-free and there are ample opportunities for exploring on foot or by bike, bus or tram.

For a listing in English of museums, festivals and current events for kids, pick up a copy of **What's On Stockholm** from the tourist office (*see p50*) or visit the Children's Stockholm section at www.stockholmtown.com. If you're planning on visiting a lot of museums, invest in a **Stockholm Card** (*see p50*); two children under seven can accompany an adult cardholder for free.

Gröna Lund.

Attractions

Fjärilshuset

*Haga Trädgård, Hagaparken (730 39 81/www.
fjarilshuset.se). T-bana Odenplan then bus 515.*
Open *Apr-Sept* 10am-5pm Mon-Fri; 11am-5pm Sat,
Sun. *Oct-Mar* 10am-4pm Mon-Fri; 11am-5pm Sat,
Sun. **Admission** 80kr; 70kr concessions; 40kr
4-16s; free under-4s. **Free with SC**. **Credit** MC, V.
In a beautiful setting at the northern end of historic
Hagaparken (see p94), the fantastic Butterfly House
– all 850sq m (3,050sq ft) of it – is the closest you'll
get to a tropical rainforest in Stockholm. Mingle with
free-flying exotic butterflies and birds, or check out
the pond full of koi carp and the Asian garden.
There's also a child-friendly café in the adjacent
greenhouse offering an extensive children's menu.

Gröna Lund

*Allmänna Gränd, Djurgården (58 75 01 00/www.
gronalund.se). Bus 44, 47/tram 7/ferry from Slussen
or Nybroplan.* **Open** *May-early June, late Aug-mid
Sept* days & times vary; call for details. *Early June-
late Aug* noon-11pm Mon-Thur; noon-midnight
Fri, Sat; noon-8pm/10pm Sun. Closed mid Sept-end
Apr. **Admission** 60kr; 40kr 4-12s; free under-4s;
one-day bracelet (all rides) 260kr. **Free with SC**.
Credit AmEx, DC, MC, V. **Map** p242 J11.
Perched on the edge of Djurgården with fantastic
views across the water, Gröna Lund is Sweden's
oldest amusement park. Built in 1883 and owned by
the same family ever since, its historic buildings and
well-preserved rides retain an old-world charm.
Older (and tamer) favourites such as carousels,
bumper cars, Ferris wheels and a fun house are on
offer alongside more modern (and daring) rides such
as Europe's highest free-fall 'power tower'. Harry
Potter fans will appreciate the park's newest ride,
'Kvasten' ('The Broomstick'), a family rollercoaster
that carries riders on suspended carriages beneath
the tracks, feet dangling in the air, giving them the
sensation of flying on a magic broomstick. The park
is also a baby-friendly place, with pram ramps on
all the stairs and a Happy Baby Centre for feeding
and soothing tots. Note that on concert nights it costs
more to get in.

Junibacken

*Galärvarvsvägen, Djurgården (58 72 30 00/www.
junibacken.se). Bus 44, 47/tram 7/ferry from Slussen
or Nybroplan.* **Open** *June, Aug* 10am-5pm daily.
July 9am-6pm daily. *Sept-May* 10am-5pm Tue-Sun.
Admission 110kr; 95kr 3-15s; free under-3s. **Free
with SC**. **Credit** AmEx, DC, MC, V. **Map** p242 G10.
A favourite haunt of local kids and a top tourist
attraction, Junibacken is a mini indoor theme park
devoted to Pippi Longstocking and other characters
created by Swedish author Astrid Lindgren (see
p164 **The politics of Pippi**). Take a fairytale train
ride (ask for narration in English) that crosses miniature fictional landscapes, flies over rooftops and
passes through quaint Swedish houses. On the
upper floor kids are welcome inside Pippi's house,

Villa Villekulla, where they can dress up like Pippi,
slide down the roof and wreak general havoc. Stories
by other writers feature, too, and activities include
storytelling and visits from some of the storybook
characters. For those who are unfamiliar with
Swedish children's books, there's a very good shop
that carries many of the better-known titles in
translation. *Photo p165.*

Skansen & Skansen Akvariet

Skansen *(442 80 00/www.skansen.se).* **Open** *Jan,
Feb, Nov, Dec* 10am-3pm Mon-Fri; 10am-4pm Sat, Sun.
Mar, Apr, Oct 10am-4pm daily. *May-mid June* 10am-
8pm daily. *Mid June-Aug* 10am-10pm daily. *Sept* 10am-
5pm daily. **Admission** 30kr-90kr; free-80kr 6-15s; free
under-6s. **Free with SC**. **Credit** AmEx, DC, MC, V.
Skansen Akvariet *(666 10 10/www.skansen-
akvariet.se).* **Open** *May* 10am-5pm Mon-Fri; 10am-
6pm Sat, Sun. *1st 3wks June* 10am-6pm Mon-Fri;
10am-7pm Sat, Sun. *Midsummer-end July* 10am-8pm
daily. *1st 2wks Aug* 10am-7pm daily. *Last 2wks Aug*
10am-6pm Mon-Fri; 10am-7pm Sat, Sun. *Sept-Apr*
10am-4pm Mon-Fri; 10am-5pm Sat, Sun. **Admission**
75kr; 40kr 7-15s; free under-7s. **Free with SC**.
Credit AmEx, MC, V.
Both *Djurgårdsslätten 49-51, Djurgården. Bus
44, 47/tram 7/ferry from Slussen or Nybroplan.*
Map p243 H12-J12.
Skansen is a zoo, aquarium, amusement park and
museum rolled into one. Young children might find
the old buildings a bit dull, but the animals are
always a hit. The regular zoo (feeding time 2pm
daily) specialises in Nordic animals, among them
brown bears and wolves. At the children's zoo,
Lill-Skansen, kids can pet Swedish farm animals.
Adventurous kids can also pet snakes and spiders in
the small aquarium (Akvariet; separate entrance fee).
The charming Galejan amusement park has rides
dating back to the 19th century. Every Wednesday
from May to September is children's day, and kids
get to ride two for the price of one. Other diversions
include guided pony rides, horse and carriage rides
and a mini-train ride. Some sights are only open during the summer. *Photo p166.*

Museums

The **Vasamuseet** (see p75) on Djurgården ,
with its amazingly preserved 17th-century
warship, is a surefire hit for children over six
who like (very) big boats. For a more hands-on
experience, take the kids on board the two
museum ships moored just outside – the ice-
breaker *St Erik* and the light ship *Finngrundet*
(entrance to these is included in the Vasamuseet
fee; see p77). Kids who love anything on
wheels will enjoy the **Spårvägsmuseet**
(Transport Museum; see p83) on Södermalm,
where they can clamber into many of the
vintage buses, train cars and trolleys, and
play at driving a tram. A good option for older
kids with an interest in the natural world is

The politics of Pippi

On 28 January 2002 nearly all of Sweden grieved over the death of Astrid Lindgren, its most famous and beloved children's author. She is best remembered for creating Pippi Longstocking, the original wild child who captured the hearts of generations of children around the world.

Lindgren was born Astrid Ericsson in 1907 in the small town of Vimmerby in southern Sweden. Like many Swedes of her generation, she grew up close to nature. She pointed to her happy childhood as the inspiration for most of her works, claiming that it superseded any later experiences. One turning point arrived when she was 19. Unmarried and pregnant, she was forced to leave her hometown for Stockholm, where she would live for more than 60 years.

After having her son, Lars, she married Sture Lindgren in 1931 and became a full-time homemaker to take care of Lars and later her daughter Karin. According to Lindgren, it was Karin who inspired the idea for Pippi, when she asked her mother to tell her a story when she was ill. In 1946 Lindgren became the children's books editor at Rabén & Sjögren, where she worked until her retirement. A prolific and multi-faceted author, she wrote some 80 books including children's and young adult fiction, detective novels, fairytales, TV and movie scripts, and fiction that blended a variety of genres.

Pippi Longstocking (1945) was condemned by some and praised by others when it first appeared. Fiercely independent, boisterous and rebellious, Pippi is an unconventional heroine who always challenges the status quo. She is anything but pretty, with red pigtails, freckles and dishevelled clothes. The richest and strongest girl in the world, she lives alone with a monkey and a horse, and throws great parties for her friends. A true humanitarian, Pippi saves children from danger, speaks up for the powerless and oppressed, and in her own way reveals the flaws in society.

Like Pippi, Lindgren herself was somewhat of a radical. In 1976, disillusioned with the governing Social Democratic party of which she was a member, she finally got fed up when they charged her 102 per cent tax on her income. She wrote a scathing letter to Expressen, disguised as a fairytale. The tax law was changed, and the incident contributed to the downfall of the government later that year.

She was always a fierce and outspoken campaigner, fighting for environmental causes, animal rights, non-violence and a more child-centred educational system.

Children can play in Lindgren's imaginary world at Junibacken (see p163) and her books are widely available in bookshops. Other favourite characters to look out for are five-year-old Emil, the Lionheart Brothers and Ronja the robber's daughter, a modern Pippi.

DO YOU KNOW Pippi LONGSTOCKING?

BY ASTRID LINDGREN WITH PICTURES BY INGRID NYMAN

Naturhistoriska Riksmusset (see p95) just north of Stockholm; as well as a Martian landscape and the regulation dinosaurs, the museum also houses an IMAX cinema.

A large part of the Musikmuseet (Music Museum; see p88) is dedicated to children; the Klånjk room (loosely translated as 'Boing!') contains quirky instruments all painstakingly made for small fingers to manage, such as a pint-sized harp and an organ where you pull rather than press the keys. In the 17th-century

vaulted cellar of Lilla Posten (the 'Little Post Office' at the Postmuseum; see p59), children can load a postal van with packages or create and post their own postcards in a replica 1920s post office scaled down to child size. Any budding artists in the family can drop into the Moderna Museet and then go to the Arkitekturmuseet (for both, see p78), housed in the same building, for a creative crafts/building session led by museum staff (noon-2pm Sundays; kids free on an adult ticket).

Nordiska Museet

Djurgårdsvägen 6-16, Djurgården (51 95 46 00/ www.nordiskamuseet.se). Bus 44, 47/tram 7/ferry from Slussen or Nybroplan. **Open** *June-Aug* 10am-5pm daily. *Sept-May* 10am-4pm Mon, Tue, Thur, Fri; 10am-8pm Wed; 11am-5pm Sat, Sun. **Admission** 60kr; free under-18s. Free after 4pm Wed. **Free with SC. Credit** AmEx, MC. **Map** p242 G11.
In the Lekstugan ('Playhouse') at Sweden's museum of cultural history, you can travel back in time to 1895 in a vivid re-creation of life in the Swedish countryside. Kids over five can try their hand at different occupations at the farm cottage, the mill, the stable and the general store. They can touch and use all the exhibits, including antique objects. The museum is recommended for children aged five to 12, and they must be accompanied by an adult; other rules are clearly signposted in Swedish and English.

Tekniska Museet

Museivägen 7, Gärdet (450 56 00/www.tekniska museet.se). Bus 69. **Open** 10am-5pm Mon, Tue, Thur, Fri; 10am-8pm Wed; 11am-5pm Sat, Sun. **Tours** *Engine Hall* adults 1pm Sat, Sun. *Mine* children 1pm Sat, Sun. *Miniature Railway* 3pm Mon-Fri; noon, 3pm Sat, Sun. **Admission** (incl Telemuseum) 60kr; 40kr concessions; 30kr 6-19s; free under-6s. Free after 5pm Wed. **Free with SC. Credit** AmEx, MC, V. **Map** p243 G14.
Sprawling across three floors, the Museum of Science and Technology is sure to keep inquisitive minds busy for hours. Although highly pedagogical, it's more like a fun house than a museum, and a great place for babies, kids and adults alike. The Minirama room will have babies cooing with special mirrors, blocks and assorted toys; in the Teknorama area, small kids can discover how machines work by using their own bodies (such as running in a huge wheel to generate electricity). For older children the machinery hall has aeroplanes suspended from the ceiling, steam-driven cars and a 1927 Harley-Davidson. In 2007 the museum unveiled Sweden's first multi-sensory cinema, CINO4 (separate admission); kids sit in special seats that shake, rattle and roll, and are equipped with 3D glasses and a personal remote control for a joltingly interactive learning experience. *See also p90.*

Outdoors

Stockholm has plenty of open spaces for active kids. The waterside **Djurgårdsbrons Sjöcafé** (*see p190*), just across the bridge on Djurgården, doubles as a boat and bike rental company. You can hire paddleboats, rowing boats, canoes, kayaks, bicycles or inline skates for a practical and fun way to explore the island and its waterways. Further into the island, at **Rosendals Trädgård**, you'll find a small but charming playground built from logs and natural materials. You can eat at the outdoor café (*see p131*) or bring along a picnic. Further

afield, there's glorious Hagaparken, whose delights include the **Fjärilshuset** (*see p163*).
If you want to experience the Stockholm archipelago, but don't have the time to explore it properly, tiny **Fjäderholmarna** island (*see p209*) is just a 20-minute boat ride away. Kids can visit an aquarium, explore a wooden playground in the form of a ship, pet bunnies in the Trädgården garden and choose from extensive ice-cream options. You can also borrow lifejackets for your kids if they want to play on the rocky shores. Boats to Fjäderholmarna are operated by **Strömma Kanal** (58 71 40 00/www.strommakanal bolaget.com) from Nybrokajen, and Stockholms Ström (20 22 60/www.rss.a.se) from Slussen.
In winter, head for the outdoor **ice-skating rinks** (skates for hire) at Kungsträdgården and Medborgarplatsen (*see p79*).

Swimming

If you're visiting Stockholm during a warm summer, forget the swimming pools – you can dive straight into the surprisingly clean water around the city. Note that lifeguards are definitely not a Swedish concept. If that sounds too chilly, try the beautiful Jugendstil bath house **Centralbadet** (*see p153*) or the child-friendly **Eriksdalsbadet** on the southern tip of Södermalm (*see p193*), which has indoor and outdoor pools.

Junibacken – for all things Pippi. *See p163.*

Arts & Entertainment

Vilda Vanadis

Sveavägen 142, Vasastaden (34 33 00/www.vilda vanadis.com). Bus 2, 40, 52, 515, 595. **Open** *May-Sept* 10am-8pm daily. Closed Oct-Apr. **Admission** 70kr; 60kr under-16s; free kids under 80cm/31.5in. **Credit** AmEx, DC, MC, V. **Map** p245 B5.

This outdoor adventure pool has got water slides, tube slides, a toddlers' pool, and free street dance lessons for kids at weekends. Adults can have a poolside massage or spa treatment. The attached hotel (*see p42*) has a dining area overlooking the pools.

Theatre, film & music

Children's theatre is hugely popular in Stockholm. There are regular performances (mostly in Swedish) at **Dramaten**, **Stockholms Stadsteatern**, **Intiman**, **Dockteatern Tittut**, **Marionetteatern** (for all, *see pp196-200* **Theatre & Dance**) and the Spårvägsmuseet (*See p83*), while **Teater Pero** (612 99 00/www.pero.se) and **Pygméteatern** (31 03 21/www.pygme teatern.com) are also worth a visit.

If you're planning a trip to the cinema, remember that children's films are usually dubbed. The **IMAX** cinema (*See p173*) at the Naturhistoriska Riksmusset offers earphones with English translation at screenings (usually documentaries; under 5s are not admitted).

Life in the slow lane at **Skansen**. *See p163.*

The **Konserthuset** (*see p187*), one of Stockholm's main venues for classical music, features a Family Saturday series during the school year when Stockholm's Royal Philharmonic plays to a boisterous crowd of toddlers and kids. Expect classical and Swedish favourites, sing-alongs and guest appearances by clowns, magicians and other characters.

Babybio

Biografen Sture, Birger Jarlsgatan 41, Östermalm (678 85 48/www.biosture.se). T-bana Östermalmstorg/ bus 1, 2, 55, 56. **Open** *Jan-June, Sept-Dec* 11am every other Fri. Closed July, Aug. **Tickets** 70kr; babies free. **Credit** MC, V. **Map** p245 E7.

This innovative concept of a 'baby cinema' was created for breastfeeding mothers who thought they'd never go to the movies again. Lock your pram outside the theatre and tow your baby and baby carrier with you (babies get their own seats inside). Dimmed lighting and sound, changing tables in the theatre and foyer, free nappies, microwaves for warming baby food, and an intermission where you can buy coffee and cakes all make for a unique experience. It's mainly for mums, but fathers are welcome too. Current films are shown in their original language every other Friday.

Babysitting

Hemfrid i Sverige

(02 00 11 45 50/www.hemfrid.se). **Open** 8am-5pm Mon-Fri. **No credit cards**.

This outfit offers an array of services, including babysitting, cleaning, laundry and cooking.

Resources & activities

Rum för Barn, Kulturhuset

4th floor, Kulturhuset, Sergels Torg (information 50 83 15 08/library 50 83 14 16/www.kulturhuset. stockholm.se). T-bana T-Centralen/bus 43, 47, 56, 59, 65. **Open** 11am-5pm Tue-Fri; 11am-4pm Sat, Sun. Workshop closes 30min before Rum för Barn. **Admission** library free; workshop 20kr. **No credit cards**. **Map** p241 G7.

The 'Room for Kids' on the fourth floor of Kulturhuset (*see p197*), the city's main cultural centre, is dedicated to activities for children aged up to 12. The beautifully renovated children's library is the main attraction; its carefully designed reading areas each cater to children of different ages and abilities, and contain hundreds of books in English and other languages. There's an arts and crafts workshop and internet access just for kids in the library. Daily events (in Swedish), such as film screenings, storytelling and poetry readings, are tailored to different age groups. Before you even step into the building, a traffic light – visible in the library window from Sergels Torg outside – warns visitors of potential queues: red means full, yellow means queuing, and green means no waiting.

Clubs

Licensed to dance.

Due to Sweden's byzantine laws and regulations – you have to have a dance licence to have people dancing and, in order to receive that, you have to have a drinking licence and, in order to have that, you have to serve food – small and intimate music bars still rule the city's nightlife. But a couple of larger venues, with professional DJs, lavish visuals and proper dancefloors, open several nights a week, have now established themselves on the scene.

The high price of alcohol, an integral part of the city's nightlife, means that people tend to go out pretty late, first having a *förfest* (pre-party) at someone's house. Once they're out on the town, if Swedes happen to dance (they must be drunk first, of course, although drugs are strictly forbidden) they generally prefer to do it to pop music with sing-along choruses.

Stockholm's nightlife is concentrated in the inner city, split between **Stureplan**, the hub of the town's VIP world of limos and neon, and **Södermalm**, the hip district where the former working-class inhabitants have been pushed out to make room for designers, DJs and musicians, with **Norrmalm** in the middle for immortals. By contrast, **Vasastaden** and **Kungsholmen** have mostly bars and cafés, while nightlife in **Gamla Stan** is a combination of the touristy and the gay scene.

Since Stockholm isn't very big and public transport is very good, it's quite easy to travel between different parts of town in one night. In Södermalm the bars tend to close around 1pm and clubs at 3am, while around Stureplan things shut down at 5am.

The best club nights tend to be slightly secretive one-offs, but you can find out what, when and where in the Friday editions of *Aftonbladet*, *Expressen*, *Metro* or *City*. Or you can check out the monthly *Nöjesguiden*, *Rodeo* or *Paus*, or visit www.kalendarium.se and www.alltomstockholm.se. Another good way to learn about the hottest nights is to pick up flyers in the clothing shops and cafés around Stureplan or on Södermalm.

Gamla Stan

Riddarkällaren
Södra Riddareholmshamn 19 (411 68 76). T-bana Gamla Stan/bus 3, 53, 55, 56, 59, 76. **Open** 10pm-3am Thur-Sat. **Minimum age** 20. **Admission** 60kr-100kr. **Credit** AmEx, MC, V. **Map** p241 J6.

On a virtually uninhabited islet, this old restaurant is home to two extremely popular clubs: Bar Brasil! on Friday, a weekly samba-soca carnival party, and gay heaven Lino on Saturday.

Norrmalm

Berns Salonger
Berzelii Park (56 63 22 22/www.berns.se). T-bana Kungsträdgården/bus 2, 47, 55, 69, 76. **Open** 11.30am-1am Mon, Tue; 11.30am-3am Wed, Thur; 11.30am-4am Fri, Sat; 11.30am-midnight Sun. **Minimum age** 23. **Admission** varies; call for details. **Credit** AmEx, DC, MC, V. **Map** p241 G8. Under the guidance of Sir Terence Conran, Berns has been redesigned as a mega entertainment palace on several floors. Since the historic interior had to stay intact, the decor is an unlikely marriage of 19th-century elegance and modern style. It has the most beautiful ballroom in town, with a 20m (66ft) ceiling, chandeliers, red velvet carpets outside and beautiful people inside dancing to house and R&B.

Café Opera
Kungliga Operan, Karl XIIs Torg (676 58 07/www.cafeopera.se). T-bana Kungsträdgården/bus 2, 47, 55, 69, 76. **Open** 6pm-3am daily. **Minimum age** 23. **Admission** 100kr after 11pm. **Credit** AmEx, DC, MC, V. **Map** p241 G8.

The best Clubs

For glam surroundings
Sturecompagniet *(see p169)* and **Berns Salonger** *(see above)*.

For Latin dance
La Isla. See p169.

For VIP excess
Spy Bar. See p169.

For music maestros
Södra Teatern *(see p169)* and **Mosebacke Etablissement** *(see p169)*.

For smooth movers
Fasching *(see p168)*, **Marie Laveau** *(see p168)* and **Teatron** *(see p168)*.

For a samba session
Riddarkällaren. See left.

Arts & Entertainment

Club class at the **Spy Bar**, a favourite with Stockholm's VIP set.

After a decade in the shadow of the places around Stureplan, Café Opera has started to take back the crown as the party king of Stockholm. The business-men with ties round their foreheads and girls in miniscule dresses are now outnumbered once more by music people, media folk, celebs and even the odd royal rumbling about.

Fasching

Kungsgatan 63 (53 48 29 60/www.fasching.se).
T-bana T-Centralen/bus 1, 47, 53, 69. **Open** 7pm-1am Mon-Thur; 7pm-4am Fri, Sat. **Minimum age** 20. **Admission** call for details. **Credit** AmEx, DC, MC, V. **Map** p240 F6.

There are gigs and jam sessions at this legendary jazz hangout six nights a week, but it's the club nights at the weekend that really lift the roof. On Friday, it's the classic reggae and dancehall bash, Club Studio One, with Micke Goulous and friends at the decks. On Saturday it's Soul!, a clubbing institution that packs the dancefloor with the best in funk, northern soul and disco.

Teatron

Regeringsgatan 61 (411 59 00). T-bana Hötorget/bus 1, 2, 43, 56, 59. **Open** 10pm-3am Fri, Sat. **Minimum age** varies. **Admission** 100kr. **Credit** AmEx, DC, MC, V. **Map** p241 F7.

A modern nightclub with a neon-lit balcony looking down on a huge dancefloor, Teatron is open several nights a week under various names (such as Go Bang! on Fridays), but always features top interna-tional DJs playing to a crowd of hysterical club kids high on life and youth. This is what Stockholm has been desperately missing for so long.

Södermalm

Debaser

Karl Johans Torg 1 (30 56 20/www.debaser.nu).
T-bana Slussen/bus 2, 3, 53, 76. **Open** 8pm-3am daily. **Minimum age** *Mon-Thur* 18; *Fri-Sun* 20. **Admission** varies. **No credit cards**. **Map** p241 J8.

This is the archetypal rock club – stylishly grim and raw, and located under a bridge in an old distillery. It's open seven nights a week with live acts and DJs, as well as a wild dancefloor. Come early (before 11pm) if you don't want to queue for hours. The music favours pop on Friday and rock on Saturday. Among the theme nights, Wednesday's Club Killers is the monthly ska and rock steady event.

Debaser Medis

Medborgarplatsen 8 (674 79 00/www.debaser.nu).
T-bana Medborgarplatsen/bus 55, 59, 66. **Open** varies. **Admission** varies. **Minimum age** varies. **Credit** AmEx, DC, MC, V. **Map** p250 L8.

This huge cultural centre is always worth a visit. With three stages, four dancefloors, five bars, a restaurant, a gallery and a cinema, there's always something going on. At least one club takes place nightly, and sometimes there are two or three hap-pening simultaneously on different floors, with music ranging from rock to techno by way of grime.

Marie Laveau

Hornsgatan 66 (668 85 00/www.marielaveau.se).
T-bana Mariatorget/bus 4, 43, 55. **Open** 5pm-midnight Mon-Wed; 5pm-3am Thur-Sat. **Minimum age** 23. **Admission** varies. **Credit** AmEx, DC, MC, V. **Map** p250 K6.

Södermalm's – and maybe Stockholm's – best club venue is a packed basement where the sweat drips from the ceiling every Friday and Saturday. During the last year ML has gone from harder electronic beats to warmer, more organic house, disco and soul, to attract a slightly older crowd.

Mosebacke Etablissement

Mosebacke Torg 3 (55 60 98 90/www.mosebacke.se). T-bana Slussen/bus 2, 3, 53, 76. **Open** 5pm-1am Mon-Thur; 5pm-2am Fri; 10.30pm-2am Sat; 10.30pm-1am Sun. **Minimum age** varies. **Admission** 60kr-80kr. **Credit** AmEx, DC, MC, V. **Map** p250 K8.
Some of the best club nights in town, such as Yes! and Raw Fusion, are held at this classic jazz joint, often with a focus on soul, disco and hip hop. The outdoor terrace is extremely popular in summer.

Södra Teatern

Mosebacke Torg 1-3 (55 69 72 30/www.sodra teatern.com). T-bana Slussen/bus 2, 3, 53, 76. **Open** varies. **Minimum age** 18-20. **Admission** 50kr-70kr. **Credit** AmEx, DC, MC, V. **Map** p250 K8.
In the foyer, bar and basement of this ever-popular cultural centre are clubs you won't find anywhere else in town: Kurdish, Balkan and Indo-Asian, and sometimes a combination of the three, with bands, poetry readings and spoken-word performances.

Östermalm

Neu

Sturegatan 4 (54 50 76 00/www.stureplans gruppen.se). T-bana Östermalmstorg/bus 1, 2, 55, 56, 91. **Open** 11pm-5am Thur-Sat. **Minimum age** 23. **Admission** 120kr. **Credit** AmEx, DC, MC, V. **Map** p241 F8.
As the name implies, this is a new venue playing the latest sounds. It's also a bit of a novelty for Stureplan as it's not just for posh brats and pretty girls, but also for music aficionados in their thirties who just don't want to go to bed (after 3am). The owners also manage the ever-popular F12 bar (*see p119*).

Riche

Birger Jarlsgatan 4 (54 50 35 60/www.riche.se). T-bana Östermalmstorg/bus 2, 47, 55, 62, 91. **Open** 11.30am-midnight Mon; 11.30am-1am Tue; 11.30am-2am Wed-Fri; noon-2am Sat. **Minimum age** 23. **Credit** AmEx, DC, MC, V. **Map** p241 F8.
Maybe not a real 'club', there's not even a dancefloor, but Riche is still a veritable riot every night of the week. A roster of theme nights, release parties and art openings keep the place buzzing with a trendy mix of media types and fashionistas, getting ready for another Spy Bar night. If you want to get to know the real Stockholm, this is a must.

Spy Bar

Birger Jarlsgatan 20 (54 50 37 01/www.thespy bar.se). T-bana Östermalmstorg/bus 1, 2, 55, 56, 91. **Open** 10pm-5am Wed-Sat. **Minimum age** 23. **Admission** 120kr. **Credit** AmEx, DC, MC, V. **Map** p241 E8.

A former favourite of B-celebrities and wannabe stars, the Spy Bar has undergone a remake and nowadays draws a trendy crowd of fashionistas, musicians and hipsters. Upstairs is a veritable labyrinth of bars and VIP rooms with plush carpets and chandeliers; outside is a very long queue of people trying to convince the bouncers that they really do know the right people.

Sturecompagniet

Sturegatan 4 (611 78 00/www.sturecompagniet.se). T-bana Östermalmstorg/bus 1, 2, 55, 56, 91. **Open** 10pm-5am Thur-Sat. **Minimum age** 23. **Admission** 120kr after 10pm Fri, Sat. **Credit** AmEx, DC, MC, V. **Map** p241 F8.
At the weekend this beautiful, three-storey, five-dancefloor party palace with an elaborate interior of marble, roses and purple is where the rich and famous play. It can make for a great night out, albeit a quite expensive one. However, only the prettiest things will make it through the doors.

Kungsholmen

La Isla

Flemminggatan 48 (654 60 43/www.isla.se). T-bana Fridhemsplan/bus 3, 4, 57, 59. **Open** 8pm-1am Wed; 8pm-3am Fri, Sat. **Minimum age** 18. **Admission** 80kr after 10pm. **Credit** AmEx, MC, V. **Map** p239 F3.
The largest and longest-running Latin disco, or 'salsoteque', La Isla is open three nights a week playing Afro-Caribbean sounds for a predominantly Latin crowd from the northern suburbs. There are also salsa courses and an excellent restaurant.

Trädgården

Flemminggatan 2-4 (50 82 67 09/www.tradgarden. com). T-bana Rådhuset/bus 1, 3, 40, 52, 62. **Open** *June-Aug* 7pm-3am Fri, Sat. Closed Sept-May. **Minimum age** 21. **Admission** varies. **Credit** AmEx, MC, V. **Map** p240 G5.
Trädgården means 'the garden', and that's pretty much what this is: an outdoor yard where you hang out playing games, sipping a cold beer or a long drink, grabbing some barbecue food before dancing under the stars (or the ceiling, if it rains). Needless to say, this is a summer hangout.

Further afield

Landet

LM Ericssons väg 27 (41 01 93 20). T-bana Telefonplan/bus 141, 142, 161, 190. **Open** 5pm-midnight Mon-Thur; 4pm-1am Fri; 5pm-1am Sat. **Credit** AmEx, DC, MC, V.
Midsommarkransen, a former working-class suburb just south of Hornstull, is the hippest part of town right now and Landet, which hosts clubs almost every night of the week, is a great place to start the night. It closes at 1am, but in this area there's almost always something fun going on, so just mix with the locals and you'll be OK.

Film

A nation of cineastes.

With a healthy home-grown market, a long and varied filmmaking history and one of the highest densities of cinemas per capita in Europe (over nine cinemas per 100,000 inhabitants, compared to approximately 1.2 in the UK), Swedes have a real passion for the silver screen.

In the 1920s, Sweden was among the world's leading filmmaking nations. Directors such as Victor Sjöström and Mauritz Stiller made an impact with films that were widely regarded as masterpieces at the time, and which are now considered to be classics. Several of these were based on books by Selma Lagerlöf (Nobel Prize laureate, 1909), including *The Phantom Carriage* (1921) and *The Treasure of Arne* (1919) by Sjöström, and *The Story of Gösta Berling* (1924) by Stiller (the film that catapulted Greta Garbo to fame). These films were groundbreaking as they were shot on location using nature as a key element, at a time when most films were still shot in studios.

The golden age of Swedish film was, however, brief, as some of the film industry's biggest stars were lured abroad – Sjöström, Stiller and Garbo all emigrated to Hollywood. The 1930s and '40s were characterised by rather provincial and burlesque comedies, and it was not until the early '50s that Swedish film again attracted the world's attention. Alf Sjöberg's version of Strindberg's play *Miss Julie* (1951) and Arne Mattsson's *One Summer of Happiness* (1952) stunned audiences in Venice and Berlin. At Cannes in 1956, Ingmar Bergman won international fame with *Smiles of a Summer Night*, and he remained in the spotlight throughout his filmmaking career.

The most successful Swedish filmmaker of all time, Bergman made more than 40 films, among which the most renowned are *Summer With Monika* (1953), *The Seventh Seal* (1956), *Wild Strawberries* (1957) and, of course, *Fanny and Alexander* (1982) – which Bergman said at the time would be his last film. He kept that

Step back into the golden age at preserved 1920s cinema **Skandia**. *See p173.*

promise for 20 years, then made *Saraband* (2003), a follow-up to his internationally successful TV series *Scenes from a Marriage*.

With the exception of Bergman, Swedish film wasn't very fertile until the late 1960s, when government funding helped a new generation of filmmakers to emerge. Directors such as Jan Troell, Bo Widerberg and Viglot Sjöman became big names in an increasingly politicised era of filmmaking.

Sweden also has the largely undeserved reputation of being the birthplace of pornographic film. Titles often referred to are: *Do You Believe in Angels?* (1961), *Dear John* (1964) and *I Am Curious: Yellow* (1967). These films were considered to be extremely daring in their time, but by today's standards they are far from pornographic. Paradoxically, along with being the first makers of 'porn', the Swedes have the oldest system of film censorship in the world, established in 1911.

These days Swedish film is less serious, fairly wordy and not sensationally erotic, and comedies, satires and farces almost always generate the most reliable audiences and the highest income. That said, an exciting new era in Swedish filmmaking began with Lukas Moodysson's excellent *Fucking Åmål* (1998). He was the first to challenge the norm by making a very different film, one that took teenagers seriously. Moreover, Moodysson showed that such filmmaking was possible on quite a small budget, paving the way for more diverse filmmaking. A wave of young immigrant filmmakers are now gaining international recognition for movies such as Reza Parsa's *Before the Storm* (2000) and Josef Fares' *Jalla! Jalla!* (2000). Other recent films worth seeing are Mikael Håfström's drama *Evil* (2003), which was nominated for an Oscar, Teresa Fabik's *Hip Hip Whore* (2004) and Tomas Alfredson's black comedy *Four Shades of Brown* (2004). Roy Andersson's *Du Levande* ('You, the Living') was screened at Cannes in 2007, and Jesper Ganslandt's *Förväll Falkenberg* ('Falkenberg Farewell') screened at several films festivals in 2006.

For more Swedish films of note, *see p229.*

THE INDUSTRY

As this edition goes to print the future of many Swedish cinemas looks uncertain. Until recently the film industry in Sweden was dominated by two huge rival companies, **SF** (Svensk Filmindustri) and **Sandrews Metronome**. Both companies controlled all aspects of film production, distribution and exhibition, and operated cinemas themselves. In 2005,

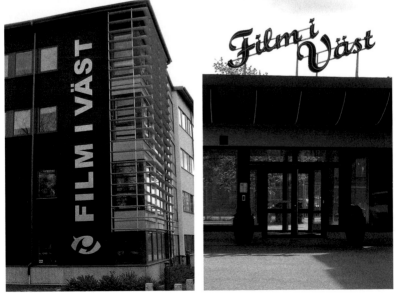

Rising star: Gothenburg's **Film i Väst** production studios. *See p172.*

Arts & Entertainment

Lasse come home

Comparisons are odious. On the one hand, we have Ingmar Bergman, the recently deceased master whose sombre and artistically rigorous studies of the human condition are honoured worldwide. On the other, we have Sweden's second best known filmmaker, whose list of features includes such probing studies of soul and spirit as *ABBA: The Movie* – a man who has lived in New York since 1995 and hasn't made a film in Swedish for 20 years.

Viewed in this light, it might be forgivable to think of Stockholm-born Lasse Hallström as the anti-Bergman, and his apprenticeship in moving images as director of Abba music videos was no promise of cinematic ambition. But in 1987 he drew the attention of the film world with *My Life as a Dog*, which earned two Oscar nominations and a Golden Globe for best foreign language film. US studios came calling, and the results have included *What's Eating Gilbert Grape*, *The Shipping News*, *Chocolat* and *The Cider House Rules* (a film billed with the perhaps apposite tagline: 'a story about how far we must travel to find the place where we belong').

Like so many foreign language filmmakers before him, Hallström answered Hollywood's siren call. It's not hard to see why – who would pass up the chance to work with everyone from Robert Redford and Johnny Depp to Julia Roberts and Judi Dench? And he's not alone: '[Lucas] Moodysson goes English', reads a May 2007 announcement on the Swedish Film Institute website (www.sfi.se), alluding to that uneven filmmaker's upcoming *Mammoth*, a film that revolves around a successful New York couple and a life-changing trip to Thailand. There's also a precedent in Victor Sjöström, the silent era master whose Tinseltown work (signed 'Victor Seastrom') was an influence on Bergman.

As we said, comparisons are odious; and if nothing else, the westward movement of Hallström and Moodysson proves that Swedish filmmakers can adapt to the very different rules of American cinema. However, it would be a great pity if they never again work in their native tongue – and a greater pity still if transfers Stateside became the norm for Sweden's most promising directors.

newcomers **Astoria Cinema** bought out Sandrews, but the company foundered and by summer 2007 it was bankrupt. The likely result of this ill-fated deal is a monopoly for SF, but the fate of the many ex-Sandrews cinemas caught up in the affair remains as yet unclear.

In film production itself, things look a bit brighter. Until fairly recently, most film production took place in Stockholm and was usually controlled by SF. But new funding initiatives have meant that much of the work has moved to production centres elsewhere, especially **Film i Väst** outside Gothenburg (*photo p171*). Virtually every recent successful film has been produced at Film i Väst, now Scandinavia's major regional film organisation. The number of films made per year is increasing, and with national funding assured until 2010 the immediate future of the Swedish film industry looks healthy.

TIMES AND TICKETS

Cinemas open one hour before the first screening (usually around 11am or 5pm). All films are shown in their original language with Swedish subtitles. Tickets usually cost between 85kr and 95kr. Listings and information can be found in the daily papers or online.

Cinemas

Astoria
Nybrogatan 15, Östermalm (660 00 25). T-bana Östermalmstorg/bus 2, 47, 62, 69, 76. **Credit** AmEx, MC, V. **Map** p241 F8.
A modern, THX-classified single-screener, this is Stockholm's leading first-run cinema.

Filmhuset
Borgvägen 1-5, Gärdet (665 11 00/www.sfi.se). T-bana Karlaplan/bus 56, 72, 76. **No credit cards**. **Map** p247 E12.
The Film House, one of the city's largest cinemas, houses the Swedish Film Institute.

Filmstaden Sergel
Hötorget, Norrmalm (56 26 00 00/www.sf.se). T-bana Hötorget/bus 1, 52, 56. **Credit** AmEx, MC, V. **Map** p241 F6.
With 14 screens to choose from, this is the place to go to imbibe a bustling multiplex atmosphere.

Grand
Sveavägen 45, Norrmalm (660 00 25/www. sandrews.se). T-bana Rådmansgatan/bus 43, 52. **Credit** AmEx, MC, V. **Map** p245 E6.
The Grand has four decent auditoriums and doors adorned with film stars in intarsia. This is the cinema Olof Palme visited just before he was shot.

Kvartersbion

Hornstulls Strand 3, Södermalm (669 19 95).
T-bana Hornstull/bus 4, 40, 66. **No credit cards**.
Map p249 L2.
Kvartersbion is run by just one person and is completely free from luxury – it looks the same as it did in the 1940s. The programme is understandably rather limited, but locals are devoted to their cinema, which has defied death yet again after funding was cut. The cinema's new saviour is the Swedish Lutheran Church.

Rival

Hotel Rival, Mariatorget 3, Södermalm (56 26 00 00/www.rival.se). T-bana Mariatorget/bus 2, 55, 191, 192. **Credit** AmEx, MC, V. **Map** p250 K6.
This classic, late 1930s 700-seat art deco cinema has been lovingly preserved, its beautifully restored interior now combined with state-of-the-art technology. Films are shown Friday to Sunday only.

Skandia

Drottninggatan 82, Norrmalm (56 26 00 00/www.sf.se). T-bana Hötorget/bus 1, 47, 52, 53, 69. **Credit** AmEx, MC, V. **Map** p241 F6.
This eccentric cinema opened in 1923. Most interiors, designed by the architect Gunnar Asplund, are still intact. Daily screenings ceased in 1996 and today it's open only for 'singalongs' and short runs. If the cinema is open during your visit, don't miss it. *Photo p170.*

Sture

Birger Jarlsgatan 41, Östermalm (678 85 48/www. biosture.se). T-bana Östermalmstorg/bus 1, 2, 55, 56. **Credit** MC, V. **Map** p245 E7.

This three-screen cinema shows art house films, as well as more commercial fare. The curtain in Cinema One was made by Ernst Billgren, one of Sweden's most famous contemporary artists.

Victoria

Götgatan 67, Södermalm (660 00 25). T-bana Medborgarplatsen/bus 59, 66. **Credit** AmEx, MC, V. **Map** p250 M8.
A modest five-screen cinema on Södermalm, showing the critics' favourites. There are some rather odd Neptune fountains outside the toilets.

Zita

Birger Jarlsgatan 37, Östermalm (23 20 20/www. zita.se). T-bana Östermalmstorg/bus 1, 2, 55, 56. **No credit cards**. **Map** p245 E7.
The only cinema in town with a bar, Zita shows films from all over the world. It frequently shows documentaries, and screens short films free of charge every day during the summer months.

IMAX

Cosmonova

Naturhistorska Riksmuseet, Frescativägen 40, Northern Frescati (51 95 51 30/www.nrm.se/ cosmonova). T-bana Universitet/bus 40, 540.
No under-5s admitted. **Credit** AmEx, MC, V.
This IMAX cinema is a paradise for families, but also worth a visit for any cinema buff. Films shown on its 11m-tall (36ft) dome-shaped screen are usually nature-based, and worth seeing. Screenings are in Swedish only, so don't forget to buy an earphone for translation when buying your tickets.

Sture.

Galleries

Head out of the centre for cutting-edge creativity.

Milliken features some of Sweden's finest emerging talents.

Over the past couple of years the Stockholm art scene has exploded to its full potential. Pursuasive and driven, it is most certainly alive and kicking. During the late 1990s, the focus was on showcasing interesting Swedish artists on the world stage, and now that exposure is reaping benefits on the local scene.

In the wake of this encouraging flow several non-profit art spaces have managed to stay alive, new ones have emerged and galleries are buying and selling as never before. A direct result of this is the **MARKET** art fair (www.market-art.se), which took place for the first time in February 2006 and aims to showcase the most exciting Swedish and Nordic contemporary art.

ART BY AREA

St Eriksplan, in the western part of the city, has recently defined itself as Stockholm's new art precinct. Featuring several of the city's hottest new galleries, it's definitely worth the trek. The Brändström & Stene gallery was the first to discover the potential of the former industrial buildings at Huddiksvallsgatan, and the new Bonniers Konsthall contemporary art institution has also opened its gates in the neighbourhood, offering modern art fans a much-needed alternative to Moderna Museet.

At the same time several galleries are abandoning the more traditional area of Östermalm, where rents are becoming astronomically high, and looking for other places to settle down.

For boho chic, the area of **Södermalm** known as SoFo (South of Folkungagatan) is still the place to be, boasting cutting-edge galleries such as CFF, ID:I Galleri and Candyland. SoFo has also become the natural link to the avant garde hotspots shooting up in the southern suburbs (*see p177* **South of SoFo**).

Moderna Museet (*see p78*) continues its sucessful blend of small monthly shows called 'The 1st at Moderna'. Since 2004 this series has presented contemporary artists, with exhibitions opening on the first of each month.

INFORMATION

One way to ensure you hit all the good spaces is to pick up a copy of *Konstguiden*. It is a free brochure, available in all major art spaces and galleries. It provides comprehensive gallery listings and is published twice a year, in spring

Arts & Entertainment

and autumn. Also check out **www.konsten. net** (Swedish only) for up-to-date reviews or **www.artinsweden.com** for information on Swedish artists and other related links. Note that many galleries are open from noon and several are closed Monday to Wednesday. During the summer most are closed from mid-June to mid-August. Admission is free unless otherwise stated.

Norrmalm

Fotografins Hus
Norra Brobänken, Skeppsholmen (611 69 69/ www.fotografinshus.se). T-bana Kungsträdgården/ bus 65. **Open** noon-7pm Tue, Wed; noon-5pm Thur-Sun. **Admission** 50kr. **Credit** AmEx, MC, V. **Map** p242 H9.
This private exhibition hall was founded in 2003, just a stone's throw from the Moderna Museet. It is the largest space in Stockholm devoted solely to photography – documentary, artistic and commercial. Fotografins Hus also runs an ambitious programme of seminars and talks.

Galleri Magnus Karlsson
Fredsgatan 12 (660 43 53/www.gallerimagnus karlsson.com). T-bana T-Centralen. **Open** noon-5pm Tue-Fri; noon-4pm Sat; 1-4pm Sun. **No credit cards. Map** p241 H7.
Magnus Karlsson moved into a new, larger location in the 17th-century Royal Academy of Art in 2005. And no wonder – this gallery has succesfully launched the careers of some of the most important contemporary painters in Sweden, including Karin Mamma Andersson and Jockum Nordström. The gallery regularly features at international art fairs.

Wetterling Gallery
Kungsträdgårdsgatan 3 (10 10 09/www.wetterling gallery.com). T-bana Kungsträdgården/bus 2, 47, 55, 62, 76. **Open** 11am-5.30pm Tue-Fri; 1-4pm Sat. **Credit** AmEx, MC, V. **Map** p241 G8.
Situated in popular Kungsträdgården Park, in the city centre, this large gallery exhibits American and British artists, such as Diti Almog, Gavin Turk and Julian Opie, along with several Europeans such as Russian Nathalia Edenmont, who recently upset the Swedish cultural establishment by exhibiting stuffed animals in her work.

Vasastaden

Also worth checking out are **Knäpper + Baumgarten** (www.knapperbaumgarten.com) and newcomer **Galleri Jonas Kleerup** (www.galleri-kleerup.se).

Andréhn-Schiptjenko
Hudiksvallsgatan 8 (612 00 75/www.andrehn-schiptjenko.com). T-bana Rådmansgatan/bus 2, 4, 42, 43, 53. **Open** 11am-5pm Tue-Fri; noon-5pm Sat. **No credit cards. Map** p245 C6.

Opened in 1991, Andréhn-Schiptjenko is one of Stockholm's leading contemporary art galleries. Its portfolio includes international artists such as Xavier Veilhan, Marilyn Minter and Abigail Lane, as well as new and well-established Swedish artists such as Annika Larsson, Annika von Hausswolff and Tobias Bernstrup.

Bonniers Konsthall
Torsgatan 19 (736 42 48/www.bonnierskonsthall.se). T-bana St Eriksplan/bus 3, 4, 42, 73, 77. **Open** 11am-8pm Wed; 11am-5pm Thur-Sun. **Credit** MC, V. **Map** p244 E4.
Bonnier Konsthall is a new venue for contemporary art in Stockholm and has rapidly become the heart of the growing Vasastaden art district. Founded by Jeanette Bonnier, this non-profit institution is run by the Bonnier Group, one of Scandinavia's biggest media concerns. The building, with an impressive glass façade, was designed by acclaimed Swedish architect Johan Celsing. Bonnier Konsthall runs a public programme with talks, seminars, artists in conversation and exhibitions. A much-needed alternative to Magasin 3 and Moderna Museet.

Brändström & Stene
Hudiksvallsgatan 6 (660 41 53/www.brandstrom stene.se). T-bana St Eriksplan/bus 3, 4, 70, 73, 77. **Open** noon-6pm Thur, Fri; noon-4pm Sat, Sun. **No credit cards. Map** p244 C3.
Brändström & Stene was the first gallery to move to this area a couple of years ago, and now you will find several others following its lead. It's one of the largest and most significant galleries in town, offering a stimulating blend of established and emerging work. It represents well-known artists such as Olafur Eliasson, Spencer Finch, Cecilia Edefalk and Isaac Julien, plus emerging stars such as Jeppe Hein and Julia Peirone.

Mia Sundberg Galleri
Gävlegatan 12 (www.miasundberggalleri.se). T-bana St Eriksplan/bus 3, 4, 70, 73, 77. **Open** times vary. **No credit cards. Map** p244 C3.
Recently decamped from Östermalm, Mia Sundberg is an excellent gallery where you'll find a mix of artists from Sweden and abroad. Keep an eye out for work by recently graduated artists, as the gallery maintains an interest in new faces.

Milliken
Luntmakargatan 78 (673 70 10/www.milliken gallery.com). T-bana Rådmansgatan/bus 2, 42, 43, 44, 52, 53. **Open** noon-5pm Wed-Sat. **No credit cards. Map** p245 D6.
Housed in old factory premises, this space has an industrial air – unusual for a gallery right in the city centre – that lends it a cool New York feel. The gallery's three high-ceilinged rooms provide great conditions for exhibiting. Milliken focuses on an international blend of artists, from emerging youngsters to big stars: you'll find Swedish duo Bigert & Bergström, Olav Westphalen, Lars Nilsson and Tris Vonna-Michell among others.

Natalia Goldin Gallery

Hudiksvallsgatan 8 (650 21 35/www.natalia goldin.com). T-bana St Eriksplan/bus 3, 4, 42, 73, 77. **Open** *11am-5.30pm Tue-Fri; noon-4pm Sat.* **No credit cards. Map** *p244 C3.*

This gallery has proved to be an exciting venue since its opening in 2003. Concentrating on young Swedish artists – several of them making their first solo exhibition at the gallery – owner Natalia Goldin has shown a keen eye for quality art. She is also one of the initiators of the new art fair in Stockholm, MARKET (*see p174*).

Djurgården

Liljevalchs Konsthall

Djurgårdsvägen 43 (50 83 13 30/www.liljevalchs. com). Bus 44, 47/ferry from Slussen or Nybroviken. **Open** *11am-5pm Tue-Sun.* **Admission** *70kr; 50kr concessions; free under-18s.* **Credit** *MC, V.* **Map** *p242 H11.*

This beautiful 1916 building next to the aquarium is a fine example of Swedish neo-classicism and is owned by the City of Stockholm. Originally built from a donation by the businessman Carl Fredrik Liljevalch, it attracts a wide audience to its 12 exhibition rooms, where you can view themed and solo shows (which change every three months) by Swedish and international artists. A very popular event is the annual open exhibition, Vårsalongen, in which a jury selects works by both established artists and amateurs, resulting in a vivid blend of high art and kitsch. Next to the building is the lovely restaurant-café Blå Porten (*see p131*).

Södermalm

Candyland

Gotlandsgatan 76 (0703 36 58 62/www.candyland.se). T-bana Skanstull/bus 2, 53, 59, 66, 76. **Admission** *varies.* **No credit cards. Map** *p251 M9.*

At this art collective, formed in 2004, ten artists exhibit their own work, as well as the work of other artists, in a rich variety of media – from installations and painting to video and photography – in an exciting, creatively interactive venue. Spring 2007 saw the launch of a new production space in Hammarby Sjöstad (*see p177* **South of SoFo**).

CFF – Centrum För Fotografi

Tjärhovsgatan 44 (640 20 95/www.centrumfor fotografi.se). T-bana Medborgarplatsen/bus 2, 53, 59, 66, 76. **Open** *noon-6pm Wed-Fri; noon-4pm Sat, Sun.* **Admission** *free.* **No credit cards. Map** *p251 L9.*

This membership association for photographers has six shows a year. Highly acclaimed international artists blend with newcomers in the yearly exhibitions of the Art Academy of Gothenburg, Valand, and the School of Photography, Gothenburg University. The website features a digital gallery where photos from members are displayed and sold.

ID:I Galleri

Tjärhovsgatan 19 (www.idigalleri.org). T-bana Medborgarplatsen/bus 2, 53, 59, 66, 76. **Open** *4-8pm Thur, Fri; noon-4pm Sat, Sun.* **No credit cards. Map** *p251 L9.*

One of the more enduring non-commercial spaces in the city, ID:I is run by 27 artists who are each in charge of the space for three weeks, during which time they are free to exhibit or invite others. United by the belief that government backing creates artistic restraints, they run the space with their own funds.

Kungsholmen

Index – The Swedish Contemporary Art Foundation

Kungsbrostrand 19 (640 60 69/www.index foundation.se). T-bana T-Centralen/bus 52, 59. **Open** *noon-4pm Tue-Fri; noon-5pm Sat, Sun.* **No credit cards. Map** *p240 G5.*

Index started out as a photography gallery, but has widened its exhibitions to include video and installation. Since moving to its new space in 2006, it is now firmly at the forefront of avant garde art, mixing international artists such as Harun Farocki, Julius Koller and Fikret Atay with Swedish beginners.

Östermalm

Galleri Charlotte Lund

Skeppargatan 70 (663 09 79/www.gallericharlotte lund.com). T-bana Karlaplan/bus 1, 42, 44. **Open** *noon-6pm Tue-Fri; noon-5pm Sat.* **No credit cards. Map** *p246 E10.*

This is one of the more reliable and interesting venues for high-profile art. The gallery's three rooms are in a first-floor apartment. You'll find both established and up-and-coming Swedish and international artists working in a variety of media.

Galleri IngerMolin

Kommendörsgatan 24 (52 80 08 30/www.galleri ingermolin.se). T-bana Stadion/bus 1, 44, 55, 56, 62. **Open** *noon-5.30pm Tue-Thur; noon-4pm Fri, Sat.* **No credit cards. Map** *p246 E9.*

For a long time Inger Molin has been working towards eliminating the line between 'art' and 'crafts'. Her gallery, which opened in 1998, shows crafts-oriented work – such as ceramics, textiles and glass – and is definitely worth a visit.

Galleri Lars Bohman

Karlavägen 16 (20 78 07/www.gallerilarsbohman. com). T-bana Rådmansgatan/bus 2, 42, 44. **Open** *11am-5.30pm Tue-Fri; noon-4pm Sat, Sun.* **No credit cards. Map** *p245 D7.*

As one of the city's most prominent galleries, Lars Bohman represents a rich range of contemporary artists, both Swedish and foreign, working in all kinds of media. The space has five rooms in all. Recent shows have included artists such as Donald Baechler, Domenico Bianchi, Ernst Billgren, Lena Cronqvist, Sabine Hornig and Dan Wolgers.

Arts & Entertainment

South of SoFo

Stockholm's suburban art scene is flourishing, with spiralling rents pushing galleries out to bigger and more attractive spaces. One of the latest initiatives to open up is **WIP** (Årstaskolgränd 14D, 84 26 47, www.wipsthlm.se), Work in Progress. It is a studio association with nearly 100 studios, hosting mostly artists but also dancers and musicians. The huge building is situated in Årsta, and used to be a warehouse for the Swedish film industry.

The best way to get a peek into the studios and meet people is to go to an opening. WIP hosts six exhibitions a year with mostly international artists. During opening nights, studios in different areas of the building are kept open and you are welcome to visit them. Other events include lectures once a month, screenings and talks. An artists' archive can be accessed in the showroom, containing a complete description of residing artists, and there is a small art bookshop in the entrance.

Hammarby ArtPort (Hammarby Fabriksväg 43, 0703 36 58 62/www. hammarbyartport.com) is another recently opened project space south of SoFo. HAP opened its doors in February 2007 as an extension to the small artist-run Candyland gallery (*see p176*).

Not being a regular exhibition space, HAP concentrates on different interactive projects and artistic production. It's housed in big premises in a newly constructed area in Stockholm called Hammarby Sjöstad, a former run-down harbour and industrial estate next to Södermalm. Surrounded by water, it has now become an idyllic district just ten minutes from the city by boat or tram. HAP runs approximately four international exhibitions a year, and also interacts with local companies, exploring different ways of presenting and working with art, including consultant services and public commissions in the area.

Hammarby ArtPort.

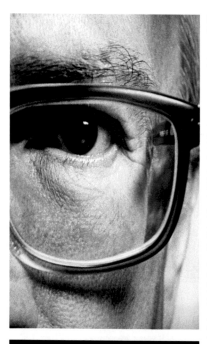

Gärdet

Magasin 3 Stockholm Konsthall

Frihamnen (54 56 80 40/www.magasin3.com).
Bus 1, 76. **Open** noon-7pm Thur; noon-5pm Fri-Sun.
Admission 40kr; 30kr concessions; free under-20s.
Credit MC, V.
Magasin 3 opened in 1987 and is housed in an old
warehouse (*magasin*) in the Stockholm port area.
Whereas other institutions suffer from a lack of
funding, Magasin 3 is one of the most rapidly
expanding privately funded art spaces in Sweden.
Previous shows have included Pipilotti Rist, Paul
Chan, Jake & Dinos Chapman and Kimsooja.

Further afield

There is a growing art scene in Stockholm's
suburbs. In addition to the galleries listed
below, the following are worth a visit:
Millesgården (*see p95*) in Lidingö;
Botkyrka Konsthall (Tumba Torg 105,
Tumba, 53 06 12 25, www.botkyrka.se), in
one of the city's rougher suburbs, which has
succeeded in attracting a wider audience to
contemporary art; local gallery **Norrtälje
Konsthall** (Lilla Brogatan 2, Norrtälje,
www.norrtalje.se); **Marabou Park
Annex** (Vasagatan 4A, Sundbyberg, www.
marabouparken.se), which has become one of
the most interesting venues in the city; and
Konsthall C (Cigarrvägen 14, Hökarängen/
Farsta, 604 77 08, www.konsthallc.se), which
works with the local community and has
society-related issues on the programme.

Färgfabriken

Lövholmsbrinken 1, Liljeholmen (645 07 07/www.
fargfabriken.se). T-bana Liljeholmen/bus 77, 133,
143, 152. **Open** noon-6pm Thur-Sun. **Admission**
40kr; 30kr concessions; free under-18s. **Credit**
AmEx, DC, MC, V. **Map** p249 L1.
The Centre for Contemporary Art and Architecture,
in the southern suburb of Liljeholmen, occupies an
important position on the Stockholm art scene.
Founded in 1995, it is housed in an old factory, with
one main exhibition space, plus three smaller rooms.
Recent projects have included a music installation
by Talking Head David Byrne and exhibitions by
Liz Cohen, Peter Geschwind and Natalie Djurberg.

Tensta Konsthall

Taxingegränd 10, Tensta Centrum (36 07 63/www.
tenstakonsthall.com). T-bana Tensta. **Open** noon-
5pm Tue-Sun. **No credit cards.**
Tensta Konsthall has been around since the mid
1990s but, after changing management in spring
2004, is now run by the successful trio of Jelena
Rundqvist, Ylva Ogland and Rodrigo Mallea Lira.
They invite Swedish and international guests to
explore the boundaries between art, music, design,
architecture, fashion and text. Well worth a visit.

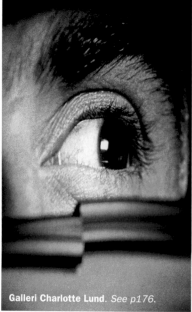

Galleri Charlotte Lund. *See p176.*

Gay & Lesbian

For gentlemen who prefer blonds.

In comparison with other European capitals, Stockholm's gay scene can seem underwhelming. There is no gay neighbourhood, a limited number of bars and clubs, and if you spend just a few days out and about you'll soon start to see the same faces. It's a mystery why gay life in the Danish capital, Copenhagen – a city much like Stockholm in terms of size and personality – is so much livelier.

To be fair, one reason for this lack of exuberance and attitude is that Stockholm is a thoroughly enlightened town. You'll see old married couples visiting gay cafés, while gay people take their straight mates out for a night

Come out: Scandinavia's biggest **Pride**.

of clubbing (and vice versa). There is less of a sense of a distinct gay life here, because if a bar or café or club is any good, everyone wants to go there.

The trick with Stockholm is not to judge it on what it lacks but to appreciate that what it offers is unique and wonderful. When the weather is good (Abba got it right: this really is a 'summer night city'), the place can be magical. Standing on the deck of Patricia and watching the sun come up, going for a post-club swim in the centre of town, sunbathing on the cliffs at Kärsön close to the royal family's home, watching the sunset with a bottle of wine on the floating deck at Mälarpaviljongen – these are the sort of experiences that only Stockholm can deliver.

TAKING PRIDE

Stockholm's annual **Pride** celebration (see p160) is the largest in Scandinavia and usually takes place in late July or early August. The focus of activity is Pride Park, an enclosure set up in one of Stockholm's parks. Inside will be a number of stalls set up by gay cafés and bars, plus a stage for performances by pop stars. To get in you need to buy a pass, which is locally known as a dog-tag. Other highlights of the event include a gay film festival, the coronation of the new Mr Gay Sweden and a parade through the city. For a full programme of events, see www.stockholmpride.org.

INFORMATION

To find out what's happening pick up **QX**, the excellent free gay newspaper. It's in Swedish but is easy to follow. QX also produces an invaluable map of gay Stockholm, which is widely available at gay and gay-friendly bars and cafés. The QX website, www.qx.se, has a guide to the city in English (and also serves as the Swedish equivalent of Gaydar). You can also listen to Radio QX online. Other popular websites include **Corky** (www.corky.se) and **Sylvia** (www.sylvia.se) for women, and **Sylvester** (www.sylvester.se) for men. All three are in Swedish, but with easy-to-follow listings.

Tune into **Stockholm Gay Radio** (95.3FM or www.gayradion.nu) to catch shows such as Ferro ('for men, about men, by men') and Happy Gay (playing 'happy party music' on Friday evenings). For gay and lesbian healthcare and helplines, see p221.

Where to stay

Two men or two women checking in together at a hotel in Stockholm won't cause so much as a raised eyebrow. There are, however, a handful of hotels that actively court gay visitors. The **Lord Nelson**, **Lady Hamilton** and **Victory** hotels (for all, *see p36*) are a trio of upmarket properties with a historic maritime theme in Gamla Stan. Also in Gamla Stan is the five-star **First Hotel Reisen** (*see p35*). The three locations of **Pensionat Oden** (www.pensionat. nu, 725kr-1,295kr double), in Södermalm (Hornsgatan 66B), Vasastaden (Odengatan 38) and Norrmalm (Kammakargatan 62), have low prices but small rooms. The **Rival** (*see p43*), on Södermalm, is both stylish and handily located for Pride events. In the city centre, close to the station and trains to the airport, is the designer **Freys Hotel** (*see p40*) and **Nordic Sea** and **Nordic Light** hotels (for both, *see p39*). **Rica Hotels** (www.rica.se) has three properties in the heart of town and is an official sponsor of Stockholm Pride.

Bars & restaurants

Leijonbaren

Lilla Nygatan 5, Gamla Stan (50 64 00 80/www. leijonbaren.se). T-bana Gamla Stan/bus 3, 53. **Open** 5pm-midnight Mon-Thur; 5pm-1am Fri-Sat. Closed mid June-mid Aug. Kitchen closes 11pm. **Credit** AmEx, MC, V. **Map** p241 J7.

A trendy gay-friendly bar in the Victory Hotel, with a good cocktail list and DJs most nights of the week. The hotel's restaurant, Leijontornet, is ranked as one of the best places to eat in the whole of Sweden, and also makes Leijonbaren's excellent bar food.

Mälarpaviljongen

Norr Mälarstrand 62, at Polhemsgatan, Kungsholmen (650 87 01/www.malarpaviljongen.se). T-bana Rådhuset or Fridhemsplan/bus 3, 40, 52, 62. **Open** *May-Sept* 11am-midnight daily, weather permitting. Closed winter. *Food served* 11am-11pm daily. **Credit** AmEx, MC, V. **Map** p240 H3.

This wonderful alfresco bistro-bar opened in 2004 and was an instant hit. The waterfront setting is lovely: a gazebo juts out over the water and there's a superb floating bar. By day, the clientele is mixed. By night, the crowd gets gayer as the hour gets later.

Naglo

Gustav Adolfs Torg 20, Norrmalm (10 27 57/www. naglo.com). T-bana Kungsträdgården/bus 2, 43, 55, 59, 62, 65, 76. **Open** 11.30am-midnight Mon-Fri; 5pm-midnight Sat. Kitchen closes 11pm. **Credit** AmEx, MC, V. **Map** p241 G7.

This tiny vodka bar is one of those places that falls into the blurry gay-straight category so common in Stockholm – the crowd tends to become gayer as the night wears on. Naglo is also known for playing lots of *schlager* music, so on a good night it can be a great final call destination.

Roxy.

Roxy
*Nytorget 6, Södermalm (640 96 55/www.roxysofo.
se). T-bana Medborgarplatsen/bus 2, 3, 53, 56.*
Open 5pm-midnight Tue-Thur, Sun; 5pm-1am Fri,
Sat. *Food served* 5-11pm daily. **Credit** AmEx, DC,
MC, V. **Map** p251 M9.
Roxy has a trendy, lounge-like interior, good food,
well-made cocktails and a cool clientele, which
includes a contingent of chic lesbians. Its slightly
out-of-the-way location in Södermalm enhances its
alternative status. Well worth a visit.

Side Track
*Wollmar Yxkullsgatan 7, Södermalm (641 16 88/
www.sidetrack.nu). T-bana Mariatorget/bus 43, 55,
66.* **Open** 6pm-1am Tue-Sat. *Food Served* 6-11pm
daily. **Credit** AmEx, MC, V. **Map** p250 L7.
A subterranean bar and restaurant popular with the
T-shirt and jeans set. Side Track is not the least bit
fashionable, and that suits the mostly male crowd just
fine. Side Track isn't for the claustrophobic, but if
you're ready to elbow your way to the bar and order
a *stor stark* (a 'big, strong beer') you'll enjoy yourself.

Torget
*Mälartorget 13, Gamla Stan (20 55 60/www.torget
baren.com). T-bana Gamla Stan/bus 3, 53.* **Open**
Bar 4pm-1am Mon-Thur; 3pm-1am Fri; 1pm-1am Sat,
Sun. Kitchen closes 11pm. **Credit** AmEx, DC, MC, V.
Map p241 J7.
Torget remains the most popular gay bar in town
and also the most cosmopolitan. For many gay visi-
tors, it's their first port of call. It has a great location

close to the T-bana station on Gamla Stan, friendly
staff and excellent food – in the early evening or
weekend lunchtime, it's one of the nicest places to
dine in the Old Town. The bar has been resting on
its laurels for some time, but until a serious rival
emerges it's still the best bet to start your weekend.

Cafés

Anna på Kungsholmen
*Drottningholmsvägen 9, Kungsholmen (652 11 19).
T-bana Fridhemsplan/bus 3, 4, 40, 57, 62.* **Open**
9am-8pm Mon-Fri; 11am-6pm Sat, Sun. **No credit
cards**. **Map** p239 G2.
Tiny, cosy and friendly, Anna's café on the island
of Kungsholmen used to attract a predominantly lesbian crowd but is now frequented by a mixed clientele. Good for home-made food, with some outdoor
seating on sunny days.

Chokladkoppen
*Stortorget 20, Gamla Stan (20 31 70/www.
chokladkoppen.com). T-bana Gamla Stan/bus 2,
3, 43, 53, 55, 59, 76.* **Open** *summer* 9am-11pm
Sun-Thur; 10am-7pm Fri, Sat. **No credit cards**.
Map p241 J7.
There's something wonderful about the fact that
the world's best gay hot chocolate café (a narrow
field, admittedly) is housed in one of Stockholm's
most photographed buildings, just across from the
Nobel Museum (*see p57*) in the heart of Gamla Stan.
As well as the rich hot chocolate, there's also superb
chocolate cake, white chocolate cheesecake and
huge sandwiches. Service can be slow, but it's worth
the wait.

Copacabana Café
*Hornstulls strand 1, Södermalm (669 29 39).
T-bana Hornstull/bus 4, 40, 74.* **Open** 10am-9pm
Mon-Thur; 10am-7pm Fri-Sun. **No credit cards**.
Map p249 M3.
A gem of a lesbian café with a Brazilian air on a quiet
side-street on Södermalm. Here you'll find the best
mango lime smoothies in Stockholm, friendly staff,
good grub and lots of old magazines to browse. On
sunny days sit outside and watch the boats go by
on the canal.

Clubs

Stockholm's gay clubbing scene is small, and
different clubs dominate different nights. The
boys head for **Connection** on Friday night
and **Lino** on Saturday. Lesbians hit Klubb
Intern at **Bysis** on Friday or Connection when
it hosts Mouse Club nights. And everyone,
absolutely everyone, goes to **Patricia** on
a Sunday. At times it can seem as though
Stockholm's entire gay population are on board.
As a patron was once heard to remark: 'If this
ship were to sink, you'd never be able to get a
haircut in this town.'

Arts & Entertainment

Patricia.

Bysis

Hornsgatan 82, Södermalm (84 59 10/www.bysis.se).
T-bana Mariatorget or Zinkensdamm/bus 4, 43, 55,
66, 74. **Open** 11am-2pm Mon; 11am-10pm Tue;
11am-3am Wed, Fri; 11am-midnight Thur; 1pm-
3am Sat; 1pm-1am Sun. **Food served** 11am-2pm
Mon-Fri; 4pm-10pm Tue-Sun. **Admission** free.
Credit AmEx, DC, MC, V. **Map** p250 K5.
This rustic tavern on Södermalm is popular with lesbians. Regulars love its courtyard, which is open until
10pm, and the fact that the DJ plays unapologetic rap
tunes instead of *schlager* or dance music. It
doesn't attract the glamorous crowd but, as a result,
is full of people of all ages having a really good time.

Lino

Restaurang Scorpio, Södra Riddarholmshamnen
19, Riddarholmen (411 69 76/www.linoclub.com).
T-bana Gamla Stan/bus 3, 53. **Open** 10pm-3am Sat.
Admission 100kr. **Credit** (bar only) AmEx, MC, V.
Map p241 J6.
Saturdays at Lino can be relied upon to deliver good
fun, with two dancefloors (one playing *schlager*,
one playing dance music), three bars and a mostly
male crowd. Inside it's the kind of club that could
be anywhere in the world, but there's an outdoor
bar where you can enjoy a beer while gazing up at
the ancient buildings of Riddarholmen. Walking
out at 3am to find it bright and sunny and then
promptly going for a swim off Norr Mälarstrand is
one of summer's treats. On Thursday nights, the
venue plays host to the popular Neos Lounge event
(www.neoslounge.com).

Patricia

Stadsgårdskajen 152, Södermalm (743 05 70/
www.patricia.st). *T-bana Slussen/bus 2, 3, 43, 53,*
55, 76. **Open** 5pm-1am Wed, Thur; 6pm-5am Fri-
Sun (Sun gay night). **Admission** free; 90kr after
10pm. **Credit** AmEx, DC, MC, V. **Map** p251 K8.
The *Patricia* was built in Middlesbrough, and once
served a stint as the royal yacht of Queen Elizabeth,
the Queen Mother, but now it's established as one
of the crown jewels of gay life in Stockholm. Every
Sunday for the past ten years gays and lesbians
have gathered here to eat, drink and dance on this
three-level party boat moored at Slussen. Sunday is
half-price food night, so book ahead to enjoy a
delicious dinner that constitutes one of the best
deals in town. The mood, food and crowd are all
excellent; the superb views from the decks are the
icing on the cake.

SLM

Wollmar Yxkullsgatan 18, Södermalm (643 31 00/
www.slm.a.se). *T-bana Mariatorget/bus 43, 55, 66.*
Open 10pm-2am Wed, Fri, Sat. **Admission**
membership 300kr per yr; non-members pay 50kr
after 11pm Sat. **Credit** MC, V. **Map** p250 L6.
Scandinavian Leather Men (SLM) is a basement
leather bar that brings a little corner of Berlin to
Stockholm. A heavy door and flight of stairs lead
down to a labyrinth of darkrooms, bars and a
dancefloor. To get in you'll have to respect the international dress code of skinhead, military, leather,
denim or construction style. Expect a cool, raw
atmosphere – not for the limp of wrist or the faint of
heart. Men only.

Other

Stockholm has several video clubs where
Bergman films are the last thing you're likely
to find. By far the biggest is **US Video** in
Norrmalm (Regeringsgatan 76, 545 158 30,
www.usvideo.nu, open 24 hours). There's also
Basement in Södermalm (Bondegatan 1, 643
79 10, open noon-6am Mon-Thur, Sun, noon-
8am Fri, Sat), **H56** in Vasastaden (Hagagatan
56, 33 55 44, www.hagavideo.nu, open 11am-
6am daily). The newest addition to the list is
10dency on Kungsholmen (Kronobergsgatan
37, 653 21 81, www.10dency.net, open noon-
midnight Mon-Thur, noon-6am Fri, Sat).

T.M.A. The Muscle Academy

Björngårdsgatan 1B, Södermalm (642 63 06).
T-bana Mariatorget/bus 43, 55, 56, 59, 66.
Open 11am-10.30pm Mon-Fri; 1-7.30pm Sat, Sun.
Day membership 100kr. **Credit** AmEx , MC, V.
Map p250 L7.
Stockholm's only exclusively gay gym is for serious
training, not cruising. It's a friendly, no-frills place
for men who want weights – and lots of them – plus
a liberal sprinkling of Tom of Finland prints. The
street name, incidentally, means 'bear yard street',
which seems appropriate.

Music

Friday night and the lights are low…

Rock, Pop & Jazz

Stockholm's live music scene is bigger than ever, and despite its out-of-the-way location, the city is a fertile ground for visiting bands from the UK and US. Then, of course, there are the homegrown stars and wannabes. Although second-generation immigrants are making themselves heard more and more, when it comes to music you will notice that Sweden is still very much a rock and pop country at heart.

The majority of the smaller clubs are located in Södermalm, where most guitar shops and cheap bars are also located. Here (as well as in St Eriksgatan, if you're looking for second-hand and vinyl) is also the place to find the city's best record shops, such as the legendary **Pet Sounds** (*see p156*) on Skånegatan, which has a popular bar with live gigs on the other side of the street, reggae oasis **Bashment** (*see p156*) on Bondegatan, or hip hop bastion Ablaze on Östgötagatan. These shops are good for flyers as well. Otherwise, check the listings in the Friday editions of *Expressen*, *Aftonbladet*, *Dagens Nyheter*, *Metro* or *City* to find out what's on. For tickets to major concerts try **Ticnet** (077 170 70 70, www.ticnet.se).

Gamla Stan

Stampen
Stora Nygatan 5 (20 57 93/www.stampen.se). T-bana Gamla Stan/bus 2, 3, 53, 55, 59, 76. **Open** 8pm-1am Mon-Thur; 8pm-2am Fri, Sat. **Admission** 100kr-120kr. **Credit** AmEx, DC, MC, V. **Map** p241 H7.
Once a pawnshop, tiny Stampen is Stockholm's best-known jazz pub. It might have passed its heyday, but interesting live acts still appear every night (9pm-12.30am), playing swing, dixie, trad jazz, blues, rockabilly and country. The crowd is more mature (and touristy) these days; younger cats prefer the somewhat hipper basement dancefloor.

Norrmalm

Fasching
Kungsgatan 63 (tickets 1-5pm Mon-Fri 53 48 29 60/club & restaurant 53 48 29 60/www.fasching.se). T-bana T-Centralen/bus 1, 47, 53, 69. **Open** 7pm-1am Mon-Thur; 7pm-4am Fri, Sat. **Admission** varies. **Credit** AmEx, DC, MC, V. **Map** p240 F6.

Nalen. *See p184.*

As the fading photos on the walls attest, many of the greats have performed at this classic jazz club (capacity 600). Gigs and jam sessions are held every night, and you'll hear jazz, Latin and even some hip hop. The crowd is a happy mix of all ages and nationalities. All in all, a cool Manhattan-style joint.

Glenn Miller Café
Brunnsgatan 21A (10 03 22/www.glennmiller cafe.com). T-bana Hötorget/bus 1, 43, 52, 56. **Open** 5pm-1am Mon-Thur; 5pm-2am Fri, Sat. **Admission** free. **Credit** MC, V. **Map** p241 E7.
This simple, cosy jazz pub has live music several nights a week. It's often packed with a mix of older fans and twentysomethings who are mates with the band. If you love jazz, and are not claustrophobic, this is your place.

Nalen
Regeringsgatan 74, Norrmalm (50 52 92 00/ www.nalen.com). T-bana Hötorget/bus 1, 2, 43, 56. **Box office** 1hr before concert. **Tickets** free-420kr. **Credit** AmEx, MC, V. **Map** p241 E7.
Since this legendary dance palace reopened in 1998, it has become the sort of wide-reaching venue that Stockholm always lacked. Built in 1888, Nalen was famous as a jazz mecca from the 1930s until the end of the '60s, when a church took over and got rid of all that sinful noise. Thoroughly renovated, Nalen now caters for all kinds of music. There are two auditoriums – Stora Salen (capacity 400) and Harlem (capacity 80) – plus a restaurant, a bar and a club room, Alcazar. *Photo p183.*

Djurgården

Cirkus
Djurgårdsslätten 43-45 (box office 66 01 02 07/ www.cirkus.se). Bus 47/tram 7/ferry from Nybroplan or Slussen. **Box office** 11am-6pm Mon-Fri & 2hrs before a show. **Tickets** 250kr-850kr. **Credit** AmEx, DC, MC, V. **Map** p243 J11.
In royal park Djurgården, Cirkus is a cylindrical wooden building built in 1892 for circus troupes. It's got seating for 1,700, as well as a bar and restaurant. Cirkus is an atmospheric place and attracts some big-name acts, but the fact that it's all-seated can be a drawback.

Södermalm

Debaser
Karl Johans Torg 1 (462 98 60/www.debaser.nu). T-bana Gamla Stan or Slussen/bus 2, 3, 43, 53, 55, 59, 76. **Open** 8pm-3am daily. **Admission** varies. **Credit** MC, V. **Map** p241 K8.
Debaser quickly became one of the leading live rock venues in the city when it opened up in 2002. Appropriately rough around the edges and located under a bridge in an old distillery, Debaser is every inch the rock club. Bands play here seven nights a week, and there's DJ action on club nights. Arrive before 11pm to avoid the (often long) queue.

Debaser Medis
Medborgarplatsen 8 (694 79 00/www.debaser.nu). T-bana Medborgarplatsen/bus 55, 59, 66. **Open** varies; call for details. **Admission** varies; call for details. **Map** p250 L8.
Former Mondo is now a part of the Debaser empire (they've also recently opened up in Malmö and Sundsvall), but it's practically the same set-up as before: at least ten concerts a week (country, pop, rock, hip hop and reggae) in three spaces (the largest holds 1,200), as well as five bars, four dancefloors, a cinema, a gallery and a decent restaurant in the heart of Södermalm. A safe bet.

Fylkingen
Munchenbryggeriet, Torkel Knutssonsgatan 1 (84 54 43/www.fylkingen.se). T-bana Mariatorget/bus 43, 55, 56. **Open** varies; call for details. **Admission** usually 80kr. **Credit** MC, V. **Map** p250 L6.
This converted brewery is the best place to hear alternative, DIY and experimental music. There is always something interesting going on, though the music might not be to everyone's taste.

Göta Källare
Folkungagatan 45 (57 86 79 00/www.gotakallare. com). T-bana Medborgarplatsen/bus 55, 59, 66. **Open** *Club* 9pm-3am Fri, Sat. *Concerts* call for details. **Tickets** 100kr-250kr. **Credit** AmEx, DC, MC, V. **Map** p250 L8.
If you aren't into Swedish 'dance bands' (oompah bands with men in golden suits playing for five hours straight), then Göta Källare is not the best bet for a night out. It works more as a plan B for gig promoters when other places are already booked. Quite cool, old-school interior, though. (Note that the entrance is by the steps leading down to the T-bana station.)

Kafe 44
Tjärhovsgatan 46 (644 53 12/www.kafe44.com). T-bana Medborgarplatsen/bus 55, 59, 66. **Open** concerts twice a wk; call for details. **Tickets** 40kr-100kr. **No credit cards**. **Map** p251 L9.

Debaser.

This hangout for Södermalm's anarchists hosts a lot of punk and rock concerts, as well as an alternative, righteous brand of hip hop. There's no minimum age limit and no alcohol is served, but with the sort of bands that play here, you won't need a drink to get a kick.

Mosebacke Etablissement

Mosebacke Torg 3 (information 55 60 98 90/ www.mosebacke.se). T-bana Slussen/bus 2, 3, 43, 53, 55, 59, 76. **Box office** 11am-4pm Mon-Fri. **Open** *Summer* 11am-1am Mon-Thur, Sun; 11am-2am Fri, Sat. *Winter* 4pm-1am Mon-Thur, Sun; 4pm-2am Fri, Sat. **Tickets** 90kr-250kr. **Credit** AmEx, DC, MC, V. **Map** p250 K8.

Many of Sweden's finest jazz artists have appeared on Mosebacke's two stages – Stora Salen and the more intimate Cornelisrummet. A lot of jazz is still performed, but the programme is more varied now – there's also pop, rock, salsa and reggae on the menu. It's next door to Södra Teatern (*see below*). *Photo p187.*

Münchenbryggeriet

Torkel Knutssonsgatan 1 (84 54 43/www.fylkingen. se). T-bana Mariatorget/bus 43, 55, 56. **Open** varies. **Tickets** 80kr-420kr. **Credit** AmEx, DC, MC, V. **Map** p241 K6.

This old brewery is now a popular medium-sized concert hall used by acts of all kinds. One night the audience is packed with Rastafarians praising Jah and raising their lighters to dancehall missionary Capleton, another you might find bespectacled types lined up for Belle & Sebastian, so check the programme before heading along. In summer, there are gigs on the stage in the open-air courtyard.

Södra Teatern

Mosebacketorg 1-3 (55 69 72 30/www.sodrateatern. com). T-bana Slussen/bus 2, 3, 43, 53, 55, 59, 76. **Box office** noon-6pm Mon-Fri; noon-4pm Sat. **Tickets** 100kr-240kr. **Credit** AmEx, DC, MC, V. **Map** p250 K8.

This cultural centre has always got something interesting going on. Built in 1859, the main auditorium, Stora Scenen (capacity 400), has red velvet chairs for low-key pop and folk concerts, while the basement, Kägelbanan (capacity 700), hosts more sing-along pop. Otherwise there's world music, plus poetry readings and spoken-word performances. Touring theatre companies also perform here on occasion.

Tantogården

Ringvägen 24 (668 22 71/www.tantogarden.se). T-bana Zinkensdamm/bus 66. **Open** varies; call for details. **Admission** varies; call for details. **Credit** AmEx, DC, MC ,V. **Map** p251 L5.

This arena (one indoor stage, one outdoor) was *the* place for indie rock in the 1990s, but it was forced to shut down for several years due to complaints from neighbours. Now open under new owners, the venue has lost its dominant position. Still, its location in Tantolunden park almost makes you feel like you are out in the countryside, and if you're into obscure punk and rock, it can be a fun night.

Further afield

Allhuset

Universitetsvägen 10, Frescati (16 20 00/www.su.se). T-bana Universitetet/bus 40. **Open** 11am-1am Mon-Thur; 11am-3am Fri. **Tickets** 60kr-240kr. **Credit** MC, V.

At this modern venue (capacity 500) on the Stockholm University campus, students wearing T-shirts adorned with their favourite band's name talk about music and drink cheap beer in a relaxed atmosphere. There are gigs from interesting Swedish and international acts, and plenty of up-and-coming bands.

Dieselverkstaden

Markusplatsen 17, Sickla (718 82 90/www.diesel verkstaden.se). Bus 71, 150, 401, 403, 404, 422, 491, 492, 496, 497/train from Slussen to Sickla Strand. **Open, admission & credit** vary; call for details.

Sounds of summer

After enduring those long winter nights, Swedes embrace summer with open arms, and nowhere is this more apparent than in the string of music festivals that crank up in and around Stockholm from the beginning of June onwards.

June

First up are the suburban **Hoodsfred** in Kista (www.hoodsfred.se), a wordplay on the big Hultsfred festival in southern Sweden, which takes place during the first weekend in June and features the best in hip hop and R&B; and the free **Re: Publik** (www.festival republik.se, formerly known as Popaganda), at the Stockholm University campus in Frescati, featuring the biggest Swedish indie talents. At the end of the month it's time for another Frescati festival, the two-day **Accelerator** (www.acceleratorfestivalen.se), featuring bands from as far afield as the US and Brazil, plus several UK acts.

July

In mid July it's time for the **Stockholm Jazz Festival** (see p160), with a wonderfully diverse line-up featuring everyone from emerging Scandinavian artists to international superstars. Past festivals have included the likes of Stevie Wonder, Lauryn Hill and Maceo Parker. The setting is beautiful – on the island of Skeppsholmen.

August

At the beginning of August, there's the annual **Pride** festival (see p160), which has much more varied music offerings than just euro-pop these days. Reggae is another Swedish summer favourite, and the **Uppsala Reggae Festival** (www.uppsalareggaefestival.se), just north of Stockholm, in the first week of August, is the largest reggae festival in Scandinavia – 2007 featured artists such as legendary Bob Marley sideman Bunny Wailer and dancehall star Beenie Man. It's as close as you'll get to the Notting Hill Carnival this near the Arctic Circle.

September

The season ends with the small, intimate and free **Pop Dakar** (www.popdakar.nu) at Frescati, before it's time to put on your coat, crawl back inside and stop talking to strangers until next summer.

Just south-east of Södermalm, in what used to be an old factory for assembling ship engines, the people who once ran the Tantogården have opened this cultural centre. Along with a good concert hall, there's also a restaurant, café, cinema, library and theatre.

Fryshuset

Mårtendalsgatan 2-8, Hammarbyhamnen (691 76 00/www.fryshuset.se). T-bana Gullmarsplan, then bus 150, 74. **Open** varies; call for details. **Tickets** 220kr-320kr. **No credit cards**.

Just south of Södermalm, in the Fryshuset youth centre (where lots of bands rehearse), lies Klubben, a key venue for hardcore, heavy metal and hip hop. Expect a young crowd, lots of headbanging and stage-diving and, since there's no bar and no age restrictions, lots of drinking in the bushes outside.

Globen

Arenavägen, Johanneshov (box office 07 71 31 00/ www.globearenas.se). T-bana Globen. **Box office** *In person* 9am-6pm Mon-Fri; 10am-3pm Sat & 2hrs before concerts. *By phone* 9am-7pm Mon-Fri; 10am-4pm Sat; 10am-3pm Sun. **Tickets** 120kr-600kr. **Credit** AmEx, DC, MC, V.

Like it or not (and many don't), you can't deny that Globen – the world's largest spherical building – is Stockholm's most recognisable structure. It's also an arena for everything from sports events to gala parties and, of course, concerts. If you're seated up high, you should probably bring binoculars or watch the giant TV screens instead. The atmosphere, as ever with large stadiums, is practically non-existent.

Landet

LM Ericssons väg 27 (41 01 93 20). T-bana Telefonplan/bus 141, 142, 161, 190. **Open** 5pm-midnight Mon-Thur; 4pm-1am Fri; 5pm-1am Sat. **Credit** AmEx, DC, MC, V.

In the vibrant suburb of Midsommarkransen, lies art school Konstfack and Designens Hus, and the area attracts lots of trendy, young people. It is also the home of Landet (meaning 'the countryside'), a laid-back restaurant and bar with an upstairs ballroom hosting clubs and concerts from fresh bands almost every night. Definitely worth a visit, but crowded at weekends so start early.

Classical Music & Opera

Despite recent raised voices from preservers of the beaux arts, Svenska Akademien, worrying about the lack of interest in traditional high culture, the classical music and opera scene in

Stockholm is still under the old social democratic cultural policy, with an aim to subsidise musical diversity and offer hundreds of free concerts every year, as well as reduced-price tickets for students and teenagers.

Stockholm may not be as extravagant as London or as grand as Vienna, but the city has far more ensembles and venues than most cities its size, boasting two full-size symphony orchestras that can compete with the best in Europe, two permanent opera houses and a healthy chamber music scene.

WHEN AND HOW

The music calendar is seasonal, running from August to June, with concerts held primarily on weekdays. In the summer, the focus of activity moves to the court theatres and parks around town. One exception is the **Stockholm Konserthuset**, which stays open in July for a four-week festival. Two other important dates are the **Stockholm Early Music Festival** (*see p159*) in July and the **Baltic Sea Festival** (www.sr.se/berwaldhallen) held in Berwaldhallen in August. The monthly English-language tourist magazine *What's On Stockholm* lists the main concerts, although the Thursday entertainment section of *Dagens Nyheter* provides better listings. Also check out the free daily papers *Metro* and *Stockholm City*. You can buy tickets by phone or online from most venues. For major venues, try **Ticnet** (077 170 70 70, www.ticnet.se).

Main venues & ensembles

Berwaldhallen

Dag Hammarskjöldsväg 3, Östermalm (box office 784 18 00/www.berwaldhallen.se). Bus 56, 76, 69. **Box office** noon-6pm Mon-Fri & 2hrs before a concert. Closed July. **Tickets** 75kr-390kr. **Credit** AmEx, DC, MC, V. **Map** p243 F11.

The Berwaldhallen was built in 1979 for the Sveriges Radio Symfoniorkester (Swedish Radio Symphony Orchestra) and the Radiokören (Radio Choir). The acclaimed modernist hall is built mainly underground. The Symfoniorkester, established in 1967, enjoyed a particularly successful period under the direction of Finn Esa-Pekka Salonen during the second half of the 1980s. The orchestra has a more contemporary touch than other Swedish orchestras, commissioning a significant amount of new music from Swedish and international composers. The Radiokören is considered to be one of the best choirs in the world.

Konserthuset

Hötorget, Norrmalm (box office 50 66 77 88/ www.konserthuset.se). T-bana Hötorget/bus 1, 52, 59. **Box office** 11am-6pm Mon-Fri; 11am-3pm Sat. Also 2hrs before concerts. **Tickets** 70kr-450kr. **Credit** AmEx, DC, MC, V. **Map** p241 F7.

Konserthuset has been the home of the Kungliga Filharmonikerna (Royal Stockholm Philharmonic Orchestra) since its inauguration in 1926. Architect Ivar Tengbom wanted to 'raise a musical temple not far from the Arctic Circle', and the bright blue structure is one of the foremost examples of early 20th-century Swedish neo-classical design. With its 1,800 seats, the Main Hall is used for major concerts, while the beautiful chamber music hall, the Grünewald Hall (capacity 460), decorated by painter Isaac Grünewald, handles smaller events. The Kungliga Filharmonikerna, which celebrated its centenary in 2002, performs here regularly. Konserthuset's repertoire is based in the classical and romantic periods, but it also hosts the internationally renowned annual Composer Festival in the autumn, focusing on living composers. *Photo p188.*

Nybrokajen 11

Nybrokajen 11, Norrmalm (box office 407 1700/ www.nybrokajen11.rikskonserter.se). T-bana Kungsträdgården or Östermalmstorg/bus 2, 47, 55, 59, 62, 69. **Box office** End Aug-mid May noon-5pm Mon-Fri. Mid May-end Aug 11am-4pm Mon-Fri. Also 2hrs before concerts. **Tickets** 100kr-200kr. **Credit** MC, V. **Map** p241 G8.

The newest venue on the Stockholm classical music scene is Nybrokajen 11, named after its address opposite the Kungliga Dramatiska Teatern. The elegant former home of the Royal Academy of Music was transformed into a permanent stage for the Rikskonserter (Swedish Concert Institute). The main hall (capacity 600) hosts mainly chamber music from all periods, with Swedish and international artists. Stallet, a converted stable, is an intimate venue dedicated to world music.

Mosebacke Etablissement. *See p185.*

Arts & Entertainment

Other ensembles

Kroumata

(54 54 15 80/www.kroumata.rikskonserter.se).
Kroumata was formed in 1978 and has since developed something of a cult status. It commissions and performs works by Swedish and international composers, and has toured widely. Since 1997 Kroumata has had its own venue, Capitol (St Eriksgatan 82), a converted theatre that serves as an intimate concert hall for a few performances a year.

Stockholm Sinfonietta

Riddarhuset, Riddarhustorget 10, Gamla Stan (www.sinfonietta.a.se). T-bana Gamla Stan/bus 3, 53. **Tickets** approx 180kr from www.ticnet.se. **Map** p241 H7.
The Stockholm Sinfonietta has worked with a host of venerable names, including conductors Sixten Ehrling and Okko Kamu, and soloists such as Catalan soprano Montserrat Caballé and Swedish cellist Frans Helmerson. The repertoire stretches all the way from baroque to contemporary and the Stockholm Sinfonietta has the sole right to perform at the marvellous Riddarhuset.

Stockholms Nya Kammarorkester (SNYKO)

Check press for concert details.
Formed by former members of the Sveriges Radio Symfoniorkester, the Stockholm Chamber Music Orchestra, commonly known by its abbreviation SNYKO, is today one of the most sought-after Scandinavian ensembles, with an international reputation for both its classical and contemporary repertoire. The orchestra performs regularly in Stockholm and tours extensively.

Opera

Folkoperan

Hornsgatan 72, Södermalm (box office 616 07 50/www.folkoperan.se). T-bana Mariatorget/ bus 4, 43, 55, 56, 74. **Box office** *June-Aug* noon-6pm Wed-Fri. *Sept-May* noon-7pm Wed-Sat. **Tickets** 250kr-375kr. **Credit** AmEx, DC, MC, V. **Map** p250 K6.
Folkoperan has been a healthy rival to Kungliga Operan (*see below*) since its founding in 1976. Its modern stagings of classic operas sung in Swedish, its unconventional and often controversial productions and the intimacy of the auditorium are among Folkoperan's distinctive features. The main season runs from September to May, when there are performances most nights of the week. The bar and restaurant are popular with a trendy young crowd.

Kungliga Operan

Gustav Adolfs Torg, Norrmalm (box office 24 82 40/ www.operan.se). T-bana Kungsträdgården/bus 2, 43, 55, 59, 62, 76. **Box office** noon-6pm Mon-Fri; noon-3pm Sat. **Tickets** 40kr-590kr. **Credit** AmEx, DC, MC, V. **Map** p241 G7.
When it opened in 1782, this opera house was considered to be one of the most modern in operation. Just 100 years later it was demolished to make way for the current opera house, which was completed in 1898. The Royal Opera has sent a string of great singers on to the international stage – among them Jenny Lind, Jussi Björling, Birgit Nilsson and Elisabeth Söderström – but, as is the case with Swedish footballers and hockey players, the most talented leave the country at a young age and rarely return to the Kungliga. It's also the home of the Swedish Royal Ballet.

Konserthuset. *See p187.*

Sport & Fitness

Everybody's doing it, from badminton to brännboll.

Sport, whether participation or spectator, is ubiquitous in Sweden. The concept of *Folkhemmet* (*see p21*) included a commitment to the development of sport and government support means that a sports hall is never far away. Consequently, indoor games such as handball, ice hockey and floorball have thrived. Outdoor activities also prosper, particularly in summer, and range from a casual game of *brännboll* to major events such as the **Stockholm Marathon** (*see p159*) and **Midnattsloppet** (*see p160*).

Football has a strong following, but the climate means the season runs from April to November, out of sync with most other parts of Europe, so there is plenty of room for other sports to make the headlines. The men's national ice hockey team attracts fanatical support, and any failure to prosper in major tournaments is regarded as a disaster. Sweden is also very prominent in world handball and the almost exclusively far northern sport of bandy (*see p190* **Anyone for bandy?**).

For more information on the sports listed here, or any others, get in contact with the **Swedish Sports Confederation** (699 60 00, www.svenskidrott.se) or the **tourist office** (*see p50*).

Participation sports/fitness

Badminton

Badmintonstadion
Hammarby Slussvägen 4, Södermalm (642 70 02/ www.badmintonstadion.se). T-bana Skanstull/bus 3, 4, 55, 74. **Open** 6am-11pm Mon-Thur; 6am-8.30pm Fri; 9am-5pm Sat; 9am-9.30pm Sun. Special summer opening times apply mid June-mid Aug; call for details. **Rates** *Per court* 100kr-130kr/hr; 80kr concessions. **Credit** MC, V. **Map** p251 O8.
Badminton is one of the most popular recreational sports in Sweden and this is the city's largest hall, with 24 courts.

Brännboll
Brännboll is a popular summer game vaguely similar to baseball or rounders. There is no pitcher; the batter simply throws up a tennis ball and hits it. The bat is often a flat, paddle shape, which helps make the game accessible to players of all levels. As *brännboll* is generally

not an organised sport, local rules can vary wildly. In short, if you're invited to play, hit the ball and run.

Cycling & in-line skating

Stockholm's compact size makes it ideal for cycling or in-line skating. There are plenty of cycle paths, some of which have very beautiful stretches, plus many cycle lanes in the city. The island of **Djurgården** is a good place for cycling – lots of green space and few cars at weekends – or try the circuit around the bay of **Riddarfjärden** (across the demanding Västerbron bridge, along Söder Mälarstrand, Centralbron and Norr Mälarstrand).

Cykel och Mopeduthyrningen
Strandvägen, Kajplats 24, Östermalm (660 79 59). Bus 47, 69, 76. **Open** *Apr-Sept* 9am-9pm daily; call for opening hours in winter. **Rates** *Bikes* from 55kr/hr; 160kr/day. **Credit** AmEx, MC, V. **Map** p242 G10.

Take the tube: **Vanadisbadet**. *See p193*.

Anyone for bandy?

Imagine standing on a concrete terrace in sub-zero temperatures for two hours – voluntarily. It might initially seem unappealing but this is what thousands of Stockholmers do several times each winter in order to watch a game of bandy.

Bandy is Sweden's third-largest sport and is essentially field hockey played outdoors on ice. Teams of 11-a-side play on an ice-rink about the size of a football pitch. Players use a stick, or occasionally their feet, to propel a bright orange coloured ball towards the goal. The game is very free-flowing, with limited physical contact, and lasts for 90 minutes. Games tend to be fairly high scoring, depending on how closely matched the two sides are – a close match might end 5-4, though if one team is dominant

it is not uncommon for them to run up a double-figure score.

Modern bandy originated in England. In winter in the late 19th century, the game was played on the frozen Cambridgeshire fens. Charles Goodman Tebbutt, a businessman from Bluntisham near St Ives, wrote down a set of rules and introduced the game to other countries, including Sweden. Goodman Tebbutt's bandy stick, on display at the Norris Museum in St Ives, is the only remaining trace of bandy in the area. Although England won the first European Championships, in 1913, the game died out soon after and it is now almost exclusively played in the most northerly parts of the world. Russia, Sweden and Finland have heavily dominated the World Championships since they began in 1957.

Hires out city bikes, mountain bikes, tandems, children's bikes and bicycle carriages, plus mopeds and in-line skates.

Djurgårdsbrons Sjöcafé

Galärvarvsvägen 2, Djurgården (660 57 57). Bus 44, 47, 69, 76. **Open** *Mar/Apr-Sept/Oct 9am-9pm daily.* **Rates** *In-line skates 60kr/hr; 200kr/day. Bikes 65kr/hr; 250kr/day.* **Credit** AmEx, DC, MC, V. **Map** p242 G10.

This is a handy place for renting in-line skates and bikes, just over the bridge on Djurgården. It's also got a pleasant waterside café.

Stockholm City Bikes

Located at 43 bicycle stands within the city, with more planned (077 444 24 24/www.stockholm citybikes.se). **Open** *6am-6pm daily.* **Rates** *Bikes 25kr/day; 200kr seven-month season ticket.* **Credit** MC, V.

Cards and tickets can be purchased from Stockholm City local transport (SL) centres at Fridhemsplan, Gullmarsplan, Tekniska Högskolan, Sergels Torg, Slussen, Täby C and T-Centralen.

This scheme is run in conjunction with Stockholm City Council to encourage cycling. The bikes are specially designed for the city, with many safety features

The domestic season in Sweden runs from November to March and its popularity in the capital has recently soared thanks to the success of local team Hammarby (www.hammarbybandy.se), who play at Zinkensdamms Idrottsplats (T-bana Zinkensdamm, bus 4, 66). Hammarby have both delighted and frustrated their supporters, usually comfortably progressing through the rather elongated league format with increasing dominance as the season progresses, only to be cursed in the grand final, held at Uppsala in April. Hammarby have never been Swedish champions but have lost in the final seven times, including six times recently in 2000, 2001, 2003, 2004, 2006 and 2007.

The quest for success has had its price however – the club looked to be in severe danger of folding in 2006-07, with debts of five million kronor (£370,000), but thanks to a vigorous campaign called 'Rädda Hammarby Bandy' ('Save Hammarby Bandy'), this figure has been reduced substantially and the club were able to participate in the 2007-08 season.

Hammarby Bandy's survival is good news indeed for the thousands who flock to Zinkensdamm to give 'Bajen' enthusiastic vocal support. Hammarby's Christmas home match – usually played on 26 December – attracts a particularly large, vocal and well-lubricated crowd. Supporters often carry bandy briefcases – an old bag containing a thermos filled with *kaffekask* (coffee well dosed with liqueur) – or at the very least a hip flask to help ward off the cold. In addition, unlimited layers of clothing and several pairs of thick socks come in very handy.

and a basket for belongings. Use of a single bike is limited to three hours but another bike can be borrowed immediately afterwards.

Fitness clubs

The number of fitness clubs in Stockholm continues to grow. The two most popular, with plentiful branches, are listed below, but for non-members these can be expensive. Alternatively, visit one of the many public swimming pools (*see p192*), some of which have gyms.

Friskis & Svettis
Mäster Samuelsgatan 20, Norrmalm (429 70 00/ www.sthlm.friskissvettis.se). T-bana Hötorget/bus 2, 43, 47, 59, 62. **Open** 6.30am-9pm Mon-Thur; 6.30am-7.30pm Fri; 9am-1pm Sat; 3-6.30pm Sun. **Rates** 90kr non-members. **Credit** AmEx, DC, MC, V. **Map** p241 F7.
Less geared to the good-looking body than SATS (*see below*), this place focuses more on general health. The telephone number is the same for all branches.
Other locations Långholmsgatan 38, Södermalm; Ringvägen 111, Södermalm; St Eriksgatan 54, Kungsholmen; Tegeluddsvägen 31, Gärdet; Sveavägen 63, Vasastaden.

SATS Sports Club
Sveavägen 20, Norrmalm (54 52 13 80/www.sats sportsclub.com). T-bana Hötorget/bus 1, 43, 47, 52, 59. **Open** 5am-10pm Mon-Thur; 5am-9pm Fri; 10am-6pm Sat; 10am-8pm Sun. **Rates** 150kr-200kr non-members. **Credit** AmEx, DC, MC, V. **Map** p241 F7.
SATS has a dozen locations in Stockholm – we've listed the most central branches here. All are well equipped and clean, with plenty of good classes. The Regeringsgatan branch has a climbing wall.
Other locations Odengatan 65, Vasastaden (54 54 28 80); St Eriksgatan 34, Vasastaden (54 55 31 40); Regeringsgatan 47, Norrmalm (50 32 80 00).

Golf

Golf enthusiasts hardly have a shortage of facilities – there are some 50 courses within an hour's drive of Stockholm – but the game's increasing popularity has led to rocketing green fees, with prices ranging from 300kr to 650kr, and a need to reserve tee times. You are allowed to play at any of the courses, despite what some of the members may think. Websites **www.golf.se** and **www.golfdigest.se** provide extensive information (Swedish only). Several pay-and-play courses suitable for beginners can be found around the city. One is **Årsta Golf**, located just south of Södermalm (81 30 00/www.arstagolf.se).

Ice-skating

Skating choices are numerous: indoor and outdoor rinks, lakes and even the frozen waters of the archipelago. The most central outdoor skating rinks are in **Kungsträdgården** in Norrmalm and at **Medborgarplatsen** on Söder. They're tiny but you can rent skates for a small fee. Popular with families, they're usually open from November to February. There are also plentiful ice hockey rinks open to the public for a few hours every day. Call the **tourist office** (*see p50*) for a full list.

Skating in the city cannot compete, however, with the lakes or archipelago. Long-distance skating (*långfärdsskridskoåkning*) is a popular sport, and Sweden has some of the best conditions in the world for it, though recent winter temperatures haven't afforded the opportunities seen in previous years. Contact the **Stockholm Ice Skate Sailing and Touring Club** (768 23 78, www.sssk.se) for details. Membership requires passing a beginner's course and long-distance skating should never be attempted without proper equipment, preparation and knowledge.

Östermalms Idrottsplats

Fiskartorpsvägen 2, Hjorthagen (50 82 83 51). T-bana Stadion/bus 55, 77, 291, 293. **Open** varies; call for details. **Admission** free. **Map** p246 B/C9.

This place usually offers an ice-rink/lane from December to the end of February, and is open to the public when there are no matches on. It's ideal for practising long-distance skating.

Jogging & running

When the sun is out, Stockholm seems to have endless beautiful jogging routes. Some of the best spots are Riddarfjärden, Långholmen, Djurgården, Hagaparken and the south side of Södermalm. If you're into a little competition, try the **Stockholm Marathon** (*see p159*) in June, attracting top-class runners and enthusiastic amateurs. Exclusively for women, and very popular, is **Tjejmilen** ('Girls' Run'), a ten-kilometre (six-mile) street race on Djurgården (54 56 64 40, www.tjejmilen.se) taking place in late August or early September. Another street race, this time on Södermalm, is the carnival-like ten-kilometre (six-mile) **Midnattsloppet** (Midnight Race; *see p160*), which takes place in August.

Kayaking & canoeing

Djurgårdsbrons Sjöcafé (*see p190*) rents kayaks and canoes, as well as pedal and rowing boats. Reliable canoeing outfits include **Svima Sport** in Solna (Ekelundsvägen 26, 730 22 10, www.svima.se) and **Brunnsvikens Kanotcentral** by Brunnsviken lake (Frescati Hagväg 5, 15 50 60, www.bkk.se).

For trips in the archipelago or around Lake Mälaren, contact the **tourist office** (*see p50*) or the following kayaking agencies: **Kajakboden Aquarius** in Tyresö (Varvsvägen 9, Tyresö Strand, 770 09 50, www.kajakboden.com); **Kayak Support** in Bromma (Nockeby backe 20, 87 73 77, www.kayak.se); **Archipelago Ljusterö Kajakcenter** on the island of Ljusterö (mobile 070 768 94 47, www.paddla.com), or **Skärgårdsgumman** on Utö (50 15 76 68, www.skargardsgumman.com).

Sailing & boats

Most outfits focus on corporate sailing tours, other companies (including Tvillingarnas Båtuthyrning; *see below*) offer smaller boats that can be rented without a skipper for a few thousand kronor per day. Rates vary depending on the type of boat you want. For nautical charts, books and other equipment, try well-stocked **Nautiska Magasinet** in Gamla Stan (Slussplan 5, 677 00 00).

Tvillingarnas Båtuthyrning

Strandvägskajen 27, Östermalm (80 68 93/www. tvillingarnas.com). Bus 44, 47, 69, 76. **Open** *Apr-Sept* 8am-1am daily. Closed Oct-Mar. **Credit** AmEx, DC, MC, V. **Map** p242 G10.

This central rental agency, located just before the bridge over to Djurgården, has a popular restaurant and hires out sailing boats and motorboats.

Skiing

Skiing is one of Sweden's most popular sports. Stockholm is relatively close to good downhill skiing, such as at **Flottsbro** (53 53 27 00, www.flottsbro.com), which is 40 kilometres (25 miles) south of the city. It's excellent for a day trip, but not very demanding for experts. About 20 kilometres (13 miles) north of Stockholm is **Väsjöbacken** in Sollentuna (35 31 85, www.vasjobacken.com), which offers good cross-country skiing. Another good spot for cross-country skiing is just south of the city at **Lida** (778 43 80, www.botkyrka.se/lida).

The best downhill skiing in the country can be found at Sweden's biggest resort, **Åre** (0647 177 00, www.skistar.com/are), north-west of Stockholm, which is close enough for a long weekend trip – SJ runs special 'ski trains' to Åre; see www.sj.se.

The website **www.skiinfo.se** offers all the information you'll need, including snow reports and accommodation options.

Swimming

When the weather's good you can take a dip in the waters around the city, thanks to a successful purification treatment in the 1960s. You can swim almost everywhere, but avoid dirty Karlbergskanalen (between Kungsholmen and Vasastaden) and leave the waves and very strong currents in Strömmen (east of Gamla Stan) to the fishermen. On Djurgården, try the small spit **Waldemarsudde** (get off bus 47 or tram 7 at Ryssviken and follow the path south to the water's edge) on the southern shore. Green Långholmen has numerous bathing spots, such as the western side of the island or the crowded little beach near the former prison (now a youth hostel/hotel). On Kungsholmen, try the southern side at **Smedsuddsbadet** opposite Långholmen, which has a sandy beach popular with families, or the south-western tip at **Fredhäll**, where you can climb down from Snoilskyvägen or Atterbomsvägen on to the rocks. **Stadshuset**, though not a designated spot, is also good for jumping in.

Eriksdalsbadet
Hammarby Slussväg 20, Södermalm (50 84 02 58/ www.eriksdalsbadet.com). T-bana Skanstull/bus 3, 4, 55, 74. **Open** 9am-8pm Mon-Thur; 9am-7pm Fri; 9am-5pm Sat, Sun. **Admission** *Indoor pool* 75kr; 50kr concessions; 35kr 4-17s; free under-4s; *outdoor pool* 60kr; 35kr concessions. **Credit** AmEx, DC, MC, V. **Map** p251 O8.
This is the main arena for Swedish swimming competitions. It also has adventure pools for children and an outdoor pool.

Forsgrenska Badet
Medborgarplatsen 6, Södermalm (50 84 03 20). T-bana Medborgarplatsen/bus 55, 59, 66. **Open** Sept-May noon-9pm Mon; 6.30am-9pm Tue, Thur; 6.30am-6pm Wed; 6.30am-7pm Fri; 9am-4pm Sat; 10am-5pm Sun. Closed June-Aug. **Admission** 60kr; 40kr concessions; 20kr 7-17s; free under-7s. **Credit** MC, V. **Map** p250 L8.
Relaxed 25m (82ft) pool, open since 1939.

Globen.

Vanadisbadet
Sveavägen 142, Vasastaden (34 33 00/www. vanadisbadet.se). Bus 2, 40, 52, 515, 595. **Open** mid May-Sept 10am-6pm daily. **Admission** 70kr; 60kr children over 80cm/31.5in; free children under 80cm/31.5in. **No credit cards. Map** p245 B5.
An outdoor adventure pool with several water slides and other family-friendly stuff. *Photo p189.*

Tennis

Eriksdal
Hammarby Slussväg 8, Södermalm (640 78 64/ www.hellas.a.se/tennis/). T-bana Skanstull/bus 3, 4, 55, 74. **Open** *Courts* 7am-9pm daily. **Rates** 100kr-120kr/hr. **No credit cards. Map** p251 O8.
Outdoor courts in southern Södermalm, which are covered during winter.

Kungliga Tennishallen
Lidingövägen 75, Hjorthagen (459 15 00/www.kltk. com). Bus 73. **Open** 7am-10pm Mon-Thur; 7am-9pm Fri; 8am-8pm Sat; 8am-10pm Sun. **Rates** *Indoor* 200kr-320kr/hr; *outdoor* 120kr/hr. **Credit** AmEx, DC, MC, V.
The Stockholm Open tournament is played at this facility, which is also open to the public.

Spectator sports

All the daily newspapers provide listings (in Swedish), usually concentrating on football, ice hockey and trotting races (*trav*). Ticket brokers (booking fee 5kr-30kr) are a good source of information. The biggest ticket broker is **Ticnet**, with an easy to navigate website in English (077 170 70 70, www.ticnet.se). Alternatively, you could try **Derbybutiken** (Mäster Samuelsgatan 46, 21 03 03).

Major stadiums

Globen
Arenavägen, Johanneshov (600 34 00/725 10 00/box office 077 131 00 00/www.globearenas.se). T-bana Globen. **Box office** *In person* Mid Aug-mid May 9am-6pm Mon-Fri; 11am-4pm Sat. Mid May-mid Aug 9am-6pm Mon; 9am-4pm Tue-Fri. *By phone* (tickets to be collected from a Globen distributor; ask for nearest) 9am-7pm Mon-Fri; 10am-4pm Sat; 10am-3pm Sun. **Credit** (in person only) AmEx, DC, MC, V.
The most famous sports hall in Stockholm is the futuristic Globen. With a capacity of just under 14,000, it hosts major competitions in tennis, ice hockey, handball, showjumping and floorball (*innebandy*), as well as concerts and other big events. It is also home to the Djurgården ice hockey team.

Råsunda Stadion
Solnavägen 51, Solna (box office 735 09 35). T-bana Solna Centrum/bus 505, 506, 509, 515. **Box office** 9am-4.30pm Mon-Thur; 9am-3pm Fri. **Credit** MC, V.

A short T-bana ride from the city centre, this is the national football stadium and home ground to AIK. Built in 1937, it has a capacity of just over 37,000. You can buy tickets for most Råsunda events via **Ticnet** (077 170 70 70, www.ticnet.se).

Stockholms Stadion

Lidingövägen 1, Hjorthagen (50 82 83 62). T-bana Stadion/bus 4, 55, 72, 73. **Map** p246 C8/C9.

The historic Stockholm Olympic Stadium, often known simply as Stadion, was built for the 1912 Olympic Games and is the home of Djurgården IF's football team. Architecturally, it's well preserved, but the old-fashioned facilities result in some practical difficulties. For tickets, contact **Ticnet** (077 170 70 70, www.ticnet.se) or other ticket outlets.

Bandy

See p190 **Anyone for bandy?**.

Football

Stockholm has four teams in Sweden's premier Allsvenskan league – **Hammarby**, **Djurgården**, AIK, plus the new kids on the block, **Brommapojkarna**. Women's football thrives in Sweden and Djurgården, Hammarby and AIK have top-flight women's teams. The official website of the Swedish Football Association, **www.svenskfotboll.se**, contains men's and women's fixtures, results, tables and a host of statistics. Hammarby's stadium, **Söderstadion**, near Globen, isn't huge (capacity 16,000), but the fans create a fantastic atmosphere. Djurgården's home is at the historic **Stockholms Stadion** (*see above*) and AIK play their home matches at a bigger arena, **Råsunda** (*see p193*), where tickets are often available.

Brommapojkarna (http://brommapojkarna. se), the largest football club in Europe in terms of active teams, is well known for its prolific youth academy and the men's team was promoted to the top flight for the first time in 2007. Brommapojkarna play at **Grimsta**, in the western suburbs of Stockholm. An exception to the above are derby matches, which are always played at Råsunda.

Those looking to find a grass-roots fan culture may be disappointed – there are several very well-run clubs below the top flight, but crowd figures for matches in the lower leagues often struggle to top double figures. The season runs from April to November.

Handball

Handball arouses enormous interest in Sweden because of the success of the national team. Since Hammarby won the premier league in 2006 and 2007, interest in handball in the capital has increased markedly. Hammarby play in **Eriksdalshallen** in southern Söder (Ringvägen 68-70, 50 84 64 90). The handball season runs from September to April. See **www.handboll.info** for national and domestic fixtures.

Horse racing & trotting

Trotting (*trav* in Swedish), in which horses pull a small two-wheeled vehicle and driver, is big business in Sweden. The 'V75' jackpot bet, when punters try to predict the winners of seven races, often with extensive permutations, is a national institution. Trotting in Stockholm takes place at the impressive **Solvalla** in Sundbyberg (635 90 00, www.solvalla.se). Solvalla also plays host to the prestigious two million-kronor Elitloppet race during the last weekend in May.

Horse racing is very much the poor relation to trotting but **Täby Galopp** (756 02 30, www.tabygalopp.se), 20 kilometres (12 miles) north of Stockholm, is worth a visit. The course, built in 1960, is modelled on American tracks and racing takes place throughout the year, with all-weather racing under floodlights in winter, and top flat and jump races on turf in summer and autumn. The season's top event is the Stockholm Cup in September.

Ice hockey

Ice hockey is the most popular sport in winter, with the national side and elite team **Djurgården** drawing big crowds to Globen (*see p193*). The season runs from September to April. See **www.swehockey.se**, the website of the Swedish Hockey Association, for fixtures and tables.

Innebandy

Innebandy (floorball) is one of Sweden's most popular participatory sports. It is an indoor six-a-side team game played with sticks and a light plastic ball. During winter, people carrying their *innebandy* stick on the T-bana and elsewhere is a common sight. While *innebandy*'s appeal as a spectator sport is limited, the bigger domestic sides and the Swedish national teams attract crowds of over 1,000. **AIK** (www.aik.se/innebandy) are Stockholm's biggest club.

Tennis

The flagship event is the **Stockholm Open** (*see p160*) at the beginning of October. It takes place at **Kungliga Tennishallen** (*see p193*).

Stockholm is built on 14 islands, so there's an awful lot of water to mess about in.

Theatre & Dance

The drama may be conventional, but the choreography is cutting-edge.

Theatre

Although national icon August Strindberg has been dead and buried for almost a century, and drama crown prince Ingmar Bergman has recently passed away, their spirits still hover over the Swedish stage, resulting in a naturalistic and serious repertoire. Themes such as death and religion are common, as are classics like *Ms Julie*.

Jugendstil building **Kungliga Dramatiska Teatern** (*see p197*), or Dramaten, is Sweden's national theatre, established in 1788. Over the years it has boasted a large number of superb actors and directors (most famous, of course, being Bergman himself). Dramaten has several stages for its productions, which range from traditional plays to more modern offerings.

The city's other key theatre, **Stockholms Stadsteatern** (*see p198*), located in Kulturhuset, also has numerous stages, but it offers a wider repertoire than Dramaten. Stadsteatern also has an ambitious children's programme, and lately it has been hosting more innovative theatre. In the summer, Stadsteatern arranges outdoor theatre, Parkteatern, which presents home-grown and international theatre and dance in parks all over the city.

Since the 1970s several experimental theatre groups, working with new forms and expressions, have sprung up. Since Stockholm is relatively small, this risk-taking theatre can be a bit of a risk-taking exercise, but **Galeasen** and **Moment** (for both, *see p199*) are two prominent groups that seldom disappoint. Just sit back and let the Swedish solemnity pump through your veins.

OTHER LANGUAGES

For the majority of casual visitors, though, all this is likely to be of little interest, since almost all theatre is performed in Swedish. Sometimes it is, of course, possible to enjoy a well-acted or

Kulturhuset.

well-known play without getting the words. Alternatively, Teater Pero has a long tradition of mime theatre. Spanish-speaking **Aliasteatern** (*see p198*) has gradually moved towards Hispanic works translated into Swedish, though there are still occasional Spanish-language performances. Touring productions in various languages appear quite regularly. Stockholm is also home to one of the world's most interesting nouveau cirque groups, **Cirkus Cirkör** (53 19 98 30, www.cirkor.se), which has its own production centre and school in the southern suburb of Norsborg.

INFORMATION AND TICKETS

'På stan', the weekly Thursday supplement of newspaper *Dagens Nyheter* (www.dn.se/sthlm) and website www.alltomstockholm.se both have up-to-date theatre listings (in Swedish). Most venues have an up-to-date website, and some have information in English. The major tourist office is located in Kungsträdgården.

Tickets are usually sold at the venue (or via their website). For major venues and bigger productions, you can also book via **Ticnet** (077 170 70 70, www.ticnet.se). Most theatres are closed on Mondays.

Major venues

The largest commercial theatre, showing large-scale musicals and comedies (in Swedish), is **Oscarsteatern** (Kungsgatan 63, box office 20 50 00, www.oscarsteatern.se). Other commercial theatres include **Göta Lejon** (Götgatan 55, box office 643 67 00, www.proscenia.se), **Maximteatern** (Karlaplan 4, box office 643 40 23, www.proscenia.se), **Intiman** (Odengatan 81, box office 30 12 50, www.wallmans.com) and **China Teatern** (Berzelii park 9, box office 56 63 23 50, www.chinateatern.se). **Cirkus** (Djurgårdsslätten 43-45, next to Skansen, box office 660 10 20, www.cirkus.se) also presents large-scale shows. **Södra Teatern** (*see p185*) is mainly a music venue, but it occasionally hosts good theatre shows.

Kulturhuset

Sergels Torg, Norrmalm (box office 50 62 02 00/ www.kulturhuset.stockholm.se). T-bana T-Centralen/ bus 47, 52, 56, 59, 69. **Box office** *Winter* noon-7pm Tue-Fri; noon-6pm Sat; noon-4pm Sun. *Summer* noon-3pm Tue-Sat.* **Tickets** 60kr-220kr. **Credit** AmEx, DC, MC, V. **Map** p241 G7.
Kulturhuset, or the House of Culture, is one of the most prominent modern buildings in Stockholm, designed by architect Peter Celsing. The building certainly lives up to its name: there are three galleries, a library (with a wide selection of foreign newspapers), activities for children, cafés and a

terrace with an impressive city view. There are two stages in the building – Kilen and Hörsalen – showing a wide spectrum of theatre, dance and music, with Kilen showing the more experimental work. The International Writers' Stage has hosted guests such as Sara Waters and Robert Fisk. The building also houses the Stockholms Stadsteatern (*see p198*), with its six stages.

Kungliga Dramatiska Teatern

Nybroplan, Östermalm (box office 667 06 80/ www.dramaten.se). T-bana Östermalmstorg or Kungsträdgården/bus 47, 55, 62, 69, 76. **Box office** *Sept-May* noon-7pm Mon-Sat; noon-4pm Sun. *June-Aug* varies; call for details. **Tickets** 120kr-300kr. **Credit** AmEx, DC, MC, V. **Map** p241 F8.
The Royal Dramatic Theatre, known as Dramaten, is Sweden's number one theatre, and some of the country's finest actors tread its boards. Ingmar Bergman was the driving force behind Dramaten from the early 1960s, directing a colossal number of productions. The main stage mounts the classics of Shakespeare and Strindberg, mixed with avant-garde dramatic works. The interior is glorious, and spending the intermission in the mirror hall or on the balcony is a real treat. When the bulbs outside show a red light, it means that the main stage is sold out. Dramaten's other stage, Elverket (Linnégatan 69) – a converted power station – has a younger profile, producing interesting modern drama, often with dance or nouveau cirque elements.

Kungliga Dramatiska Teatern.

Arts & Entertainment

Stockholms Stadsteatern

Sergels Torg, Norrmalm (box office 50 62 02 00/ www.stadsteatern.stockholm.se). T-bana T-Centralen/ bus 47, 52, 56, 59. **Box office** *Aug-mid June* noon-7pm Tue-Fri; noon-6pm Sat; noon-4pm Sun. *Mid June-July* noon-3pm Tue-Sat. **Tickets** 60kr-230kr. **Credit** AmEx, DC, MC, V. **Map** p241 G7.

With six stages in all, plus its successful summer Parkteatern programme, Stadsteatern is one of Scandinavia's largest theatrical institutions. Like Dramaten, it has a largely conventional repertoire. There are exceptions, though, such as *Det allra viktigaste*, an extraordinary four-hour play with a gay theme, directed by Suzanne Osten. The smaller stages offer more experimental drama often for a younger audience. The Marionetteatern puppet theatre, created in the 1950s by puppet master Michael Meschke, also has its home at Stadsteatern. The adjacent puppet museum, Marionettmuseet, contains puppets from all over the world.

Smaller venues & groups

Aliasteatern

Hälsingegatan 3, Vasastaden (box office 32 82 90/www.aliasteatern.com). T-bana Odenplan or St Eriksplan/bus 4, 47, 72. **Box office** *Aug-June* noon-5pm Mon-Fri. Closed July. **Tickets** 60kr-250kr. **No credit cards. Map** p244 D4.

This small theatre has been Stockholm's link to Spanish-language drama since 1978. In the past decade, however, it has mainly performed the works of Spanish-speaking dramatists in Swedish. The programme includes music and children's plays.

Dockteatern Tittut

Lundagatan 33, Södermalm (box office 720 75 99/ www.dockteatern-tittut.com). T-bana Zinkensdamm/ bus 4, 66. **Box office** *Sept-May* 9am-5pm Mon-Fri. Closed June-Aug. **Tickets** 60kr. **No credit cards. Map** p249 K4.

This puppet theatre in Söder has been making high-quality shows for children (aged from two) for more than 25 years, combining puppet and shadow play. Performances are held in the daytime.

Fria Teatern

Önskehemsgatan 15, Högdalsplan, Högdalen (box office 99 22 60/www.friateatern.se). T-bana Högdalen/bus 143, 165, 744, 745, 746. **Box office** 10am-4pm Mon-Fri; 10am-7pm on performance days. **Tickets** 70kr-200kr.

This suburban theatre has been threatened by financial crisis ever since it opened in 1968, but it always manages to survive, keeping its political edge and continuing to show high-quality theatre for adults and children. A smaller affiliated stage, Lilla Scenen, at Bergsgatan 11 on Kungsholmen, opened in 2002.

Fylkingen

Münchenbryggeriet, Torkel Knutsonsgatan 2, Södermalm (84 54 43/www.fylkingen.se). T-bana Mariatorget/bus 4, 43, 55, 66. **Box office** 10am-5pm Mon-Fri. **Tickets** free-80kr. **No credit cards. Map** p240 K6.

Founded way back in 1933, Fylkingen is the place to be if you're into new music and intermedia art. It's always been committed to new and experimental forms: 'happenings', musical theatre and text-sound compositions were prominent during the 1960s. In recent years, an increasing amount of ambitious performance art and dance have been presented. Fylkingen holds several festivals every year; check the website for details of forthcoming events.

Intercult

Offices: Nytorgsgatan 15, Södermalm (box office 644 10 23/www.intercult.se). **Box office** 9am-5pm Mon-Fri. **Tickets** 100kr-220kr. **Credit** varies, depending on where performance is held.

Intercult is more of a production group than a conventional theatre, with a strong international focus. It's a highly political forum, with the spotlight mainly trained on the Balkans and the Baltic region – and it holds a wide range of cultural gatherings and guest performances.

Judiska Teatern

Djurgårdsbrunnsvägen 59, Gärdet (box office 667 90 13/information 660 02 71/www.judiskateatern.org). Bus 69. **Box office** *Oct-May* 6-7pm Wed, Thur; 2-7pm Fri; 5-6pm Sat; 3-4pm Sun. Closed June-Sept. **Tickets** 90kr-180kr. **Credit** AmEx, MC, V.

The Jewish Theatre is not as focused on religion as the name might suggest. The actors perform finely crafted poetic theatre, mainly new work, in a beautiful old building with a very modern interior. Well worth a visit.

Art of the avant-garde: **Orionteatern.**

Moment

Gubbängstorget 117, Gubbängen (box office 50 85 01 28/www.moment.org.se). T-bana Gubbängen.
Tickets 160kr. **No credit cards.**
This cultural centre, a converted 1940s cinema in the suburb of Gubbängen, is run by a group of young artists and directors. The programme includes new drama, music, art exhibitions and cinema. It's 20 minutes by T-bana from the city centre.

Orionteatern

Katarina Bangata 77, Södermalm (information 640 29 70/box office 643 88 80/643 37 16/www.orion teatern.se). T-bana Skanstull/bus 3, 59, 76.
Box office *Sept-Midsummer* 5-7pm Mon-Thur. Closed Midsummer-Aug. **Tickets** 100kr-230kr.
Credit DC, MC, V. **Map** p251 N10.
The Orion Theatre, Stockholm's largest avant-garde theatre company, was formed in 1983, and has since collaborated with the likes of Peking Opera from Shanghai and Theatre de Complicité from London. The building, once a factory, is an unusual and effective theatre space.

Strindbergs Intima Teater

Barnhusgatan 20, Norrmalm (box office 20 08 43/www.strindbergsintimateater.se). T-bana T-Centralen or Hötorget/bus 1, 47, 53, 65. **Box office** 2hrs before performance. **No credit cards.**
Map p240 F5.
Founded by August Strindberg back in 1907, this small theatre used to show the dramatist's plays exclusively. Nowadays the programme, co-ordinated by Strindbergsmuseet, is more varied and includes guest performances and theatre for children.

Teater Brunnsgatan Fyra

Brunnsgatan 4, Norrmalm (box office 10 70 50/ www.brunnsgatanfyra.nu). T-bana Östermalmstorg/ bus 1, 2, 55, 56. **Box office** *Sept-June* 5-7pm Wed-Sat; 2-4pm Sun. Closed July, Aug. **Tickets** 200kr-220kr. **No credit cards. Map** p241 E7.
Kristina Lugn – one of Sweden's best, and best-known, poets and dramatists – took over this small theatre when its creator, actor Allan Edwall, died. Some of Sweden's most prominent actors and dramatists can be found working in this stone cellar, among them Erland Josephson, Lena Nyman and Staffan Westerberg. Often sold out.

Teater Galeasen

Slupskjulsvägen 32, Skeppsholmen (box office 611 00 30/611 09 20/www.galeasen.se). Bus 65. **Box office** *Mid Jan-June, Aug-mid Dec* 10am-4pm (10am-8pm on performance nights). Closed July, mid Dec-mid Jan.
Tickets 150kr-200kr. **Credit** MC, V. **Map** p242 H9.
In the 1980s and early 1990s this was the hip spot for theatregoers. Nowadays, things have changed and actors of that generation are now household names. But Galeasen has continued to be a nursery for young actors and directors, and the work on show here is still high quality.

Teater Giljotin

Torsgatan 41, Vasastaden (box office 30 30 00/ www.teatergiljotin.com). T-bana St Eriksplan/bus 3, 4, 72, 77. **Box office** 1hr before peformance.
Tickets 160kr-220kr. **No credit cards.**
Led by director Kia Berglund and musician Richard Borggård, this outfit produces well-directed and often new Nordic plays.

Everything from ballet to street dance at **Dansens Hus**. *See p200.*

Arts & Entertainment

Teater Pero

Sveavägen 114, Vasastaden (box office 612 99 00/www.pero.se). T-bana Rådmansgatan/bus 2, 4, 42, 52, 53, 72. **Box office** 11am-2pm Sat; 1hr before performance. **No credit cards.** **Map** p245 C6.

Teater Pero has a strong tradition of mime, and has been producing shows for children and adults for over 20 years.

Teater Scenario

Odengatan 62, Vasastaden (box office 643 71 82/ www.teaterscenario.com). T-bana Odenplan/bus 3, 40, 62. **Box office** 1hr before performance. Closed mid June-mid Aug. **Tickets** 80kr-170kr. **No credit cards.** **Map** p245 D5.

A small theatre company featuring a new generation of exciting dramatists, notably Daniela Kullman and Dennis Magnusson.

Teater Tribunalen

Hornsgatan 92, Södermalm (box office 84 94 33/ www.tribunalen.com). T-bana Zinkensdamm or Mariatorget/bus 4, 43, 55, 66. **Box office** Early Aug-May 1hr before performance. Closed June-early Aug. **Tickets** 100kr-160kr. **No credit cards.** **Map** p250 K5.

Angry, political, radical theatre with an ideological outlook inherited from the 1970s. Brecht and Fassbinder are the house gods, and productions here often receive critical acclaim from the press.

Dance

Whereas the theatre scene, perhaps because of the language barrier, is a somewhat stagnant world of mostly national interest, the Stockholm dance scene is considerably more vibrant and international in outlook. At least outside **Kungliga Balletten** (the Royal Ballet at **Kungliga Operan**, *see below*). Stockholm's dance audience has grown steadily during the last decade. **Moderna Dansteatern** (*see below*), in Skeppsholmen, has been the home base for many freelance dancers and choreographers for over 20 years, as is the studio **WELD** (formerly ELD) for more conceptual stuff. The **Cullberg Balett** (www. cullbergbaletten.com), a truly international company with a solid reputation, is also based in Stockholm. Mats Ek, founder Birgit Cullberg's son, no longer leads the company, but he is still active as a freelance choreographer.

The most significant modern dance scene, however, is at **Dansens Hus** (House of Dance; *see below*), which opened in 1990. Its extensive programme includes visiting companies from around the world, and the quality is consistently high. The award-winning Finnish-Swede choreographer Kenneth Kvarnström took over the helm in 2004. Dansens Hus hosts some of the most interesting and creative local choreographers around, including Cristina Caprioli, Örjan Andersson, Virpi Pahkinen and Helena Franzén.

Dance theatre also has a strong position in Sweden – award-winning Birgitta Egerbladh with her Pina Bausch-inspired, humorous choreography now has her base at Stockholms Stadsteatern. For dance listings, check the Swedish-language magazine *Danstidningen* (www.danstidningen.se) or 'På Stan', the Thursday supplement of *Dagens Nyheter*.

Venues

Venues

Dansens Hus

12-14 Barnhusgatan, Norrmalm (box office 50 89 90 90/www.dansenshus.se). T-bana Hötorget or T-Centralen/bus 1, 47, 53, 69. **Box office** Mid Aug-Midsummer 2pm-6pm Mon-Fri. 2pm-7pm Mon-Fri, 2pm-7pm Sat when there is a performance. Closed Midsummer-mid Aug. **Tickets** 160kr-280kr. **Credit** AmEx, DC, MC, V. **Map** p241 E6.

The House of Dance is the major venue for Swedish dance. This is where you'll find the Cullberg Ballet when they're in town, and the international guest list might include the likes of Anna Teresa de Keersmaeker's company Rosas, Nederlands Dans Theater and Akram Khan. The Swedish dance group Bounce! has also been a huge success here, with its funny, street dance-inspired shows drawing large audiences. *Photo p199.*

Kungliga Operan

Gustav Adolfs Torg, Norrmalm (box office 24 82 40/www.operan.se). T-bana Kungsträdgården/ bus 2, 43, 55, 59, 62, 76. **Box office** Sept-May noon-6pm Mon-Fri; noon-3pm Sat. Closed June-Aug. **Tickets** 40kr-580kr. **Credit** AmEx, DC, MC, V. **Map** p241 G7.

The Royal Opera, founded in 1733 and one of Europe's oldest opera houses, is home to Sweden's finest classical company, the Royal Ballet. The dancers are outstanding and, though the repertoire is usually traditional, there is occasionally some modern work on show. For example, eminent choreographer Birgitta Egerbladh has visited, flexing the feet of some astonished classical dancers. The interior is completely over the top – the chandelier weighs two tons and the Golden Room is simply stunning.

Moderna Dansteatern

Slupskjulsvägen 32, Skeppsholmen (box office 611 32 33/www.mdt.a.se). Bus 65. **Box office** 30mins before performance. **Tickets** 180kr. **No credit cards.** **Map** p242 H9.

The small Modern Dance Theatre was founded by Margaretha Åsberg, the grande dame of Swedish dance, and has single-handedly provided a space for postmodern and avant-garde dance in Stockholm. More recently, performance art has also found a refuge here.

Trips Out of Town

Vaxholm. *See p210*.

Trips Out of Town

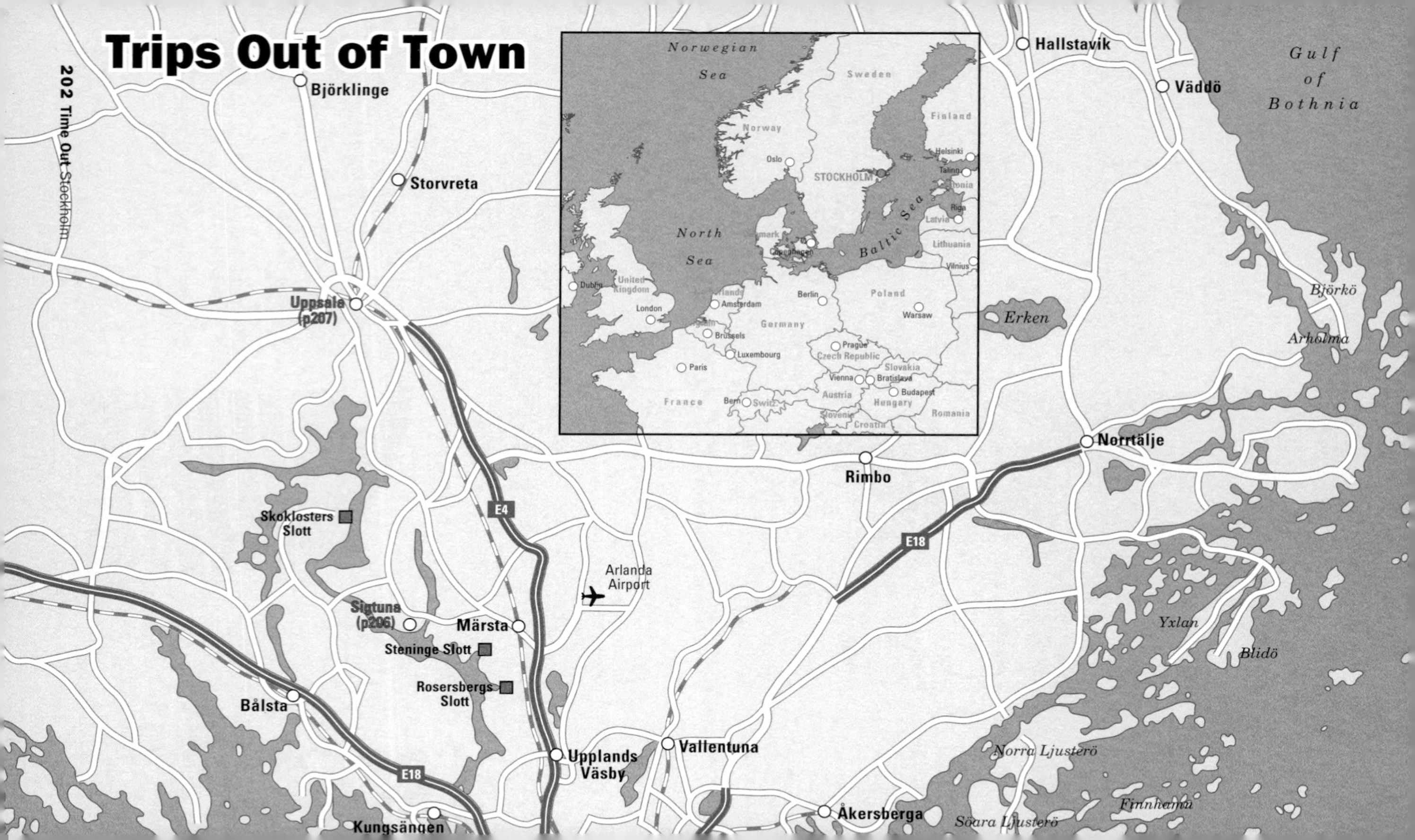

Björklinge
Storvreta
Uppsala
(p207)
Hallstavik
Väddö
Gulf
of
Bothnia
Björkö
Arholma
Erken
Norrtälje
Rimbo
E4
E18
Skoklosters
Slott
Arlanda
Airport
Sigtuna
(p206)
Märsta
Steninge Slott
Rosersbergs
Slott
Bålsta
Upplands
Väsby
Vallentuna
Åkersberga
Kungsängen
Yxlan
Blidö
Norra Ljusterö
Södra Ljusterö
Finnhamn
Norwegian
Sea
North
Sea
Baltic Sea
Sweden
Norway
Finland
STOCKHOLM
Oslo
Helsinki
Tallinn
Riga
Latvia
Lithuania
Vilnius
Copenhagen
Dublin
United
Kingdom
London
Amsterdam
Berlin
Poland
Warsaw
Germany
Brussels
Luxembourg
Paris
France
Prague
Czech Republic
Slovakia
Vienna
Bratislava
Budapest
Austria
Hungary
Bern
Switz.
Slovenia
Croatia
Romania

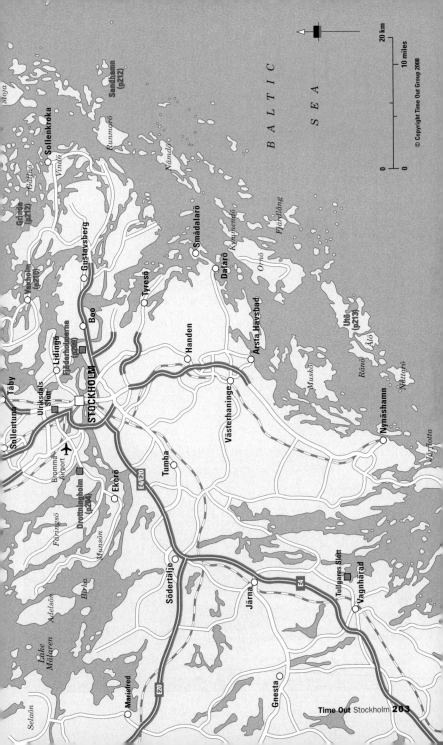

Moja

Sandhamn
(p212)

B A L T I C

S E A

© Copyright Time Out Group 2008

20 km

10 miles

Runmarö

Sollenkroka

Vindö

Grinda
(p212)

Nämdö

Gustavsberg

Vaxholm
(p210)

Tyresö

Smådalarö

Kymmendö

Ornö

Fjärdlång

Dalarö

Boo

Lidingö
Fjäderholmarna
(p209)

Sollentuna

Täby

Ulriksdals
Slott

STOCKHOLM

Handen

Årsta Havsbad

Musko

Utö
(p213)

Ålö

Ränö

Nåttarö

Bromma
Airport

Drottningholm
(p204)

Ekerö

Västerhaninge

Nynäshamn

Järflotta

Färingsö

Munsön

Tumba

E4/E20

Birka

Adelsön

Södertälje

Tullgarns Slott

Vagnhärad

Järna

E4

Lake
Mälaren

Mariefred

E20

Gnesta

Selaön

Day Trips

How the other half lived.

Drottningholm

The grand palatial estate of Drottningholm – the permanent residence of the Swedish royal family since 1981 – attracts more than 100,000 visitors annually. Located ten kilometres (six miles) to the west of central Stockholm, on the sparsely populated island of Lovön, it is an essential excursion from the city. The very well-preserved grounds – 300-year-old trees frame the statues and fountains of the French garden behind the palace – and some excellent 17th- and 18th-century architecture, including a functioning theatre from 1766 and exotic **Kina Slott** at the western end, led UNESCO to add the entire site to its World Heritage List back in 1991.

Constructed at the height of Sweden's power in Europe during the mid 17th century, **Drottningholms Slott** was built to impress – and impress it certainly does. Wealthy dowager Queen Hedvig Eleonora financed the initial phase of the palace's construction, which lasted from 1662 to 1686. The royal architect Nicodemus Tessin the Elder modelled the

waterfront residence on the Palace of Versailles. Highlights include the monumental staircase, Ehrenstrahl drawing room and Hedvig Eleonora's state bedchamber.

The palace's second period of growth began after Lovisa Ulrika married Crown Prince Adolf Fredrik in 1744. She was a great lover of the arts and it was at her commission that architect Carl Fredrik Adelcrantz constructed **Drottningholms Slottsteater**. The theatre, with its original stage sets and hand-driven machinery in place, is the world's oldest working theatre – concerts, ballets and operas are still held here in the summer.

Behind the palace is the long rectangular **French Baroque Garden**, laid out in five stages separated by lateral paths. Its bronze statues are copies of early 17th-century works by the Dutch sculptor Adriaen de Vries. The originals were moved across the street to the **Museum de Vries**, which opened in 2001. The statues – spoils of war from Denmark's Fredriksborg Palace and Prague – are arranged in the former royal stable in the same pattern as those in the garden.

Drottningholms Slott.

North of the baroque garden is the beautiful, lake-studded **English Park**, so named because it followed the English style of naturalistic landscaping that was fashionable at the time. It was added by Gustav III after he took over the palace in 1777.

Kina Slott stands near the end of the garden down a tree-lined avenue. As a surprise for Lovisa Ulrika's 33rd birthday in 1753, Adolf Fredrik had a Chinese-inspired wooden pavilion built here. Ten years later it was replaced by this rococo pleasure palace, also designed by CF Adelcrantz. The palace, which was carefully and extensively renovated between 1989 and 1996, has been repainted in its original red colour with yellow trim and light-green roofs; guided tours are available.

Across from Kina Slott is the small **Confidencen** pavilion. When the royal family wanted to dine in complete privacy, they sat in the top room and servants hoisted up a fully set table from below. Down the road behind the palace is the former studio of the 20th-century Swedish artist **Evert Lundqvist** (402 62 70, open for guided tours in Swedish 4pm daily May-Aug, 60kr).

Drottningholms Slott

402 62 80/www.royalcourt.se. **Open** *May-Aug* 10am-4.30pm daily. *Sept* noon-3.30pm daily. *Oct-Apr* noon-3.30pm Sat, Sun. Closed mid Dec-early Jan. Guided tours in English daily mid June-Sept; weekends Oct-May. **Admission** 70kr. **Credit** AmEx, MC, V. **Free with SC**.

A combined ticket to Kina Slott and Drottningholms Slott costs 90kr, and includes a discount on tickets to the theatre.

Kina Slott

402 62 70. **Open** *May-Aug* 11am-4.30pm daily. *Sept* noon-3.30pm daily. Closed Oct-Apr. Guided tours weekends May-mid June; daily mid June-Sept. **Admission** (incl tour) 50kr.

Museum de Vries

402 62 70. **Open** guided tour only (call for times). Closed Sept-mid May. **Admission** 60kr.

Slottsteater

Administrative office May-Sept 759 04 06/Oct-Apr 55 69 31 07/www.drottningholmsslottsteater.dtm.se. **Open** (guided tours only) *May* noon-5pm daily. *June-Aug* 11am-5pm daily. *Sept* 1-4pm daily. Closed Oct-Apr. **Admission** 60kr.

Where to eat

First-class restaurant **Drottningholms Wärdshus** (759 03 08/81, www.drottningholmswardshus.se, main courses 220kr-245kr, closed dinner Sept-May) occupies an 1850s building across the street from the estate, near the jetty. There's also a bar, conference facilities and tables outside in the garden during the summer.

Drottningholmspaviljongen (759 04 25, www.drottningholmspaviljongen.com, main courses 100kr-225kr, weekends only Oct-Dec, closed Jan) offers daily lunch specials, including Swedish *husmanskost*.

Drottningholm's only café, **Kina Slotts Servering** (759 03 96, closed dinner & Nov-Mar), is located near Kina Slott.

Prices at these eateries are quite high, so you may want to opt for a picnic on the lawns.

Getting there

By metro/bus

T-bana to Brommaplan, then bus 177, 178, 301-323.

By boat

Between May and early Sept you can travel by steamboat from Stadshusbron near Stadshuset on Kungsholmen (100kr single, 130kr return); the journey takes 1hr. The most frequent service is between early June and mid Aug. Contact **Strömma Kanalbolaget** (*see p210*) for more information.

By car

From Kungsholmen take Drottningholmsvägen west towards Vällingby, then at Brommaplan follow the signs to Drottningholm. It's about a 15-minute drive.

By bicycle

There is a well-signposted cycle path from outside Stadshuset in Stockholm to Drottningholm; the ride takes about 50mins.

Sigtuna

A thousand years ago this small town by Lake Mälaren was the most important in Sweden. Founded around 980 by King Erik Segersäll, Sigtuna was a major trading port during Viking times.

Later the town became the centre of activity for Christian missionaries. After King Gustav Vasa's Reformation, when he demolished many churches and monasteries, Sigtuna fell into ruin. Virtually all that is left from its great period are the remains of three 12th-century granite churches (from an original seven) bordering the town centre, and a collection of artefacts in the Sigtuna Museum.

Many of the buildings date back to the 18th and 19th centuries. The **Rådhus**, in the central square, was built in 1744 and is the smallest town hall in Sweden. The **Sigtuna Museum** is built on the site of a former king's residence and has an excellent exhibition on the Vikings. It also runs the Rådhus and **Lundströmska Gården**, a middle-class house where a merchant lived with his family. Stop by the tourist office on Stora Gatan to book a tour of the town.

Off the main street, you can take a melancholy stroll through the church ruins and cemeteries of **St Lars**, **St Per** and **St Olof**. The church of **St Maria**, which looks quite new compared to the others, was actually built by the Dominicans in the 13th century and is one of the oldest brick buildings in Sweden.

Down by the water, you can rent canoes and bicycles, take in the view from a café or stroll along the path. Summer is the ideal time to visit Sigtuna, but seeing frozen Lake Mälaren during winter is breathtaking.

Sigtuna Museum

Stora Gatan 55 (59 78 38 70/www.sigtuna.se/museer). **Open** *June-Aug* noon-4pm daily. *Sept-May* noon-4pm Tue-Sun. **Admission** 20kr. *Lundströmska Gården, Stora Gatan 39.* **Open** *June-Aug* noon-4pm daily. **Admission** 10kr. *Rådhus* **Open** *June-Aug* noon-4pm daily. **Admission** free. **Credit** AmEx, DC, MC, V.

Where to eat

For a good meal in a charming 18th-century pub, head two blocks west of the town square to **Amandas Krog** (Långgränd 7, 59 25 00 24, main courses 125kr-225kr). You can order a lunch special of fish, meat or pasta, or something fancier such as crayfish soup or grilled venison. The **Båthuset Krog & Bar** (59 25 67 80, main courses 165kr-2695kr, closed Mon, dinner only) is located out on the water from Ångbåtsbryggan; a wooden dock leads to the restaurant, which serves hearty portions

Trips Out of Town

of fresh mussels and cod. For one of the best waterfront views, visit the terrace at the **Sigtuna Stadshotell**'s top-notch restaurant (Stora Nygatan 3, 59 25 01 00, mains 165kr-295kr, closed 4wks July, Aug), serving Swedish *husmanskost* with an international touch.

Tourist information

Sigtuna Turism

Stora Gatan 33 (59 48 06 52/www.sigtuna.se/ turism). **Open** *June-Aug* 10am-6pm Mon-Sat; 11am-5pm Sun. *Sept-May* 10am-5pm Mon-Fri; noon-4pm Sat, Sun. Closed Christmas.

Getting there

By train/bus

Take the Pendeltåg commuter train (www.sl.se) or the Uppsala train (www.tim-trafik.se) to Märsta. The Uppsala train is faster, but make sure it goes via Märsta and not Arlanda. From Märsta, take bus 570 or 575 to Sigtuna bus station, near the town centre. From Stockholm Central Station the trip takes 1hr.

By car

Head north on the E4 for about 30km (18 miles) then exit on the 263 and follow the signs to Sigtuna. Drive about 10km (six miles) west until you come to a roundabout, where you turn towards Sigtuna Centrum. The entire journey takes about 50 mins.

Sigtuna was the most important town in Sweden a thousand years ago.

Uppsala

The historic city of Uppsala, Sweden's answer to Cambridge or Oxford, is home to the oldest university in Scandinavia – dating back to 1477 – and some 30,000 students. It's a bustling, charming city, situated at the northern tip of Lake Mälaren, about 70 kilometres (40 miles) north of Stockholm, with ancient buildings, plenty of cafés and beautiful parks.

The city's magnificent Domkyrkan, Scandinavia's largest cathedral, stands on a ridge to the west of the downtown area beside a 16th-century brick castle. The small Fyrisån river runs along a man-made stone channel through the centre of town. One block to the east is a pedestrian shopping street and the busy main square of **Stora Torget**. The former home and garden of the famous botanist Carl Linnaeus (whose face adorns the 100kr note) are located nearby, along with several other university museums.

Uppsala was founded slightly to the north of its present location; it moved southwards in the 13th century as construction began on the **Domkyrkan**, today the city's most striking landmark by far. This red brick Gothic cathedral, completed in 1435, was built on a cross plan. The building is as tall as it is long, with two western towers rising up to a neck-craning 118.7 metres (389 feet); more than half a million people visit each year. Inside there's an enormous vaulted ceiling, a floor covered with gravestones and Sweden's largest baroque pulpit, designed by Tessin the Younger. It's also the last resting place of some famous Swedes. Linnaeus and the philosopher Emanuel Swedenborg are buried here, and Gustav Vasa is entombed beneath a monument depicting him and his two queens.

The buildings of Uppsala University are scattered throughout the city. Across from the cathedral stands the **Gustavianum**, formerly the university's main building, now a museum. Beneath its copper onion dome are exhibits on the history of science and the university, an old anatomical theatre, some Nordic, classical and Egyptian antiquities, and the curiosities of the Augsburg Art Cabinet.

Up the hill from the cathedral is the huge, earth-red **Uppsala Slott**, built by Gustav Vasa in the late 1540s as a fortress. His sons later added to the building, although much of it was destroyed in the city fire of 1702. It houses an art gallery and the county governor's residence, **Vasaborgen**, but is not as spectacular as you

Trips Out of Town

might expect. The castle's freestanding bell tower, Gunillaklockan, has become a symbol of Uppsala; it strikes at 6am and 9pm.

The university's grand **Botaniska Trädgården** (Villavägen 8, 018 471 28 38, www.botan.uu.se), west of the castle, includes a tropical greenhouse, baroque formal garden and 11,000 species of plants. To see where the university's first botanical garden stood, visit **Linnéträdgården**, situated one block north of pedestrianised Gågatan. Carl von Linné (1707-78), better known as Linnaeus, restored the garden in 1741 soon after taking up a professorship at the university. One of the world's most famous scientists, Linnaeus developed a method of classifying and naming plants and animals that was adopted by scientists around the world and is still in use today. His attempts at growing coffee, cacao and bananas here – in an attempt to make Sweden more economically independent – were unsurprisingly thwarted by the Swedish winter. He lived in the small house on the corner of the property, now the **Linnémuseet**, which has a permanent exhibition on his life and work. Linnaeus Week takes place in early August every year, when 18th-century costumed characters roam the streets, and there are lectures and botanical tours

Gamla Uppsala (Old Uppsala), two kilometres (1.2 miles) to the north of Uppsala, is the site of the original settlement. The **Gamla Uppsala** museum opened in 2000, and features informative exhibits about Viking history and myths.

Domkyrkan
Domkyrkoplan (018 18 71 73/www.uppsala domkyrka.se). **Open** *Cathedral* 8am-6pm daily. *Treasury* May-Sept 10am-5pm Mon-Sat; 12.30-5pm Sun. Oct-Apr 11am-3pm Tue-Sat; 12.30-3pm Sun. **Admission** *Cathedral* free. *Treasury* 30kr.

Gamla Uppsala
Disavägen (018 23 93 00/group bookings when closed 018 23 93 12/www.raa.se/gamlauppsala). Bus 2 or 110 from central Uppsala. **Open** *May-Aug* 11am-5pm daily. *Sept-Apr* noon-3pm Wed, Sat, Sun. Closed 3wks from mid Dec. **Admission** 50kr; 30kr concessions, 7-18s; free under-7s.

Gustavianum
Akademigatan 3 (01 84 71 75 71/www. gustavianum.uu.se). **Open** 11am-4/5pm Tue-Sun. **Admission** 40kr; 30kr concessions; free under-12s.

Linnéträdgården & Linnémuseet
Svarbäcksgatan 27 (museum 018 13 65 40/ www.linnaeus.uu.se). **Open** *Garden* May-Sept 9am-7/9pm daily. Closed Oct-Apr. *Museum* May-mid Sept 11am-4pm Tue-Sun. Group bookings all year. **Admission** *Garden & Museum* 50kr.

Uppsala Slott
018 727 24 85. **Open** *Castle* (guided tours only) *June-Aug* Swedish 12.15pm, 2pm daily; English 1pm, 3pm daily. Closed Sept-May. *Art gallery* noon-4pm Tue-Fri; 11am-5pm Sat, Sun; noon-8pm 1st Wed every month. **Admission** 80kr.

Vasaborgen
018 50 77 72/www.vasaborgen.se. **Open** *May-Aug* 11am-4pm daily. Closed Sept-Apr. **Admission** 40kr.

Where to eat

The city's finest dining can be found at **Domtrappkällaren** (St Eriksgränd 15, 018 13 09 55, www.domtrappkallaren.se, main courses 135kr-295kr, closed Sun), which serves excellent Swedish and French cuisine in a 13th-century vault near the cathedral steps. If you want the same atmosphere at a cheaper price, try the pub lunch. One block east is **Hambergs Fisk** (Fyristorg 8, 018 71 21 50, main courses 85kr-260kr, closed Mon, Sun & July), which specialises in seafood.

To watch the pedestrian traffic at Stora Torget, visit **Restaurang Rådhussalongen** (Nos.6-8, 018 69 50 70, main courses 95kr-200kr), and for an excellent vegetarian lunch, try **Fröjas Sal Vegetarisk Restaurang** (Bäverns Gränd 24, 018 10 13 10, set menus 65kr-80kr, closed Sat, Sun June-Aug) opposite the bus station. One of Uppsala's most justly famous old-fashioned cafés is **Ofvandahls Hovkonditori** (Sysslomansgatan 5, 018 13 42 04, closed Sun July), founded in the late 19th century, where you can stock up on pastries and marzipan sweets.

Tourist information

Uppsala Tourism
Fyristorg 8 (01 87 27 48 00/www.uppland.nu). **Open** 10am-6pm Mon-Fri; 10am-3pm Sat.

Getting there

By train
Several trains a day leave for Uppsala from Stockholm's Central Station; see www.sj.se or call 07 71 75 75 75 for times.

By bus
Swebus Express's (www.swebusexpress.se) bus 899 departs several times a day from Stockholm's City terminal (Cityterminalen). The journey takes about 1hr and costs 60kr one way.

By car
Follow the E4 north from Stockholm for about 50mins. The highway passes through the eastern half of Uppsala, from where you follow the signs to Uppsala Centrum to the west.

Trips Out of Town

The Archipelago

Leave the city in your wake.

Fjäderholmarna is the closest archipelago island to the capital.

The Stockholm archipelago begins just a few miles east of the capital, covering about 140 kilometres (90 miles) from north to south. Only 150 of the islands are inhabited, but many Stockholmers have summerhouses in the archipelago and visitor numbers swell in the warmer months, especially July. The landscape varies tremendously, from the more populated, thickly wooded inner archipelago to the bare, flat rocks of the central and outer islands.

The archipelago is best visited from mid June to mid August – during the rest of the year many hotels, restaurants and other facilities are closed, ferries are few and far between, and some islands pretty much shut down to visitors. Always book ahead to ensure there will be accommodation available.

During the summer the archipelago often gets more sunshine than the mainland, but it's still a good idea to pack a raincoat and sweater. Sunscreen and mosquito repellent are also recommended. Take provisions as shops are not always open, and remember that cashpoints are few and far between.

The easiest way to get out to the islands is by ferry – we've listed the three main companies below:

Cinderellabåtarna

58 71 40 00/www.cinderellabatarna.com.
Ferries leave from Strandvägen. **Map** p242 G9.

Strömma Kanalbolaget

58 71 40 00/www.strommakanalbolaget.com.
Ferries leave from Strandvägen. **Map** p242 G9.

Waxholmsbolaget

679 58 30/www.waxholmsbolaget.se. Ferries leave from opposite the Grand Hôtel, Strömkajen. **Map** p241 G8.

Fjäderholmarna

The four islands that make up Fjäderholmarna are the closest archipelago islands to Stockholm – just six kilometres (four miles) east of downtown. Ferries drop visitors off at the main island of **Stora Fjäderholmen**. A paved walking path circles the island, passing the restaurants, small museums and handicraft boutiques on the northern and eastern shores, and the forested area and flat rocks to the west. About a dozen people live on **Ängsholmen** and Stora Fjäderholmen. The smaller islands of **Libertas** and **Rövarns Holme** provide sanctuary for birds, but there's no way to get to them unless you have your own boat. The shops and boat museum usually close around 5-5.30pm, while the restaurants are often open until midnight, leaving time to catch the last boat back to Stockholm.

When the weather is good, the northern cliffs of Stora Fjärderholmen are flooded with sunbathing Stockholmers and tourists, and the place can feel a bit cramped. Swimming options are limited, with no easily accessible beaches. The ferries from Stockholm dock on the northern shore next to the guest harbour and the **Östersjöakvariet** aquarium (718 40 55, closed Oct-Apr), which is housed in a cave dug out by the military to store ammunition. The shop doubles as the tourist office.

The **Spiritum Museum** (Vodka Museum; 55 67 88 20, www.spiritum.se, guided tours 50kr), which focuses on the island's place in the history of vodka distillation, is next door to the aquarium, while further along the path the **Allmogebåtar Museum** (Boat Museum; 070 477 98 51, admission free) on the eastern side of the island is devoted to boats.

Following the path, you come across the **outdoor theatre**, which puts on plays every summer against the beautiful backdrop of boats. Further round, on the southern shore, a small street contains an **art gallery** and studios where artists make and sell pottery, linen goods and wooden handicrafts. At **Åtta Glas** (716 11 24) you can watch glass being blown and then buy the finished article in the little shop next door.

Where to eat

As you step off the ferry, the **Rökeriet** (716 50 88, www.rokeriet.nu, main courses 65kr-250kr) is on your left along the water's edge. The indoor restaurant has a beautiful view over the neighbouring islands. The nearby **Fjäderholmarnas Krog** (718 33 55, www.fjaderholmarnaskrog.se, main courses 195kr-335kr) offers an upmarket menu, and has a harbour view. For dessert, try **Systrarna Degens Glasstuga** (716 78 01, closed Oct-Apr), which specialises in ice-cream and smoothies. **Fjäderholmarnas Magasin** (718 08 50, closed Oct-Apr, main courses around 95kr), located on the southern shore, serves typical lunch specials and salads.

Tourist information

The island doesn't have a tourist office, but information is available from the **Östersjöakvariet** (718 40 55; *see above*). You can usually pick up a free brochure and map on the ferry.

Getting there

By boat

Strömma Kanalbolaget (*see p209*) ferries leave from Nybroplan (every 30mins 10am-8.30pm mid May-end Aug; every hr 10am-11.30pm early May-mid May; every hr 10am-8pm, then 9.30pm, 10.30pm, 11.30pm end Aug-early Sept; 6 times each afternoon early-end Sept, return 80kr). **Fjäderholmslinjen** (21 55 00, www.rss.a.se/fjaderholmslinjen) depart every hour from Slussen 10am-10pm daily May-early Sept; return 90kr.

Vaxholm

The island of Vaxholm, just 3.5 kilometres (two miles) long, is by far the most populated and easily accessible island in the archipelago. It is located about 17 kilometres (11 miles) north-east of Stockholm and is connected to the mainland by highway 274. The place is overrun in summer, when roughly a million visitors come for Vaxholm's waterfront restaurants, handicraft shops and art galleries. Ferries from Stockholm dock at Vaxholm's historic downtown, located on the island's south-east corner. The town has a lively, beach-side feel and frequent outdoor events in the summer. On the main street of Hamngatan, to the north, you'll find all the conveniences you might expect in a small town.

Gustav Vasa founded the city of Vaxholm in the 1540s after winning Sweden's war with Denmark. The city supplied food and water to the newly constructed fortress and tower located on the small island to the east. Several additions were made to the fortress during the 19th century, and today it contains the **Vaxholms Fästnings Museum** (54 17 21 57, www.vaxholmsfastning.se, open 11am-5pm daily June-3rd wk Sept, guided tours in Swedish only, admission 50kr). The museum is easily reached by a two-minute boat trip (40kr return) from Vaxholm wharf.

West of Hamngatan is **Vaxholm Kyrka**, designed in the 1760s by Carl Fredrik Adelcrantz, who also built several churches in Stockholm. It hosts concerts in the summer. The city's old **Rådhuset** (Town Hall) is now home to the tourist office, and the cobbled square outside has stalls selling handicrafts in summer. Every year Vaxholm harbour hosts a steamboat festival, **Skärgårdsbåtens Dag**, on the second Wednesday in June.

Where to eat

There's a good choice of restaurants along the wharf, including seafood, Italian and Chinese. For fine dining with a view of the water, try

Waxholms Hotell (*see below*; main courses 140kr-275kr, closed dinner Sun), serving dishes such as turbot stuffed with truffles and lobster. For more down-to-earth fare, take a seat on the outdoor patio of the popular **Hamnkrogen** (Söderhamnen 10, 54 13 20 39, main courses 80kr-180kr). You will also find pizzas and hamburgers in abundance.

On Trädgårdsgatan you'll find **Strömingslådan**, a small red kiosk in a garden which sells herring prepared in every way possible and plenty of local specialities for takeaway (Trädgårdsgatan 12, 54 13 02 47, closed Sept-May).

Vaxholm.

Where to stay

The sole hotel, **Waxholms Hotell** (Hamngatan 2, 54 13 01 50, www.waxholms hotell.se, 1,175kr-1,650kr double), built in 1901, has light, tastefully decorated rooms and satellite TV. Alternatively, you can book B&Bs (around 250kr per person per night) through the Vaxholm tourist office (*see below*). **Vaxholms Strand & Camping** (54 13 01 01, closed Oct-Apr) is located at the western end of the island and its sandy beach is a good spot for families.

Tourist information

Vaxholms Turistbyrå & VisitVaxholm AB

Rådhuset (54 13 14 80/www.vaxholm.se). **Open** *June-Aug* 10am-6pm Mon-Fri; 10am-2pm Sat, Sun. *Sept, May* 11am-4pm Mon-Fri; 11am-3pm Sat, Sun. *Oct-Apr* 10am-3pm Mon-Fri; 10am-2pm Sat, Sun. Stop by the tourist office to get hold of island maps, fishing licences and an events schedule. The website gives general information on facilities and attractions.

Getting there

By metro & bus

T-bana Tekniska Högskolan, then bus 670 to Vaxholm. The whole journey takes about 1hr.

By boat

Waxholmsbolaget boats (*see p209*) from Strömkajen are the best option; they run several times a day all year (single 65kr). **Cinderellabåtarna** boats (*see p209*) from Strandvägen are less frequent, running up to three times a day mid June-end Aug (60-90mins, single 90kr).

By car

Head north on the E18 for 15km (9 miles) then exit at the Arninge Trafikplats on to highway 274. Follow signs to Vaxholm, which will lead you through Stockholmsvägen and Kungsgatan to downtown.

Trips Out of Town

Have lunch in one of **Grinda**'s award-winning restaurants (or catch your own).

Grinda

Grinda, just over an hour away by boat from Stockholm and accessible year-round, is one of the archipelago's most popular islands. Visitors come for the peaceful surroundings, swimming, good restaurant dining and pine forests.

In 1906 Henrik Santesson, the first director of the Nobel Foundation, bought the island and commissioned architect Ernst Stenhammar to design a summer residence. The result was a beautiful art nouveau stone house, the present-day **Grinda Wärdshus** (*see below*).

Grinda Gård is the starting point for a path through the forest to Grinda's highest point, Klubbudden, 35 metres (115 feet) above sea level.

Grinda has plenty of good swimming spots; Källviken, along the path to the guest harbour and the inn, has a shallow sandy beach, ideal for children. There are also some popular spots between Källviken and the guest harbour, and by the northern and southern piers.

Where to eat

Award-winning **Grinda Wärdshus** (*see below*; mains 110kr-315kr, booking essential) is open year-round and is the island's best restaurant; try speciality poached catfish. **Framfickan** (54 24 94 91, closed end Aug-mid June, mains 80kr-150kr), by the guest harbour, offers lighter pasta dishes, and has an outdoor veranda.

Where to stay

Grinda Wärdshus (54 24 94 91, www.grinda wardshus.se, 900kr per person per night) has 30 double rooms in the red wooden houses, built in 2003, beside the restaurant. The rooms have no telephone or TV, but are light and stylish. **Grinda Stugby & Vandrarhem** (54 24 90 72, www.grinda.nu, closed Nov-Apr, cottages

600kr-900kr, hostel 225kr, campsite 80kr per person per night) runs 31 basic cottages, as well as a hostel with 44 beds and the campsite. Camping is only allowed in the designated area.

Getting there

Cinderellabåtarna (*see p209*) boats depart twice a day from Strandvägen (mid June-end Aug, single 90kr-110kr) and stop at the south pier. **Waxholmsbolaget** (*see p209*) boats run all year (single 80kr) to both piers. There are several crossings a day during the summer.

Sandhamn

For archipelago beauty without total isolation, opt for Sandhamn. The island (officially named Sandön, but known as Sandhamn) boasts a hotel and conference centre, various restaurants and bars, bustling nightlife and a long, sandy beach. Pine forests cover most of the island, but the village dates back to the 1600s and has a few shops, a post office and a small museum.

Many of the island's points of interest are near the ferry dock. The **Hembygdsmuseum** (closed Sept-Midsummer) stands by the water in a small, red 18th-century storehouse, containing equipment from the toll station and an exhibit on alcohol smuggling. The **Tullhuset** (Toll House) is nearby; it operated until 1965 but is now leased out to private residents. In the 1870s August Strindberg lived with his wife in a building, now called **Strindbergsgården**, overlooking the harbour.

There are beaches at **Fläskberget**, to the west of the village, and at **Dansberget** to the east, but you should really take the 20-minute walk through the forest to the beautiful sandy beach at **Trouville** in the south. Bikes can be rented at the **Viamare Sea Club** (57 45 04 00, www.viamareseaclub.com), which also has an outdoor pool, bar and café.

Where to eat

For an upmarket choice try the **Seglarrestaurangen**, at the Sandhamn Hotell & Konferens (*see below*), with its veranda and views of the harbour. The historic **Sandhamns Värdshus** (57 15 30 51, www.sandhamns-vardshus.se, main courses 110kr-250kr) serves fish and wild game in a cosy environment. An even livelier time can be had at **Dykarbaren** (57 15 35 54, www.dykarbaren.se), a popular bar with a restaurant upstairs. The **Sands Hotell** (*see below*) also has a restaurant.

Where to stay

The **Sandhamn Hotell & Konferens** (57 45 04 00, www.sandhamn.com, 1,895kr double), overlooking the guest harbour, has 81 luxurious rooms, pool, fitness centre and sauna. The **Sands Hotell** (57 15 30 20, www.sands hotell.se, 1,850kr double) enjoys splendid views, and is smartly decorated within. For B&Bs, contact **Sandhamns Turistinformation** on 57 15 30 00.

Getting there

By boat

Sandhamnspilen (765 04 70, www.sandhamn.com) run boats from Strandvägen to Sandhamn (2hrs, single 120kr). The other option is to catch bus 434 from Slussen to Stavsnäs (1hr), which arrives in time for the ferry to Sandhamn (25mins, single 65kr). **Waxholmsbolaget** and **Cinderellabåtarna** boats (for both, *see p209*) depart several times a day from Stockholm during the summer.

Utö

Utö is one of the largest islands in the archipelago, and over the summer it receives about 300,000 visitors. The main harbour is **Gruvbryggan**, where ferries from Stockholm arrive and most of the island's facilities can be found, including the tourist office, the only hotel, restaurants, shops and the guest harbour. Ferries also stop at Spränga and on the adjoining island, Ålo, connected to Utö by road.

Utö is ideal for swimming and some of the best beaches can be found on the southern shore. Families should head for **Barnesbad**, a child-friendly beach 1.5 kilometres (one mile) north of Gruvbryggan harbour. At the harbour you can also play tennis, beach volleyball, miniature golf, football and boules. The best way to get around Utö is by bike, which you can rent at Gruvbryggan during high season (get there early as it's popular). The tourist

office also rents out bikes and these can be booked in advance. Alternatively, hire a kayak or rowing boat to explore the coast.

Where to eat

Gourmet cooking is served up at the beautiful **Utö Värdshus** restaurant (50 42 03 00, www.uto-vardshus.se, main courses 130kr-235kr), which is frequently voted the best restaurant in the archipelago. A short stroll after dinner will bring you to **Bakfickan** (closed mid Aug-May), a popular cellar bar.

In summer, you can eat at **Seglarbaren** (50 42 03 00, closed mid Aug-mid June, main courses 80kr-160kr), a restaurant on the waterfront by the main harbour. The island's bakery, **Utö Bageri** (50 15 70 79, closed Sept-May), near the harbour, sells great pastries, sandwiches and coffee, as well as its own special sailors' bread, Utölimpa, which stays fresh for three weeks if stored in a cool, dark place. The adjoining restaurant, **Dannekrogen** (same phone), is a homely place.

Where to stay

A five-minute walk uphill from Gruvbryggan is **Utö Värdshus** (*see above*), the island's only hotel. It offers a variety of accommodation in scattered historic buildings, including four-person **wooden cottages**. Utö Värdshus also runs the **STF Youth Hostel** (50 42 03 15, 330kr per person per night, closed Oct-Apr), with 64 beds. You can also rent basic cottages through the tourist office (*see below*) – most are around Spränga. Camping is available near the harbour (contact the marina office).

Tourist information

Utö Turistbyrå

Gruvbryggan (50 15 74 10/www.utoturist byra.se). **Open** usually 10am-4pm daily.

Getting there

By boat

Waxholmsbolaget boats (*see p209*) run from Strömkajen several times a day May-Aug (2.5-3hrs, single 120kr). Boats also stop at the next-door island of Ålö, so if you phone ahead you can arrange for a bike to be waiting there and cycle north to Uto.

By train, bus & boat

From Central Station take a pendeltåg train to Västerhaninge (about 35mins), then bus 846 to Årsta Havsbad (SL passes valid on the train and bus), then a boat (single 55kr) to Utö. The journey takes about 1.5hrs to Gruvbryggan, and another 15mins to Spränga.

Stockholm ‹ › Arlanda Airport

20 minutes
4–5 times/hour
200 km/hour

Directory

Features

Directory

Getting Around

Arriving & leaving

By air

Four airports serve Stockholm: Arlanda, Bromma, Skavsta and Västerås.

Arlanda Airport

Flight information 797 61 00/other enquiries 797 60 00/www.arlanda.se.
Stockholm's main airport, the largest in Scandinavia, is 42km (27 miles) north of the city centre and serves over 15 million passengers a year. International flights arrive and depart from terminals 2 and 5. Domestic flights depart from terminals 3 and 4.

It's a light, spacious, well-designed place, and the facilities are good. For currency exchange there is Forex (terminal 2), X-Change (terminal 5) and SEB exchange (terminal 5), as well as Handelsbanken and SEB banks in the Sky City shopping and eating area (which connects terminal 5 with 3 and 4). There are ATMs at terminals 2, 4, 5 and Sky City. There is a pharmacy (open 7am-7.30pm Mon-Fri, 8am-5pm Sat, 8am-7.30pm Sun) in Sky City. All terminals have cafés and bars, but head for Sky City for more serious eating.

The fastest way to get into Stockholm is on the bright yellow **Arlanda Express** train service (020 22 22 24/www.arlanda express.com), which arrives at its own terminal next to Central Station (the main station for trains and the Tunnelbana). Trains depart 4-6 times an hour, from Arlanda 5.05am-12.35am daily, and from Central Station 4.35am-12.05am daily. Journey time is 20mins; single fare is 200kr (100kr under-25s; four under-18s free with each full-price passenger). Buy tickets from the yellow automatic ticket booths at Arlanda or Central Station, or on the train (for 50kr extra). The booths take all major credit cards.

Alternatively, **Flygbussarna airport buses** (600 10 00/www. flygbussarna.se) leave about every 10mins from all terminals to Cityterminalen (the main bus station next to Central Station, *see right*). Buses run from Arlanda 4.50am-12.30am daily, and from Cityterminalen 4am-10pm daily.

The journey takes around 40mins. A single fare is 95kr (four under-18s free with each full-price passenger). There are also plenty of taxis at the airport – the usual fixed rate to the city is 450kr, but make sure you ask the driver first since many taxi firms set their own prices.

Bromma Airport

797 68 74/www.lfv.se.
Stockholm city airport, Bromma, is 8km (5 miles) west of the city centre. Its location makes it popular, but only 11 airlines operate from it.

You can get into the city centre on **Flygbussarna airport buses**. They run from Bromma 7.30am-10pm Mon-Fri; 10am-2.45pm Sat; 10.20am-8pm Sun. To Bromma 6am-8pm Mon-Fri; 7.50am-3.20pm Sat; 9am-6.45pm Sun. Single fare is 69kr and the journey takes about 15mins to Cityterminalen. Taking a taxi into town will cost you around 200kr.

Skavsta Airport

0155 28 04 00/www.skavsta-air.se.
Skavsta serves Stockholm even though it's 100km (62 miles) to the south. It's the airport of choice for budget airlines. Airport facilities include a Forex exchange bureau, restuarant, café, bar, playground and tax-free shops. **Flygbussarna airport buses** (single 130kr) take 80mins to reach the centre of Stockholm, and leave Skavsta 20mins after each arriving flight and Cityterminalen about 2hrs before a departing flight. If you can't find a taxi at the airport, you can order one, but the trip to Stockholm will set you back about 1,300kr.

Västerås Airport

021 80 56 10/www.vasteras flygplats.se.
Ryanair flies into Västerås, located 110km (68 miles) north-west of Stockholm. Facilities include a small café (open 6am-6pm daily), bar, tax-free shop and car hire. The **airport bus** (single 130kr, journey 75mins) leaves 20mins after an arriving flight for Cityterminalen in Stockholm; it returns about 2hrs before departing flights. There are trains every hour to the city (but you'll have to take a bus or taxi to the train station first). A taxi ride to Stockholm will cost around 1,300kr.

Airlines

Air France 51 99 99 90/ www.airfrance.com
Austrian Airlines 02 00 72 73 73/ www.aua.com
British Airways 02 00 77 00 98/ www.britishairways.com
Finnair 07 71 78 11 00/ www.finnair.com
Flynordic 58 55 44 00/ www.flynordic.com
Iberia 07 71 61 60 68/ www.iberia.com
KLM 58 79 97 57/ www.klm.com
Lufthansa 07 70 11 10 10/ www.lufthansa.com
Malmö Aviation 07 71 55 00 10/ www.malmoaviation.se
Ryanair 0900 20 20 240/ www.ryanair.com
SAS 07 70 72 77 27/797 40 00/ www.sas.se
Sterling 58 76 91 48/ www.sterlingticket.com

By train

The major rail travel company in Sweden is **SJ** (www.sj.se). International, domestic and commuter trains arrive and depart from Stockholm's main train station, Central Station. Just below the station is T-Centralen, the main station for the Tunnelbana system, and taxis are available outside.

SJ

Central Station, Vasagatan, Norrmalm (07 71 75 75 75). T-bana T-Centralen/bus 3, 47, 53, 62, 65. **Open** *Domestic tickets* 6am-10pm Mon-Fri; 8am-10pm Sat, Sun. *International tickets* 9am-6pm Mon-Fri. **Map** p241 G6.
To book tickets from abroad, call +46 771 75 75 75 or visit www. swedenbooking.com. Tickets can only be picked up in Sweden or sent by post to Norway and Denmark.

By bus

Most long-distance coaches (national and international) stop at **Cityterminalen**, Stockholm's main bus station, next to Central Station. T-Centralen is an escalator ride away, and there are always plenty of taxis outside.

Eurolines

Klarabergsviadukten 72, Norrmalm (762 59 60/timetable service from abroad +46 362 90 80 00/www. eurolines.se). T-bana T-Centralen/bus 3, 47, 53, 62, 65. **Open** 9am-5.30pm Mon-Fri. **Map** p241 G6.
Operates buses to more than 500 European cities.

Swebus Express

Cityterminalen, Klarabergsgatan, Norrmalm (07 71 21 82 18/www. swebusexpress.se). T-bana T-Centralen/bus 3, 47, 53, 59, 62, 65. **Open** 8am-8pm Mon-Fri; 9am-6pm Sat, Sun. **Map** p241 G6.
One of the larger Swedish bus companies, Swebus Express covers Sweden's major cities, along with Oslo and Copenhagen. Tickets can be purchased online and by phone up to 1hr before departure and at Cityterminalen until departure.

By car

Stockholm's highway links with Europe have been made easier thanks to the Öresund toll (300kr) bridge between Sweden and Denmark, which opened in 2000 and is crossed by more than 10,000 cars daily. It's 615km (382 miles) from Stockholm to Malmö; 475km (295 miles) to Göteborg. Driving in Sweden is relatively safe – Swedish roads are in great condition and there are no other tolls.

By sea

If you arrive in Stockholm by sea, you have most likely come from Finland or Estonia. These are the main companies operating ferries to and from Stockholm:

Birka Cruises

Södermalmstorg 2, Södermalm (702 72 30/www.birka.se). T-bana Slussen/bus 2, 3, 53, 76, 96. **Open** 8.30am-6pm Mon-Fri; 10am-2pm Sat, Sun. **Map** p241 K8.
Daily cruises in summer to Gotland, Finland, Tallinn, Riga and Poland. The boat terminal, Stadsgårdskajen, is right next to Slussen.

Silja Line

Kungsgatan 2, Norrmalm (440 59 90/www.tallinksilja.se). T-bana Östermalmstorg/bus 1, 2, 55, 56, 91. **Open** 9am-6pm Mon-Fri; 11am-3pm Sat. **Map** p241 F8.
Ferries to/from Finland. Boats dock at Värtahamnen just north-east of the city centre. The terminal has parking, luggage lockers, an ATM, a kiosk and a café. There are taxis at the terminal and Silja Line has its own bus connection to Cityterminalen

(single 25kr). Signs show you how to walk the 5-10mins to the nearest T-bana station, Gärdet (as well as from Gärdet to the terminal).

Tallink

Kungsgatan 2, Norrmalm (440 59 90/www.tallinksilja.se). T-bana Östermalmstorg/bus 1, 2, 55, 56, 91. **Open** 9am-6pm Mon-Fri; 11am-3pm Sat. **Map** p241 F8.
Ferries go to and from Estonia. Boats dock at the Frihamnen terminal, to the north-east of the city centre. It is served by taxis and has its own bus service between the terminal and Cityterminalen (single 25kr).

Viking Line

Cityterminalen, Klarabergsgatan, Norrmalm (452 40 00/452 40 75/www.vikingline.se). T-bana T-Centralen/bus 3, 47, 53, 59, 62, 65. **Open** 8am-7pm Mon-Sat; noon-7pm Sun. **Map** p241 G6.
Ferries go to/from Finland, and from Helsinki to Tallinn. Boats dock at Vikingterminalen on Södermalm. The terminal has parking and luggage lockers. There are taxis at the terminal but many prefer to walk the 10mins to Slussen. Viking Line also has its own bus link to Slussen and Cityterminalen (return 50kr).

Public transport

The **Tunnelbana** (abbreviated to **T-bana**) metro system is the quickest, cheapest and most convenient way of getting around the city. The efficient, comprehensive bus network operates around the clock and covers areas not reached by the metro or the commuter trains. Both the Tunnelbana and city buses are run by **Statens Lokaltrafik**, or **SL** (600 10 00/www.sl.se).

SL Center

Central Station, T-Centralen, Norrmalm. T-bana T-Centralen/bus 3, 47, 53, 59, 62, 65. **Open** 6.30am-11.15pm Mon-Sat; 7am-11.15pm Sun. **Map** p241 G7.
This information centre can answer any questions you might have about public transport. It is located on the floor below the main concourse at Central Station. You can pick up maps and timetables here. Another branch is at Sergels Torg.
Other locations Slussen, by Saltsjöbanan (open 7am-6pm Mon-Fri, 10am-5pm Sat); Fridhemsplan (open 7am-6.30pm Mon-Fri, 10am-5pm Sat); Tekniska Högskolan (open 7am-6.30pm Mon-Fri, 10am-5pm Sat).

Fares & tickets

Tickets can be purchased in the T-bana but not on the bus. Some bus stations have ticket machines. Single tickets cost 20kr-60kr depending on how far you're travelling, and are valid for 1hr from when the trip starts. It is cheaper to buy multi-ticket coupons or travel cards, available from Pressbyrån kiosks and SL Centers. Coupons are available in sets of 16 (160kr); ask for a *remsa*, Swedish for coupon strip. A 24hr pass with unlimited travel costs 90kr; a 72hr pass is 190kr. A 30-day unlimited travel pass is 620kr. There is also the **Stockholm Card**, which includes unlimited travel on public transport, admission to over 70 museums and sights, sightseeing by boat and more (for more details, *see p51*).

Tunnelbana

The three metro lines are identified by colour – red, green or blue – on maps and station signs. All three lines intersect at T-Centralen. At interchanges, lines are indicated by the names of the stations at the end of the line, so you should know in which direction you're heading when changing between lines. The T-bana runs from around 5am to midnight Mon-Thur, Sun; 5.30am-3am Fri, Sat.

Buses

Most bus routes operate from 5am to midnight daily. You board at the front, and get off through the middle or rear doors. Single tickets can be bought on board; get pre-paid tickets stamped by the driver. Travel passes should also be shown to the driver.

Night buses

Most night buses run from midnight until 5am, when the regular buses take over. The main stations are Slussen, T-Centralen, Odenplan, Fridhemsplan and Gullmarsplan.

Ferries

Many ferry companies operate on Stockholm's waterways. Some routes are used daily by people commuting to work, while others are designed for sightseeing or excursions into the archipelago. SL travel passes are not valid on the archipelago ferries.

Cinderella Båtarna

58 71 40 00/www.cinderellabatarna. com. **Credit** AmEx, DC, MC, V.
Ferries to Vaxholm, Grinda, Möja, Sandhamn and more. Boats depart from Nybrokajen on Strandvägen. Tickets can be purchased on board.

Djurgårdsfärjan
Year-round ferry service operated by Waxholmsbolaget (*see below*) within Stockholm harbour. It runs between Slussen and Djurgården (stopping at Allmänna Gränd, next to Gröna Lund), Skeppsholmen and Nybroplan. From May to August the ferry also stops at the Vasamuseet. Buy tickets in ticket booths before boarding; single 30kr. SL travel passes are valid.

Strömma Kanalbolaget
58 71 40 00/www.strommakanal bolaget.com. **Credit** MC, V.
Departs from Stadshusbron (next to Stadhuset) to Birka and Drottningholm, and from Strandvägen to Fjäderholmarna, Vaxholm and Sandhamn. Tickets can be purchased on the boat (cash only) or in the ticket booths next to the departure points.

Waxholmsbolaget
679 58 30/www.waxholmsbolaget.se. **Credit** MC, V.
Waxholmsbolaget ferries cover the whole archipelago, from Arholma in the north to Landsort in the south. Boats depart from Strömkajen outside the Grand Hôtel, opposite the Royal Palace. Tickets can be purchased on the boat. The useful website (in English) includes timetables that you can download.

Local trains
For trips into the suburbs and surrounding towns, there are commuter trains run by SL. The same tickets may be used on these trains as on the T-bana. The main commuter train station is Central Station, and will take you to as far north as Bålsta and Kungsängen and as far south as Södertälje, Nynäshamn and Gnesta.

Maps
Stockholm street maps are included at the back of this guide, starting on *p238*; there's also a Tunnelbana map on *p256*. The tourist office has good free street maps, which mark museums and sights; a free map is also available from the round information kiosk on the concourse of Central Station. Bus and Tunnelbana timetables (with maps at the back) can be picked up for free at **SL Centers** (*see p217*) and ticket booths.

Taxis
Taxis are easy to find in Stockholm. They can be ordered by phone, online or hailed on the street, and there are taxi ranks near railway and bus stations. Taxi services offered in private, unmarked cars are illegal in Sweden and should be avoided. Fares (starting at around 30kr) are quite steep; current rates and supplements should be displayed inside each cab.

Taxi companies
The firms listed below take bookings 24hrs a day.
Flygtaxi (airport taxis) 020 97 97 97/www.flygtaxi.se
Taxi Kurir 30 00 00/www.taxikurir.se
Taxi Stockholm 15 00 00/www.taxistockholm.se
Top Cab 33 33 33/www.topcab.com

Driving
Driving in Stockholm can be a hassle. There's a lot of traffic, free parking is difficult to find and fuel is expensive. A car is rarely a time-efficient form of transport in town, and it's only out in the country that it becomes an asset. It is wise to familiarise yourself with the do's and don'ts of Swedish road travel; visit the Swedish road administration (www.vag verket.se) for the lowdown on Swedish driving laws.

Breakdown services
If your car breaks down, look up *Bilreparationer* in the Yellow Pages. If it's a rental car, contact the rental firm directly.

Motormännens Riksförbund
Breakdowns 020 21 11 11. **Open** 9am-4pm Mon-Fri. **Office** *Sveavägen 159, Norrmalm (690 38 00/www.motormannen.se). Bus 2, 40, 52, 515, 595.* **Open** 8.30am-5pm Mon-Fri. **Map** p245 B5.
The Swedish equivalent of the British AA, with reciprocal arrangements with most European motoring organisations. Call the toll-free number if you have a problem.

Parking
Parking is not easy in the city centre. If you have parked illegally or not paid the right fee, you'll get a hefty fine from parking attendants or the police. *Parkering Förbjuden* means 'parking prohibited', and it's illegal to park closer than ten metres (33 feet) from a pedestrian crossing. Car parks (*parkering*), indicated by a white 'P' on a blue sign, charge 20kr-50kr per hour.

Vehicle rental
You have to be 25 years of age to rent a car in Sweden, and you will need a credit card.

Avis
Vasagatan 8, Norrmalm (20 20 60/ 020 78 82 00/www.avis.se). T-bana T-Centralen/bus 3, 47, 53, 59, 62, 65. **Open** 6am-9pm Mon-Fri; 9am-4pm Sat, Sun. **Credit** AmEx, DC, MC, V. **Map** p241 G6.
Other locations Ringvägen 90, Södermalm (644 99 80); Arlanda Airport (797 99 70); Bromma Airport (28 87 00).

Europcar
Vasaplan 1, Norrmalm (53 48 03 80/020 78 11 80/www.europcar.se). T-bana T-Centralen/bus 3, 47, 53, 59, 62, 65. **Open** 6.30am-7pm Mon-Fri; 10am-4pm Sat; noon-6pm Sun. **Credit** AmEx, DC, MC, V. **Map** p241 H6.
Other locations Fiskartorpsvägen 20, Östermalm (20 44 63); Arlanda Airport (55 59 84 00); Bromma Airport (80 08 07).

Hertz
Vasagatan 26, Norrmalm (454 62 50/020 21 12 11/www.hertz.se). T-bana T-Centralen/bus 3, 47, 53, 59, 62, 65. **Open** 7am-6pm Mon-Fri; 9am-3pm Sat, Sun. **Credit** AmEx, DC, MC, V. **Map** p241 G6.
Other locations Arlanda Airport (797 99 00); Bromma Airport (797 99 14).

Cycling
Stockholm is very bike-friendly. For good places to cycle and bike rental places, *see pp189-190*.

Walking
Stockholm is a compact city, and walking is often the best way to get around. For details of walking tours, *see p50*.

Directory

Resources A-Z

Addresses

In Sweden, addresses are written with the building number after the street name. Also, as in the UK, but not the US, the first floor is the floor above street level. The floor at street level is *bottenvåning*, often abbreviated to 'BV'.

Age restrictions

The legal drinking age is 18, but you must be 20 years old to buy alcohol at the state-owned monopolistic off-licence Systembolaget.

You can smoke and drive at 18. At 15 teens become *byxmyndig*, which, loosely translated, means they are 'in charge of their pants'. In other words, they can legally have sex.

Business services

Stockholm is a great city for doing business, but remember that most businesses are closed for July. Many hotels cater mainly to business travellers (hence higher rates Sunday to Friday) and many venues can be hired for conferences and meetings.

Conventions & conferences

There is one main trade fair/conference centre just on the edge of Stockholm: **Stockholmsmässan**, Mässvägen 1, Älvsjö (749 41 00/www.stofair.se).The website www.fairlink.se provides plenty of useful information.

Many bureaux can help with events in the city – look under *Konferensarrangörer* (conference organisers) or *Konferenslokaler* (conference venues) in the Yellow Pages.

Amica (02 01 12 22 22/www.amica.se) organises conferences of any size, while **Svenska Möten** (07 71 50 55 00/www.konferensportalen.se) has 100 conference locations.

Couriers

Look in the Yellow Pages under *Budservice* for a list of couriers. Prices vary but to have a small package delivered on the same day within Stockholm costs around 200kr with the following companies:

DHL

54 34 50 00/toll-free customer service 07 71 34 53 45/www.dhl.se. **Open** 24hrs daily. **Credit** AmEx, DC, MC, V.

TNT

625 58 00/toll-free 020 96 09 60/www.tnt.com. **Open** 8am-6pm Mon-Fri. **Credit** AmEx, MC, V.

UPS

Toll free 020 120 22 55/020 78 87 99/www.ups.com. **Open** 8am-7pm Mon-Fri; 9am-1pm Sat. **Credit** AmEx, MC, V.

Office & computer services

Årsta Park Kontorshotell

Byängsgränd 14, Årsta (651 86 00/www.arstaparkkontorshotell.se). T-bana Enskede Gård. **Open** 8.30am-4.30pm Mon-Fri.
Offices available at reasonable rents in the city.

Megabyte System Svenska

Drottninggatan 94, Norrmalm (55 51 11 11/www.megabyte.se). T-bana Hötorget/bus 1, 47, 52, 53, 69. **Open** 10am-6pm Mon-Fri. **Credit** AmEx, MC, V. **Map** p245 E6.
Computer software, components and servicing.

Translation services

Semantix

Stureplan 4A (50 62 25 50/www.semantix.se). T-bana Östermalmstorg/bus 1, 2, 55, 56. **Open** 8am-5pm Mon-Fri. **No credit cards** (bank transfers only). **Map** p241 E5.
A language services provider.

Useful organisations

Ministry of Foreign Affairs

405 10 00/www.utrikes.regeringen.se.

National Tax Board

0771 56 75 67/www.skatteverket.se.

Stockholm Migration Board

011 15 60 00/www.migrationsverket.se
Handles all issues related to immigration, including work visas.

Sveriges Riksbank

787 00 00/www.riksbank.com.
Economic and financial data.

Swedish Stock Exchange

405 60 00/www.stockholmsborsen.se.

Customs

You must be at least 18 years old to bring in tobacco products, and 20 to bring in alcohol. Visitors from the EU can bring in alcohol and tobacco for private use without incurring customs duty. Check **Swedish Customs** website www.tullverket.se for details of the cut-off points between private and commercial use.

Disabled visitors

It is not usually a problem for disabled visitors to get around Stockholm; facilities were always good compared to much of Europe, and recent legislation means that all public buildings must be accessible to the disabled and visually impaired.

The streets are in good condition and have wide pavements, and kerbs have ramps for wheelchairs. Wheelchair-adapted toilets are common, and many hotels even have allergy-free rooms.

The public transport system is quite wheelchair-accessible, especially the Tunnelbana, which has plenty of elevators, and most buses can 'kneel' at bus stops – although wide gaps between trains and platforms remain a common complaint.

Travel advice

For current information on travel to a specific country – including the latest news on health issues, safety and security, local laws and customs – contact your home country's government department of foreign affairs. Most have websites with useful advice for would-be travellers.

Australia
www.smartraveller.gov.au

Canada
www.voyage.gc.ca

New Zealand
www.safetravel.govt.nz

Republic of Ireland
http://foreignaffairs.gov.ie

UK
www.fco.gov.uk/travel

USA
http://travel.state.gov

Most taxis are large enough to take wheelchairs, but check before you order a cab. Try **Taxi Stockholm** (15 00 00).

De Handikappades Riksförbund

Katrinebergsvägen 6, Liljeholmen (685 80 00/www.dhr.se). T-bana Liljeholmen/bus 77, 133, 143, 152. **Open** *Aug-June* 8.30am-noon, 1-4pm Mon-Fri. Closed July. **Map** p249 M2.
Supplies information on facilities for the mobility-impaired. The website has an English version with tips about accessible hotels, restaurants, cinemas, museums and theatres.

Drugs

Drugs, including cannabis, are nowhere near as widely accepted in Sweden as in some parts of Europe. Possession of any controlled drug, including medicine for which you do not have a prescription, is illegal and you can be heavily fined for the very smallest amounts.

Electricity

Sweden, along with most of Europe, has 220-volt AC, 50Hz current and uses two-pin continental plugs. The 220V current works fine with British-bought 240V products with a simple plug adaptor (available at airports or department stores). With US 110V equipment you will need to use a current transformer.

Embassies & consulates

Many foreign embassies are clustered in Diplomatstaden, near Ladugårdsgärdet. A full list of embassies can be found in the phone book under *Ambassader*, and embassy locations are on the tourist office website (www.stockholm town.com). There is no New Zealand consulate or embassy in Stockholm: a representative in the Hague (+ 31 703 658 037) oversees Sweden.

Australian Embassy

Sergels Torg 12, Norrmalm (613 29 00/www.sweden.embassy.gov.se). T-bana T-Centralen/bus 47, 52, 56, 59, 65. **Open** 8.30am-12.30pm, 1.30-4.30pm Mon-Fri. **Map** p241 G7.

British Embassy

Skarpögatan 6-8, Östermalm (671 90 00/www.britishembassy.com). Bus 69. **Open** *Visas* 9.30am-noon Mon-Fri. *Consulate and information* 9.30am-noon, 2-4pm Mon-Fri. **Map** p243 F12.

Canadian Embassy

Tegelbacken 4, Norrmalm (453 30 00/www.canadaemb.se). T-bana T-Centralen/bus 3, 53, 59, 62, 65. **Open** 8.30am-noon, 1-5pm Mon-Fri. **Map** p241 H6.

Irish Embassy

Östermalmsgatan 97, Östermalm (661 80 05/irish.embassy@ swipnet.se). T-bana Karlaplan/bus 4, 42, 44, 72. **Open** 10am-noon, 2.30-4pm Mon-Fri. **Map** p246 E10.

Emergencies

To contact the police, ambulance or fire service in an emergency call **112** (free of charge, including from public pay phones). For emergency rooms at hospitals, *see p221* **Accident & emergency**. For central police stations, *see p224* **Police & security**.

Gay & lesbian

Organisations

Gaystudenterna

Universitetet, Nobelhuset, Frescati (674 62 31/16 55 03/www.sus. su.se/gaystudenterna). T-bana Universitetet.
This group of gay activist students (non-students also welcome) works for gay awareness in education.

RFSL

Sveavägen 59, Vasastaden (50 16 29 00/www.rfsl.se). T-bana Rådmansgatan/bus 43, 52. **Open** *Phone enquiries* 10am-3.30pm Mon-Fri. **Map** p245 D6.
The National Association for Sexual Equality, Sweden's gay, lesbian and trans rights group has its main office here.

Healthcare

For an HIV-positive support group, *see p221* **AIDS/HIV**.

Lesbisk Hälsomottagning

Södersjukhuset, Ringvägen 52, Södermalm (616 11 44). Bus 3, 4, 55, 74. **Open** *Phone enquiries* 10-11am Tue; 3-4pm Thur. **Map** p250 N6.
Free gynaecological healthcare for lesbians only. Call ahead to book an appointment.

Venhälsan

Södersjukhuset, Ringvägen 52, Södermalm (616 25 00/www.hiv.nu). Bus 3, 4, 55, 74. **Open** 5-8.30pm Tue, Thur. **Map** p250 N6.
Free healthcare for both bi- and homosexual men. Located on the fifth floor; take elevator D.

Health

For advice on minor illnesses or prescription drugs, call the 24-hour **Healthcare Information Service** (32 01 00/www.vardguiden.se); stay on the line when the automatic answering service kicks in and you will be connected to a nurse.

For advice related to prescription medicine call the **Läkemedelsupplysningen** (medicine information office) toll-free on 020 66 77 66, and press 2. It is open 24 hours daily and staff speak English.

Accident & emergency

The following hospitals have 24-hour emergency rooms:

St Görans Sjukhus
Sanktgöransplan 1, Kungsholmen (58 70 10 00). T-bana Fridhemsplan/bus 57, 59, 74.

Södersjukhuset
Ringvägen 52, Södermalm (616 10 00). Bus 3, 4, 55, 74. **Map** p250 N6.

AIDS/HIV

The **AIDS Helpline** (020 78 44 40) can direct you to the closest hospital for tests, treatment and information.

Noaks Ark
Eriksbergsgatan 46, Östermalm (700 46 00/www.noaksark.redcross.se). T-bana Östermalmstorg/bus 1, 2, 55, 56. **Open** *June-Sept* 9am-4pm Mon-Fri. *Oct-May* 9am-5pm Mon-Fri. **Map** p245 F6.
The Red Cross's HIV and AIDS organisation.

Posithiva Gruppen
Tjurbergsgatan 29, Södermalm (720 19 60/www.posithivagruppen.se). T-bana Skanstull. Bus 3, 4, 43, 55, 74. **Open** 6pm-midnight Wed; 7pm-midnight Fri, Sat.
Support group for HIV-positive bi- and homosexual men.

Alternative medicine

Alternative medicine, especially massage, is very common in Sweden. The use of other complementary treatments is also rapidly increasing in popularity.

AAA Kliniken Norr
Surbrunnsgatan 61, Vasastaden (31 21 00). T-bana Odenplan/bus 2, 4, 40, 42, 53, 72. **Open** Phone enquiries 8am-8pm Mon-Fri. **No credit cards. Map** p245 D5.
A clinic offering acupuncture, massage and chiropractic treatments. Appointments required in advance. **Other locations** AAA Kliniken Söder, Götgatan 101, Södermalm (640 27 50).

Family planning

You can buy condoms in grocery stores, pharmacies, 7-Elevens and in vending machines at some bars and clubs. You'll need a prescription to get the Pill, though. Abortions are legal until week 18; after that there must be a serious medical reason – non-residents may have difficulty getting abortions at any time.

Mama Mia
Karlavägen 58-60, Östermalm (50 64 90 00/www.mamamia.se). T-bana Stadion/bus 42, 44, 55, 56, 62. **Open** *Phone hours* 8am-5pm Mon-Thur; 8am-3pm Fri. **Map** p246 E9.
Family planning and postnatal care. Call in advance for an appointment. **Other locations:** Götgatan 83E, Södermalm (55 69 37 70).
Phone hours 8am-4pm Mon-Thur; 8am-noon Fri.

Dentists

Dentists can be found in the Yellow Pages under *Tandläkare*. No appointment is needed for emergency dental care. Try the **Emergency Dental Clinic** at St Eriks Sjukhus, Polhelmsgatan 46, Kungsholmen (54 55 12 20/28), open 7.45am-8.30pm daily. Rates vary, but start at 490kr; if you arrive after 7pm, prices increase by 50 per cent. No appointment needed.

Afta Akuttandvård
Sergels Torg 12, Norrmalm (20 20 25). T-bana T-Centralen/bus 47, 52, 56, 59, 65. **Open** *Drop-in patients* 8am-6pm Mon-Fri; 9am-3pm Sat, Sun. **Map** p241 G7.

Akut tandvården i Stockholm
Kungsgatan 29, Norrmalm (10 92 93). T-bana Hötorget/bus 1, 43, 52, 56. **Open** 8am-5pm Mon-Thur. **Map** p241 F7.

Doctors

Call beforehand to set up an appointment with these general practitioners.

Dr Akut
Strandvägen 7B, Östermalm (660 73 44/www.doktorakut.se). T-bana Östermalmstorg/bus 47, 62, 69, 76. **Open** 7am-7pm Mon-Fri.

Husläkarjouren
Sabbatsbergs Sjukhus, Olivecronas Väg 2, Vasastaden (672 39 90). T-bana Odenplan/bus 4, 40, 47, 53, 72. **Open** *Phone enquiries* 4.30-10pm Mon-Fri; 8am-8pm Sat, Sun. **Map** p244 E4.
Overnight GP. Call first to make an appointment.

Sturehälsan
Birger Jarlsgatan 43, Östermalm (20 37 00/www.sturehalsan.se). T-bana Rådmansgatan/bus 2, 42, 43, 44. **Open** *Oct-June* 9am-5pm Mon, Wed, Fri; 9am-7.30pm Tue, Thur; 11am-3pm Sat. *July-Sep* 9am-5pm Mon, Wed-Fri; 9am-7.30pm Tue.

Insurance

EU nationals should obtain a European Health Insurance Card, which facilitates free medical care under the Swedish national health service. Visitors of other nationalities should arrange insurance prior to their trip.

Opticians

For details of Sweden's main chain of opticians, *see p152.*

Pharmacies

Pharmacies (*apotek*), identified by a green and white J-shaped sign, can be found all over the city. Most are open 10am-6pm Mon-Fri, and closed at the weekend. For details of two pharmacies with extended opening hours, *see p152.*

Helplines

Alcoholics Anonymous
720 38 42. **Open** 11am-1pm, 6-8pm daily.

Children's Helpline (BRIS)
0200 23 02 30. **Open** 24hrs daily.

Narcotics Anonymous
Helpline 411 44 18/toll free 0771 13 80 00/answering service with information in English 411 44 18 (press 2 for English).

Poison & Medications Hotline
33 12 31. **Open** 24hrs daily.

ID

Swedes have national identity cards, but most people use their driving licence as ID. It is a good idea to carry some form of identification when you go to bars and clubs if you're under 25 or look like you could be. Also, ID will be needed if you want to pay the lower price sometimes offered at museums for people under 25 or over 65.

Internet

Stockholm is a world-leader in e-commerce, new media and software development, and has the highest internet use per capita in the world. For useful websites, see p230. If you're staying for a long time and your business hasn't set you up with internet access, try the main phone company **Telia** (90 200/www.telia.com).

Internet cafés

There are quite a few cybercafés in the city centre. You can also surf the net at libraries (free of charge), and many hotels, hostels, 7-Elevens, newspaper kiosks and grocery stores. **Sidewalk Express** (www.sidewalk express.se) has computer terminals offering access around the city, including Cityterminalen; they all cost 19kr per hour.

Café Access
Basement, Kulturhuset, Sergels Torg, Norrmalm (20 52 10/www. kulturhuset.stockholm.se). T-bana T-Centralen/bus 47, 52, 59, 65. **Open** 11am-7pm Mon; 10am-7pm Tue-Fri; 10am-5pm Sat; 11am-5pm Sun. Closed Sun in July, Aug. **No credit cards. Map** p241 G7.

Internet Café
3rd floor, PUB, Hötorget 13-15, Norrmalm (24 57 59). T-bana Hötorget/bus 1, 52, 56. **Open** 10am-7pm Mon-Fri; 10am-5pm Sat; noon-5pm Sun. **No credit cards. Map** p241 F6.

M@trix
Hötorget T-Bana station, Norrmalm (20 02 93/www.matrix-se.com). T-Bana Hötorget/bus 1, 43, 52, 56. **Open** 10am-midnight Mon-Thur, Sun; 10am-3am Fri, Sat. **Credit** AmEx, DC, MC, V. **Map** p241 F7.

Left luggage

There are left-luggage lockers available in Arlanda Airport, and also at the bus, train and ferry terminals.

Arlanda Airport
See p216. Lockers **Rates** 20kr-30kr per 24hrs. *Manual left luggage storage* **Open** 6am-10pm Mon-Fri; 6am-6pm Sat, Sun. **Rates** 280kr per wk for a suitcase.

Central Station
See p216. **Open** 5am-12.30am. **Rates** 25kr-35kr per 24hrs.

Silja Line Terminal
See p217. **Open** 8am-8.15pm daily.

Viking Line Terminal
See p217. **Open** 6.15am-8.15pm daily.
Lockers can be used for a maximum of 24hrs.

Legal help

Information about legal help can be obtained from the police, trade unions or legal advisers. Lawyers' offices are found in the Yellow Pages under *Advokater*. They are not obliged to help you but most will at least make recommendations.

Libraries

Stockholm's libraries are open to anyone for reference, but if you want to take a book out, you will need ID and an address in Sweden (a hotel address will not do).

Kungliga Biblioteket
Humlegården, Östermalm (463 40 00/www.kb.se). T-bana Östermalmstorg/bus 2, 42, 44, 55, 56. **Open** 9am-8pm Mon-Thur; 9am-7pm Fri; 10am-5pm Sat. The library closes 2hrs earlier mid June-mid Aug. **Map** p246 E8.
Mainly oriented towards research.

Stockholms Stadsbiblioteket
Sveavägen 73, Vasastaden (50 83 11 00/www.ssb.stockholm.se). T-bana Odenplan/bus 2, 4, 40, 42, 52, 53, 69, 72. **Open** 9am-9pm Mon-Thur; 9am-7pm Fri; noon-4pm Sat, Sun. Check the website for updated summer times. **Map** p245 D5.

Known mostly for its its architecture, but has books in many languages.

Utrikespolitiska Biblioteket
Lilla Nygatan 23, Gamla Stan (696 05 27/www.ui.se). T-bana Gamla Stan/bus 3, 53. **Open** 9am-5pm Mon-Fri. **Map** p241 J7.
Specialises in international politics.

Lost property

Both of Stockholm's two main public transport companies have lost-and-found centres.

SL
Klara Östra Kyrkogata 4, Norrmalm (610 00 00). T-bana T-Centralen/bus 3, 47, 53, 59, 62, 65. **Open** noon-7pm Mon-Fri; noon-4pm Sat. **Map** p241 G6.
For objects lost on the Tunnelbana, city buses and commuter trains.

SJ
Central Station, Vasagatan, Norrmalm (07 71 60 60 00/762 25 02). T-bana T-Centralen/bus 3, 47, 53, 59, 62, 65. **Open** 9am-6pm Mon-Fri. **Map** p241 G6.
Lost and found for long-distance trains.

Media

International newsstands

Copies of most of the major foreign newspapers and magazines, especially English-language ones, can be found in the city.

NK Press
NK department store, Hamngatan 18-20, Norrmalm (762 87 80). T-bana Kungsträdgården or Östermalmstorg/bus 43, 47, 55, 59, 69. **Open** 10am-7pm Mon-Fri; 10am-5pm Sat; noon-5pm Sun (June, July noon-4pm Sun). **Credit** AmEx, DC, MC, V. **Map** p241 F7.

Press Stop
Götgatan 31, Södermalm (644 35 10/www.press-stop.se). T-bana Medborgarplatsen or Slussen/bus 43, 55, 59, 66. **Open** 10am-7pm Mon-Fri; 10am-5pm Sat; noon-5pm Sun. **Credit** AmEx, MC, V. **Map** p250 L8.
This branch of Press Stop sells magazines specialising in art, architecture and design.
Other locations Gallerian, Hamngatan 37, Norrmalm (723 01 91); Västermalmsgallerian, St Eriksgatan 45, Kungsholmen (21 91 13).

Magazines

For the latest in lifestyle trends and fashion, buy the English-language glossy **Stockholm New** (www.stockholmnew.com) or the new English-language version of trendy art and fashion magazine **Bon** (www.bonmagazine.com). For insight into Scandinavian culture, buy the quarterly **Nordic Reach** (subscribe online at www.nordic reach.com). House-proud Swedes choose from several magazines on interior design, of which **Sköna Hem**, **Elle Interiör** and **Lantliv** are very popular. **Cosmopolitan** arrived on the scene a few years ago but **Amelia**, **Damernas Värld** and **Vecko-Revyn** are the main contenders for female readership. Men's magazines **Café** and **Slitz** focus on music, fashion and celebrity interviews. **Sonic** and **Groove** have the lowdown on the music scene, and **ETC** offers left-wing political criticism. **Situation Sthlm**, about the city's street life and politics, is typically sold in T-bana stations by homeless people.

Architecture and design magazines include **Forum**, **Arkitektur** and **FORM**. Sweden's biggest art magazine is glossy **Konstperspektiv** (www.konstperspektiv.nu), while the magazine **Paletten** (www.natverk stan.net/paletten) takes a theoretical approach to contemporary art.

Newspapers

The two main daily papers are **Dagens Nyheter** (738 10 00, www.dn.se), and the right-leaning **Svenska Dagbladet** (13 50 00, www.svd.se). On public transport, you're likely to see people reading **Metro** (402 20 30, www.metro.se/metro), **Stockholm City** (50 65 63 98, www.stockholmcity.se) or **Punkt SE** (725 20 00,www.aftonbladet.se) which are free daily papers distributed at T-bana stations. **Aftonbladet** (725 20 00, www.aftonbladet.se) and **Expressen** (738 30 00, www.expressen.se) are popular evening tabloids with the latest scandals and gossip, as well as weekly TV guides.

On Fridays Aftonbladet publishes **Klick** and Expressen publishes **Fredag**, which are weekly entertainment listings; DN's equivalent is **På Stan** (On the Town). DN's På Stan website has an excellent search engine and calendar.

The monthly publication **Nöjesguiden** (www.nojesguiden. se) features stories about the Stockholm scene and events listings.

It's available free from shops, cafés and newsstands.

For Swedish news in English, **SR Radio Sweden International** lists brief summaries on its website (www.sr.se/rs/red/ind_eng.html). Alternatively, there is **The Local** (www.thelocal.se), which provides a round-up of Swedish-related news in English.

Radio

E-FM
107.5 MHz
Soul and dance classics from the 1970s and '80s.

NRJ
105.1 MHz
The latest hits.

Radio Sweden
89.6 MHz
Check the schedule (www.sr.se/rs) for English programming, generally including sport and political topics.

Sveriges Radio P2
93.8/96.2 MHz
Classical, jazz and opera.

Television

The state channels of **SVT 1** and **SVT 2** were the first to broadcast in Sweden and still earn the highest ratings. Their commercial-free programmes are varied enough to appeal to all ages.

Deregulation during the mid 1980s ended the state's television broadcasting monopoly and allowed for the creation of several private channels. The most successful of these is the terrestrial **TV4**, with news, soap operas, sitcoms and game shows. Similar programming can be found on **TV3** and **Kanal 5**, both of which are broadcast from abroad and – much to the chagrin of the government – do not always adhere to the Swedish broadcasting regulations.

Hip youths with carefully dishevelled hair present the entertainment programming at popular **ZTV**.

Foreign-made programmes and films are shown in their original language with Swedish subtitles.

Money

The Swedish krona (plural kronor, abbreviated to kr or SEK) is divided into 100 öre. It comes in coins of 50 öre, 1kr, 5kr and 10kr, and notes of 20kr, 50kr, 100kr, 500kr and 1,000kr. At the time of going to press: £1 = 13.6kr, $1 (US) = 6.8kr, €1 = 9.2kr.

In 2003 Sweden voted against joining the European Monetary Union (EMU). However, euros are accepted in many shops, restaurants and hotels, at least in areas popular with tourists.

ATMs/cash machines

There are two types of ATM: **Bankomat** (the joint system of the business banks) and **Uttag** (which belongs to Swedbank). Don't forget that banks tend to charge commission. You'll find ATMs all over the city, in department stores, shopping centres and at banks.

Average climate

Month	Max temp	Min temp	Rainfall
Jan	0°C/32°F	-5°C/22°F	39mm/1.5in
Feb	0°C/32°F	-5°C/22°F	27mm/1.1in
Mar	3°C/38°F	-3°C/26°F	26mm/1in
Apr	8°C/48°F	1°C/33°F	30mm/1.2in
May	15°C/59°F	6°C/44°F	30mm/1.2in
June	21°C/70°F	11°C/52°F	45mm/1.8in
July	22°C/71°F	13°C/56°F	72mm/2.8in
Aug	20°C/68°F	13°C/56°F	66mm/2.6in
Sept	15°C/59°F	9°C/50°F	55mm/2.2in
Oct	10°C/50°F	5°C/43°F	50mm/2in
Nov	4°C/40°F	0°C/32°F	53mm/2.1in
Dec	1°C/33°F	-3°C/26°F	46mm/1.8in

Directory

Banks & bureaux de change

You can change money in the city at banks, many hotels and specialist bureaux de change, such as **Forex** and **X-change**; the latter tend to be best because they often provide a more favourable exchange rate and have numerous offices in the city centre. There are exchange offices in the tourist office, Central Station and at Arlanda Airport (Terminals 2 and 5).

Banks are usually open 9am-3pm Mon-Fri, and some stay open until 6pm at least once a week. All banks are closed at weekends and on public holidays, as well as the day before a public holiday.

Forex

NK, Hamngatan 18-20, Norrmalm (762 83 40/www.forex.se). T-bana Kungsträdgården/bus 47, 55, 59, 62, 76. **Open** 10am-7pm Mon-Fri; 10am-5pm Sat; noon-4pm Sun. **Map** p241 G7.
Other locations Kungsgatan 2, Östermalm (611 51 10); Central Station, Norrmalm (411 67 34); Cityterminalen, Norrmalm (21 42 80); Vasagatan 14, Norrmalm (10 49 90); Arlanda Airport, Terminal 2, Terminal 5 and Sky City (59 36 22 71).

X-change

Kungsgatan 30, Norrmalm (50 61 07 00/www.x-change.se). T-bana Hötorget/bus 1, 52, 56. **Open** 8am-7pm Mon-Fri; 9am-4pm Sat. **Map** p241 F7.
Other locations PUB, Hötorget 13-15, Norrmalm (10 30 00); Arlanda Airport, 3 locations in Terminal 5 (797 85 57); Central Stationen, Norrmalm (54 52 30 30).

Credit cards

Major credit and debit cards are widely accepted. If you pay by credit card in a shop, you may be asked for photo ID. Banks will advance cash against a credit card, but prefer you to use an ATM.

For lost or stolen credit cards, phone one of the following 24-hour numbers:
American Express 429 56 00/ 429 54 29.
Diners Club 14 68 78.
MasterCard 020 79 13 24.
Visa 020 79 31 46.

Money transfers

Local banks don't do money transfers unless you are a customer of the bank. **Forex** (see above; fee from US$20) and **Western Union** are your best bets for money transfers to and from Sweden, and have branches all over Stockholm.

Western Union

020 74 17 42, press 9 for English/www.westernunion.com. **Open** 8am-8pm Mon-Fri; 8am-5pm Sat; 10am-4pm Sun.
Call the toll-free number to find your nearest branch.

Tax

The sales tax for most commodities is 25 per cent. There is a 12 per cent sales tax on food and hotel bills, and six per cent sales tax on books, movie and concert tickets and transport (taxis, flights, trains). The sales tax is always listed separately on the bill but is included in the displayed price.

Non-EU residents can reclaim tax on purchases above 200kr in shops displaying a 'Tax-Free Shopping' sticker. All you have to do is ask for a tax-free receipt when paying for an item. When you leave the EU, show your purchases, receipts and passport to customs officials and have your Global Refund cheques stamped. The refund can be collected from any Global Refund office or credited to your own bank account. Call **Global Refund** (020 74 17 41, 54 52 84 40, www.global refund.com).

Travellers' cheques

Travellers' cheques are accepted as payment in the more touristy areas, but do not expect to be able to use them in smaller shops or restaurants. All major travellers' cheques are accepted these days, except for Eurocheques.

Opening hours

Normal opening hours for shops are 10am-6pm Mon-Fri; 10am-5pm Sat; noon-4pm Sun. Some smaller shops close earlier on Saturdays and do not open on Sundays. All shops used to be closed on public holidays, but this is changing more and more. Many grocery stores are now open 365 days per year.

Restaurant opening hours vary greatly. They are usually open by 11am if they serve lunch; otherwise they'll open some time in the afternoon (usually 4 or 5pm). Closing time is around midnight unless the restaurant has a bar, in which case they may stay open until 1am or even later. Note that many restaurants close in July.

Office hours are generally 8.30am-5pm Mon-Fri. For bank opening hours, see left **Banks & bureaux de change**. For post office opening hours, see below **Postal services**.

Police & security

The police are not that common a sight in Stockholm, but can always be spotted at concerts or any special events. They speak English and are friendly and helpful. If you are the victim of a crime, call the police on 112. But Stockholm is considered a very safe city, so the chance of that happening is small. Still, it's wise to take the usual city precautions: don't openly flaunt money or jewellery, keep a close eye on your surroundings and be careful in dark areas late at night.

Pickpocketing does occur in crowded places. Muggings are rare and there are no particular areas considered dangerous, but it's best not to walk in dimly lit areas such as parks at night (an increasing number of muggings have taken place in Humlegården, Berzelii Park and Kungsträdgården).

Police HQ

Kungsholmsgatan 43, Kungsholmen (401 01 00). T-bana Rådhuset/bus 3, 40, 52, 62. **Map** p240 G4.
This is the main police station (also the place where people suspected of committing a crime are kept until the trial). Sub-station Torkel is at Knutssonsgatan 20, Södermalm (401 13 00).

Postal services

Most post offices are open 10am-6pm Mon-Fri, 10am-2pm Sat; they have a yellow sign containing a blue crown and horn symbol. You can also buy stamps at tobacco kiosks, 7-Elevens, and the tourist office *(see p226)*.

Posten
Central Station, Vasagatan, Norrmalm (020 23 22 21/www. posten.se). T-bana T-Centralen/bus 3, 47, 53, 59, 62, 65. **Open** 7am-10pm Mon-Fri; 9am-6pm Sat, Sun. **Map** p241 G6.
This handy post office inside Central Station has long opening hours.

Poste Restante

Letters sent Poste Restante can be sent to any post office and there is no extra charge. Items will be kept for a month, and you'll need some form of ID to collect. For the nearest post office (*Postkontor*) to you, look under *Posten* in the Yellow Pages or www.posten.se.

Religion

Most Swedes are nominally members of the Church of Sweden, which is Evangelical Lutheran, but less than ten per cent of the population attends church regularly. Many other Christian sects are represented in Stockholm, and around 50,000 Muslims and 10,000 Jews live in or near the city.

The service and opening times listed below often change in summer, so call ahead to double-check.

Immanuelskyrkan (Evangelical)
Kungstensgatan 17, Vasastaden (58 75 03 31). T-bana Rådmansgatan/ bus 42, 43, 46, 52. **Services** *English* 11am Sun. **Map** p245 D6.

Katolska Kyrkan (Catholic)
Folkungagatan 46B, Södermalm (640 15 55). T-bana Medborgarplatsen/bus 59, 66. **Open** *Winter* 7.30am-6pm daily. *Summer* 7.30am-noon, 2-6pm daily. **Services** 5pm, 8pm Mon-Fri; 9am, 5pm Sat; 10am, 11am Sun. **Map** p250 M8.

St Jacob (Ecumenical Church of Stockholm)
Västra Trädgårdsgatan 2, Norrmalm (723 30 00). T-bana Kungsträdgården/bus 46, 55, 59, 62, 76. **Open** 24hrs daily. **Services** *English* 6pm Sun. **Map** p241 G7.

Stockholmsmoskén (Muslim)
Kapellgränd, Södermalm (50 91 09 00). T-bana Medborgarplatsen/bus 59, 66. **Open** 10am-6pm daily. **Map** p251 L8.
Stockholm's only mosque, on Söder; *see also p83.*

Stora Synagogan (Jewish)
Wahrendorffsgatan 3, Norrmalm (58 78 58 00). T-bana Kungsträdgården/bus 46, 55, 59, 62, 76. **Tours** 10am, noon, 2pm Mon-Fri, Sun. **Services** 9am-midnight Sat (bring a passport in order to be let in). **Map** p241 G8.
The Great Synagogue is conservative/liberal.

Storkyrkan (Protestant)
Trångsgrund 1, Gamla Stan (723 30 16). T-bana Gamla Stan/bus 43, 46, 55, 59, 76. **Services** 11am Sat, Sun. **Map** p241 J8.
Stockholm's 700-year-old cathedral; *see also p59.*

Smoking

Sweden passed a law on 1 June 2005 that banned smoking in all public places where food or drink is served.

You can't smoke in most other public places either, including bus stop cubicles and all Tunnelbana stations.

Study

Many students come from abroad to study in Sweden. To find schools, look up *Utbildning* in the Yellow Pages.

Universities & colleges

Berghs School of Communication
PO Box 1380, 111 93 Stockholm (58 75 50 00/www.berghs.se).
Offers programmes in journalism, media, advertising and PR.

Handelshögskolan
PO Box 6501, 113 83 Stockholm (736 90 00/www.hhs.se).
Stockholm's School of Economics, the city's main business school, was founded in 1909. The school has an exchange programme with 155 places each year.

Konstfack
Visiting address: LM Erikssonsväg 14, Hägersten.
Postal address: PO Box 3601, 126 27 Stockholm (450 41 00/www.konstfack.se).
The University College of Arts, Crafts and Design.

Kungliga Tekniska Högskolan
Valhallavägen 79, 100 44 Stockholm (790 60 00/international@admin. kth.se/www.kth.se).
The Institute of Technology is nearly 200 years old and has 18,000 students. It provides one third of Sweden's technical research and has established exchanges all over the world.

Stockholms Filmskola
Hornsgatan 65, 118 49 Stockholm (616 00 35/www.stockholmsfilm skola.com).
A private school offering pre-university foundation courses (lasting two years) in film studies.

Stockholms Musikpedagogiska Institut
Visiting address: Eriksbergsgatan 8B, Östermalm.
Postal adress: PO Box 26164, 100 41 Stockholm (611 05 02/611 52 61/www.smi.se).
A small, independent college that specialises in music and the arts.

Stockholms Universitet
106 91 Stockholm (switchboard 16 20 00/international office 16 28 45/study@sb.su.se/www.su.se).
Stockholm University – north of the city centre, with its own T-bana stop, Universitetet – has about 35,000 undergraduate students and 2,200 postgraduate students.

Telephones

International & local dialling codes

To make an international call from Stockholm, dial 00 and then the country code, followed by the area code (omitting the initial 0, if there is one) and the number. The international code for the UK is 44; it's 1 for the US and Canada; 353 for the Irish Republic; 61 for Australia; and 64 for New Zealand.

To call Stockholm from abroad, dial 00, then 46 for Sweden, then 8 for Stockholm, then the number. Stockholm phone numbers vary in the number of digits they contain.

Directory

The area code for Stockholm (including the archipelago) is 08, but you don't need to dial it if you're within the area. All phone numbers in this guide are given as dialled from within Stockholm.

Swedish mobile phone numbers begin with 07. Numbers beginning 020 are always toll-free lines.

Operator services

All operators in Sweden speak English or will connect you to someone who does.
National directory enquiries 118 118
International directory enquiries 118 119
National and international operator 90 200
Telephone charges/faults helpline 90 200
Telegrams 020 0021
Time 90 510
Wake-up calls 90 180 – or dial *55* and then the time at which you want to be woken, in four figures according to the 24hr clock, then dial #. To delete the command, press #55#.

Public phones

Public phones, operated by partly state-owned phone company Telia, are not as widespread as they used to be because of the rise in the use of mobile phones. The newest phones accept coins (both SEK and euro). All phones accept credit cards and pre-paid phonecards, which are available in 30, 60 or 100 units and can be bought at most newsagents and tobacconists. One unit buys one minute of a local call; long-distance calls cost two units per minute.

Instructions are given in English. You can make reverse-charge (collect) calls from all public phones (key 2 then enter the number you are calling including the area code), and call emergency services (on 112) for free.

Mobile phones

Sweden is on the worldwide GSM network, so compatible mobile phones should work without any problem.

Komab

Norrlandsgatan 15, Norrmalm (412 11 00/www.komab.se). T-bana Östermalmstorg/bus 2, 47, 55, 56, 59, 69. **Open** 9.30am-6pm Mon-Fri; 10am-3pm Sat. **Credit** MC, V. **Map** p241 F8.
Seriously low prices on mobile phones – cheaper, in fact, than the price of renting one for a week.

Time

Stockholm is one hour ahead of GMT, six hours ahead of US Eastern Standard Time and nine ahead of Pacific Standard Time.

Summer time (an hour later) runs from late March to late October, with the same changeover days as the UK.

Tipping

There are no fixed rules about tipping in Sweden because the service charge is almost always included. In restaurants, most people leave 5-15 per cent, depending on how satisfied they are. Rounding up the bill is usually sufficient when you pay a bartender (at the bar) or a taxi driver.

Toilets

Public toilets (*toalett*; small, green booths) are usually found near or in parks. They cost 5kr and are clean.

There are public toilets and showers at Central Station and at Sergels Torg by the entrance to the T-Centralen T-bana station (open 7.15am-10.30pm daily, toilets 5kr, shower with towel 20kr).

Tourist information

Stockholm Tourist Centre

Sverigehuset (Sweden House), Hamngatan 27 (main entrance from Kungsträdgården), Norrmalm (50 82 85 08/www.stockholm town.se). T-bana Kungsträdgården/bus 2, 45, 47, 55, 56, 62. **Open** 9am-7pm Mon-Fri; 10am-5pm Sat, 10 am-4pm Sun. **Map** p241 G7.
This is the main tourist office in Stockholm, with huge amounts of useful information, plus free books and maps and the free monthly magazine *What's On Stockholm*. You can also buy the Stockholm Card (in person or online – *see p51*) and theatre and concert tickets. There is also a Forex exchange bureau.

Hotellcentralen

Concourse, Central Station, Vasagatan, Norrmalm (50 82 85 08/online booking www.stockholm town.se). T-bana T-Centralen/bus 3, 47, 53, 59, 62, 65. **Open** *June-Aug* 8am-8pm daily. *Sept-May* 9am-6pm Mon-Sat; noon-4pm Sun. **Map** p241 G6.
The tourist office's hotel booking centre can find and book hotels in all price brackets. If you ring them to arrange a hotel booking, it's free; if you visit it costs 75kr (25kr for youth hostels). Staff can only make same-day bookings for youth hostels.

Swedish Travel & Tourism Council

(www.visitsweden.com).
The Swedish tourism council has an excellent website with all the information you could possibly need in a variety of languages. There are plenty of useful links and telephone numbers.

Visas & passports

Sweden is one of the European Union countries covered by the Schengen agreement, meaning many shared visa regulations and reduced border controls (with the exception of the UK and Ireland, the Schengen zone takes in the entire EU, and also extends to Norway and Iceland). To travel to Schengen countries, British and Irish citizens need full passports; most EU nationals usually need only carry their national identity card when travelling between Nordic countries but it is wise to carry a passport as well since some airlines require passports.

Passports, but not visas, are needed by US, Canadian, Australian and New Zealand citizens for stays of up to three months. Citizens of South Africa and many other countries do need visas, obtainable from Swedish consulates and embassies abroad (or in other Schengen countries that you are planning to visit).

Visa requirements can change, so always check the latest information with your country's Swedish embassy.

Weights & measures

Sweden uses the metric system. Decimal points are indicated by commas, while thousands are defined by full stops. Throughout this guide, we have listed measurements in both metric and imperial.

When to go

Most people choose to visit between May and September, which is when most sights and attractions have extended opening hours. The time around Midsummer weekend (nearest 24 June) is the big summer holiday weekend, when many people leave town and much of the city is closed. July is the main holiday month for locals, and many restaurants, bars and shops close for some or all of the month. Mosquitoes can be a nuisance outside the city between June and late September, especially at dusk out in the archipelago.

Winter (November-March) brings short days and cold temperatures, but snow doesn't usually stay on the ground long. The city looks stunning just after a snowfall, especially on clear, crisp, sunny days, which are relatively common.

Public holidays

On public holidays, virtually all shops, banks and offices, and many restaurants and bars, are closed. Banks are also closed the day before a public holiday. Public transport runs a limited service on Christmas and New Year's Day.
Annual public holidays are:
Nyårsdagen 1 January
(*New Year's Day*)
Trettondedagsafton 5 January
(*Eve of Epiphany*)
Trettondedag Jul 6 January
(*Epiphany*)
Skärtorsdagen 20 March 2008
(*Maundy Thursday*)
Långfredagen 21 March 2008
(*Good Friday*)
Påskdagen 23 March 2008
(*Easter Sunday*)

Annandag Påsk 24 March 2008
(*Easter Monday*)
Valborgsmässoafton 30 April
(*Walpurgis Night*)
Första Maj 1 May (*May Day*)
Krist Himmelfärds Dag
1 May 2008 (*Ascension*)
Nationaldagen 6 June
(*National Day*)
Midsommarafton 20 June 2008
(*Midsummer's Eve*)
Midsommardagen 21 June 2008
(*Midsummer's Day*)
Alla Helgons Dag
1 November (*All Saints' Day*)
Julafton 24 December
(*Christmas Eve*)
Juldagen 25 December
(*Christmas Day*)
Annandag Jul 26 December
(*Boxing Day*)

Women

Great measures have been taken in Sweden to guarantee equal opportunities for men and women. Today, women in Sweden can combine having a family and working thanks to the state-sponsored childcare programme; almost 80 per cent of all women work and around 75 per cent of children aged one to six use the state childcare system. Swedish women still earn less than men, however, partly because of the professions they choose and the fact that many mothers work part-time.

It is unlikely that female visitors will face any kind of harassment, and Stockholm is a very safe city to walk around, although the normal precautions are always recommended.

Kvinnoforum (56 22 88 00/www.kvinnoforum.se) works to enhance the empowerment of women, while **KvinnorKan** (723 07 07/www.kvinnorkan.se) demonstrates and encourages women's knowledge.

Working in Stockholm

If you want to work in Stockholm, but you're not yet in the country, the best way to

find a job is to register at some of the many online recruiting companies, such as **Academic Search** (www.academic search.se), **Monster** (www.monster.se), **Stepstone** (www.stepstone.se) and **Topjobs** (www.topjobs.se).

The European Employment Services network, **EURES** (http://europa.eu.int/eures/ home.jsp?lang=en) provides a database of job vacancies throughout the EU and useful information about working conditions.

If you're already living in Sweden, you can start looking for a job by going to the state employment agency, **Arbetsförmedlingen**; it has a lot of information and offers free guidance for people seeking work.

Arbetsförmedlingen

Norrtullsgatan 6, Vasastaden 113 29 Stockholm (50 88 22 00/www. ams.se). T-bana Odenplan/bus 2, 4, 40, 42, 53, 72. **Open** *Phone enquiries* 8am-4.30pm Mon-Fri. *Office* 9.30am-3.30pm Mon-Fri. *Self-service (use of computers)* 8am-3.30pm Mon-Fri. **Map** p245 D6.

Work permits

All EU nationals can obtain a work permit in Sweden; non-EU citizens must apply for a work permit abroad and hand in the application to a Swedish embassy or consular representative. The rules for obtaining work permits vary for different jobs. EU citizens can stay in Sweden for three months, after which they must apply for a residence permit (which can take a month to process, so it's best to apply as soon as you arrive). Non-EU citizens must apply for a residence permit from outside Sweden. You'll need to produce a valid ID or passport and other documents depending on your status (employee, job-seeker, self-employed, student, etc). Contact the **National Immigration Authority** (Migrationsverket; 011 15 60 00/ www.migrationsverket.se).

Useful organisations

The EU has a website (http:// europa.eu.int/citizensrights/) with information on your rights, and useful numbers and addresses.

Directory

Vocabulary

It will only take a few minutes in Stockholm to realise that just about everyone speaks strikingly good English and is happy to oblige you by using it. However, as anywhere else, any attempts you make to learn a few basic phrases will be met with pleasure – or hilarity (Swedish is notoriously difficult to pronounce).

Vowels

Swedish vowels include the standard a, e, i, o, u and sometimes y along with three additional vowels: å, ä and ö. Vowels are long when at the end of a word or followed by one consonant, and short when followed by two consonants.
å – as in tore
ä – as in pet
ö – as in fur
y – as in ewe
ej – as in late

Consonants

g (before e, i, y, ä and ö), j, lj,dj and gj – as in yet
k (before e, i, y, ä and ö), sj, skj, stj, tj and rs – all more or less like sh, with subtle differences
qu – as in kv (though q is hardly ever used in Swedish)
z – as in so

Alphabetical order

Swedish alphabetical order lists å, ä and ö, in that order, after z.

Useful words & phrases

yes ja (yah); no nej (nay); please/thank you tack; hello hej (hay); goodbye hej då (hay daw); excuse me ursäkta (ewr-shekta); I'm sorry förlåt (furr-lawt); do you speak English? talar du engelska? (tah-lar dew engelska?); how are you? Hur är det (hewr eyre day?)

Sightseeing

entrance ingång (in-gawng); exit utgång (ewt-gawng); open öppen (ur-pen); closed stängd (staingd); toilet (women/men) toalett (too-a-let) (kvinnor/män); where var; when när (nair); near nära (naira); far långt (lawngt); (city) square torg (tohrj); church kyrka (chewr-ka); art gallery konstgalleri; town hall stadshus; street/road gata/väg;

palace slott; metro tunnelbana; ticket to... biljett till... (bill-yet till); how much is this/that? hur mycket kostar den/det? (hewr mewkeh costar den/det?); which way to...? hur kommer jag till...? (hewr comer yah til...?)

Accommodation

hotel hotell; youth hostel vandrarhem; I have a reservation jag har beställt ett rum (yah har bes-telt ett room); double room dubbelrum; single room enkelrum; double bed dubbelsäng; twin beds två sängar; with a bath med bad; with a shower med dusch

Days of the week

Monday måndag; Tuesday tisdag; Wednesday onsdag; Thursday torsdag; Friday fredag; Saturday lördag; Sunday söndag

Numbers

0 noll; 1 ett; 2 två (tvaw); 3 tre (trea); 4 fyra (few-ra); 5 fem; 6 sex; 7 sju (shew); 8 åtta (otta); 9 nio (nee-oo); 10 tio (tee-oo); 11 elva; 12 tolv; 13 tretton; 14 fjorton (fyoor-ton); 15 femton; 16 sexton; 17 sjutton (shew-ton); 18 arton; 19 nitton; 20 tjugo (chew-goo); 21 tjugoett (chew-goo-ett); 30 trettio (tretti); 40 fyrtio (fur-ti); 50 femtio (fem-ti); 60 sextio (sex-ti); 70 sjuttio (shew-ti); 80 åttio (otti); 90 nittio (nitti); 100 hundra (hewndra); 1,000 tusen (tews-sen); 1,000,000 miljon (milly-oon)

Eating out

have you got a table for...? har ni ett bord för...? (hahr nee ett boord furr...?); bill notan (noo-tan); menu meny (men-ew); wine list vinlista (veen-lista); breakfast frukost (frew-cost); lunch lunch (lewnch); dinner middag (mid-daag); main course huvudrätt (hew-vew-dret); starter förrätt (fur-et); bottle flaska; glass glas; restaurant restaurang; cake shop konditori; bakery bageri; bar-restaurant krog

Basic foods & extras

ägg egg; bröd bread; gräddfil sour cream; ost cheese; pommes frites chips/fries; potatis potatoes; ris rice; senap mustard; smör butter; smörgås sandwich; socker sugar.

Swedish specialities (husmanskost)

ärtsoppa split pea and pork soup; black & white steak and mashed potato; fisksoppa fish soup; Janssons frestelse gratin of

anchovies and potatoes; kåldolmar stuffed cabbage rolls; köttbullar meatballs; lufsa pork dumpling with smoked salmon; potatissallad potato salad; pytt i panna fried meat and potato hash with a fried egg and pickled beetroots; rimmad oxbringa lightly salted brisket of beef; sillbricka an assortment of herring dishes; smörgåsbord typical self-service buffet, starting with herring, followed by cold dishes, then hot dishes, then dessert.

Fruit & veg (frukt & grönsaker)

apelsin orange; ärtor peas; bönor beans; citron lemon; hallon raspberry; hjortron cloudberry; jordgubbar strawberries; kål cabbage; lingon lingonberry; lök onion; morötter carrots; nötter nuts; persika peach; smultron wild strawberries; svamp mushrooms; vindruvor grapes; vitlök garlic

Meat & game (kott & vilt)

älg elk; biff beef; fläsk pork; kalvkött veal; korv sausage; kyckling chicken; lammkött lamb; rådjur roe deer; ren reindeer; skinka ham

Fish (fisk)

ål eel; blåmusslor mussels; forell trout; gös pike-perch; hummer lobster; kräftor crayfish; lax salmon; räkor prawns; sjötunga sole; strömming/sill (inlagd/sotare) herring (pickled/blackened); surströmming fermented Baltic herring; torsk cod

Cakes & desserts (bakverk & desserter)

dammsugare confectionery made with green marzipan and chocolate; glass ice-cream; kaka/tårta cake (kaka can also mean cookie); lussekatt saffron bun with raisins; ostkaka Swedish cheesecake; pepparkakor gingerbread biscuits; plättar miniature pancakes served with jam and cream; semla whipped cream and almond-paste buns

Drinks (drycker)

brännvin schnapps; varm choklad hot chocolate; fruktjuice fruit juice; glögg fortified mulled wine; kaffe coffee; mineral-vatten mineral water; mjölk milk; öl beer; punsch sweet arak-like spirit; rödvin red wine; te tea; vitt vin white wine.

Further Reference

Books

For books about Sweden in English, you should visit the Swedish Institute's **Sweden Bookshop** *(see p139)*, or the book sections in department stores NK or Åhlens *(for both, see p137)*.

Architecture, art & design

Claes Caldenby & Olof Hultin *Architecture in Sweden 1995-9* (2001) With text in both English and Swedish.
Katrin Cargill *Creating the Look: Swedish Style* (1996) A guide to achieving the Swedish design look.
Courtney Davis *A Treasury of Viking Design* (2000) Scandinavian Viking design in ceramics, textiles, woodwork and so on.
Ralph Skansen Edenheim *Traditional Swedish Style* (2002) Illustrated presentation of the interiors of Skansen's buildings from a cultural and historical perspective.
Charlotte Fiell *Scandinavian Design* (2002) In-depth illustrated guide focusing on 200 designers and design companies.
Groth Hakan & Fritz van der Schulenburg *Neoclassicism in the North: Swedish Furniture and Interiors 1770-1850* (1999) Excellent photographs trace the evolution of the neo-classical style in Sweden.
Susanne Helgeson *Swedish Design* (2002) A survey of Swedish designers. Offers insight into Swedish design philosophies.
Olof Hultin, Bengt Oh Johansson, Johan Mårtelius & Rasmus Waern *The Complete Guide to Architecture in Stockholm* (1999) This guide introduces the reader to 400 of the most notable buildings in the Stockholm area.
Derek E Ostergard & Nina Stritzler-Levine *The Brilliance of Swedish Glass 1918-1939* (1997) Illustrated essays that put Swedish glass production into perspective.
Lars & Ursula Sjöberg *The Swedish Room* (1994) Illustrated guide to interior design.
Michael Snodin & Elisabet Stavenow-Hidemark (eds) *Carl and Karin Larsson: Creators of the Swedish Style* (1998) Numerous essays by experts.
Barbara Stoeltie, René Stoeltie & Angelika Taschen *Country Houses of Sweden* (2001) Coffee-table book with lovely photographs of Swedish country houses from a variety of periods.

Biographies

Maaret Koskinen *Ingmar Bergman* (2007) An overview of the late, great filmmaker.
Sharon Linnea *Raoul Wallenberg: The Man who Stopped Death* (1993) Biography of the famous Swedish diplomat who saved the lives of 100,000 Hungarian Jews during World War II and then mysteriously disappeared after going into Soviet custody.
Joe Lovejoy *Sven-Göran Eriksson* (2002) For football lovers only.
Eivor Martinus *Strindberg and Love* (2001) In-depth biography of the dramatist, focusing on the four most important women in his life.
Carl Magnus Palm *From ABBA to Mamma Mia: The Official Book* (2000) The first book published with the co-operation of the band, with lots of good photos.

Fiction & autobiographies

Frans G Bengtsson *The Long Ships* (1945) A true Swedish classic, this novel enchants its readers with the adventures of a fictional Viking.
Ingmar Bergman *The Magic Lantern: An Autobiography* (1989) Memoirs of the film master's career and childhood.
Karin Boye *Kallocain* (1940) A bleak vision of a future totalitarian world state.
Eyvind Johnson *Dreams of Roses and Fire* (1949) Novel by the winner of the 1974 Nobel Prize for Literature.
Selma Lagerlöf *The Wonderful Adventures of Nils* (1906) One of Sweden's best-loved modern folk tales, written to teach Swedish schoolchildren about the geography of their country. Tiny Nils explores the Swedish landscape on the back of a goose and lives through many hair-raising experiences.
Astrid Lindgren *Pippi Longstocking* (1945) Fantastic series of children's books about a girl who does exactly as she pleases.
John Ajvide Lindqvist *Let the Right One In* (2007) A bestseller in Sweden, this is a unique fusion of social novel and vampire legend.
Henning Mankell Best-selling crime writer most famous for his series of detective stories starring Inspector Kurt Wallander from southern Sweden.
Vilhelm Moberg *The Emigrants* (1949) Moving story about what it was like to emigrate from Sweden to the US in the 19th century, later made into a film.
Mikael Niemi *Popular Music* (2004). A witty, compelling coming-of-age story set in northern Sweden in the 1960s.
August Strindberg *Miss Julie and Other Plays* (1998) Contains some of the dramatist's key plays: *Miss Julie*, *The Father*, *A Dream Play*, *Ghost Sonata* and *The Dance of Death*.
Mary Wollstonecraft *Letters Written during a Short Residence in Sweden, Norway and Denmark* (2004) Early feminist Wollstonecraft describes her travels through Scandinavia in 1795.

History, politics & society

Peter Berlin *The Xenophobe's Guide to the Swedes* (1999) An amusing book explaining the complex rules that govern Swedish social interaction.
Lisa Werner Carr & Christina Johansson Robinowitz *Modern-day Vikings: A Practical Guide to Interacting with the Swedes* (2001) Discussion of the Viking beginnings of the Swedish character.
Ake Daun *Swedish Mentality* (1996) Focuses on the development of Swedish culture and society.
Matz Erling *Glorious Vasa: The Magnificent Ship and 17th-century Sweden* (2001) Fascinating book that provides a great insight into what life was like in 17th-century Stockholm.
Stig Hadenius *Swedish Politics during the 20th Century* (1999) Authoritative treatment of all the dramatic political changes that took place between 1900 and 1999.
Istvan Hargittai & James Watson *The Road to Stockholm: Nobel Prizes, Science and Scientists* (2002) Discusses the selection process for the scientific laureates and the ingredients for scientific discovery and recognition.
Mikael af Malmborg *Neutrality and State-building in Sweden* (2001) The history and future of Swedish neutrality.
Byron J Nordstrom *The History of Sweden* (2002) Swedish history from prehistoric times to the present.
Jan Öjvind Swahn *Maypoles, Crayfish and Lucia: Swedish Holidays and Traditions* (1997) A guide to Swedish customs and festivals published by the Swedish Institute.

Film

Before the Storm (Reza Parsa, 2000) Excellent thriller.
The Best Intentions (Bille August, 1992) The story of Ingmar Bergman's parents, written by Bergman himself.
Elvira Madigan (Bo Widerberg, 1967) Beautiful-looking film about a doomed love affair.
The Emigrants (Jan Troell, 1970) First of two films – the second is *The New Land* – dealing with Swedish emigrants to America.
Evil (Mikael Håfström, 2004) Oscar-nominated film about a young rebel in a Swedish private school in the late 1950s.
Fanny and Alexander (Ingmar Bergman, 1982) Family saga seen through the eyes of a small boy.
The Father (Alf Sjöberg, 1969) Film version of Strindberg's play about a battle between husband and wife, descending into madness and death.
Four Shades of Brown (Tomas Alfredson, 2004) Black comedy interweaving four lives.
Fucking Åmål (US title *Show Me Love*, Lukas Moodysson, 1998) All-girl twist to the high-school romance genre, which won multiple awards.
House of Angels (Colin Nutley, 1992) Prejudice and conflict in rural Sweden.
I am Curious: Yellow (Vilgot Sjöman, 1967) Sexually frank but morally involved tale mixing reportage and fiction.
Jalla! Jalla! (Josef Fares, 2000). Culture clash comedy.
Lilja 4-ever (Lukas Moodysson, 2002) Moodysson darker than usual but very popular in Sweden.
My Life as a Dog (Lasse Hallström, 1985) A witty and touching story of a young boy in 1950s rural Sweden.
Persona (Ingmar Bergman, 1966) An actress refuses to speak, while her nurse chatters away about her sex life.
The Seventh Seal (Ingmar Bergman, 1956) Unforgettable medieval allegory, with plague sweeping through an apocalyptic Sweden and Max von Sydow's knight playing chess with Death.
Songs from the Second Floor (Roy Andersson, 2000) Loosely connected vignettes deal with traffic jams and redundancy in a surreal black comedy.
Together (Lukas Moodysson, 2000) Excellent comedy about life and love in a 1970s commune.
The Treasure of Arne (often called *Herr Arnes Pengar*, Mauritz Stiller, 1919) Bravura premonition-laden drama set in Sweden in the 16th century.
Tsatsiki, Mum and the Policeman (Ella Lemhagen, 1999)

Engaging story of a young Stockholmer who longs to meet his Greek father.
Under the Sun (Colin Nutley, 1998) Sweet and satisfying film based around an unconventional love story.
Wild Strawberries (Ingmar Bergman, 1957) Warm story of an academic who rediscovers his youth.
Wings of Glass (Reza Bagher, 2000) Involving film about a Swedish-Iranian family's conflict between their Muslim roots and Swedish environment.

Music

Classical

Hugo Alfvén (1872-1960) Composer of the ballet *Bergakungen* ('Mountain King'), five symphonies and numerous songs.
Franz Berwald (1796-1868) Wrote operas, chamber music and four symphonies.
Daniel Börtz (born 1943) Composer whose contemporary chamber music and solo pieces reflect earlier periods.
Anders Eliasson (born 1947) Composer of complex orchestral works.
Håkan Hardenberger (born 1961) Internationally renowned trumpeter.
Anders Hillborg (born 1952) Most famous for his *Celestial Mechanics* for solo strings.
Christian Lindberg (born 1958) Trombone virtuoso.
Wilhelm Peterson-Berger (1867-1942) Composer of operas and piano miniatures with a strong folk influence.
Allan Pettersson (1911-80) Composer most renowned for his *Symphony No.7*.
Hilding Rosenberg (1892-1985) Wrote numerous string quartets.
Wilhelm Stenhammar (1871-1927) Composed chamber music, operas and orchestral pieces.
Jan Sandström (born 1954) Renowned for his *Motorbike Concerto* for trombone and orchestra.
Sven-David Sandström (born 1942) Composer of complex orchestral works, ballets and percussion pieces.
Anne Sofie von Otter (born 1955) The world-famous mezzo-soprano.

Pop & rock

Abba Their phenomenally successful albums include *Waterloo* (1974) and *Super Trouper* (1980).
The Cardigans Pop band formed in 1992, with *Life* probably their most well-known album.
The Concretes *Hey Trouble* (2007) was the third album from eccentric Stockholm-based rockers.

Europe Remembered for the terrible 1986 hit 'The Final Countdown'.
The Hellacopters US-tinged Swedish rock.
The Hives Internationally successful punk fivesome; albums include *Your New Favourite Band*, *Barely Legal* and *Tyrannosaurus Hives*.
Sahara Hotnights Garage-rock girl band.
Soundtrack of Our Lives Successful six-piece rock outfit hailing from Gothenburg.

Websites

City of Stockholm
www.stockholm.se
Official information on the city's government, services and history, with useful links.
Destination Stockholm
www.destination-stockholm.se
Discounted accommodation, plus restaurant reviews and useful city information. In multiple languages.
Nobel Prizes
www.nobel.se
Everything you ever wanted to know about the Nobel Prizes, their history and the winners.
Royal Family
www.ritva.se
Unofficial and quite amusing fan site about the Swedish royal family.
Scandinavian Design
www.scandinaviandesign.com
The products and personalities of Nordic design, plus information on museums, magazines and design schools.
Scandinavica
www.scandinavica.com
An English-language website dedicated to Nordic culture.
Stockholm Guide
www.stockholmtown.com
Official tourist office site with good information on events, activities and attractions in the city and archipelago.
Stockholm Map
www.map.stockholm.se/kartago
A zoom-in, zoom-out map of the city, with instructions in Swedish.
Sweden
www.sweden.se
'The official gateway to Sweden', with well-written articles and fact-sheets on elements of Swedish culture.
Swedish Institute
www.si.se
Essential source of information about Sweden, Swedes and Swedish culture, plus information about studying in Sweden.
Yellow Pages
www.gulasidorna.se
Online Swedish Yellow Pages, also plots locations on maps. Swedish only, but easy to follow.

Index

Advertisers' Index

Please refer to the relevant pages for contact details

Major sight or landmark	▮
Railway station	▮
Park	▮
College/Hospital	▮
Main Shopping Street	
Area Name	GÄRDET
Subway Station	Ⓣ
Tourist Information	ⓘ

Maps

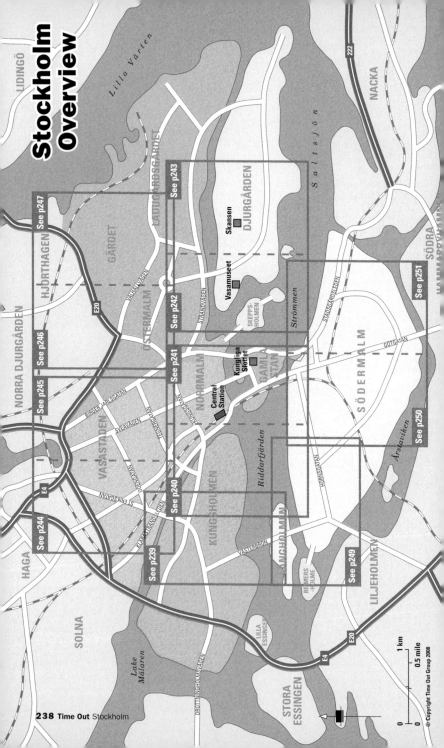

Stockholm Overview

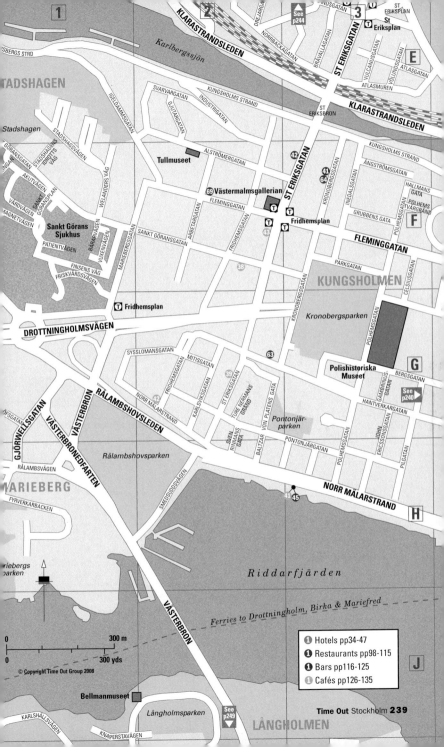

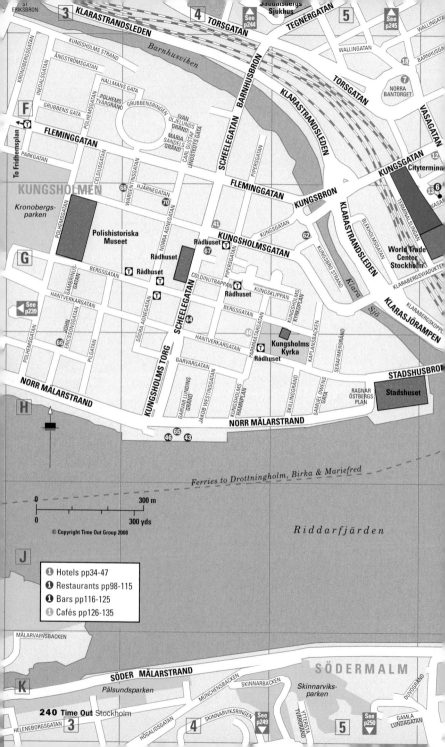

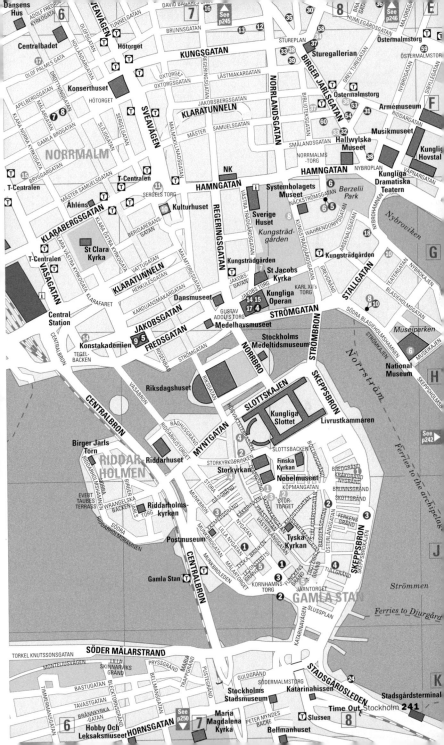

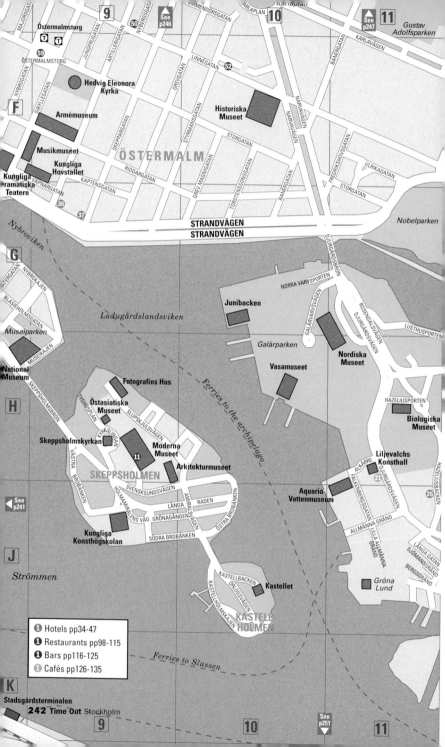

See
p247

TAPTOGATAN

OXENSTIERNSGATA

TV-Huset

VALHALLAVÄGEN

LADUGÅRDSGÄRDET

Gärdet

0   300 m

0   300 yds

© Copyright Time Out Group 2008

F

To Kaknästornet →

Radiohuset

GÄRDESGATAN

SKARPÖGATAN

**British
Embassy**

US Embassy

DAG HAMMARSKJÖLDS VÄG

61

DJURGÅRDSBRUNNSVÄGEN

40

MUSEIVÄGEN

Berwaldhallen

LABORATORIEGATAN

NOBELGATAN

**Sjöhistoriska
Museet**

**Tekniska
Museet**

**Etnografiska
Museet**

Djurgårdsbrunnsviken

G

ROSENDALSVÄGEN

37

ROSENDALSTERRASSEN

**Rosendals
Slott**

Skansen

22

**Rosendals
Trädgård**

ORANGERIVÄGEN

VALMUNDSVÄGEN

H

DJURGÅRDEN

SIRISHOVSVÄGEN

Cirkus

**Skansen
Akvariet**

SINGELBACKEN

SOLLIDSBACKEN

BECKHOLMSVÄGEN

DJURGÅRDSVÄGEN

DJURGÅRDSVÄGEN

BERGSJÖLUNDSVÄGEN

J

NORDENSKIÖLDS
-GATAN

RYSSVIKSVÄGEN

PRINS EUGENS VÄG

BECKHOLMSBRON

**BECK-
HOLMEN**

Waldemarsviken

**Prins Eugens
Waldermarsudde**

K

Time Out Stockholm **243**

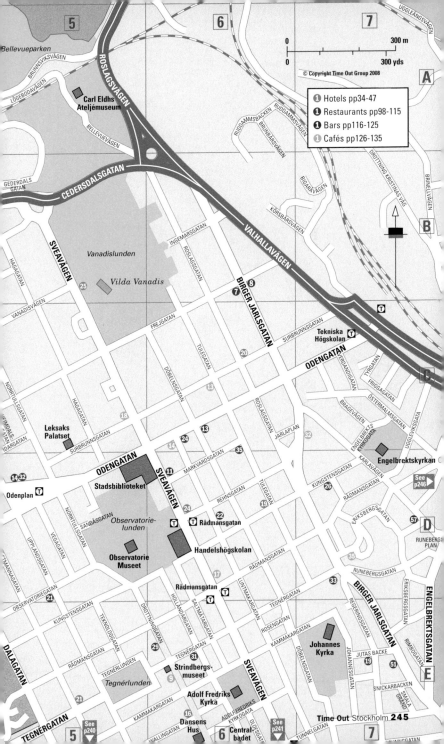

Bellevueparken

0   300 m
0   300 yds
© Copyright Time Out Group 2008

A

1 Hotels pp34-47
1 Restaurants pp98-115
1 Bars pp116-125
1 Cafés pp126-135

UGGLEVIKSVÄGEN

ROSLAGSVÄGEN

BRUNNSVIKSVÄGEN

LÖGEBODAVÄGEN

Carl Eldhs
Ateljémuseum

BELLEVUEVÄGEN

GEDERDALS-
GATAN

CEDERSDALSGATAN

RUDDAMMSBACKEN
RUDDAMMSVÄGEN
BRUNBARSVÄGEN

BIGARÅVÄGEN

DROTTNING KRISTINAS VÄG

BRINELLVÄGEN

B

SVEAVÄGEN

HAGAGATAN

Vanadislunden

INGEMARSGATAN
ROSLAGSGATAN

VALHALLAVÄGEN

KÖRSBÄRSVÄGEN

KÖRSBÄRSVÄGEN

Vilda Vanadis

25

BIRGER JARLSGATAN

8

7

VANADISVÄGEN

FREJGATAN

DÖBELNSGATAN

TULEGATAN

SURBRUNNSGATAN

SURBRUNNSGATAN

Tekniska
Högskolan

T

ODENGATAN

VALHALLAVÄGEN

T

C

NORRTULLSGATAN

HAGAGATAN

SURBRUNNSGATAN

20

13

16

ROSLAGSGATAN

JÄRLAPLAN

32

ENGELBRANDIGATAN

FRIGGAGATAN

TYRGATAN

ÖSTERMALMSGATAN

BRAGEVÄGEN

ENGELBREKTS
KYRKOGATAN

UGGLEVIKSGATAN

Leksaks
Palatset

ODENGATAN

14

24

SVEAVÄGEN

11

MARKVARDSGATAN

35

13

Engelbrektskyrkan

KARLAVÄGEN

KUNGSTENSGATAN

RÅDMANSGATAN

See
p246

14 32

Odenplan T

Stadsbiblioteket

Observatorie-
lunden

REHNSGATAN

TULEGATAN

19

26

ERIKSBERGSGATAN

57

D

RUNEBERGS
PLAN

NORRTULLSGATAN

UPPLANDSGATAN

VEGAGATAN

SANDÅSGATAN

SVEAVÄGEN

T Rådmansgatan

22

T

Handelshögskolan

RÅDMANSGATAN

35

RUNEBERGSGATAN

BIRGER JARLSGATAN

ERIKSBERGSGATAN

ENGELBREKTSGATAN

DALAGATAN

OBSERVATORIEGATAN

STMANNAGATAN

Observatorie
Museet

17

Rådmansgatan

HOLLÄNDARGATAN

SALTMÄTARGATAN

LUNTMAKARGATAN

TEGNERGATAN

33

REGERINGSGATAN

RIMBOGATAN

E

21

KUNGSTENSGATAN

TEKNOLOGATAN

DROTTNINGGATAN

T

ROSENGATAN

KAMMAKARGATAN

Johannes
Kyrka

JOHANNESGATAN

JUTAS BACKE

19

SNÄLLA
SNÄLLA

51

RÅDMANSGATAN

TEGNERLUNDEN

29

TEGNÉRGATAN

31

DÖBELNSGATAN

SNICKARBACKEN

21

Strindbergs-
museet

8

Tegnérlunden

SVEAVÄGEN

Time Out Stockholm **245**

KAMMAKARGATAN

Adolf Fredriks
Kyrka

ADOLF FREDRIKS
KYRKOGATAN

TEGNÉRGATAN

See
p240

5

16

Dansens
Hus

WALLINGATAN

6

Central-
badet

DÖÖSGATAN

See
p241

7

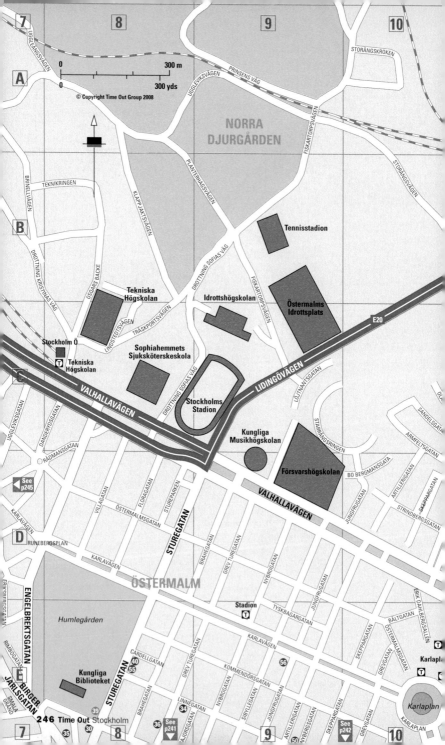

7 8 9 10

A

© Copyright Time Out Group 2008

0   300 m
0   300 yds

NORRA
DJURGÅRDEN

UGGLEVIKSVÄGEN
PRINSENS VÄG
STORÄNGSKROKEN

UGGLEVIKSVÄGEN

STORÄNGSVÄGEN

FISKARTORPSVÄGEN

B

BRINELLVÄGEN
TEKNIKRINGEN
DROTTNING KRISTINAS VÄG
KLAPPJAKTSVÄGEN
PLANTERHAGSVÄGEN
OSCARS BACKE

Tennisstadion

DROTTNING SOFIAS VÄG

LINDSTEDTSVÄGEN
TRÄSKPORTSVÄGEN

Tekniska
Högskolan

Idrottshögskolan

FISKARTORPSVÄGEN

Östermalms
Idrottsplats

E20

C

Stockholm Ö

Tekniska
Högskolan

VALHALLAVÄGEN

DROTTNING SOFIAS VÄG

Sophiahemmets
Sjuksköterskeskola

Stockholms
Stadion

LIDINGÖVÄGEN

LÖJTNANTSGATAN

SANDELSGATAN

ARMFELTSGATAN

Kungliga
Musikhögskolan

STJÄRNÄNGSRINGEN

ARTILLERIGATAN

VALHALLAVÄGEN

Försvarshögskolan

BO BERGMANSGATA

JUNGFRUGATAN

STRINDBERGSGATAN

See
p245

UGGLEVIKSGATAN
DANDERYDSGATAN

Rådmansgatan

VILLAGATAN

FLORAGATAN

STUREPARKEN

ÖSTERMALMSGATAN

STUREGATAN

BRAHEGATAN

GREV TUREGATAN

NYBROGATAN

D

KARLAVÄGEN

Runebergsplan

KARLAVÄGEN

ENGELBREKTSGATAN

ÖSTERMALM

ERIK DAHLBERGSALLÉN

ÖSTERMALMSGATAN

BÄLTGATAN

Karlapla

ERIKSBERGSGATAN

RIMBOGATAN

Humlegården

Stadion

TYSKBAGARGATAN

KARLAVÄGEN

56

Karlaplan

E

Kungliga
Biblioteket

STUREGATAN

CARDELLGATAN

40
55

GREV TUREGATAN

KOMMENDÖRSGATAN

JUNGFRUGATAN

SKEPPARGATAN

GREVGATAN

KARLAPLAN

BIRGER JARLSGATAN

ENGELBREKTSGATAN

SMÅLA GRÄND

39

BRAHEGATAN

LINNEGATAN

34

NYBROGATAN

SIBYLLEGATAN

ARTILLERIGATAN

NYBERGSGATAN

SKEPPARGATAN

GREVGATAN

See
p242

246 Time Out Stockholm

35   30

36   See
p241

MAJORSGATAN

50

7 8 9 10

1 Hotels pp34-47
1 Restaurants pp98-115
1 Bars pp116-125
1 Cafés pp126-135

WENSTRÖMSVÄGEN
AHLSELLVÄGEN
ÄLVKARLEÖVÄGEN
UNTRAVÄGEN
TRÖLLHÄTTEVÄGEN
MOTALAVÄGEN
PÖRJUSVÄGEN
KRÅNGEDEVÄGEN
LANFORSVÄGEN

SKÖGVAKTARGATAN
ARTEMISGATAN
KOLARGATAN
JÄGMÄSTARGATAN

HJORTHAGEN

MIDSKOGSGRÄND

NORRA HAMNVÄGEN
HAMNPIRSVÄGEN

LIDINGÖVÄGEN
YTTRE HAMNPIRSKAJEN

E20

Kungliga Tennishallen

Silja Line Terminalen   *Ferry to Helsinki*

TEGELUDDSVÄGEN

SÖDRA BASSÄNGKAJEN
SÖDRA HAMNVÄGEN
FÖRSTA BASSÄNGVÄGEN
HANGÖVÄGEN
ANDRA BASSÄNGVÄGEN
TREDJE BASSÄNGVÄGEN
FJÄRDE BASSÄNGVÄGEN

STUDENTBACKEN
TROPPSTIGEN
SMEDSBACKSGATAN
E20
Gärdet T

PATRULLSTIGEN
LIVRYTTARSTIGEN
FURUSUNDSGATAN
VÄRTAVÄGEN
SANDHAMNSPLAN
MALMVÄGEN
LAGERHUSGRÄND

Gärdet T
KAMPEMENTSGATAN

ERIK DAHLBERGSGATAN
RINDÖGATAN
BRANTINGSGATAN
SANDHAMNSGATAN
ÖRESUNDSGATAN
RÖKUBBSGATAN
TEGELUDDSVÄGEN C

GILLÖGAGATAN

PETRIGATAN
BLANCHEGATAN
ASKRIKEGATAN
T **Gärdet**

BLANCHEGATAN
ÖSTHAMMARSGATAN

ERIK KÄLLSKÄRSGATAN
Tessinparken
DR GEIJERSGATAN
ÄNGSKÄRSGATAN

GÄRDET

HEDINSGATAN
STORSKÄRSGATAN

STRINDBERGSGATAN

T **Karlaplan**

SEHLSTEDTSGATAN D
Danshögskolan

VÄRTAVÄGEN
BANERGATAN
VALHALLAVÄGEN

Filmhuset
BORGVÄGEN
LINDARÄNGSVÄGEN

Konstfack
GREVE VON ESSENS VÄG
E

LÜTZENGATAN
TYSTAGATAN
WITTSTOCKSGATAN
RIGI...

LADUGÅRDSGÄRDET

KARLAVÄGEN
BANERGATAN
Gustav Adolfsparken
See p242 ▼ **11**

TV-Huset
TAPTOGA...
VALHALLAVÄGEN
See p243 ▼ **12**

Time Out Stockholm **247**
13

11   12   13   A

The best guides to enjoying London life

(but don't just take our word for it)

'More than 700 places where you can eat out for less than £20 a head... a mass of useful information in a geuinely pocket–sized guide'

Mail on Sunday

'Armed with a tube map and this guide there is no excuse to find yourself in a duff bar again'

Evening Standard

'I'm always asked how I keep up to date with shopping and services in a city as big as London. This guide is the answer'

Red Magazine

'Get the inside track on the capital's neighbourhoods'

Independent on Sunday

'A treasure trove of treats that lists the best the capital has to offer'

The People

Rated 'Best Restaurant Guide'

Sunday Times

Available at all good bookshops and timeout.com/shop from £6.99

100% Independent

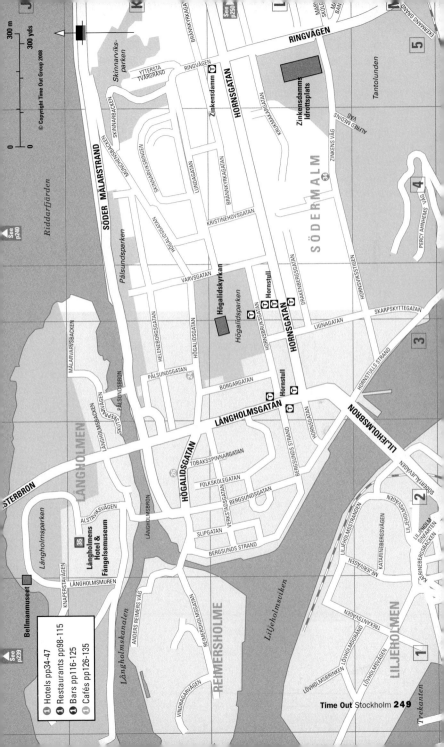

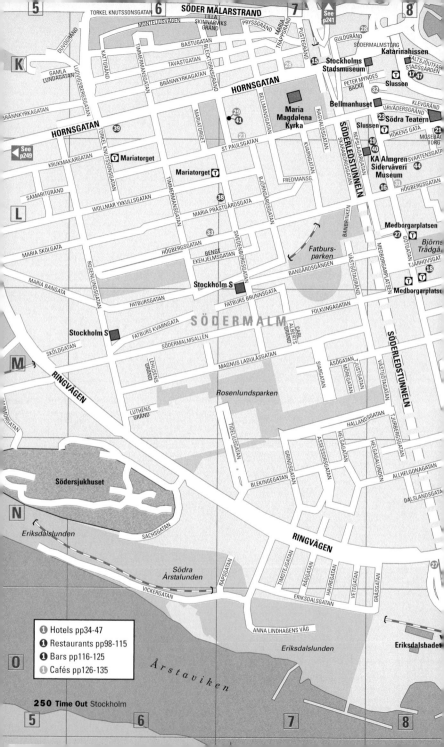

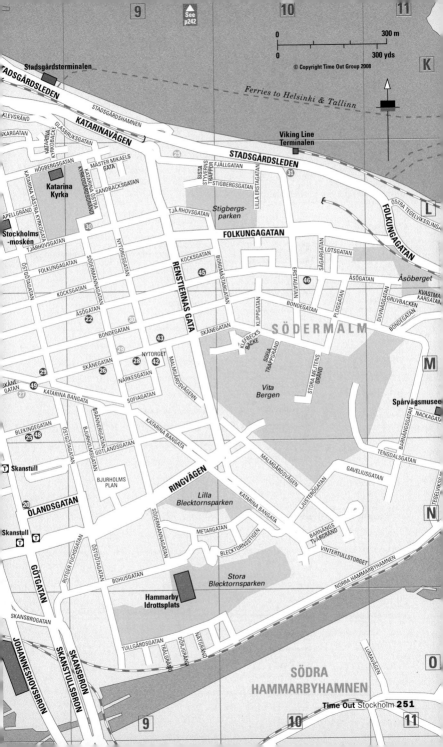

Street Index

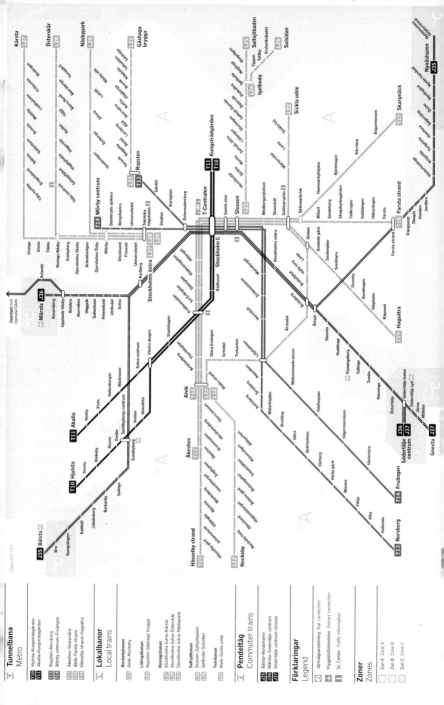